Family Theories

An Introduction

Fifth Edition

To our families.

Family Theories

An Introduction

Fifth Edition

James M. White

The University of British Columbia

Todd F. Martin

Trinity Western University

Kari Adamsons

University of Connecticut

Los Angeles | London | New Delhi
Singapore | Washington DC | Melbourne

FOR INFORMATION:

SAGE Publications, Inc.
2455 Teller Road
Thousand Oaks, California 91320
E-mail: order@sagepub.com

SAGE Publications Ltd.
1 Oliver's Yard
55 City Road
London EC1Y 1SP
United Kingdom

SAGE Publications India Pvt. Ltd.
B 1/I 1 Mohan Cooperative Industrial Area
Mathura Road, New Delhi 110 044
India

SAGE Publications Asia-Pacific Pte. Ltd.
18 Cross Street #10-10/11/12
China Square Central
Singapore 048423

Printed in the United States of America

ISBN: 9781506394909

This book is printed on acid-free paper.

FSC
www.fsc.org
MIX
Paper from
responsible sources
FSC® C005010

Acquisitions Editor: Joshua Perigo
Editorial Assistant: Alexandra Randall
Production Editor: Kimaya Khashnobish
Copy Editor: Patrice Sutton
Typesetter: C&M Digitals (P) Ltd.
Proofreader: Susan Irwin
Indexer: Kathy Paparchontis
Cover Designer: Dally Verghese
Marketing Manager: Katherine Hepburn

18 19 20 21 22 10 9 8 7 6 5 4 3 2 1

Brief Contents

Detailed Contents

Foreword

I n 1973, a fellow graduate student at the University of Minnesota, Peter Torsiello, and I prepared a lengthy manuscript on theory construction and its application to families. These ideas remained dormant until 1990, when I teamed up with Dr. James White, who provided the necessary intellectual breadth and energy to attempt a textbook project. To the earlier theory construction ideas, we added coverage of the field's then existing major theoretical frameworks. The result was the first edition of this book, published in 1996.

It always has been important to have stories about families, ways to understand, explain, and predict what happens in them. But scientific interest in family theories didn't really develop until after World War II ended in 1945.

Research became more important for academic scholarship, and resources increasingly became available to develop and apply sophisticated methods of research. The problem was how to integrate rapidly expanding research findings to create a coherent body of knowledge. At first, conceptual frameworks and then theories provided a useful structure for the integration.

This book has preserved several useful themes across editions. One is the dual meaning of framework, both as a pre-theoretical set of concepts and assumptions, and as a set of similar theories. All editions also have attended to intellectual traditions, to major variations within theories, to specific topic applications, and to the personal lives of readers, as well as to each perspective's limitations.

Along the way, the authors have taken on the difficult task of trying to effectively reach the needs of both beginning and advanced students. This remains a challenge.

Other themes have been constant across editions. Where families appear in a theory is important. Do we want to explain how families work or use something about families to explain how individuals or societies work? Families as groups relate to their members and to societies in various ways. Some theories about families are limited in their usefulness to relatively narrow topics, while other theories have broader application.

Changes across editions of this book also have been important. Four kinds of changes stand out. First, feedback from students and instructors has led to changes in emphasis and detail. Second, changing the mix of coauthors has added new voices and perspectives.

A third change across editions reflects changes in families themselves. While the last quarter century has witnessed fairly subtle family life changes in most respects, any shift in the central tendency or variability of family life raises new questions for theorists to address. While some theories are better able than others to explain changes in families, periods of rapid social change always pique interest in how to understand and explain them.

The fourth major contributor to changes across editions of this book has been innovations in theories and in theorizing. The picture here is mixed. Some theoretical frameworks have been elaborated and refined. Some have become marginalized, whether being empirically attacked or just ignored. One positive newer trend may be combining similar or even very different theories into a coherent whole.

Unfortunately, two aspects of family theorizing have not been particularly productive across the life span of this book.

First, a theory should be rejected if it fails to be logically and empirically supported in comparison with a rival theory. Family scientists have not designed and executed such critical tests. So the appeal of any specific theory has remained mostly a matter of subjective personal preference. We need more rigorous research on how popular each theory has been and why some have been more popular than others.

Second, applying and combining existing theories has been considerably more popular than creating new theories. While both combining and creating certainly can be desirable, there is no broadly acceptable standard for doing either well. Theorizing, and communication about methods of theorizing, eventually needs to be governed by acceptable scientific standards and routinely communicated in published reports.

The authors of this book care deeply about the future of family scholarship. Hopefully, readers will care as much.

David Klein
July 2018

Preface

S uccessive editions of a popular book are more difficult undertakings than they may appear. While researching chapter topics on the web, we encountered wonderful PowerPoint slide shows and a variety of other teaching materials that instructors had produced. While we were impressed and heartened by this material, we were also cautioned that any new edition should have considerable continuity with past editions. At the same time, we realized how important it is, especially to students, that the material seems up to date. This too provided difficulties because there were many major theoretical contributions in the 1990s and earlier that were before our current cohort of undergraduates were born!

Theoretical Frameworks Versus Applications

We have tried to first and foremost be guided by providing an accurate and coherent view of the theories in this book. We continue with the "frameworks" approach as what we regard as the best pedagogical tool for achieving this end. This point is worthy of some elaboration. Fine and Fincham (2013) have edited an excellent volume of issue-oriented applications of theory. They believe that students will be best served by learning theory as it is applied to these empirical topic areas such as work and family or acquiring gender. We would argue, however, that the framework approach that we use in this volume is more strongly recommended for several reasons:

1. The framework approach ties the current theory to the intellectual traditions and history that inform this particular theoretical avenue of thought. For example, there is little dispute that rational choice theory is tied to the intellectual wellsprings of utilitarianism in the 1800s and also to the hedonists (300 BCE) and the pre-Socratic sophists. This intellectual tradition is alive and well in economics, sociology, history, and many other disciplines. The arguments launched by these schools of rationalism also appear in jurisprudence, criminology, and political discussions. We think that students using *Family Theories* deserve an entrée to this world of ideas as both future scholars and researchers as well as future citizens trying to understand a very complex world.

2. Another reason we believe that the framework approach used in this book is superior to topic applications is that the student is exposed to the broad, general, and abstract concepts and propositions of the theories. The topics approach might expose students to only those propositions that are useful in understanding the particular phenomenon under consideration.

The problem is that this may only give the student an incomplete picture of the theory. It may neglect the important assumptions of the theory and how the theory deals with different levels of analysis. For example, if we applied life course theory to individuals in a particular role (perhaps mothers), we would not have need to explain how this theory functions for cohorts or becomes institutionalized or deals with social change. Indeed, it is our hope that by introducing the more general propositions of the theory, we give the student a chance to see the internal logic and coherence of the theory. Applications of a theory are not applications of the entire theory to a phenomenon (since that would seldom be required) but only a limited "slice" of the theoretical pie.

3. The last argument we make in this regard is based on a much bigger difference between our pedagogical goals and those favoring an applied approach. One of the pedagogical goals we have for this book is to invite our students and readers into the world of ideas. Ideas have a life of their own. Certainly they can be applied to research, but they can also help you read the *New York Times* or assist you in thinking through arguments in a courtroom where you are a juror. Complex ideas such as the nature and origin of social norms, the limits of individual motivation, and even the nature of an explanation are beyond any applications approach. As we say in the last sentence of this book, we believe that entering the world of ideas has intrinsic benefits to the individual. We feel compelled to say that there are also extrinsic benefits to a society in producing a truly intellectual and educated group of young adults.

Major Changes to This Edition

The two biggest changes to this edition are the retirement of David Klein as a coauthor and the addition of Kari Adamsons as one of the coauthors of this work. Dr. Adamsons has a marvelous background in many areas relevant to this book. She brings a wealth of teaching experience and academic research to our team.

It is of course a loss to have David Klein retire as an active participant in this enterprise. His years of involvement have left an indelible legacy to this book and family scholarship in general. He will be missed.

There have been several other major changes to this edition. The introductory Chapter 1 has become more focused, and students are briefly introduced to the notion of scientific *facts*. Chapter 2 has been radically changed to deal with classical social theories such as Weber and Durkheim as well as the themes from classical social theory that constantly emerge in the frameworks discussed in subsequent chapters. In addition, Chapter 2 deals with theoretical assumptions tied to philosophies of science and a brief history of the ways family theory has changed over the last 70 years.

We also added a newly revised Chapter 10 on theory construction and emerging theories. For a long time, we have wanted to capture more of the process dimension of theories to complement the product orientation that such books as this necessarily assume. This new chapter addresses this grievance, and we anticipate that students and instructors will welcome this change.

Certainly, there are a myriad of changes such as the updating of empirical applications and theoretical progress. One major change is the reintroduction of study questions. We have tried to keep a truly intellectual flavor to these questions while making them relevant to the current context of world affairs. There are other small changes too numerous to cite here. The overall structure of the chapters remains the same as in previous editions. We hope that students and instructors will continue to find this book simultaneously stimulating and approachable.

Organization of the Book

The first chapter of this book provides a general introduction to the topic of family theory and theory in general. The second chapter deals more with philosophy of science issues and a brief history of family theory. The next seven chapters covering the theoretical frameworks are organized using the same headings. We now briefly examine the headings used to organize these chapters. Each theoretical framework is introduced by a brief fictional account or vignette about some aspect of family life. These accounts serve to focus the reader on the particular form of behavior and interaction that the theoretical framework is intended to explain.

The first subheading the reader encounters in these seven chapters is *Intellectual Traditions*. This section introduces the reader to a brief and non-exhaustive historical perspective on the ideas in the theoretical framework. This section should be especially valuable for assisting students to integrate this material with material they encounter in other courses in the social sciences and humanities.

The second subheading to be encountered is *Focus and Scope Assumptions*. All theories contain basic assumptions, but most important among these are the assumptions that set the boundaries for the theory. Each theoretical framework sets boundaries on explanations and, just as important, focuses on some particular elements or processes in families. Understanding the focus and scope of a theoretical framework assists in understanding the explanatory power of a theory.

The third subheading is *Concepts*. Concepts are the building blocks of any theory. In theories, concepts are used to provide meaning and to help classify phenomena. Meanings are provided by formal definitions.

Classification is achieved by placing a particular act or event in the broader category of a concept. Concepts also assist explanation when they are used in propositions.

The fourth subheading is *Propositions*. In this section, a modest and nonexhaustive list of theoretical propositions gives the reader a simple idea of how explanation might proceed. The propositions are best understood as the way that a particular theory relates its concepts to each other. Explanation then is when an observation is covered by one of these propositions. This is the most abstract area of each chapter.

The fifth section is *Variations*. In this section, a small set of theoretical variations is discussed. These variations are selected to capture the range of differences that the theoretical framework may accommodate. We have attempted to include what we regard as the major variants, but there is certainly some room for debate. Instructors and students may, of course, add variants to their class discussions, and this would further enrich the understanding of the framework.

The sixth subheading is *Empirical Applications*. One or two examples are discussed, and the more general theoretical framework or one of its variations is used to explain and interpret an empirical research finding or small set of findings in a topical area. The principal goal here is to demonstrate how the theory interacts with research.

The seventh subheading is *Critiques and Discussion*. This section covers the major flaws or weaknesses of the framework. Our treatment is aimed at enhancing the student's depth of understanding of the theory rather than to encourage rejection of the theory. A *Conclusion* section provides a brief synopsis of the major thrusts of the theory and our perspective on the theory. The *Study Questions* we have added can be used for study and class discussions.

The penultimate chapter of the book is an expansion of some of the ideas about theory as process that were suggested in the first chapter. The final chapter of the book, the *Epilogue*, presents a typology for analyzing and comparing the seven theoretical frameworks. This chapter also takes stock of where we are in the field and the directions we see for the future.

We hope that all of our readers—students, faculty, and researchers—are as profoundly influenced by the ideas in this book as we have been. We believe that your life will be enriched by these ideas and that good research and thinking about families requires good ideas.

James White, Todd Martin, and Kari Adamsons

Acknowledgments

We express our gratitude to our students and numerous colleagues for their support and encouragement. We acknowledge the many people who have provided support, criticism, and encouragement for previous editions of this project.

We would like to express our deepest gratitude to the folks at SAGE starting with Josh Perigo for his unwavering support for this project. Finally, we would like to thank our spouses and families for their continuing support over the years.

We would also like to thank the following reviewers for this fifth edition:

Diann Moorman, University of Georgia

Mark A. Fine, University of North Carolina at Greensboro

Katie Heiden-Rootes, Saint Louis University

Michelle Sherwood, Eastern Illinois University

Duane Alan Dowd, PhD, Central Washington University

Ruth Miressi, Park University

Richard N. Pitt, Vanderbilt University

Lauren Dick, MS, Carthage College

Dr. Stephanie Irby Coard, University of North Carolina at Greensboro

CHAPTER

1

What Is a Theory?

> "Bill, why do you think Rod and Michelle are getting divorced? There was no infidelity, and they have always seemed to be so good together."
>
> "Actually, Jill, I would have predicted it. Rod and Michelle were perfect together when they first got married, but over the past 2 years, they have gone in very different directions. Rod is totally absorbed with his job and all the travel that is required, but Michelle has become more bored with her job and has talked more about having kids. I think their goals as a couple are very far apart. Rod just wants a companion when he comes home tired from work and travels, and Michelle wants a family."
>
> Jill thought for a moment and then asked Bill, "So you think that a couple should share some common goals?"
>
> Bill immediately responded, "Yes, and that way they can see the future of their relationship and where it is going."
>
> Jill faced Bill squarely and said, "That's an interesting theory. What would it say about us?"

Bill has a theory about couple dynamics and longevity. Indeed, as we watch TV shows, read the paper, and attend classes, we are confronted with informal and partially formulated theories and theoretical propositions every day. Bill's theory is that couples should have common goals. He believes that not having such goals is associated with couple dissolution. Certainly, marital and couple dissolution involve many other factors such as social support, economic well-being, intimacy, and so on. A fully developed theory of marital dissolution would have to include a wider set of concepts and processes than just the couple sharing goals. This example, however, shows how much of our everyday life and concerns actually involve theoretical propositions.

There are similarities in the way in which we develop and articulate theories in our everyday life and the way we do so in our professional life. Likewise, scientific theory bears similarities to our everyday theories, but seldom could these two be equated because the differences are distinct and important. In articulating our everyday theories, we often assume our definitions are shared by others rather than to consider beginning by defining our terms. For example, when Jill says "There was no infidelity" does she mean sexual infidelity or emotional infidelity? If it were sexual infidelity, does that mean only sexual intercourse or other forms of physical intimacy as well, such as kissing and holding hands? The foundation of Bill's theory rests on the idea that couples who do not share goals will drift apart emotionally and physically. Since scientific theories are not on a case by case basis (scientific theories are nomothetic and general instead of individual case and idiographic), we would need some precision regarding such terms as *infidelity*, *shared goals*, and *drifting apart*. In our everyday theories, we seldom frame them so that they would include most couple relationships rather than the particular one we might be discussing.

Another important difference is that our everyday theories are often sloppy in regard to the logic of what we are saying. For example, Bill's argument about sharing common goals so that a couple can envision their future may seem intuitively obvious for some people. The problem is that Bill's propositions about sharing common goals and envisioning a future may need further specification. Certainly, children may represent a common longer term goal, but couple agreement on which wine to have with a meal may not be of the same degree. It would probably help if Bill added some proposition about the long-term and short-term goals, couple versus individual goals, and the overall salience or importance of goals to both rather than one individual. Scientific theories usually demand a more precise and structured logic so that propositions are linked into a coherent argument.

Yet another difference between our everyday theories and those of science is in the area of prediction. Bill says he could have predicted the breakup of Rod and Michelle, but this is clearly after the breakup has happened. This kind of explanation is called "after the fact," or in Latin, ex post facto, explanation. The problem with such after the fact explanations is that they lack the defining ingredient of prediction in which the explanatory propositions yield a prediction that has not yet come to pass but will in a specified time come to pass. In other words, we expect scientific theories to yield before the fact, or a priori, explanations for an event. The weakness of explaining something after it has occurred is that there are an infinite number of other explanations that might also be true. Scientific methods are often designed to eliminate these other possible theories by using experimental designs and predicting from the theory before the event has occurred.

Now that we have seen how different our everyday theoretical musings are from scientific theories, we should also recall the similarities. We want all of our theories to be credible and plausible. We expect that our theories should make sense not just to ourselves but also to others. Since humans emerged from medieval times into the Renaissance and Enlightenment, the nature of facts and data changed dramatically. Before the Renaissance, facts were established by religious or political fiat. Gods and goblins were invoked to explain facts, and facts were construed so that these explanations could seem possible. Such explanations as the "gods are angry" or superstitions such as "garlic will keep demons away" were seen as equal to Copernican views of celestial mechanics. What slowly changed and brought us into the Enlightenment is the view that facts are methodological in design. This view suggest that when two persons have a disagreement about a fact such as does Earth orbit the Sun or does the Sun orbit Earth, the way to resolve this is not to imprison the nonbeliever or have them beheaded. Such resolutions to facts were quite common before the Enlightenment. There are many societies today that still revert to such tactics such as what the emperor or president says is a "fact." But it was the emergence of facts as methodologically resolvable that was the hallmark of science and reason in the Enlightenment. Returning to the two views about Earth-Sun orbits, a methodology can be developed that will resolve one view as superior to another because it predicts and it explains other phenomena. Modernity has pursued this way of resolving disputes, and those that respect facts do so because any alternative claim can be subjected to the same methodological tests. Certainly, every discipline and science has more particular methods of argumentation, logic, and proof, but all facts rest on this methodological view. There is also no doubt that all of these methods become more refined over time, but such evolution and change is reason for celebrating human progress in regard to knowledge.

As we have already argued in the discussion of Bill's theory about Rod and Michelle's divorce, science and scientific theory would favor a more universal and methodological approach. It is probably the case that in areas such as love, relationships, marriage, and family where we all have experience and some biases, a methodological approach to our theories about such areas is of paramount importance. Universality keeps us from being too idiosyncratic, and logic, definitions, and well-specified relations ensure that there are ways of testing which theories might be more predictive and explain more. To understand how this is possible, we now turn to the way in which scientific theory is assembled.

Architecture of a Scientific Theory

Attitudes that scientists have about theory depend on the philosophy of science that they endorse. We will deal with philosophical differences in the next chapter. Here, we assume the most conventional and probably the most popular perspective.

Box 1.1 What Is a Theory?

"A scientific theory might be likened to a complex spatial network: Its terms are represented by the knots, while the threads connecting the latter correspond, in part, to the definitions and, in part, to the fundamental and derivative hypotheses included in the theory. The whole system floats, as it were, above the plane of observation and is anchored to it by rules of interpretation. These might be viewed as strings, which are not part of the network but link certain points of the latter with specific places in the plane of observation. By virtue of those interpretive connections, the network can function as a scientific theory: From certain observational data, we may ascend, via an interpretive string, to some point in the theoretical network, thence proceed, via definitions and hypotheses, to other points, from which another interpretive string permits a descent to the plane of observation" (Hempel, 1952, p. 36).

"A theory is nothing—it is not a theory—unless it is an explanation. One may define properties and categories, and one still has no theory. One may state that there are relations between the properties, and one still has no theory. One may state that a change in one property will produce a definite change in another property, and one still has no theory. Not until one has properties, and propositions stating the relations between them, and the propositions form a deductive system—not until one has all three does one have a theory. Most of our arguments about theory would fall to the ground, if we first asked whether we had a theory to argue about" (Homans, 1964, p. 812).

"Deductive theory can be described briefly as an attempt to increase human understanding by providing explanations of why certain things occur. It provides this explanation by having a set of propositions and then deducing that, if these propositions are true, and if certain other conditions are met, certain specific and observable events occur. The more specific events are then 'explained' by the more general propositions that have been used as premises in deducing that the specific events occur. The explanation is only as valid as the propositions and logic that are used in the deduction, but one of the goals of science is to gradually eliminate invalid propositions and increase the number of useful, valid ones" (Burr, 1973, p. 3).

"Theorizing is the process of systematically formulating and organizing ideas to understand a particular phenomenon. A theory is the set of interconnected ideas that emerge from this process" (Doherty, Boss, LaRossa, Schumm, & Steinmetz, 1993, p. 20).

One useful way to understand theoretical arguments is to examine their basic components. We start with the idea that a theory is a systematic collection of concepts and relations. This is consistent with all four of the quotes in Box 1.1. Because there is an endless variety of ways to organize ideas, we will limit ourselves to the requirements for a *scientific* theory. Such theories contain systematically related propositions that are empirically testable (Rudner, 1966). Thus, there are several components that we need to discuss in further detail: (a) concepts, (b) relations between concepts, (c) propositions, (d) relations between propositions, and (e) connections between propositions and the empirical world of observed data. Before we look at each of these components, we must distinguish between ideas and data.

Ideas and Data

Science is fundamentally concerned with ideas, data, and relationships between them. Theory exists in the realm of ideas. Research takes place in the realm of data. A science advances to the extent that its theories and its studies (i.e., its empirical research) are productive and mutually reinforcing. For knowledge to be scientific, scientists must explain empirical observations by ideas or theory. *Theories explain by treating particular observations as examples of general principles or processes.* For example, there may be certain conditions, such as first intercourse, that encourage dating couples to become more serious and less casual about their relationship. This would constitute a hypothesis or testable conceptual proposition if data have not yet been examined in this regard. If, however, we have a great deal of data suggesting that first intercourse has a specific effect on couples' "probability of marriage," then that general proposition is what we often regard as a scientific fact. So a scientific fact is a relation between two concepts or measurements that is replicated over time and shows stability.

The linkages between ideas and data can be organized in different ways. If research produces empirical generalizations, the data might inductively lead to the development of a new theory, or the data might be interpreted in terms of an existing theory. When the process goes from data to ideas, we think of it as being *inductive*. Sometimes, a researcher starts with an existing theory, derives expectations about the data (i.e., hypotheses), and then makes observations to see how well the data fit. When the process goes from ideas to data, we think of it as being *deductive*. Theoretical ideas in science are developed both inductively and deductively. In either case, the ideas and the data must fit together in a meaningful way for the theory to be judged adequate.

Parts of a Theory

All scientific theories use the same basic building blocks. These building blocks are assumptions, concepts, relations, and propositions. The section below discusses each of these central ideas.

Assumptions are orienting constructs that are necessary for knowledge. For example, if we want to add numbers, we must make assumptions such as each number can be reduced to a primary unit (1) such that all 1s are of equal value. With that assumption, we can add $1 + 1 = 2$ or $2 + 2 = (1 + 1) + (1 + 1)$. If we wish to have negative numbers or fractions, still other assumptions have to be made. In theory, we have to make assumptions as well. In social theory, these assumptions are often about primitive units such as persons. For example, many social theories assume that "persons" will act out of self-interest (e.g., conflict theories and rational choice theories). There are other theories that don't make assumptions about individuals but about more macroscopic units, such as history or evolution, and individuals just act as instances of those forces. Every student of social theory should critically examine the foundational assumptions undergirding a theory. If you do not agree with the assumptions or have others to propose, the theory will turn out to look like a very different product.

Concepts are abstractions. A concept is not the thing; rather, it stands for the abstract class of things, ideas, or entities. Concepts are essential to theories because they enable us to organize experience. We do not invent a new concept every time we refer to a unique event. For example, we do not need a new term for marriage or a new meaning for the event called marriage every time a wedding takes place. Instead, we think of getting married in a more abstract way. We say that all weddings have certain defining properties. If we want to distinguish different kinds of weddings, we might establish categories. We could distinguish elopements from formal weddings and church weddings from civil wedding ceremonies. The categories remain abstractions, however, in that they all refer to occasions of a particular type, not to specific instances of weddings.

In science, the more explicit the definition for a concept, the better we can determine when it applies and when it does not apply. A scientific concept can mean only what a community of interacting scientists agrees that it means. Although scientists sometimes argue about the "proper" meaning of concepts, a theory tends to gain a footing in the scientific community once scholars settle on meanings for the time being. Many concepts in scientific theories refer to states of affairs with fairly stable properties. For example, we cannot have a coherent theory about the distribution of housework responsibilities if the meaning of *housework* changes every time we use this word.

Many but not all concepts can correspond to a set of empirical measures. A *variable* is any measure that can have two or more values, such as yes or no, *strongly agree* to *strongly disagree*, or even a range of values such as the Centigrade scale of temperature. For example, we may measure housework by hours of work within the house or by a specified set of tasks, such as doing laundry, toilet cleaning, and so on. Variables that might measure housework could be the hours a person spent doing the work, the economic value of the work, and so on.

Relations play the role of verbs in a theory. To relate concepts to each other, we need connecting relations asserting how the concepts are related. All relations have properties (symmetry, reflexivity, and transitivity). So, for example, we could use the same concepts but with different relations, and the truth of the statement will change completely. The statement immediately below is true:

John is a relative of George.

George is a relative of Bill.

Therefore,

John is a relative of Bill.

But the next statement below is false:

John is the father of George.

George is the father of Bill.

Therefore,

John is the father of Bill.

In these two cases, one relation is transitive (is a relative of), and the other is not transitive (is the father of). This simple difference in the properties of relations makes all the difference in the validity of the final statement. Relations often can be formalized in simple terms such as greater than or less than, and definitions are signified by identity or equals. As we shall see shortly, this fact provides a key link between theory and research.

Propositions exist when a concept is linked in a meaningful way by a relation to another concept. So we could say that among dual-earner couples, *the social class status of the husband is positively related to the amount of housework he performs.* This would be a theoretical proposition. The first concept is *social class status of the husband.* The second concept is the *amount of housework.* The relation in this proposition says that the greater a husband's social class status (relative to other husbands), the greater the husband's amount of housework. This relation can be mathematically expressed (modeled) as a function:

$$Amount\ of\ housework = f\ (Social\ class\ status).$$

As we shall see shortly, our first approximation of this functional relation (f) between a husband's social class status and amount of housework is usually a straight line with either a positive or negative slope. When a proposition asserts covariation between variables; the relation between concepts includes a sign (positive or negative), indicating that increases either occur together or go in opposite directions. When a relation asserts causal influence, the relation also makes clear which variable (independent) is influencing which other variable (dependent).

Defining Theory

Earlier in this chapter, we defined a scientific theory as "a set of systematically related propositions that are empirically testable" (Rudner, 1966, p. 10). Now that we have the building blocks in place, we can discuss the meaning and implications of this definition in greater detail.

Systematically related propositions. A theory usually comprises several propositions. Indeed, one proposition alone would not constitute a theory but would simply be a "conceptual hypothesis." Not only must a theory have at least two propositions, but these two propositions must be also systematically linked by relations. The way we link one theoretical proposition to another is by logical form. Although there are many mathematical and logical systems at our disposal, we will use simple syllogisms to show what we mean by form and relations. Note that the mini theory below is used only for an example of logical form and should not be regarded as empirically adequate.

Imagine that we have two propositions, but they may at first appear unrelated. For example, from a set of propositions about the intergenerational transmission of social class, we find the following:

> *The greater the family of orientation's values on education, the greater the son's social class status.*

If we combine this with our previously discussed proposition about amount of housework, we get a mini theory with two related propositions. Furthermore, we can deduce a third, new, and interesting proposition from these two.

> *The greater the family of orientation's values on education, the greater the son's social class status.*

> *The greater the husband's social class status, the greater the amount of housework performed.*

Therefore, the greater the family of orientation's values on education, the greater the amount of housework performed by the son (husband) in his family of procreation.

Now, the above mini theory is in the form of a syllogism. These deductive arguments are constructed so that if the first two propositions (called premises) are true, then the deduction (called the conclusion) is necessarily logically true (although not necessarily empirically true). It is much more important that if the conclusion is false, then we know that at least one or both of the premises are also false (falsification). These properties hold only if the correct form is followed. In regard to syllogisms, the correct form is that the middle term B (below) must appear at the end of the first premise and at the beginning of the second premise. This is called the rule of distributed middle.

A is a subset of B

B is a subset of C

Therefore, A is a subset of C.

Regardless of whether these ideas are in the correct form, what we want to know is if our theory as a whole is accurate. In logic, if we showed that our conclusion is true, that would not mean that the two premises are also true. Indeed, when we make such an assertion, it is called the "fallacy of affirming the consequent." In reality, we have to work backward. What we try to do is to disprove our conclusion. If we show that our conclusion is false, then we also know that at least one of the premises is false. We get much greater intellectual power out of using this reverse logic (*modus tollens*). This is one of the major theoretical reasons we use the null hypothesis in testing our theories.

Empirically testable. For a set of propositions to qualify as a scientific theory rather than religious or literary or political, it must be capable of being empirically tested. That does not mean that all our scientific theories have been empirically tested but that a theory that is not capable of being empirically tested is *not* a scientific theory. Now we turn to the question "What does it mean to say that a theory is capable of being empirically tested?"

The proposition in the conclusion of our mini theory used above can be used as an example. It states that the degree to which the husband's family of orientation values education is related to the amount of housework the husband will perform. This concluding proposition will now become our research focus. When we decide to research a particular proposition, it becomes the *conceptual hypothesis* in addition to being the deduced conclusion of a theoretical argument.

The first thing we must do to research this conceptual hypothesis is to find ways to measure its components as variables. That means that we must find or develop measures for the first concept, husband's family of orientation's values on education, and the second concept, amount of housework performed. Finally, we must not forget that we must find a way to demonstrate (or operationalize) the relation between these concepts. We might operationalize or measure the family of orientation's values on education by asking the husband several questions about his perception of his mother's and father's values about education and how much financial assistance they offered for his education. Both of these measures would have problems of validity and reliability because of faulty recall, halo effects, and so on. We might measure amount of housework by either the number of hours spent on various household tasks or the economic value of tasks performed by the husband. Both of these measures would have problems. Which tasks should we list? Would the husband inflate his estimate of the time spent? If we had the husband list the tasks and then assigned the economic value at the cost of a plumber for plumbing jobs, a babysitter for child care, and so on, would we find that this correlates poorly with the measure of amount of time spent on household chores? Indeed, there are always problems and questions regarding how accurately our empirical operationalizations measure our concepts in our conceptual hypothesis.

The last component of our conceptual hypothesis to be operationalized is the *relation*. As we indicated previously, we hypothesize that amount of housework is a function of family's values on education. What is this function? In most social research, the first functional form that we test is that of a straight line. You may recall the slope-intercept formula for a straight line ($y = b[x] + a$). Indeed, this simple mathematical model is the basis for much of our analysis of relations in the social sciences. The formula for a straight line is a *mathematical model,* and it has a corresponding *statistical model* expressed in the formula ($Y = a + b[X] + e$). Basically, the application of the statistical formula in the analysis of the data allows us to examine the linear relation between amount of housework (Y) and the family's values on education (X). The strength and direction (positive or negative) of that relation will be given by the regression (correlation) coefficient (b).

Once all the measures are in place, we have, in effect, two hypotheses. Our theoretical proposition represents the conceptual hypothesis, and our measures and the relation between them represent the *measurement hypothesis*. The architecture of the empirical test of a theory is portrayed in Figure 1.1.

Finally, if we were to conduct our study on husbands in dual-career couples, we would have to control for several variables that might account for the relationship, such as number of children, maid service, wife's level of housework, and income level. After we analyze the results, we might

Figure 1.1   Conceptual and Measurement Hypotheses

THEORY PROPOSITIONS

↓

Derived Theoretical or Conceptual Hypothesis (proposition)

↓

CONCEPT X	**RELATION**	**CONCEPT Y**
Family of orientation's value on education	→ *is a function of* →	*Husband's amount of housework*

	process of operationalization	
↓		↓
↓	↓	↓
↓	↓	↓

Measurement Hypothesis

Measure of Concept X	**Measure of Relation**	**Measure of Concept Y**
Husband's perception of his family	→ $Y = \beta X + e$ →	*Husband's self-reported hours of housework*

find that there is no relationship between the variables we measured. If we can satisfy our critical colleagues that we have valid and reliable measures of the concepts and relations in the conceptual hypothesis, then we could conclude that the theoretical proposition is false. Because this is a deductive system (syllogism), we would also know that at least one of our premises is also wrong. As a result, it would be time either to recast and modify the theory significantly or even to discard it completely.

On the other hand, what if our results are supportive of the conceptual hypothesis? If we can satisfy our colleagues regarding the validity and reliability of our measures and procedures, then we might want to say that the theory is true. However, as we said previously, this would be committing the fallacy of affirming the consequent. If the proposition seems to hold, it does not mean that the other propositions (premises) are true because it is logically possible to deduce the conclusion from several other sets of premises. We can never determine which possible set of premises might be true. As a result, science and theory achieve a great deal by disproving hypotheses and theoretical propositions rather than ever proving anything. All our scientific knowledge is tentatively held until we disprove it. Scientists are not true believers but skeptics.

Functions of Theory

Scientific theories serve many purposes. Here, we emphasize how they contribute to understanding. It is widely recognized, however, that knowledge for its own sake is not the only worthwhile goal in life. We all want to do something with our knowledge. In our preceding example, if we had some confidence in our theory about housework, a young woman searching for a helpful mate might want to examine the educational values of the family of orientation of prospective spouses. More seriously, for those in one of the helping professions, theories about the family may provide knowledge to improve their services as therapists, program evaluators, or social policy advisers. For those who are political activists, agitators for modest or revolutionary causes or the reduction of major social problems or even staunch defenders of the world as it is or once was, theoretical knowledge about families can be put to fruitful use. Without meaning to diminish the importance of any of these practical uses of theories, we concentrate here on the ways in which theories contribute to the immediate goals of science.

1. *Accumulation.* Theories assist in the accumulation and organization of research findings. Much of the pursuit of knowledge involves the collection and analysis of empirical facts, filtered through the lenses of researchers. A body of empirical knowledge, however, is just a pile of findings. Theories tell us how to select and arrange research findings into meaningful groupings. If no existing theory is available for this purpose, new theories can be constructed from findings through a process of tentative generalization.

2. *Precision.* Theories articulate ideas in more carefully specified ways than everyday language allows. Thinking theoretically forces one to clarify what concepts and relations really mean and what they include and exclude. This precision facilitates communication so long as the communicators are trained in the language of science.

3. *Guidance.* Theories direct researchers to develop and test measurement hypotheses (i.e., empirical statements about what the data are expected to look like). Because theoretical ideas entail abstract, plausible, and tentative arguments, they must be checked against the empirical evidence for confidence in them to grow. Theories point to new kinds of relevant evidence for which findings do not currently exist. It is relatively easy to find or create evidence in support of a theory that one likes, however. Theories, therefore, also promote a critical spirit of inquiry. Efforts are made to refute theories, not just to support them. If a field contains two or more theories that yield incompatible hypotheses, it may be possible to design a study or a series of studies that help decide which theory is better.

4. *Connectedness.* Theories demonstrate how ideas are connected to each other and to other theories. Theories are systematic sets of ideas. The parts of a theory fit together in a coherent way. Knowing what the parts are and how they fit together helps distinguish one theory from other theories. This also helps us see what two or more theories share or how they could be connected or combined by bringing together elements of each.

5. *Interpretation.* Theories help make sense of how the phenomena they cover operate. There are at least two aspects of sensibleness in interpretation. One is essentially descriptive: A theory should enable a good description of the subject matter with which it is concerned. This does not necessarily mean that the theory must fit our intuitive judgments of the way things work. In fact, a theory may challenge many intuitions or commonsense views of the world. Rather, to enable us to describe a subject, a theory provides a plausible picture of structures or processes that we can accept as reasonable given the assumptions in the theory. The other feature of interpretation is that theories evoke or promote stories about the way things work. If we can visualize concrete or even general scenarios of how things work, the theory is providing an interpretation.

6. *Prediction.* Theories point to what will or can happen in the future. If a theory helps us understand what has happened in the past or is happening now, this is, of course, desirable. To continue to be useful, however, a theory must contain propositions equally applicable to future events and experiences. This does not mean that any theory accurately foretells the future, only that it should make some relevant propositions regarding future outcomes. If we know what a theory predicts, this can contribute to the guidance function mentioned earlier. If a theory predicts something that is subject to human intervention and alteration, future actions may invalidate the theory. Normally, however, a theory is expected to hold up in the future to the extent that its predictions are confirmed. Even if predictions are not confirmed, the theory may be basically correct, and only the conditions under which it works may require revision.

7. *Explanation.* Theories provide answers to *why* and *how* questions. As the quotes in Box 1.1 from Burr (1973) and Homans (1964) suggest, explanation is often considered the single most important function of a theory. Because explanation is so central to the functioning of theories and because it has a variety of different meanings, we need to address this topic in more detail. Without theories, we cannot determine why and how things happen the way they do. In our everyday lives, we may be satisfied by saying that one specific event, say, a divorce between two friends, happened because of one or more other events that took place before the divorce. Such reasoning captures some of what goes into a scientific explanation, but it overlooks the most important aspect. Scientific theories explain by relying on

deductive arguments. Specific events and the connections between them must be derived from more general statements for us to say that the events and the connections between them have been explained.

Explanation is provided by a general statement (sometimes called a "covering law") that includes (or covers) the specific instance we want to explain. So, for example, if you drop this book and it falls to the floor, we could ask you to explain why it fell. You would simply cite the law of gravity as explaining why the book fell. This is to say that the particular phenomenon is part of a generally understood pattern we call *gravity*. Now, this is not to say that, in reality, our understanding of gravity is simple; indeed, it involves complex theories of electromagnetism, mass, space, and time. But the law derived from these complex theories covers the specific phenomenon of the falling book. Thus, to explain why someone got divorced (a particular instance) would be to provide the general theoretical propositions (covering laws) explaining divorce.

It is crucial to remember that although functions or goals such as those we have listed represent ideals, this is no guarantee that a particular theory will fulfill such ideals. In fact, we can use the seven listed functions as standards against which to measure the performance of a theory at any stage of its development. A theory may perform well in some respects but less well in others. Determining such facts helps us decide where our energies need to be directed to improve the theories that we have or invent better ones.

Theories About Families

Ideas about human families can come from many sources, including scientific disciplines concerned with the study of entities that are not families, as well as personal experiences with our own families. No potential source should be dismissed, although we should be aware that those sources selected likely will affect key features of the theory that emerges. Most of the family theories that exist today draw on ideas from external sources. Family theories are not insulated sets of ideas, and family theorists do not merely talk to each other about family ideas.

For a theory to be about families, there must be at least one family concept in the theory. We cannot decide what a family concept is, however, unless we first decide what a family is. Indeed, foundational assumptions are often definitions of such important terms. Therefore, let us begin by thinking of a family as a social group. We need to identify the distinguishing features of this group. Following are some of the major ways that families differ from such groups as associations of coworkers and networks of close friends.

1. *Families last for a considerably longer period of time than do most other social groups.*

Of course, some relationships in families are not enduring. Marriages can be broken by divorce or death fairly soon after they are formed. Yet we normally think of our own families as lasting throughout our lifetimes. We actually are born into a family that already exists. Our parents remain parents even after we become adults. We add members to the family when we marry and become parents. Our siblings remain siblings throughout our lifetimes. Although it is possible for coworkers and close friends to maintain relationships for long periods of time, families are the only groups that virtually require lifetime membership, even though some members are added and subtracted along the way. Belonging to a family is involuntary in the sense that we do not choose which parents are going to give birth to us. Other groups tend to be much more voluntary, in that we have some choice about joining them in the first place.

2. *Families are intergenerational.*

Through the act of giving birth, families include people who are related as parents and children. If elders live long enough, we have ties to grandparents and maybe even to great-grandparents and great-great-grandparents. At some point, we ordinarily have living members of both older and younger generations, and we may eventually become grandparents or great-grandparents ourselves. Other kinds of groups may include people with fairly large age differences, but families are the only groups that virtually guarantee this.

The fact that the human infant at birth is a helpless creature and cannot approach self-sufficiency for almost 20 years means that the intergenerational bond is particularly crucial to human survival. Every child needs some sort of caretaker and caregiver, whether it is a biological parent, an adoptive or foster parent, or somebody else who takes the responsibility for providing nurturance during the early years of life. It is no accident that our image of family includes an intergenerational component.

3. *Families contain both biological and affinal (e.g., legal, common law) relationships between members.*

It is the biological act of birth that creates the fundamental family tie. This act also means that we share at least some inherited characteristics or proclivities with family members who are directly or indirectly related to us by birth. At least until humans perfect the cloning of adults, and perhaps even then, the process of becoming a person will be based to some degree on biology. Families are in the business of producing and sustaining persons and personhood. Even though work groups or friendship groups may sometimes contain biologically related members, such groups tend to have other purposes.

There is also a social side to this process of creating persons. No society leaves the biological act of birth or the rearing of children to chance. Personhood is achieved through a process of socialization. That socialization is subject to secular and religious rules about how the process should be carried out. Pursuant to these rules, family members have rights and obligations that tend to be codified in both laws and informal agreements.

Aside from adoption, the major legal provision about families concerns marriage. We may not think of a marriage in itself as constituting a family, but we recognize marital relationships as part of families. Some families are conjugal, in that they contain one or more marriages. It might even be argued that if humans didn't have families, they wouldn't need marriages, although families may often function well without marriage. In any case, marriage itself involves rights and obligations under the law, and it also creates family ties in law. Some of our family members join and leave the group either because of our own marriages and divorces or because of the marriages and divorces of other family members.

Other kinds of groups are subject to regulation by laws (e.g., contracts) and informal agreements, of course. Such regulations may exclude as well as include people in work and friendship groups, and they govern proper conduct within such groups. What such groups do not have, however, are relationships anything quite like, for example, cousins or aunts and nephews, which arise because our mother's sister is married.

4. *The biological (and affinal) aspect of families links them to a larger kinship organization.*

It follows from what we already have said that families are not just small groups of closely related individuals who live together or interact on a frequent basis. Families extend outward to include anybody sufficiently related to us by blood, marriage, or adoption. This kinship group may have the identifiable boundaries of a clan, or it may be loosely organized and diffuse. Everybody stops counting distant relatives as family members at some point along the periphery. Nevertheless, the ties of kinship create the potential for lineages and collateral (i.e., within-generation) family relationships that can become quite extensive. Through kinship, families are tied to history, tradition, and multiple generations of group members. In some societies, these kinship groups are major features of the social, cultural, political, and economic landscape. Work and friendship groups tend to be much more temporally and spatially encapsulated.

To answer the questions in Box 1.2, we likely will find ourselves asking other questions. Do we visualize the people listed in each example as all being part of one family, or do they belong to two or more different families? Are the listed persons the only ones in the family, or could there also be others (i.e., is this a whole family or just part of one)? Should we think of these persons as members of an actual family, or are they a family in either a symbolic sense or in the way they function in their relationships? Are we thinking of how common or uncommon a grouping is in a particular society, either in frequency or in what is expected as normal, natural, and acceptable by law or custom? And are both affinal and consanguineous relationships identified as family relationships?

Box 1.2 Which of These Is a Family?

- A husband and wife and their offspring
- A single woman and her three young children
- A 52-year-old woman and her adoptive mother
- A man, his daughter, and the daughter's son
- An 84-year-old widow and her dog, Fido
- A man and all his ancestors back to Adam and Eve
- The 1979 World Champion Pittsburgh Pirates (theme song: "We Are Family")
- Three adult sisters living together
- Two lesbians in an intimate relationship and their children from a previous marriage of one woman and a previous relationship of the other woman with a male friend
- Two children, their divorced parents, the current spouses of their divorced parents, and the children from previous marriages of their stepparents
- A child, his stepfather, and the stepfather's wife subsequent to his divorce from the child's mother
- Two adult male cousins living together
- A 77-year-old man and his lifelong best friend
- A childless husband and wife who live 1,000 miles apart
- A widow and her former husband's grandfather's sister's granddaughter
- A divorced man, his girlfriend, and her child
- Both sets of parents of a deceased married couple
- A married couple, one son and his wife, and the latter couple's children, all living together
- Six adults and their 12 young children, all living together in a communal fashion

We could discuss additional arguments about the distinctive features of families as groups. For example, we could draw attention to certain qualities of social interaction that are commonly found in families but not elsewhere. One of these is that family members supposedly care about one another as whole persons (cf. Beutler, Burr, Bahr, & Herrin, 1989). Whichever criteria are considered, however, the distinctiveness of family groups tends to be only a matter of degree. Nonfamily groups, such as networks of friends or coworkers, usually have some family properties but fewer of these properties or in less obvious amounts.

It also is worth noting that we can conceptualize the family not only as a concrete group or social organization but also as a social institution. As an institution, family includes all the beliefs and practices of and about all the families in a particular society or geopolitical context. It also includes the ways in which different families are connected to each other and to other social institutions. For example, in most modern and well-developed societies, families tend to have a private character, each one walled or fenced off from other families and from public view much of the time. There also are expected and experienced linkages between families and schools, families and the workplace, families and governments, families and the mass media, and so on. Because members of families often share economic resources and collaborate in both productive labor and the consumption of resources, it is also useful to consider families as being involved in a society's system of social stratification. Thus, some families have more wealth, power, and status than do other families.

With an idea of the meaning of family, we can begin to envision what counts as a family concept. Some of these concepts describe the composition, or size and configuration, of family membership. Some describe the structures and processes of interaction that take place between family members. Some describe the ways that families relate to their environments. Some describe the whole family as a group, the family as an institution, or the nature of the ties between two or more members within the family group.

We believe that for a theory about human relationships to be a family theory, one or more ideas (concepts or variables) about families must be included in the theory. The family idea may appear in either or both of two places: (a) as part of the explanation (e.g., parental discipline helps explain juvenile delinquency), (b) as the phenomenon to be explained (e.g., the state of the economy in a country helps explain the divorce rate in that country), or (c) both (e.g., marital communication styles help explain marital satisfaction).

Thus, we can distinguish two general kinds of family theories, those that are "about the family" or explaining how families work (b and c above) and those that consider family ideas to be useful explanations (a and c above).

Of course, a wide variety of ideas, some familial and some not, may be needed in combination to adequately explain family life (e.g., marital affection plus the economy influence the odds of divorcing). Likewise, the forces that help explain family life may also help explain other things (e.g., the state of the economy may influence stock prices as well as the divorce rate). When assessing the family theories of others, or when creating one yourself, it helps to locate where the family ideas are, or at least where you think they belong.

Theorists can adopt narrow, intermediate, or broad definitions of what constitutes a family, why they exist, and what they do. Because families have changed historically, and likely will change in the future, we favor an inclusive definition of family, not because of personal preferences but because we advocate improving our theoretical understanding of family diversity and change.

Evaluation of Theory

While there is no one acceptable way to evaluate a particular theory or to compare the merits and shortcomings of two or more theories, it is very helpful to be able make judgments about the quality of the theories that exist. We have tried to be very cautious here about making final judgments about the adequacy of any theory, but members of the scientific community do look to certain standards for discriminating between theories as they exist at a given point in time.

Table 1.1 lists and defines in descending order of importance the 13 most frequently endorsed criteria, from a longer list of 32 criteria, based on a survey of a diverse group of more than 100 family scientists (Klein, 1994). Although there will always be some disagreement over the salience or importance that the various evaluative criteria receive, the following includes most of the criteria that have been used in recent times for the evaluation of theory and the relative weights used by scholars. We believe that even the systematic application of the first three or four of these criteria to the frameworks and theories in this book will assist the reader in developing his or her critical capacity in regard to family theory.

Frameworks

In light of the current situation, a precaution is in order as we prepare to explore in some detail nine of the currently important theoretical frameworks in the family studies. Our own map of the alternatives is not the

Table 1.1 Criteria for Evaluating Family Theories

1. **Internal consistency:** A theory does not contain logically contradictory assertions.

2. (Tie with 3) **Clarity or explicitness:** The ideas in a theory are expressed in such a way that they are unambiguous. They are defined and explicated where necessary.

3. **Explanatory power:** A theory explains well what it is intended to explain.

4. **Coherence:** The key ideas in a theory are integrated or interconnected, and loose ends are avoided.

5. (Tie with 6) **Understanding:** A theory provides a comprehensible sense of the whole phenomenon being examined.

6. **Empirical fit:** A large portion of the tests of a theory have been confirmatory or at least have not been interpreted as disconfirming.

7. **Testability:** It is possible for a theory to be empirically supported or refuted.

8. **Heuristic value:** A theory has generated or can generate considerable research and intellectual curiosity (including a large number of empirical studies, as well as much debate or controversy).

9. **Groundedness:** A theory has been built up from detailed information about events and processes observable in the world.

10. **Contextualization:** A theory gives serious consideration to the social and historical contexts affecting or affected by its key ideas.

11. **Interpretive sensitivity:** A theory reflects the experiences practiced and felt by the social units to which it is applied.

12. (Tie with 13) **Predictive power:** A theory can successfully predict phenomena that have occurred since it was formulated.

13. **Practical utility:** A theory can be readily applied to social problems, policies, and programs of action (i.e., it is useful for teaching, therapy, political action, or some combination of these).

Source: Klein (1994).

only possible one, nor is it necessarily complete and otherwise adequate. In 1950, only the functional and symbolic interactional perspectives, among the theories we cover, would likely have been widely recognized. Until the mid-1960s, two other perspectives that we do not cover as distinctive were commonly identified (institutional and situational). By this time, the developmental perspective had gained recognition, but several others were either widely rejected or absorbed into other points of view. When Nye and Berardo (1966/1981) attempted to comprehensively cover conceptual frameworks at the end of this period, they even added six more, each roughly representing an academic discipline (i.e., anthropology, psychoanalysis, social psychology, economics, legal studies, and Western Christian studies).

When Broderick (1971) reviewed the theoretical developments of the 1960s, he saw several new possibilities. Of these, the exchange and systems perspectives have continued to thrive, and they are represented in our following chapters. By the end of the 1970s, a similar review by Holman and Burr (1980) added conflict, behavioral, ecological, and phenomenological perspectives as being of at least secondary importance. Of these, we give major attention only to the conflict and ecological perspectives. When Nye and Berardo (1966/1981) reissued their 1966 book, they added exchange, systems, and conflict theories in their introduction, as well as "social individualism" and "transactional analysis," neither of which seem to have progressed thereafter. Finally, the most recent comprehensive treatment includes more than a dozen chapters on distinct theoretical perspectives (Boss, Doherty, LaRossa, Schumm, & Steinmetz, 1993), with the notable addition of feminist theory.

A fruitful typology of theories is only partially in the eye of the beholder. Some threads seem to be common to the various alternative classifications, and some reflect historical changes in the field regarding the popularity and promise of the alternatives. Nevertheless, each mapping of the territory is at least somewhat dependent on the purposes and viewpoint of the author. In our case, we aim for relative simplicity to meet the needs of readers. We capitalize on the existing complexity mainly by covering some of the varying and more recent emphases within the broader traditions.

We use an organizational concept throughout this book: that of *theoretical framework*. What we mean by theoretical framework is that there exists in each scientific field a core of theoretical assumptions and propositions. We do not simply refer to these as theories, because although they are theories, they also are sufficiently general to have given rise to a number of theoretical variants. In this one sense, these theoretical frameworks are like families, with the core theory providing sufficient richness for the development of offspring.

STUDY QUESTIONS ———————————————

1. What is a fact?

2. Why and how do scientific facts change?

3. Can you construct a theory without making assumptions?

4. Why do scientific theories want to be logical? (Hint: Do illogical arguments offer an appealing explanation; for instance, "he was in this room and the room next door at the same time"?)

5. Can a theory explain but not predict, or predict but not explain? (Hint: Think of a prediction model based on past behaviors but not having any discussion on *why* something happens.)

6. In this book, what is a framework?

2

Classical Social Theories and Family Theories

Matt and Sarah were arguing about why Amanda and Drew broke up. Matt argued that they never had "chemistry" from the beginning, and so they lacked the "glue" to stay together. Sarah disagreed. She maintained that Amanda was very "romantic" and that Drew was simply too practical and mundane. As they both argued their perspectives, Sarah suddenly said, "Wait a minute! Matt, our argument is not about Amanda and Drew but about larger assumptions. You think that relationships are basically driven by biological forces, whereas I think relationships are formed by compatible personalities."

What Sarah has noticed about the argument is that our explanations of relationships, or anything else for that matter, are founded on assumptions. In the first chapter, we discussed "assumptions as a basic construct in the architecture of theories." Behind every explanatory theory of why or how something happens is a set of assumptions about the nature of causation and the processes that produce the outcomes we wish to explain. This chapter explores the nature of some of these assumptions captured as "philosophies" and how these assumptions have been expressed over the history of theories about families.

Philosophies of Science

The term *philosophy* can refer to two different things. On the one hand, a philosophy might refer to the values and way of thinking of a person. We might say that someone who likes to shop is a *materialist*, meaning that he or she values material objects. The other meaning of philosophy refers to the academic discipline of philosophy. Both meanings are important in understanding the emergence and growth of family theories and frameworks, but for the moment, we focus on the importance and relevance of academic philosophy, especially the academic philosophy of science, for scientific theories.

The methods of philosophy are logic and other forms of discursive reasoning. In general, philosophers do not use the empirical methods of science to establish the credibility of their ideas. Some philosophers, known as philosophers of science, examine the principles by which scientists work through reconstructing the logic of scientific processes. Whereas sociologists of science systematically study the behaviors and thoughts of scientists and the social organization of the sciences, philosophers of science explore what science should or could be like in terms of abstract ideas. There are several ways in which this philosophical study is important.

The discipline of philosophy was historically prior to the scientific disciplines. The ancient Greek philosophers and oriental philosophers had many creative ideas about human affairs and the workings of the natural world. It was out of the Enlightenment philosophy of the 18th and 19th centuries that the modern sciences in the Western world were born. During this period, it was common for individual scholars to be both philosopher and scientist at the same time or to easily shift back and forth between the two. It was only during the 19th and 20th centuries that the various scientific disciplines branched into special fields to which a person could devote an entire career.

The historical legacy of philosophy as a precedent to the sciences has meant that philosophy, as a formal discipline, has influenced all sciences. Many of the influences have been indirect. The so-called physical sciences, such as physics and chemistry, emerged first. Between 1850 and 1900, the philosophical principles embedded in these earlier sciences spilled over into the biological sciences, such as botany and zoology, and the social sciences, such as psychology and sociology. During the 20th century, family studies emerged as a subspecialty within several of the social sciences. Now, in the early 21st century, some scholars think of family studies as a distinct field with an interdisciplinary character or even as a unique discipline in its own right.

In philosophy, as in other academic disciplines, new ideas are constantly being proposed and debated. A particular philosophy of science may be popular at a given moment, but later it may be challenged and some other philosophy may take its place at or near the top of the heap. Scientists, including family scientists, frequently turn to the literature produced by philosophers to see what the current issues are. When scientists need to justify the basic principles guiding their search for answers to important questions, they sometimes seek guidance from philosophers of science or from other philosophers.

It is now often asserted that there are different, if not rival, philosophies of science. This is apparent in professional philosophy itself and, more important for this book, among family scholars as well. The philosophies we adopt influence the way we conduct our scientific practice, including the theories we create and our attitudes toward the theories of others. We sketch below a few of the central philosophical views that may help distinguish family theorists and other family scholars from one another.

Key elements of three philosophies of science appear in Box 2.1. We have called these *positivistic, interpretive,* and *critical* philosophies of science (e.g., Neuman, 1994). We do not claim that these are the only three alternatives in family science. Indeed, we discuss other alternatives such as feminism and postmodernism in subsequent chapters. At this juncture, we present Box 2.1 to illustrate the nature of philosophical assertions.

The divergence from positivism can be traced to two major influences. First, a group of philosophers working in Vienna in the early part of the 20th century argued that knowledge claims are either true or false and that the job of scientists is to verify the true claims. Another philosopher, Sir Karl Popper, disputed this view. Popper (1959) argued that empirical knowledge claims could be shown to be false but that there is no way to prove them to be true. Popper's position has become influential among not only philosophers but also practicing social scientists. Whether or not family scholars have read Popper, his ideas have indirectly influenced family theorizing, helping usher in what is sometimes called a postpositive era in the philosophy of social science (Thomas & Wilcox, 1987).

The second major influence was a work by historian and philosopher of science Thomas Kuhn (1962/1998) titled *The Structure of Scientific Revolutions.* Kuhn launched many important arguments (see White, 2004), and among these was the interpretation that science did not proceed on the basis of rational evidence and the elimination of competing hypotheses as much as it proceeded by the political processes similar to any other social organization. Successful theories were seen as developed by winning adherents rather than careful proof and investigation. The effect of this interpretation was to undermine the credibility of positivistic science and to put forth a relativistic position that "truth" is decided by whoever holds power.

Relativistic positions have seldom been popular in the philosophy of science because they fly in the face of facts such as the usefulness of scientific knowledge, medical science, and technology. Indeed, the major reactions against relativism have come from *pragmatists* (e.g., Peirce, Rorty, & Haack) who hold that although knowledge is social, it nonetheless is guided by principals that set standards for what we regard as acceptable evidence, whether it be in a court of law or in a scientific laboratory. While the pragmatist position does not admit absolute truth, it maintains a far less relativistic position regarding scientific knowledge than many interpretivist and critical theorist positions (see Box 2.1). Today, most family scholars would probably fall into this perspective, which might be described as *pragmatic positivism.*

Box 2.1   Three Philosophies of Science Applied to Family Theories

Positivist View

View of knowledge: There are accepted methods that differentiate more adequate claims about families from those that are less adequate. Although the older versions of positivism would have claimed access to objectivity, most current formulations argue a less absolute position in terms of truth and objectivity (see White, 2004).

Goals of family theory: Explanation and prediction of family phenomena and events

Interpretive View

View of knowledge: All knowledge is gained by interpreting the meanings that family members assign to an event or behavior. Truth is relative to each actor's meanings and the context in which these meanings occur. Interpretive knowledge tends to be relativistic and reflexive.

Goals of family theory: Understanding, empathy

Critical View

View of knowledge: Truth is imposed by those who control the power to shape knowledge. There is a plurality of theories, but the theories that acquire truth status are those that support and maintain the prevailing power system. Knowledge is always defined by those in power to serve their purposes.

Goals of family theory: Emancipation and empowerment of oppressed social groups

Source: Adapted from Neuman, 1994.

Values in Science

One of the key reasons that positivistic science emerged historically as a way of thinking and working that is somewhat different from the arts, religion, and politics was concern about the distortions in knowledge along with considerable human suffering that seem to result when reasonableness, fairness, and facts are devalued. Science is not without its faults, just as no individual human being or social organization is faultless. The *value neutrality* sometimes advocated by scientific positivists is similar in at least some ways to value tolerance or respect for value diversity. But this is a matter of degree, and the value-relevant and value-laden positions of the critical and interpretive perspectives (see Box 2.1) may push the ideals of tolerance and diversity to an extreme point of complete relativism.

Writing several decades ago about science as a vocation, sociologist Max Weber made some interesting comments:

> Today one usually speaks of science as free of presuppositions. Is there such a thing? All scientific work presupposes that the rules of logic and method are valid. Science further presupposes that what is yielded by scientific work is important in the sense that it is worth being known. In this, obviously, are contained all our problems. For this presupposition cannot be proved by scientific means. It can only be interpreted with reference to its ultimate meaning, which we must reject or accept according to our ultimate position toward life. (quoted in Gerth & Mills, 1946, p. 143)

More recently, Christensen (1964) provided an analysis of the value issue in family science. His assessment was quite Weberian. Christensen advocated neither the rejection nor the espousal of nonscientific values by theorists and other scientists. Rather, he advocated the identification and separation of nonscientific values from scientific values. Indeed, the values of positivistic science are, for the most part, methodological. That is, positivism values knowledge that can be empirically replicated, knowledge that has distinct observable components, and knowledge that is more general and law-like than an individual case or instance. This may continue to be the most common view among family scientists, but it is not the only view. Those perspectives that do not distinguish methodological rules for separating more from less adequate knowledge claims end up with only a set of beliefs often called ideology.

The notion of ideology has three major meanings: (a) a set of beliefs; (b) the systematic study of a set of beliefs, their nature, and their origin; and (c) visionary speculation, often about ideals and with an action agenda for achieving the ideals. There is no question that systems of belief about families can be part of a family theory or that carefully studying those beliefs might improve a family theory. There is also no doubt that beliefs about family science can affect family theories. Even visionary speculation has creative potential for theories. Our caution is only that ideologies among family scholars that are philosophical or political may be usefully connected with a particular family theory, but they are not within or constitutive of the theory itself. So, if a scientific theory argues that *X* causes *Y*, the truth of this does not depend on whether we like or dislike *X* or *Y*. The theory may suggest how to change *Y* if the direction of change is consistent with our values and ideology, but scientific theory should be equally useful for someone with exactly the opposite values and ideology.

As citizens and professionals, we may want to help someone or eradicate a certain type of behavior such as bullying or date rape based on our moral values. These values may motivate social scientists to study certain areas rather than others. When it comes to taking action, however, professionals are constrained by the code of ethics of their profession and the common legal understanding that professionals are not liable as long as they follow the best practices of their profession. For almost all professions, *best practices* are defined as following actions informed and justified by scientific findings. From social work to medicine, best practices entail evidence-based practice where evidence is defined scientifically. For professional interventions, therefore, the importance of relatively objective and reliable scientific findings is a critical part of helping others or changing the world. It is important to note that data that are twisted to fit particular values would not be useful for evidence-based practice and would fail to meet scientific standards of reliability and validity.

To summarize, philosophical ideas establish principles that help frame the ways that family theories and other aspects of scholarship are created and used. Philosophical ideas are themselves foundations for scholarship, but they cannot be scientifically proven true or false. In many ways, scholars either consciously or unconsciously adopt a particular philosophical stance in regard to research by the way they do their research. Those who attempt not to use their research as a vehicle for their own values, the values of their religion, or their political values would be clearly identified as positivist. Although those holding interpretive and critical philosophies have criticized this perspective, the positivist approach remains the hallmark of scientific work and scholarly accountability. Indeed, the public expects family scientists to present their research findings independent from their religious and political beliefs. In science, it is expected that any research finding can be replicated by other researchers regardless of whether they have the same or different political and religious beliefs. This is as close as we may be able to get to scientific "objectivity."

What Is an Explanation?

We have stated that our explanations of relationships, families, or anything else for that matter are founded on assumptions. In the previous section, we argued that some of the assumptions we make are guided or misguided by the epistemologies we assume, and these were summarized as the positivist view, the interpretive view, and the critical view. In this section, we take a slightly different approach to the issue about the assumptions we make. Pragmatism would suggest that the assumptions we make would be formed by the goal or purpose we have in mind. In the pragmatic tradition, we argue that family scholarship and research are trying to produce knowledge and explanation. The assumptions we make should, therefore, be useful in moving us toward our goal of producing knowledge and acquiring explanations.

Of course, this raises the obvious question of what we mean by knowledge and explanation. One of us (White, 2013) has argued that historically knowledge has been characterized as being true and factual. Such a characterization of knowledge throws us into philosophical debates about the nature of truth and the nature of reality. To avoid these debates, one might focus on the nature of scientific knowledge rather than the more generic and vernacular meanings of knowledge. Scientific knowledge is knowledge that is acquired by using the scientific method.

The more specialized approach to knowledge as established by the scientific method is not without its own special problems and somewhat flies in the face of the common vernacular definition. First, science is largely based on disconfirmation of hypotheses, and as such, any fact or truth can be viewed only as tentative rather than everlasting. Second, the scientific method, as a criterion for scientific knowledge, is less than clear. In fact, scientific methods are diverse. Archaeology uses naturalistic field methods that are distinct from the laboratory experiments of cellular biologists yet no less scientific. Indeed, over the history of science, the appropriate methods are principally defined by whatever criteria are accepted by the community of scientists in each field in each time period (see Kuhn, 1962/1998; Hellemans & Bunch, 1988). So what makes scientific knowledge scientific is not completely clear.

The sociologist Robert Merton (1973) argues that there are a set of values that underlie the methods of scientists. Following Merton, Allchin (1998) and later White (2004) argue that these values are epistemic rather than teleological values. *Teleological values* focus on a final end or purpose such as the "betterment of humans." *Epistemic values* are values about the principles that guide our acquisition of knowledge. These authors argue that scientific knowledge is knowledge that is acquired by methods that reflect values on honesty, skepticism, universalism, open communication, and evidence. All these values are represented in various historical periods, whether it be in the work of scientists such as Copernicus, Newton, Einstein, or Crick and Watson. In any one historical period, the community of scientists defines scientific methods based on these values.

Although the inclusion of epistemic values might help clarify what scientific knowledge is, the questions regarding knowledge and explanation remain. White (2013) claims that given the "universalistic" values of science, knowledge is something we tentatively hold that has the capacity to generalize across time periods and contexts. For example, the theory of gravitational forces in contemporary physics is one such type of knowledge. It must be kept in mind that such knowledge is always being modified and changed depending on research and lacks the stability of other forms of knowledge such as religious truths. Religious truths require beliefs, but scientific knowledge requires evidence.

It is perhaps easier to understand the universalistic criterion in science if we briefly examine "scientific explanation." Most of the discussions about scientific explanation focus on the argument made by Hempel and Oppenheim (1948) commonly known as the "covering law" model of scientific explanation. The covering law model supposes that an explanation of a given phenomenon is a deduction from premises composed of at least one general law-like statement and specific conditions. For example, if you were to hold this book above the ground and drop it, the explanation would be provided by the general laws of gravity plus the specific mass of the book and the mass of Earth and any other relevant conditions such as air pressure, wind velocity, and so on. Indeed in this perspective, an explanation is a logical explanation of a phenomenon that has occurred and that the explanation was able to predict.

Salmon (1984) has been one of the major critics of the covering law model, arguing instead for a causal model of explanation. The causal model of scientific explanation works well for some areas of science such as chemistry and physics but less well for more descriptive sciences such as natural history, biology, and archaeology. In addition, the deterministic thinking in the causal model is somewhat at odds with contemporary thinking about multiple causality and equifinality as it is with stochastic and probabilistic models. It can also be effectively argued that causal explanations are simply a specific form of the more general covering law model. The law-like statement in the covering law is simply replaced with a general causal statement. So in effect, we now have a fair degree of consensus as to what a scientific explanation entails.

Returning to the pragmatic position, what then would be the assumptions that would move us toward the goal of acquiring scientific knowledge and explanation? First, the epistemic values of honesty, skepticism, open communication, universalism, and evidence would be a foundation for our knowledge. Second, we are focused on acquiring information that is sufficiently general so as to allow us to construct explanations as either covering laws or causal models. Not all the theories we cover in this book are necessarily at the same stage of development. Some theories are very close to offering us covering law or causal models, whereas others are still progressing from using metaphors in order to explain. Most of the theories in this book would agree with the epistemic values that underlie scientific knowledge and increasingly secular knowledge in the 21st century.

Classical Social Theories

Classical social theory can be traced back to the pre-Socratic philosophers of Greece and the moralistic philosophers of China, such as Confucius. Much of the most relevant classical theory is from the period of early Modernism (1800–1900). It was during this time that scientific methods moved from the empirical inductionism of Francis Bacon's *Novum Organum* (1620) to a more deductive approach strongly influenced by Isaac Newton's *Philosopiae Naturalis Principia Mathematica* (1687). Whereas Bacon advocated that science should observe, record, and generalize from empirical events, Newton's method emphasized the importance of rational thought and mathematics in creating laws from which we could explain events. Although as we shall see, there is even today a strong inductionist influence in the social sciences (e.g., phenomenology, grounded theory), most of the social sciences focus on the Newtonian approach that is more deductive. Today when we say theory is inductive, we mean that it attempts to reach generalized laws or regularities by observing particulars. Deduction on the other hand usually means that we generate laws by thought and then generate hypotheses from our theory for testing our thinking against empirical data. Clearly, these two approaches can be used in very compatible ways, and many scholars today would see theoretical methods as a mixture of these two.

What is important for us is to understand that during the period of early Modernism, theories were formed using either one or both of these approaches. We now turn to an examination of some of the most influential of these social theories. As we shall see, these theories have formed the broad strokes of the contemporary social theories and family theories that you study today. These classical theories tended not to focus on the family but instead viewed family as just like other social groups. Certainly, this changed in the 20th century, and we shall see this change as we get to contemporary iterations of theory.

Marx and the Sweep of History

Most students are familiar with the work of Karl Marx once he and Engels were contracted to write the *Communist Manifesto* pamphlet (1848; *The Communist Manifesto* book was written later, 1867/1971). Certainly, the political pamphlet inflamed sensitivities of Victorians and established Marx and Engels as ideological socialists. However, Marx's academic writing (often with F. Engels) encompassed historiography (*The German Ideology*, 1845/1932), historical political analysis (*The Eighteenth Brumaire*, 1852/1963) and, later, political economy (*Capital*, vol.1, 1867/1992). Although political scientists and economists might see Marx's contributions to social thought in a different perspective, we emphasize Marx's contribution to macroscopic historiography. This contribution is evident in early writings such as *The German Ideology* but is also well documented in Marx's influence on Engel's *The Origin of the Family, Private Property, and the State* (1884/1946) published after Marx's death.

In terms of historiography, Marx is well known for the concept of *dialectical materialism*. This concept was clearly derived from the philosophy of history identified with G. W. F. Hegel and known as German idealism or absolute idealism. While Hegel argued that a dialectic of ideas explains political and economic history, Marx turns this on its head and argues that it is not ideas that drive the world but our relation to physical material. His dialectic incorporated two such relations: owning or controlling the means of production or laboring for those that own or control. For Marx, all of history could be explained by these two relations.

It was only after Marx's death that Engels applied this Marxian dialectic to the family in *The Origin of the Family, Private Property and the State* (1884/1946). It is in this book that the original dialectic is envisioned as being between the sexes. Although early ethnographies of hunter-gather groups led to somewhat erroneous conclusions regarding which sex, male or female, controlled the means of production, this work's breadth and vision contributed significantly to contemporary theories in both the Feminist and Conflict Frameworks. In addition, Marx's work remains a significant influence on contemporary economic theories (see Piketty, *Capital in the Twenty-First Century*, 2014).

The overall effect on contemporary theory goes far beyond any particular concept. The Marxian vision is one in which the power and sweep of history is responsible for outcomes rather than individuals or groups. Indeed, individuals are at the mercy of forces greater than themselves or even their country. Historical period and the dialectical forces of history are causal. Even though we need not use dialectical materialism as an explanation, we can see this perspective—that history is a macroforce—in perspectives such as environmental theory (climate change), inevitability of social conflicts (Huntington's *Clash of Civilizations and the Remaking of World Order*, 1996/2007), and evolutionary ecology (e.g., Chapter 9). The basic idea that humans are being swept along by forces larger than themselves is basic to such approaches.

Durkheim's Norms and Social Change

Emile Durkheim is certainly one of the most influential early contributors to social analysis. His works include *The Rules of Sociological Method* (1895), *Division of Labour in Society* (1893), and *Suicide* (1897). His perspective is that the study of social groups and societies is based on what he called "social facts." A social fact is composed of the norms, beliefs, and values held by the collective, external to an individual, that have coercive power over the individual. For example, if it is a hot day and you would like to take off your clothes, you are constrained by the social norms of others, depending on whether you are at a nudist camp or a downtown shopping center. Durkheim argued that these elements (social facts) could contribute to integration and social solidarity or to disorganization and dysfunction. In his classic work on suicide, Durkheim argued that societies with low integration and social cohesion were more likely to have higher rates of suicide. The major contributions of Durkheim are diverse. He demonstrated that societies could be studied scientifically as advocated earlier by his colleague Comte. He founded the *institutional* approach with the idea of *social facts*. Finally, Durkheim is often credited as an early champion of *functionalism*.

Although Durkheim's contributions are many, we focus on one major contribution that has been important for the development of social theory of the family. This is the concept of *norms*. This concept has been interpreted by many theorists as explaining patterns of family formation and structure. This concept is applied to rule-governed patterns of behavior within families (e.g., bedtime) and external to any one family (e.g., societal laws about child abuse and spanking). The social psychological dimension of this concept is often identified as "expectations," whereas the institutional dimension is often called informal and formal norms. In both of these senses, norms are the social expectations for behavior in a social group, organization, or society.

Durkheim also discussed situations where norms break down and become vague or ambiguous as social disorganization for groups and anomie (or lack of guidance) for individuals. While recognizing that social disorganization brings difficulties for social groups and individuals, Durkheim also argues that social change comes about by such disorganization and the resulting reorganization of social groups. Certainly, this is relevant to the increasing diversity of family forms we find in society today. Many critics see this increasing diversity as a sign of social breakdown and disorganization. However, it seems clear from the scientific research on cohabitation that this newer stage of mate selection has become accepted and expected in much of the world. Such an argument owes a great deal to Durkheim's early efforts.

Weber's Methodological Individualism and the Protestant Ethic

Max Weber is well known as an advocate of interpretive approaches to understanding social behavior. This means that while Durkheim and Comte were advocating scientific procedures for explanation, Weber was advocating understanding, or *verstehen*. This approach emphasized contextual interpretation of symbols and meanings. This was a familiar approach during this historical period and had been used for some time by religious scholars as the hermeneutics or contextual interpretation of religious texts. It is not surprising that Weber's most famous work deals with religion, *The Protestant Ethic and the Spirit of Capitalism,* (1904), and that he also wrote separate books on the religions of China, India, and Judaism. At the same time, Weber was trained in jurisprudence as well as economics and contributed to our understanding of the ongoing process of rationalization and bureaucratization of societies in such works as *Economy and Society* (1978/1922).

Throughout Weber's work, there is a strong methodological commitment to understanding how individuals behave by understanding beliefs and values within the historical context. This devotion to methodological individualism can be seen as a form of reductionism except that Weber also strongly argued for macro-level forces. It is in his 1904 work that this is perhaps most clear. Weber argues that capitalism would not have developed if it were not for the particular *soteriology,* or salvational ethics, that developed among early Protestant sects. Especially important is the need to establish one's *elect* status by economic success, while not being able to enjoy or show off that wealth in any way (no dancing, only plain clothes, etc.). As a result, profit was reinvested as capital rather than enjoyed. The comparative method that Weber preferred was used to show that capitalism developed only where such a salvational ethics existed and his studies of the religions of China and India and Judaism were used to demonstrate his thesis.

Although we could argue about the accuracy of his thesis, the methodology of contextual interpretation is well demonstrated in this work. Not only does Weber identify macro-level religious beliefs but he shows also that when those religious beliefs are incorporated in the individual, particular individual economic behavior (investing) results. This economic behavior reinforces the macro-level religion and provides funds (tithing) for the further success of the religion. So Weber successfully ties individual behavior with aggregated macro-level outcomes. As a result, Weber's insistence on the individual as the basis for causal interpretation in the social sciences seems plausible.

Weber's methodological individualism and religious studies are important to interpretive approaches to the family and the relation between family and society. Although Weber was not the only early social scientist to discuss problems with levels of analysis, he may well have been the most committed to keeping these individual levels and the macro level of social organizations distinct from one another. Today, Weber's work is a clear example of interpretive understanding mixed with positivism.

Spencer and Parsons Functional Social Systems

The basic ideas of functional explanation have been around for centuries. Every time we ask *how* something works instead of *why* something exists, we are asking for a functional explanation. Indeed, a key to understanding this theory is its concern with how the social world is constructed. Despite the long history of this tradition, we believe that the clearest progenitor of the 20th-century versions of the functionalist framework in the biological and social sciences is the evolutionary theories (Darwin, 1880) that developed during the middle of the 19th century and were incorporated into the work of Herbert Spencer on biology (1864), psychology (1855) and sociology (1874). Although functionalist thinking preceded Spencer, prior explanations had been limited. With the advent of evolutionary theory, it became plausible to expand functional arguments to explain not only why a set of functions developed but also how they might end. This dynamic argument became available through the concepts of *adaptation* and *selection*. Now scholars could talk about functions that were adaptive because they survived and dysfunctions were "selected" out of the population. Indeed, this meant that the original *how* question addressed by functional arguments moved increasingly close to also providing an explanation as to *why* a given structure exists. That is to say, a structure exists because it has been part of a functional system that has successfully adapted to the environment.

Early social theorists such as Spencer (1820–1903) and Durkheim (1858–1917) recognized how organic functionalism might be used to explain various social institutions and behaviors. For example, the family could be seen as supplying various functions such as reproduction to the larger social whole. Indeed, it was Durkheim (Lamanna, 2002) who believed that the parts of the social system had to be understood as functioning for the whole.

Although Spencer was among the first to adopt functionalist explanations, they were quickly followed by social and cultural anthropologists pursuing explanation of why and how different cultural traditions exist in various social systems. Among the leaders of the functionalist framework were two anthropologists who were to have a lasting effect on the logic of functionalism: A. R. Radcliffe-Brown (1881–1955) and Bronislaw Malinowski (1884–1942). Radcliffe-Brown's contribution to functionalism was to make it relative to the environment in which the society must adapt. He argued that a structure developed to serve a particular system within the parameters of an environment and its demands. Hence, Radcliffe-Brown moved functionalism to a much broader and more evolutionary perspective where social and cultural variation might be incorporated (Turner, 1991, p. 43). Malinowski (1944, cited in Martindale, 1960) really added the dimension of levels of social systems, and this was to prove to be integral to many of the major theoretical works such as Talcott Parsons's (see Martindale, 1960, and Turner, 1991).

Much of the scholarly world principally identifies functionalism with the enormous body of theoretical work produced by Talcott Parsons (1902–1979). Parsons's perspective on the family is best understood within the architecture of his larger theory of social systems. Parsons divided up the social world into three systems. The cultural system is composed of shared symbols and meanings. The social system is composed of organized social groups and institutions. Finally, the personality system is composed of the species generic types of personalities. For Parsons, much of the personality system was drawn from Freudian psychoanalysis. The great bulk of Parsons's thinking was devoted to the social system. His work on family, however, also encompassed the socialization processes needed for the social system and the ways in which the integration of adult individuals into the group or social system maintained the institutional social system (see Parsons & Bales, 1955; Turner, 1991, p. 61).

Parsons (1937, 1951) argued that every social system needed to achieve a state of order or system equilibrium. Subsystems such as institutions functioned to assist in achieving this system order. He posited four "functional imperatives" that all systems require: adaptation, goal attainment, integration, and latency (or maintenance of morale and motivation). This system of functions is commonly referred to by the acronym A-G-I-L. Every system must have subsystems that function for the adaptation of the system. Every system must satisfy the goals of the system and must integrate its members. Finally, every system must ensure that motivation for action (latency) remains above a certain level.

Parsons's major work on the family resides in his essays in the Parsons and Bales (1955) book on the family. Parsons suggests

> that the basic and irreducible functions of the family are two: the primary socialization of children so that they can truly become members of the society into which they have been born; second, the stabilization of the adult personalities of the population of the society. (pp. 16–17)

Parsons's view was that these two functions were intimately related because a child could be socialized into a society only if the society were institutionalized and organized into expected role structures and adults received stability from such role structures. Although Parsons (1954) had previously argued that industrialization and urbanization had caused the erosion of extended kinship for the American family, he nonetheless is emphatic that the family is still a strong and stable institution capable of performing these two basic functions.

Critics of Parsons, such as Robert Merton, argued that his grand theory was too ambitious for the current state of the social sciences (Merton,

1968, p. 6). Others such as William Goode embraced functionalism and extended it to the international evolution of family structure. Goode's work (1959) expanded Parsons's notion that the American family was losing its extended kinship as a result of the effects of industrialization and urbanization. Goode extended this argument by noting that as children became an economic liability as societies moved from agrarian to industrial economies, the married couple would increasingly be the focus of family life. This movement was further in evidence in modern societies by the rise of romantic love and voluntary mate selection, and the overwhelming emphasis on marriage rather than children. Thus, as family functions changed, the structure of the family changed. Goode's extension provided a middle range theory of family change that remains popular.

Metaphors From Classical Theory

Many students might ask why we bother with classical theory. Examining our intellectual past provides us with understanding that is less trapped by our own historical period and political climate. For the purpose of this book, we are indebted to the broad analyses of theories and ideas discussed by Lillegard (2003) and subsequently by White (2004). The analyses here are different in focus.

Our discussion of classical theory brings out several somewhat confusing ideas. For example, we might ask if social causation is really dependent on what is going on in macroeconomics or historical events (Marx), or do individual choices and personalities have some causal efficacy (Weber). We do not pretend to resolve such big picture questions at this juncture, but we can identify some significant themes or metaphors that might provide useful heuristics for understanding theories.

1. *Macro-Level Explanations.* Certainly, those explanations that argue for the efficacy of historical forces, whether ideas (Hegel) or material (Marx), would belong in this group. There are other theories that may or may not belong here such as evolutionary theories, social class theories, and conflict theories. For example, some feminist theorists might see sex as a social class (Firestone, 1970), whereas others might see it as more of a purely social construction (de Beauvoir, 1953). Macro-level explanations see individuals and groups as being driven by powers outside their control and sometimes even unknown to them. The clearest example of this is the view from sociobiology that although you think and act, you are really driven to get your genes to the next generation.

2. *Normative-Conformity and Deviance.* One of the major ways sociologists explain the social world is by the existence and power of social

rules or norms, both informal and formal. You do not always wear clothes because of the temperature but wear clothing because it is appropriate. Likewise, social change comes about only when a significant number of people deviate from an existing social norm thus creating a new norm. Certainly, socialization dependent theories, such as symbolic interaction (Mead, 1934) use norms as a major conceptual tool. However, normative explanations are often found as a part of functional theory (Durkheim, 1897) in some important forms of rational choice theory (Coleman, 1990). In addition, norms are a significant component of Parsonian functionalism. Hence, we can expect this type of conceptualization to surface in many theories.

3. *Individual Motivation.* Although focusing on individual motivation is often seen as either a form of psychological reductionism or a form of the "great human" theory of history, it appears in many theories. Weber's methodological individualism proposes that any macro-level social force should be explainable at the level of the individual. Such a view suggests that individual values, beliefs, and cognitions are important for an explanation to make sense. Furthermore, Weber's view suggests that theorists need to pay attention to how they will move from individual causation up to macro-level events (levels of analysis problem). Some of the theorists who have encountered this problem are exchange theorists (Homans, 1961), rational choice theorists (Coleman 1990), and economic theorists (Adam Smith, 1776).

4. *Social Systems and Functions.* There is little doubt that functional explanations are popular in the social sciences, but these explanations have become more sophisticated as they became united in the "system" approach in the later work of Parsons and with advent of system thinking from cybernetic and information theories. The simple way of viewing functional theory is through the "organic" analogy (the heart pumps blood for the circulatory system). However, contemporary systems approaches are much more complex and may focus on functional relations within a state, changes of state by a system, and dynamics of systems. Certainly, we see such approaches in individual level neurological theories, family stress theories (Boss, 1988), family resiliency theories (McCubbin & Patterson, 1983), and ecological theories (Hawley, 1986).

These four themes emerge and reemerge throughout this book. The themes provide a way for you to compare and contrast these theories as well as understand them. These themes are not exclusive of other newer concepts that are emerging in the study of the family such as levels of analysis and the role of history in explaining who we are and who our family is.

A Brief History of Family Theory

Each theory in family science has its own historical legacy, as we discuss further in subsequent chapters. Our focus here is on major themes and examples of how family theory has been important to scholarship throughout history. We refer to several useful accounts of this history and recommend them for greater depth of coverage.

Adams and Steinmetz (1993) surveyed contributions of the classics, which encompass ideas up to the 20th century. Early philosophers were often interested in prescribing ways of living, according to their own values. Adams and Steinmetz called attention to this infusion of ideology, and they noted that it sometimes was accompanied by efforts to describe families in more dispassionate ways. Only scattered references to family life per se are contained in the classical works, with little resemblance to the kind of scientific explanation we have now come to expect of scholarship.

Much of the early work centered on attempts to find the origins of marriage as an institution and to trace its evolution as societies moved toward a more modern form (Adams & Steinmetz, 1993, pp. 76–78). Some scholars searched for the ultimate purposes of marriage or the family. Some saw progress or at least the adaptation of family life to changing social circumstances. Some lamented the declining importance of the family, especially as industrialization and urbanization gripped the Western world in the 19th century. Adams and Steinmetz (1993, p. 86) conclude that the closest these social philosophers came to a real theory was a model of parental socialization that resulted in positive outcomes for children and the meeting of needs for both generations when parents became elderly. For the most part, however—whether obvious or subtle—ideology in the classics, Adams and Steinmetz (1993) found, is seldom totally absent, although its presence makes a theory neither right nor wrong (p. 93).

Howard (1981) examined the history of U.S. family sociology from 1865 to 1940. He also noted the early emphasis on evolutionary thinking, as well as the interest of "moral reformers," in doing something about the problems families seemed to be facing because of the Industrial Revolution. Howard considered the period between 1890 and 1920 a progressive era. Even as moral reformers and charity workers expanded their initiatives, the idea that families could adapt to changing environments became popular. An emphasis on the psychosocial interior of family life took hold, and educational programs to foster the socialization of children seemed promising. If families were sometimes struggling and disorganized, it was because they were caught between two conflicting value systems, one emphasizing traditional images of the family and the other based on the requirements of the modern democratic and capitalistic state.

The years 1920 to 1940 constitute the latest period Howard described in detail. In these years, the key theme in family scholarship shifted from ecology to interaction among family members, with the goal of personal adjustment. In 1924, the American Sociological Society (now the American Sociological Association) established its Family Section, and at about the same time, Ernest Groves developed the first systematic college course in family life education at Boston University. Howard also noted as a countertheme during this period a renewed emphasis on the institutional level of analysis, with studies of families in a community context and attention to cultural diversity on a broader scale. In a chapter published in Howard's book, van Leeuwen (1981) noted that European family scholars remain more interested in the institutional, or macroscopic and historical, levels. On both continents, however, the norm developed that family scholars should refrain from moral and political evaluations as they increasingly relied on empirical data collected through fieldwork (van Leeuwen, 1981, p. 133).

Reflecting on much of the same body of work mentioned above, Christensen (1964) concluded that systematic theory building in the family field did not begin until about 1950. Concepts and rough orientations were taking shape in the first half of the century, along with a growing industry of empirical research, but without formalized explanations meeting the requirements of propositional theory. Although not highlighted in any of these historical accounts, an upswing in scholarly interest about families within many academic disciplines appeared before 1950, with contributions by sociologists, anthropologists, psychologists, home economists, and social workers, among others. Yet Christensen's designation of 1950 as a turning point seems to be basically correct. An inspection of the *International Bibliography of Research in Marriage and the Family, 1900–1964* (Aldous & Hill, 1967) shows that of almost 4,000 entries before 1950, only 7 contain theory or a cognate term in their titles. Of the 12,000 entries for the 1950 to 1964 period, 93 entries contain such terms. By comparison, for the 2-year period from 1991 to 1993, 264 of 7,600 entries in a subsequent inventory (Touliatos, 1994) pertain to family theory. Interestingly, the largest proportion of theoretical works before and during the 1950s dealt with courtship and mate selection. This was the first topic to receive systematic and cumulative theoretical treatment.

Aside from the increasing attention to family theory in the scholarship of the field since 1950, the last half of the century can be subdivided into three stages, each with its own set of themes.

Conceptual Frameworks: 1950–1966

The single most prominent theme in family theorizing during the 1950s and early 1960s was an emphasis on identifying conceptual frameworks. This emphasis is evidenced by a series of works devoted to the topic (Christensen, 1964; Hill, 1951; Hill & Hansen, 1960; Nye & Berardo, 1966/1981). The number and character of the particular frameworks varied, but the basic idea remained the same. As research on family life accumulated, most analysts attempted to give explanations for their findings. The explanations often were narrowly focused, and it was difficult to see how various studies fit together. The attempt to identify frameworks was a search for underlying principles that might help in the construction of general theories for the field. It was not claimed that such theories already existed nor was it often assumed that a single integrated theory would be practical. Rather, the idea was that by comparing the currently fragmented works with respect to the concepts and assumptions they used, scholars might be able to work toward the building of family theories in a more coordinated way.

Christensen (1964) captured the spirit of this period well in the closing remarks of his introductory essay in the *Handbook of Marriage and the Family:*

> As has been said several times, there is urgent need for better theory. Critics of family research have described it as being amateurish, trivial, scattered, often sterile, and sometimes moralistic. . . . There is still need for correcting what Goode (1959, p. 186) spoke of as a hornet's nest of conceptual and terminological problems. There is still need to isolate and then integrate, insofar as seems feasible, the theoretical frameworks which can guide the discipline. And there is still need to find and then specify the relationships among empirical generalizations in order to constitute true theory. (pp. 29–30)

Formal Theory Construction: 1967–1979

A change in tone characterized the next several years of work on family theory. Following Hill's (1966) address after receiving the first Burgess Award for a career of scholarly achievement in the family field, attention turned toward methods of deductively and inductively creating theories, using a clearly delineated propositional format. Many examples of this type of work emerged. Nye and his colleagues presented a propositional theory of family stability (Nye, White, & Frideres, 1969), followed by a propositional theory of age at marriage (Bartz & Nye, 1970). Goode and his colleagues published a massive volume listing hundreds of propositions relevant to scores of family topics (Goode, Hopkins, & McClure, 1971).

The most important works of this period, however, were those spearheaded by Burr (Burr, 1973; Burr, Hill, Nye, & Reiss, 1979, Vols. 1 & 2). In his 1973 volume, Burr applied the principles of deductive, propositional theory building provided by philosophers and sociologists to 11 topical areas of research. In the first volume of Burr, Hill et al. (1979), Burr and his colleagues applied the same procedure to twice as many areas, involving experts in those areas as chapter authors. In Volume 2, Burr, Hill et al. (1979) focused on five general theories that were not substantively limited. The editors noted that the second volume was not comprehensive in its coverage of general theories, and they acknowledged difficulties in linking the two volumes. Inductively integrating materials from the first volume proved difficult because of the lack of semantic equivalence across domains, the complexity of models in the first volume, and the lack of a way to bridge macro- and micro-level propositions (Burr, Hill et al., 1979, Vol. 2, pp. xii–xiv).

Organizational developments within the National Council of Family Relations (NCFR) also were important during this period. In his Burgess address, Hill (1966) had called for the creation of a Theory Section to parallel the existing Research Section. Although his initiative was defeated, by the late 1960s NCFR had created the joint Research and Theory Section that continues today. Hill did not relent in his effort to give visibility to theorizing as a major professional activity, however. With the help of Nye and others, he created the Workshop on Theory Construction, which began with meetings at the NCFR annual conference site just before the regular NCFR conference. The workshop served as a training ground for both students and more advanced family scholars, allowing them to nurture and demonstrate their talents in theory building. In 1975, the name of the workshop was expanded to Theory Construction and Research Methodology. This workshop also survives today. In its first 24 years, more than 560 papers were presented, and more than 730 participants appeared on its programs. It is interesting that both the section and the workshop evolved to combine theoretical and research interests. This symbolizes the extent to which family scholars see the two enterprises as fundamentally connected.

Pluralism: 1980–1999

The publication of the two edited volumes by Burr and colleagues (Burr, Hill et al., 1979) seems to represent the high-water mark, if not the culmination, of the theory construction movement. The pluralism of the most recent decades has several possible interpretations. It can be seen as a continuation of the quantitative growth of contributions by scholarly participants in family theory and research. It can also be taken to be a furthering of fragmented and specialized interests. Or it can be viewed as a new respect and tolerance for diverse philosophies, theories and theory building methods, and research strategies.

Doherty, Boss, LaRossa, Schumm, and Steinmetz (1993) provide a cogent summary of nine main trends, although they give these developments somewhat more recent origins than we would. We excerpted their list from a more detailed discussion:

1. The impact of feminist and ethnic minority theories and perspectives

2. The realization that family forms have changed dramatically

3. The trend toward greater professional (multidisciplinary) inclusiveness

4. The trend toward more theoretical and methodological diversity

5. The trend toward more concern with language and meaning

6. The movement toward more constructivist and contextual approaches

7. An increased concern with ethics, values, and religion

8. A breakdown of the dichotomy between the private and public spheres of family life and between family social science and family interventions

9. Greater recognition by family scholars of the contextual limits of family theory and research knowledge (pp. 15–17)

To be sure, Doherty et al. (1993) see challenges posed by, and potential problems with, these emergent developments, but their basic posture is laudatory and optimistic. Nonetheless, any idealistic hope on the part of some leaders in the field that we would eventually converge around one grand theoretical scheme to explain everything about families has now been completely dashed and discarded. What we see is the continuing proliferation of theories, the eclectic combination of elements from different theories, and variations and transformations within existing theories. It is as common now, if not more common than ever before, for theorizing to be narrowly focused on particular topics and issues. Countless mini theories, middle-range theories, and models of mostly causal processes, all closely linked to Hempel's (1952) plane of observation, characterize the literature, particularly in professional journals and in the proceedings of conferences and workshops.

The other main trend in recent years has been a vigorous questioning of the philosophical foundations in the field (cf. Osmond, 1987; Thomas & Wilcox, 1987). The result has been a turn toward interpretive and critical philosophies (see Box 2.1) and away from at least some elements of the positivistic philosophy (see Cheal, 1991; White, 2004). It is important to remember, however, that the entire scholarly community does not move in unison in any one direction. Some theorists attempt to blend and integrate, whereas others find one philosophy or even one theory compelling and the others inadequate.

Science in the Post-Postmodern Era: 2000–Present

The current scene is a curious and shifting mixture of consensus and conflict over theories and theory-building methods. Yet we believe that there might be some glimpses of the direction we are headed. Certainly, the *Sourcebook of Family Theory and Research* (Bengtson, Acock, Allen, Dilworth-Anderson, & Klein, 2005) still showed much of the pluralism and confusion from the previous era. Although the 2005 *Sourcebook* shows the diversity of theoretical thinking in family studies, we are less sure that it is representative of the theory we see in first-tier journals in our area. Furthermore, theoretical entries do not follow the more rigorous and formal format and discussions in Bengtson and Allen's 1993 *Sourcebook* and the 1979 two-volume Burr, Hill et al. *Contemporary Theories*. Even though there seemed to be little consensus on the evaluation of theories or the role of values in theory, several chapters in the Bengtson et al. (2005) *Sourcebook* offered either theoretical or methodological advances. The overall tone, however, was continued diversity and tolerance for a multitude of ways of thinking that many scholars from previous decades might not have wanted to accommodate as "scientific progress."

At almost the same time as the 2005 Bengtson et al. *Sourcebook* was being finalized in late 2004, White published *Advancing Family Theories* (2004). This book attempted to correct many of the misperceptions inherent within the "postmodern movement," and White argues for a return to distinctions such as adequate and inadequate theory and competing knowledge claims. Such a stance removes the basic assumption of pluralism and relativism by saying that although we might not be able to know absolute truth or falsity, we can certainly know which arguments and theories are better able to predict and explain based on methodological criteria. White also argues against a free-for-all of value orientations in the social sciences by saying that a methodological approach assumes that one does not bend the method (and data) to fit one's ideological biases. Interestingly, White is not alone in his attempt to return to more disciplined theory and propositions, as many social scientists in North America react strongly to the excesses of the past 30 years of pluralism (e.g., see Gross & Levitt, 1994; O'Neill, 1995).

The 2004 publication of the Chibucos, Leite, and Weis *Readings in Family Theory* sent a clear message that theories were research oriented and scientific. This was followed by the simultaneous publication of the *Handbook of Marriage and the Family* (3rd ed., Peterson & Bush, 2013) and the *Handbook of Family Theories: A Content Based Approach* (Fine &

Fincham, 2013), both of which emphasized the empirical and generalizing characteristics of theory. It is important to note that the postmodern era of pluralism and lack of consensus in the social sciences was necessary to admonish those that uncritically expounded about "privileged" knowledge claims in the sciences. The overall perspective today seems that family scholarship has largely moved beyond the years of pluralism and relativism in the late 20th century and that the new consensus follows the tenets of our discussion of the pragmatic and tentative nature of scientific knowledge and explanation.

Conclusion

In many ways, the history of theory in the study of the family has brought us full circle from the naive acceptance of science in the 1950s to a much more social and tentative understanding of our knowledge today. Despite this evolution, we are experiencing renewed consensus on basic criteria for evidence and scientific methods based on pragmatic positivism. This evolution was necessary so that a more nuanced understanding of science, its values and understandings, could come to the practice of social science and family scholarship.

STUDY QUESTIONS

1. How would a fact be treated in each epistemological view point: the positivist view, interpretive view, and the critical view? If you were a despot or dictator, which viewpoint would you prefer?

2. What is "methodological individualism" ?

3. Parsons argued that family performs two basic functions for societies. What are these two? Do you think these can be adequately performed by other social structures?

4. History teaches us that theories proposed about the social world are influenced by the historical periods in which they are constructed. That being said, theories within any historical period may show great variety. For example both Marx and Comte, Weber and Durkheim shared historical periods but represented very different perspectives. What influences do you think might shape today's new theories?

The Rational Choice and Social Exchange Framework

Kevin and Sarah have been dating seriously for about 6 months. Both agree that they have a close relationship with a lot of warmth and support. After going to a romantic movie, Kevin and Sarah go back to Kevin's apartment and are in the middle of some pretty serious petting when Sarah says, "Kevin, if we are going to do it, I want you to use a condom. I have one in my purse." Kevin says, "Are you serious? Don't you trust me? I mean, it's not as though I have AIDS or something." Sarah seems to be caught off guard and pauses for a moment before responding. "Kevin, I know how you feel about me, and I trust you, but a condom makes good sense because it is easy for anyone to pick up a sexually transmitted disease. Some of these diseases are hard to detect and even harder to cure, especially for women. I don't want to end up not being able to have children when I am ready to as a result of carelessness." Kevin quickly blurts, "But these things are so plastic. You know, Sarah, a guy doesn't feel anything if he wears one of those!" Sarah's voice carries a tinge of anger or bitterness. "Kevin, I wanted to make love with you, but now I feel you are just after your own pleasure and don't really care about the possible consequences for me. I'm the one who could get pregnant, I'm the one who has to get an abortion or carry the baby for 9 months, and in the end, I am now the one who has to ask for a commonsense preventive measure that would protect both of us." Kevin's tone becomes disappointed but still angry. "Come on, and I'll take you home."

This sketch of Kevin and Sarah's interaction provides us with an illustration of two people pursuing their self-interests. Kevin's self-interest is to maximize his sexual pleasure. Sarah's self-interest is to avoid the costs associated with unprotected sex. From this standpoint, often called *utilitarianism*, both Kevin and Sarah are acting rationally, but they are operating on different values.

The essence of utilitarianism is that individuals rationally weigh the rewards and costs associated with behavioral choices. They choose those activities that maximize their rewards. Utilitarianism is a philosophical perspective that has heavily influenced exchange theories in the social sciences. The central focus of exchange theory is on motivation. Human beings are viewed as motivated out of self-interest. What does it mean to say that utilitarianism focuses on motivation? Motivation is what induces a person to act. The focus, therefore, is on the person and what propels that person to choose a particular action. Theories inspired by utilitarian thinking are based on the assumption of individual self-interest. This in turn means that we as social scientists can understand a person's actions by understanding the individual's interests or values. These interests allow the individual to account for both costs and rewards and to make choices that maximize the actor's utility or profit. The basic notion, then, is that rational actors choose a course of action that produces the greatest benefit.

Exchange theorists usually explain the existence and endurance of social groups, such as the family, by their appeal to the self-interest of individual members. Individuals come together in groups so as to maximize their rewards. Of course, membership in social groups may also necessitate compromise and even costs to the individual member. If the costs of group membership exceed the rewards, then membership in the group is no longer a rational choice. Thus, the family group is usually conceptualized as a source of rewards for the individual members.

Intellectual Traditions

Social exchange and rational choice originated in what is known as *utilitarian thinking*. Utilitarianism actually refers to several varieties of theory, all of which share a common theme. The common theme is that humans are motivated and act so as to maximize those outcomes they most value. Some examples of utilitarian thinking are the ethical utilitarianism of the Epicureans and later Jeremy Bentham and John Stuart Mill, psychological hedonism, and the ideal utilitarianism of G. E. Moore. A complete picture of all the variants of utilitarian thinking would require volumes rather than pages. We direct our attention to the forms of utilitarian thinking found in the social sciences, particularly in the area of family studies.

Because utilitarianism is concerned with achieving outcomes that are valued, most social science theories are voluntaristic, or interest, theories of value. In these variants, great emphasis is placed on the unfettered choice of individuals. One of the originators of this perspective, Adam Smith, held an economic view of humankind based on the belief that people act rationally to maximize benefits, or utility. When choice was externally controlled or determined, however, actors could not make rational choices because their rationality was constrained by external limits on choice. This view was the basis for laissez-faire economics and, in addition, much of the utilitarian theory in the social sciences today.

In current social science, utilitarian thinking is quite obvious in microeconomic theory of the family (Becker, 1981), social psychology (Emerson, 1976; Homans, 1961; Nye, 1979), organizational sociology (Blau, 1964), and rational choice theory (Coleman, 1990; Hechter, 1987). There are major differences of emphasis among these authors, especially in how they unite individual motivation to macroscopic processes of reciprocity and social change. The focus of all these theories, however, is on the rational utilitarianism of the individual.

Many of these theories have been termed *exchange theories*. This has led to some confusion with a group of theories that is structural and not at all focused on individual motivation. For example, the French anthropologists Claude Lévi-Strauss (1969) and Marcel Mauss (1954) are often called exchange theorists, but their focus is on the institutional norm of reciprocity and the social functions of exchanges in terms of group solidarity and the formation of group alliances. Other theorists such as John Scanzoni (1970) and Randall Collins (1975) have a conflict-resource orientation; they fit only marginally into our characterization of utilitarianism because of their additional emphasis on macroscopic structures. In the study of the family, utilitarian thinking (maximization of individual profit) is generally referred to as rational choice and exchange theory, and we follow this convention. It is certainly possible, however, to argue the macroexchange position that patterns of human motivation are responsible for the emergence of social structures to regulate those motivations and construct institutions that constrain the individual choices that led to their origin in the first place. This argument for the emergence of social structures from individual profit motives is most recently associated with the rational choice theory of James Coleman (1990).

In the contemporary study of the family, Ivan Nye (1969, 1976, 1979, 1981) has been the foremost proponent of exchange theory. Nye's (1979) formal propositional statement of exchange theory relied heavily on the social-psychological approach of his predecessors from psychology, Thibaut and Kelley (1959). Although Nye's (1979) version of utilitarianism does include the norm of reciprocity and group-level exchanges, these macrosocial concepts are not well integrated with the social-psychological utilitarianism that is his principal focus. Nye (1979) titles his chapter "Choice, Exchange, and the Family," thus emphasizing the voluntarist assumption guiding his version of utilitarianism. In our treatment of social exchange, we rely on Nye's statement of utilitarianism applied to the family as well as more recent summaries of exchange theory (Sabatelli & Shehan, 1993) and conceptual additions from rational choice theory (Coleman, 1990).

Focus and Scope Assumptions

The individual is real. The assumption that the individual is real is technically referred to as *methodological individualism*. This assumption implies that group phenomena, social structure, and the normative culture are constructed by the actions of individuals. Thus, if we understand the actions of individuals, we will also understand these macrosocial phenomena. In regard to the family, this is an important and perhaps tenuous assumption. In exchange theory, the family is viewed as a collection of individuals. But we are all aware that mate selection, parenting, and many other family matters are regulated by both formal norms (laws) and informal ones. This is the task set by the assumption of methodological individualism. The age-old problem for utilitarian theories is that social norms and social order must be explained by individual profit. James S. Coleman (1990), in the first chapter of his book *Foundations of Social Theory,* tackles this question from a utilitarian, or rational choice, perspective. Although we will discuss Coleman's position, we nonetheless recommend his discussion to readers as supplying one of the best direct confrontations with the challenges of methodological individualism for the macroscopic study of social groups and institutions.

Prediction and understanding come about by understanding the individual actor's motivation. Although not all theorists who assume methodological individualism attempt to understand individuals' actions through motivation, rational choice and microexchange perspectives usually do expect that individual motives are explanatory. Although these theorists acknowledge that individuals are always constrained in their choices, within these constraints any choice can be understood as based on the actor's motivation rather than exogenous forces or constraints. In this sense, exchange theory is a voluntaristic theory in the same way in which Adam Smith's theory was voluntaristic. This insight led Nye (1979) to state that the basic theory is about choice (p. 4) and has led other theorists to suggest rational choice explanations for family behavior (Coleman, 1990). Because families are a relatively long-lasting social group, the voluntaristic assumption leads exchange theorists to assume that families are rewarding to individual members. The fact that children do not voluntarily choose their parents may provide some difficulties for the theory, however.

Actors are motivated by self-interest. Even with the assumption that the actor's motivation explains behavior, a theorist could still assume that motivation is multidimensional or not conscious (as in the concept of the subconscious) or founded on inherent drives such as those that Freud proposed. But microutilitarian exchange theories usually include the assumption that individuals are unilaterally motivated by self-interest; individuals seek things and relationships they regard as beneficial for themselves. The notion of self-interest raises some interesting questions regarding what we commonly know as altruism. Even some variants of ethical utilitarianism have been based on the assumption that we should act to accrue the greatest good for the greatest number. But for family exchange theorists, such as Nye (1979), collective interests and altruism are derived and explained by the self-interests of individuals. So although self-interest is not necessarily the hallmark of all forms of utilitarian thinking, it is a basic assumption in regard to exchange and choice theory.

Actors are rational. It is easy to agree with the assumption that actors are rational. All of us like to think that we are rational human beings. But how often do we stop and think about what it means to be rational? This is a more complex assumption than we initially might have thought.

To be rational is to have the ability to calculate the ratio of costs to rewards. This is an analytic ability. One crucial dimension of rationality is that it is the same for all actors. Any two rational actors in identical situations with identical values and identical information would necessarily reach the same result in their calculations and thus pursue the same behavior. This assumption of rational actors is as important for microeconomics as it is for choice and exchange theory because it allows the interchangeability of actors and the concept of general rational actors captured in notions such as "the consumer."

The idea of rational actors evolved from the rationalist philosophies of the Age of Enlightenment. Many students will recall that the Enlightenment was characterized by a newfound confidence in the ability of humans to reason. What was meant by reason was deduction or analytic thought. Such analytic thinking was believed to be independent of experience or sense data. Many philosophers such as the French philosopher René Descartes believed human rationality provided unequivocal knowledge that was true (*quod erat demonstratum*). Indeed, the view of humans as rational actors originating in the work of Enlightenment philosophers, such as John Locke, provides much of the rationale for our current legal system. For example, juvenile offenders are treated differently from adults because they are believed to have not yet fully developed the ability to calculate rewards and costs. The rational assumption also provided the basis for much of the economic theory of Adam Smith.

It is easy to confuse rationalism with other words that share the same root but have very different meanings. For instance, *rational* is not interchangeable with *rationalization*. A rationalization is an attempt to provide an apparently rational justification for one's behavior *after* the behavior occurred; it is not proof of a choice but rather an ex post facto fabrication (after the fact). Later, we further discuss the ex post facto nature of rationalization, which critics of exchange theory raise as an objection.

Concepts

Reward and Cost

A *reward* is anything that is perceived as beneficial to an actor's interests. A simple way to conceptualize cost is as the inverse of reward. It is also possible to conceptualize *costs* as the negative dimension of rewards. It is important, however, to include as costs or negative rewards the opportunities for rewards that might be missed or forgone that are associated with any specific choice. The dialogue between Sarah and Kevin might be extended to include the costs to Sarah if she became pregnant and had to forgo opportunities such as completion of high school and postsecondary education. Indeed, such forgone opportunities might constitute very significant costs.

It would be naive to assume that the concepts of costs and rewards are unique to utilitarian theories. Certainly, Watsonian and later Skinnerian psychology emphasize rewards and punishments. Although the basic notions are similar, the theories differ because the assumption of cognitive rationality is largely absent from these behavioristic psychological theories. Indeed, behaviorists deny that conceptual processes need to be included in explanations of human behavior and posit that only behavioral patterns of stimulus and response need be examined. This view is at odds with the cognitive emphasis in exchange theory on rationality.

Microeconomics is focused on economic rewards and costs. Family exchange and choice theorists view rewards and costs as being formulated from a much broader array of values than is used in economic theory. For example, Nye (1979), Blau (1964), and Foa and Foa (1980) each list six sources of rewards and costs, although each list includes some different sources. We consider these general sources of costs and rewards in greater depth below.

When we examine the basic concept of rewards more deeply, we find definitions referring to things or relationships that bring pleasure, satisfaction, and gratification. Such definitions come uncomfortably close to a naive *hedonistic calculus* weighing pleasure and pain. Such a hedonistic view falls apart rapidly when the complexities of decisions are examined. For example, one may climb a mountain because it is gratifying, but it also involves risk and hardship. Indeed, it is doubtful that mountain climbers would find the task as gratifying if it did not contain the risk and hardship. Many of our most gratifying experiences are gratifying in part because not everyone is willing to undertake the hardship or risk.

Profit or Maximizing Utility

The notions of reward and cost alone do not explain behavior. If one attempts to explain that an actor behaves in a certain way because it is rewarding, the resulting explanation is overly simplistic and fails to account for the many elements that were rationally calculated by the actor. Indeed, reward and cost alone supply us with little other than a form of behaviorism.

It is the concept of profit, or utility, that allows the theory to avoid such criticisms. Profit is defined as the ratio of rewards to costs for any decision. Actors rationally calculate this ratio for all possible choices in a situation and then choose the action that they calculate will bring the greatest rewards or the fewest costs. Thus, the mountain climber weighs the rewards of climbing a mountain, such as the social approval of other climbers and the aesthetic enjoyment of the climb, against costs such as the risk of being killed or injured in a rockfall or avalanche. From this example, you can see that it is the notion of rational calculation of profit that makes exchange theory more than naive hedonism.

Comparison Level (CL) and Comparison Level for Alternatives (CL+)

In complex situations, the evaluation of profit available to an actor may be divided into two comparison levels. The first is the comparison (CL) of what others in your position have and how well you are doing relative to them. The second comparison (CL+) is how well you are doing relative to others outside of your position but in positions that supply an alternative or choice.

The role of comparisons in the evaluation of choices has mainly been emphasized by Thibaut and Kelley (1959) and Nye (1979). This perceptual orientation is especially useful for family researchers wanting to explain phenomena such as timing of children or the decision to divorce. The decision to divorce provides a good illustration of the two comparison levels. For example, a husband may compare (CL) his profit ratio for his marriage with what he perceives other husbands he knows are receiving in their marriages. The second level of comparison (CL+) would be to compare his profit as a husband with the profit he perceives in other possible, unmarried positions, such as divorced and remarried husbands. According to the theory, if he were to calculate greater profit for an alternative position, he is more likely to choose a divorce.

For family researchers, evaluation levels represent one of the more attractive components of the theory because they allow us to understand changes of marital and family status. Comparison levels can be used to understand a choice such as divorce, and they can also be used to understand the degree of satisfaction or gratification an actor associates with an outcome. Sabatelli and Shehan (1993) propose that the notion of comparison level could help us understand why young couples with children experience lower marital satisfaction than couples in other stages of family life (e.g., Rollins & Feldman, 1970). Sabatelli and Shehan (1993) point out that couples with young children are in a period of family life that follows a stage (early marriage) marked by high satisfaction, thus constituting a high comparison level. Demands and expectations associated with childrearing take time and energy away from fulfilling the high marital expectations in the way they were satisfied before children. Hence, the comparison of present rewards with what one has previously received is linked to greater dissatisfaction with marriage.

Rationality

We have previously discussed rationality as a basic assumption necessary for the calculation of the ratio of rewards to costs. If you think about things and relationships that you find rewarding in your life, however, you will probably notice that the value of these rewards changes with time and situation. In addition, you would surely note that not all rewards are equally weighted. For example, you might be thirsty and want a drink, but not all liquids that would quench your thirst are equally valuable (as any cola commercial attests). Furthermore, the value of a reward may decrease as you gain more of it (marginal utility); a dollar to a rich person has less value than a dollar to a poor person. To deal with the changing value of rewards and costs, it is necessary to add the idea of the importance, salience, or weight of alternatives. To understand any actor's choice as rational, we need to know what the person considers rewarding and costly, and in addition, we have to know the relative weights (or salience) for each of the rewards and each of the costs.

A simple example might clarify this idea. Imagine that your family is trying to decide on a destination for a summer vacation. You have narrowed down the choices to backpacking in the backcountry near Jackson Hole, Wyoming, or visiting the campgrounds along the Oregon coast. To reach this stage, each family member has to compare the possible alternatives, such as taking individual vacations rather than a joint vacation. This is similar to the second comparison level, or what Thibaut and Kelley (1959) called the comparison level for alternatives. Is it a reward or cost to go on a family vacation? Do you enjoy being together, or is it more valuable to spend some time away from family members? After there is agreement that a family vacation is more valuable, the next step is to decide on the destination. Do you value hiking in the mountains or walking miles of uncluttered beaches? Do you want the adventure of backpacking or the more placid contentment of watching the Pacific Ocean? Are there activities for all family members in both spots? Each value, such as adventure and diversity of opportunities for other family members, is weighted by the importance, or salience, of this for you. Finally, you make a choice based on the maximization of profit for you. Of course, your family as a whole might choose the other alternative.

This example raises a critical question. How could a researcher ever examine the complex decisions of family members in one family, let alone a large sample of families? Certainly, the theory appears too cumbersome for a detailed accounting of rewards, costs, and relative weights for each individual, for every decision in each and every family. Exchange theory can be used in such investigations by making two assumptions. One assumption we have already discussed: Because actors are rational, they are interchangeable. This assumption means that given the same rewards, costs, and weights, any actor would make the same choice as any other. The second assumption is one we have not discussed in any detail. It is the assumption that for large numbers of actors, we can assess the rewards, costs, and weights as those that would be held by a modal, or average, actor. In other words, we assume that for most people in a social group or social system, rewards, costs, and weights are relatively uniform. There may be variation in how people look at rewards and costs, but there is great overall uniformity and little systematic variation.

Exchanges and Equity

The rational weighing of costs and rewards in an unconstrained environment seldom happens in reality. Usually, we live in a social system characterized by social interdependencies; some of the rewards we may desire are dependent on the cooperation of others, or we may need to trade with others something we have of lower value in exchange for something of higher value. This is an economic view of society. In most instances, maximizing profit entails exchanges with others. Social relationships that last over some period of time do so in part because they offer profits. A rational person is willing to incur some losses to maintain such profitable relationships. Marriage may be one such relationship, in which inequities over a period of time are tolerated because of the expectation of future and longer term rewards from the relationship. Certainly in families, vacations are planned not so as to optimize the profit for any individual but rather to distribute fairly and equitably rewards to all family members.

In a few exchange perspectives (Scanzoni, 1970, 1972; Sexton & Perlman, 1989; Walster & Walster, 1978), the principle of equity is viewed as being central to the maintenance of social relationships and groups. After all, siblings play together because of a set of negotiated and agreed-on exchanges perceived by them to be a fair exchange. Families decide on a vacation spot based not on any one individual's profit but on an equitable distribution of rewards for all members. Husbands and wives can be viewed as in a fair exchange situation, and when the situation becomes unfair or imbalanced, we expect divorce or separation. As we shall see later, marriages are seldom exactly equitable at any point in time, and some people may be so committed to marriage that inequity is not an issue. Indeed, if equity generally operated in marriage, we would not have so much literature on division of household labor in the family (e.g., Pina & Bengtson, 1993).

It is useful to keep in mind two precautions. First, equity can be defined as *fairness* or *justice*, and relations do not need to be exactly equal to be fair or just but can be perceived to be so. Social norms in a given place and time may require inequality, such as women being expected to subordinate their self-interests for the good of men and children. So it is possible that an unequal division of household labor is viewed as fair or equitable. Second, rationality may not be uniform across social actors. A person cannot know how rewarding or costly something is to others in a group, or what comparison levels other group members have, without adequate information and experience.

Human Capital and Social Capital

Most exchange theorists support the idea that profitable exchanges are valued and maintained. This fact seems to imply that individuals in such exchanges have resources to exchange (economic and human capital), and the network of profitable exchanges is itself a form of resource (social capital). Becker (1964) first developed the idea of human capital, and it has become a central concept in the rational choice approach. Coleman (1990) states that "human capital is created by changing persons so as to give them skills and capabilities that make them able to act in new ways" (p. 304). Some familiar sources of human capital would be educational institutions and information media, but these sources should not be considered other than as the medium by which individuals acquire human capital. Indeed, human capital refers to the knowledge, skills, and techniques acquired by the individual. Knowledge and skills have economic value for the individual because they increase the individual's wages or opportunities. We often measure human capital by years of formal education or training, workshops, apprenticeships, Graduate Record Exams, and so on.

Social capital is a more recent concept than human capital. Although social capital was first posited by Bourdieu (1980), most North American scholars were introduced to the term by Coleman (1988). Coleman (1990) argues that social capital is created when the relations among persons change in ways that facilitate action, which is in turn tied to economic value. Social capital, then, refers to the network of relationships with others. Such exchange networks facilitate action (potential and actual exchanges) that allows for the acquisition of the more concrete types of capital: human and financial. A network of individuals ties together the human capital of individuals. Coleman (1990) describes the individuals as being the nodes of the network and the social capital being the lines connecting individuals. Furthermore, he argues that these networks have properties that describe and predict their utility for individuals. Furstenburg (2005) largely agrees that social capital is a structural concept with network properties. These network properties suggest that some networks are more than just size of membership. For example, if two groups have the same number of members and are equal in regard to other forms of capital, the group with the greatest trust among its members should be able to achieve more than groups with less trust (Coleman, 1990). White (2004), however, points out that Coleman argues that children must not only be connected to adults in a network; the adults must have the human capital required for the development of the child as well. Thus, for families, human and social capitals are both intimately linked together.

Generalizable Sources of Rewards

The concept of a set of general rewards and costs for actors in a specific social system is absolutely necessary if exchange theory is to be applied to groups and large numbers of people and families. Of course, some of the most interesting research questions are not about one family or person but about why people in general behave in a certain way. For instance, we may want to know why married couples delay childbearing or why people wait until their late 20s to get married. Examining why one person, say, Martha Jones, delayed marriage would not give us the answer we seek. Martha was hospitalized with a major disease from her 20th birthday until she was 30 years old. We doubt that this explains why most people delay marriage. The answer to our question would usually come from representative survey research using large numbers of respondents. If we attempt to explain our respondents' choices by maximization of profit, then the question arises as to how we can compute the ratio for all these actors in our sample.

The notion of general sources of costs and rewards enables us to compute a general accounting of saliencies, costs, and rewards and to establish a general choice that would be most profitable for actors in a social system. Indeed, the relative stability of general costs and rewards in a social system allows actors to make rational decisions. Various theorists have proposed different general sources of rewards and costs. Homans (1961) originally emphasized social approval as the most general source of rewards and costs. Other theorists have felt a need for the inclusion of other sources.

Blau (1964) proposed the social rewards and costs of personal attraction, social acceptance, social approval, instrumental services, respect, and power. Foa and Foa (1980) proposed love, status, services, goods, information, and money. Nye (1979) proposed social approval, autonomy, predictability, ambiguity, security, agreement, and equality of resources. Nye makes the claim that many of these sources are culture free and may be used anywhere in the world, but he fails to tell us which ones have such universal generalizability. None of the exchange theorists has spent his or her energies addressing general salience weights for these general costs and rewards, but in specific applications, he or she usually makes an argument as to why one set of rewards or costs is more salient than another. Because salience may change dramatically with the situation, the question is perhaps best left open at the general theoretical level.

Because most social exchange theorists identify social approval as a reward or cost, we can use that source for a general example. Let's return to the question "Why do people delay marriage?" and see what kind of answer we can formulate according to exchange theory, using the broad category of social approval for rewards and costs. We must first postulate the profit linked to marriage. In North America, most people marry at least once. According to exchange theory, a rational actor would marry to maximize profit. We must all agree that marriage is socially approved more than alternative forms of relationships, such as cohabitation or singlehood. Our parents, religious institutions, and political institutions view marriage as the appropriate relationship between coresident heterosexual adults.

It is not difficult to make the argument that social approval is one of the major reasons we marry. Why are young people delaying marriage? Very simply, marriage roles and responsibilities (especially pregnancy and child care) interfere with the social approval attached to other early life course expectations, such as finishing education and getting started in a career. Today, as opposed to only a few decades ago, these educational and work expectations apply to both men and women as sources of social approval. Thus, young men and women delay marriage so that they may first achieve these other socially approved statuses. After all, most of us had parents, teachers, and clergy who advised us to finish our education and get a job before getting married. Although there are many gaps in our explanation, it nonetheless serves to illustrate the way in which general sources of reward might be used to explain social patterns, such as delay of marriage.

Propositions

Rational choice theorists explain individual and family phenomena by identifying general propositions that seem to cover the particular phenomenon of interest. This is, of course, the procedure for all deductive theories. In the case of exchange theory, the general propositions required for any explanation are few in number. According to theory, social phenomena can be explained with little conceptual and propositional baggage. When a theory leads to successful explanations with very little baggage, we call it *parsimonious*. This simplicity is seen as an asset in comparing competing theories. Let's examine the propositions called for in exchange theory.

Actors in a situation will choose whichever behavior maximizes profit.

The simplest and most powerful proposition in exchange theory is simply that an actor will choose the course of action that offers the greatest rewards relative to costs. One implication of this proposition is that actors may not necessarily choose options that provide the greatest rewards if the costs are high relative to costs associated with other choices. A less rewarding option may be selected because the costs are lower. This fact should caution us that unlike the case in behaviorism, in exchange theory, profit rather than reward determines behavioral choices.

Actors in a situation in which there are no rewards seek to minimize costs (principle of least costs).

Some of you might ask, What if there are only potential costs in a situation and no rewards? The theory actually incorporates this concern but in an implicit rather than explicit way. Implicit in exchange theory is the concept of reward and cost being interchangeable because of the notion of calculation of profit. If profit is the ratio of rewards divided by costs, then clearly a fraction results when costs exceed rewards. Because division is the same operation as subtraction (the dividend is how many times you can subtract the denominator from the numerator), we can see that costs are mathematically equivalent to negative rewards. Indeed, a cost is a negative reward. Implicitly, then, the proposition regarding maximization of profit becomes the minimization of costs. This rule, or proposition, about minimization of costs can then be applied to the special case in which there are zero rewards but different costs associated with choices.

One of the more vexing problems for exchange theory has been the computation of long-term costs and rewards versus short-term costs and rewards. We give up many immediate rewards to achieve long-term rewards. For example, those who believe that a university education has the purpose of getting a good job might sacrifice 4 years of income while they are in a university, and many other immediate rewards, for what they perceive as higher rewards after they graduate. In a marriage, one spouse might pass up the satisfaction of making an angry response to an affront from the other spouse for the marriage to last over the longer term.

Compared with school groups and work groups, families are relatively lengthy in duration. The analysis of long-term rewards and costs is essential to understanding the behavior of its members. We can extrapolate two general propositions in this regard from Nye (1979, p. 6):

When immediate profits are equal, then actors choose according to which alternative provides the most profit in the long term.

When long-term profits are equal, then one chooses the alternative that provides the most profit in the short term.

These two propositions allow us to gain some perspective on the calculation of profit by interjecting time as a complicating variable. We still have to add the relative salience to the actor of immediate rather than deferred gratification. And of course, these propositions tend to provide guidelines for analysis rather than predictions, as it is doubtful that we would often encounter situations in which profits are equal.

Coleman (1990) extends the propositions above and argues that actors adopt norms and regulated behavior so that they might maximize their marginal utility. As a result, the maintenance of social organization enhances longer term profits. In this sense, Coleman views the family as one such social structure.

Actors will prefer stable structures where rational calculations of profit are possible and hence will support structural norms enhancing stable structures.

It should be noted that this proposition from rational choice theory allows for exchange and choice theorists to move from micro-level analyses to more macro-level analyses concerning social structures and norms. For example, the family can be viewed as a social institution that maintains exchanges of the human capital of parents to the children. The network that facilitates this exchange is a variable (social capital) such that some family structures may impede the transfer of knowledge and skills while other family structures optimize that exchange. The exchange can be measured by the increasing human capital of the children. At a broader social level, this leads to Coleman's proposition regarding social capital:

Social structures and networks produce varying amounts of social capital depending on the properties of the network structure (e.g., closure, membership).

There are several properties that Coleman (1990) discusses in relation to social capital. In his application to families, he tends to stress closure and membership. Networks with more members bring greater social capital simply because there is greater potential for and ties with other networks. For example, if one were in a network of 10 people, the potential to hear about rewards such as job opportunities would be greater than if the network only numbered two, all other things being equal. Likewise, closure is a property where members are all connected to one another. Such internal connectivity allows for the maximum potential for the group to develop and enforce social norms, whether these be external norms from community or school, such as "do your homework," or internal family norms, such as "it is your bedtime."

The propositions in this section suggest that choice and exchange theory are deterministic. If we knew all the values and salience weights composing an actor's calculations, we could accurately predict the actor's choice and behavior in any given situation. The obstacles to such accurate predictions would not just be errors in our measurements but would also be the fluid and dynamic nature of social groups and social norms. In the end, this leads the theory to deal with probabilities rather than necessary causation. Nonetheless, at the individual level, this is a causal perspective in which the actor's perceptions, values, and calculation of profit compose the causal variables, and the actor's choice and behavior are the effect variables. As a result of this individual level deterministic view, exchange theorists might, for example, argue that those actors who choose to get married calculate that marriage is more rewarding than remaining single.

If people are basically selfish (motivated by self-interest), how is social order possible? In particular, how can family members cooperate, live in harmony, and invest themselves in each other's welfare? Exchange theorists and macrorational choice theorists, such as Coleman (1990), tend to argue that individuals learn to increase the profits of others to increase their own profits. Thus, relationships become bargaining processes, each party exchanging rewards valued by other parties. Bargaining can eventually lead to "contracts," or promises, by each to mutually reward the other at acceptable costs to both. Over time, trust and commitment develop out of fair exchanges (social capital). We trust that the rewards we give to others will be reciprocated in due course, and we commit to enduring investment costs for the moment with the assurance that relationship partners will repay our investment. When a group such as a family has a stabilized pattern of exchanges, such that commitment, trust, and profit are operating to the mutual benefit of all, then a spokesperson for the group can engage in exchanges with spokespersons of other groups. So macroexchanges can be viewed as the bargaining process between or among groups.

Variations

We have largely been following Nye's (1979) version of exchange theory and Coleman's (1990) rational choice theory, but it is important to note the diversity within exchange theories. We classify the many variants on the basis of whether they are microsocial or macrosocial. You may recall that a microsocial theory includes the assumption that the individual is the active unit of analysis, whereas in macrosocial theories, the active unit of analysis is the social group or institution. Although all theorists would like to think that they have successfully bridged the chasm between micro- and macroperspectives, there are, in reality, few theories for which one can confidently make such a claim. Individual exchange theories usually involve simply adding up all the individual motivations and calling that *group motivation* or developing a "great man" theory whereby one actor is responsible for social change, and therefore, only one motive need be analyzed (Homans, 1967). Macroexchange theories examine the exchanges between groups and the resulting social solidarity and alliance formation. Individuals are largely lost in the larger social group and in most ways are unidentifiable and unrecoverable as part of an explanation.

Microexchange Theories

In our characterization of exchange theory, we have followed the microsocial perspective associated with Nye (1979), Levinger (1982), Lewis and Spanier (1979), Sabatelli (1988), Thibaut and Kelley (1959), and Sabatelli and Shehan (1993). There are other variants of this microsocial perspective, but these have not been developed as family theories. For example, Coleman (1990) and Hechter (1987) have both authored variations on a type of utilitarianism referred to as *rational choice theory*. Both of these authors take the individual as the basic unit of analysis and attempt to construct macrosocial applications through a notion that some rewards can be achieved only by groups and social organization. There have been attempts at applying parts of the Coleman approach to the study of the family, using the concept of *social capital* (e.g., Furstenburg, 2005; Teachman, Paasch, & Carver, 1997). This is a concept added to the concepts of human and economic capital that evolved from an earlier work by the Nobel Prize–winning economist Gary Becker (1981), whose work *A Treatise on the Family* presented a rational actor economic theory of the family. Becker (1981) and his followers have met with considerable criticism that their approach is both too focused on economic motivation and too individualistic. Despite these criticisms, economic theories of the family and family behaviors, such as mate selection and divorce, tend to be widespread in the economic literature. In addition, following the pioneering work of Kahneman and Tversky

(1979) on the seeming irrationality of human choices, there has been and continues to be critical questioning of the ideas of "choice" and "rationality" within microeconomics and psychology (Kahneman & Tversky, 1984; Laibson & Zeckhauser, 1998). We have more to say about these criticisms of exchange theories in the next section.

Other examples of a microexchange variant are the theoretical work of Emerson (1962, 1976) and the work of Cook (1975; Cook & Yamaguchi, 1990) dealing with the *relative balance,* or ratio, of rewards in social relationships. Cook and Emerson use the relationship rather than the individual as a unit of analysis. The relationship has stable characteristics of exchange such that the ratio of rewards and costs in the relationship between actors indicates the power balance between actors. This approach has given rise to both the economic interpretation found in Becker (1981) and the network approach found in Coleman (1990). Although this microsocial approach might be suitable to the study of the family, there has been only limited research applications of this work directed specifically at studying families (see Haveman & Wolfe, 1994; Teachman, Paasch, & Carver, 1997).

One of the more important variants of exchange theory used to study family relationships is *equity theory.* Although equity theory is directly derived from exchange theory propositions, it contains the additional proposition that fair exchanges are more profitable to relationships than are unfair exchanges. If A and B are in an unfair relationship, then the social norm of reciprocity is not maintained, and the relationship is likely to be discontinued by one of its members. Thus, whenever a relationship provides profitable outcomes, it is essential for the maintenance of the relationship that exchanges be equitable. One can immediately see how equity might be applied to exchanges between marital partners and in family relations. Indeed, family scholars have used equity theory to study such longer term family relationships (e.g., Scanzoni, 1972; Sexton & Perlman, 1989; Walster & Walster, 1978). It is interesting to note that several investigators of equity in marriage (e.g., Pina & Bengtson, 1993; Sexton & Perlman, 1989) and in dating couples (Sprecher, 2001) have concluded that, at best, equity appears to have restricted explanatory value for these close relationships.

Macroexchange Theories

As we said in our introductory remarks to this chapter, we are mainly concerned with presenting the microsocial exchange perspective, because that is the perspective generally applied to the study of the family. We do not want to leave the impression, however, that macrosocial exchange theorists have totally ignored the study of the family. You may have noted that our previous discussions of microexchange theories focus mainly on the individual's choices and decision making. Certainly, such decision making can be applied to decisions such as the selection of a mate or the choice between divorce and staying married. Macroexchange theories tend to be focused more on the group or organization, however.

The transition from a microexchange to a macroexchange perspective is achieved by the addition of several concepts to those we have already reviewed. First, most macroexchange theorists identify two types of exchanges: *restricted* and *generalized* exchanges. Restricted exchanges take place at one point in time and involve little trust. For example, when you buy something in a store, you hand money to the salesperson, who then gives you the item you have selected. On the other hand, generalized exchanges take place over a longer period of time and therefore require more trust. An example of a generalized exchange is lending money to a friend or relative and trusting that repayment will be made at some future date. The trust required in generalized exchanges is buttressed by the *norm of reciprocity* as discussed above in regard to equity theory. That individuals find the relationships in a family group profitable is in part because the family group maintains profitable exchanges with other social organizations, such as schools, churches, and the economy. The essence of macroexchange perspectives is the view that these group and organizational exchanges are more central than individual decision making.

In structural exchange theories, the individual's choices are viewed as being determined by the macroexchanges between groups and organizations. Note that this is just the opposite of the view in microexchange theories, such as rational choice theory, that the individual's decisions determine the group's exchanges.

Perhaps the best example of macroexchange thinking applied to the family is provided by the work of the French structuralist Claude Lévi-Strauss (1969), who developed a theory that the fabric of societies is constructed by norms that require generalized social exchanges between groups. At the heart of these generalized exchanges are the exchanges between kin groups and clans. Prescriptive mating norms require the formation of alliances between groups through the exchange of mates. For example, in a moiety, or two-clan system, if you are a member of the Bear clan and want to form a political, social, and economic alliance with the Eagle clan, you could create a mating rule, such as "Bear women must marry Eagle men." The strongest expression of this alliance rule would be a totemic incest taboo, for example, forbidding an Eagle man to marry an Eagle woman. Lévi-Strauss's (1969) work has been criticized as not being applicable to voluntary mate selection systems, such as our own, but his work has led to some interesting applications, such as Harrison White's (1963) book examining mathematical models of kinship. In general, the more macrosocial utilitarian theories have not been applied to the family as a unit of analysis but rather to larger kinship groups, such as clans. As a result, North American family scholars have tended to favor the more microsocial variants of utilitarian thinking.

It should be useful to remember that exchanges need not be dyadic (between two people). In groups with three or more members, such as most families, the interests of all members need to be accommodated so that no member's personal interest dominates. Also, in groups with three or more members, the exchanges may be indirect. For example, I may help my wife, who helps her mother, and her mother may then do something nice for me because I helped her daughter. Or various groups of in-laws may take turns hosting holiday celebrations. And as we know from even casually thinking about inheritance patterns, the accumulated benefits of one generation may be passed along to the next generation ad infinitum. I may be eligible for inheritance not by promising to pay back my parents, but by assuring my parents that I won't break the chain and will pass on inheritance myself to my parents' grandchildren (Ekeh, 1974).

Empirical Applications

One way to understand a theory is to apply it to some examples. In this section, we apply exchange theory to two areas of research in the study of the family: divorce and sexual relations.

Divorce

Over the past half century, divorce in North America has increased dramatically. The past three decades have seen a slowing and stabilizing of divorce rates, but the risk of divorce is sometimes estimated to be as high as one divorce out of every two marriages. Divorce means difficult and painful adjustments for children as well as the husband and wife in a family. It is not surprising, then, that the explanation of why partners separate and divorce continues to occupy the attention of a significant number of family scholars.

Among the many possible explanations of divorce, exchange theory appears to offer one of the more promising roads to understanding. Briefly, according to exchange theory, each spouse analyzes the marriage by using the two comparison levels. First, a spouse compares profits relative to other marriages. If he or she feels deprived relative to other marriages, then the marital satisfaction of that spouse would be low, creating a motive for choosing separation and divorce. As Lewis and Spanier (1979) have aptly pointed out, however, many unhappy spouses remain married because of other constraints. Exchange theorists view these other constraints as costs associated with divorce. In the second comparison level, the spouse calculates the rewards and costs (profit) associated with possibilities other than marriage, for example, being single and divorced. Among the possible costs to this alternative would be child support, alimony, peer disapproval, the church's disapproval, kinship group disapproval, sexual deprivation, loss of interaction with one's children, role loss, and so on. Some of the possible rewards might be finding a more compatible partner, freeing family members from a confrontational and conflict-ridden home life, and freeing oneself from family responsibilities. The computation of the perceived alternatives to marriage depends on a diversity of variables, such as the gender ratio of the community in which one lives and the ages of one's children.

George Levinger (1965, 1966) assessed the likelihood of divorce in terms of *attractions*, *barriers*, and *alternatives*. If attractions to one's spouse and barriers to divorce are both low, and if alternatives are attractive, then divorce is more likely. Because all three factors are important, it is not sufficient to explain divorce in terms of any one of them alone. This application should remind us that it is important to know if the subjective calculations of both partners must be taken into account. Is divorce more likely if only one partner perceives a "poor deal" by staying married, or must both partners be getting a poor deal? In some societies, it may not be possible for one partner to end the relationship unilaterally if the other partner is unwilling to do so. Thus, when applying the exchange perspective to divorce, we need to specify the conditions under which miserable spouses can be expected to stay married.

One of the major stumbling blocks for successfully applying this exchange theory explanation to divorce is that the rewards and costs in the two comparison levels seem to change over the life span of the individual. This is evident in the paradoxical finding pointed out by White and Booth (1991) that the great bulk of divorces (30%–40%) occur in the first 5 years of marriage, the very point in the life span that is associated with the highest marital satisfaction. Furthermore, as marital satisfaction declines over the life course, so does the risk of divorce. It seems a paradox that we should find the greatest number of divorces when marriages are the happiest! However, the comparison levels for happiness are highest early in a relationship, and it is easier to become disappointed when expectations are not fulfilled. Sabatelli and Ripoll (2004) have further suggested that even generalized rewards may change importance over historical period and cohorts. Dew (2009) indirectly implies that rewards are gendered and that few of our choice models have incorporated this distinction. Clearly, we can see the importance of a permanent life mate may be different for each gender and that it may have declined over the last 50 years just as has the importance of religion. As society and technology change, so too do the things we consider to be rewarding. The question remains as to the pace, rapidity, and extent of changes in reward salience and if these changes make the context for choice so unstable as to make these choices nonrational. One example of this is suggested by South (2001) where the effect of women's employment on divorce changes across periods of time.

White and Booth (1991) explain this paradox by proposing that as marriages proceed through the spouses' life course, the importance of marital happiness tends to decline; in addition, longer duration marriages have relatively high costs for dissolution (barriers). White and Booth (1991) proposed that longer marriages with high costs for dissolution require high levels of marital unhappiness to propel spouses to divorce, whereas early marriages with few costs to divorce require greater levels of marital happiness to keep them together. Thus, the life course changes in salience and the ratio of rewards and costs explain the paradox. Lewis and Spanier's (1979) model of marital stability has been challenged by a competing exchange model offered by Thomas and Kleber (1981), who propose that regardless of marital quality, marital stability will be high when there are few alternatives and high barriers to dissolution. White and Booth (1991) feel that in addition to solving the paradox between high divorce rates and marital satisfaction, their data resolve the debate in favor of Lewis and Spanier's (1979) model. We believe grounds remain for further research on these competing models.

Gender Differences in Sexual Behavior

Our second application of exchange theory is drawn from propositions presented by Nye (1979) regarding sexual behavior, although we focus not on the formal propositions but on what the explanation would look like. But first, what is it that we want to explain about gender differences in sexual behavior? In most, if not all, cultures, sex seems more actively sought after by males than females. Although there may exist a biological answer to why this is the case (see Chapter 8; also, for a popular review, see Bergner, 2013), most authors assume that the biological drive is malleable in how it is satisfied. Furthermore, many of the behaviors that could be associated with a higher sex drive in one gender, such as prostitution, are usually labeled social rather than biological problems.

Nye (1979) argues that males are more likely to exchange rewards (especially money or marriage) for sexual access. Because exchange theory is essentially a motivational theory, Nye posits that sex is more profitable for males than it is for females. Nye is not assuming a more vital sex drive for males than females. Such an assumption would place the entire explanation on the shoulders of the biological importance, or salience, of sex for males over females. As a social scientist, Nye seems to assume that the biological drive for the two genders is equal, and he therefore searches for a social explanation.

First, Nye argues that in all cultures, women take the major responsibility for the children they bear. Unwanted pregnancy is thus more costly to women than it is to men. Even in the most modern societies, paternity is still difficult and expensive to prove. Contraceptives can be used to prevent the potential outcome of unwanted pregnancy, but contraception also is usually left to the female partner. These are real and potentially high costs to intercourse. A second differential is that men for the most part report better outcomes from sex than do women. Men are more likely to achieve orgasm than are women, and women are more likely to experience frustration from sexual relations.

The result of these differential costs and rewards is that relative to women, men, in general, find that sex offers greater rewards and fewer costs. As a result, men must either have sexual relations with those who find it as rewarding as they do (homosexuality), or they must increase the rewards for women. Nye says that the usual ways in which these rewards are increased for women is for men to offer either money or the probability of marriage. Other rewards such as status and security might be more salient at various points in the life course.

Nye's application of exchange has great scope and breadth. For example, it could explain female adornment as a sexual attractor that functions to increase the value of the exchange. Because married persons have already struck a bargain, we would expect much less difference between men and women in postmarital sexual relations. This prediction is consistent with the fact that a difference of less than 10% exists between male and female extramarital affairs (Blumstein & Schwartz, 1983). Furthermore, we can make some general predictions, such as that when the costs of contraception (inconvenience and medical complications) are equally distributed among both genders and sexual knowledge is shared among both genders so that both genders enjoy the same level of outcome, then we would expect less sexual bargaining with marriage and money. Keep in mind that Nye's (1979) theory remains to be tested and must be shown to provide a better explanation than competing theories, but this example does illustrate exchange theory's potential breadth of explanation. Indeed, Chibucos, Leite, and Weis's (2004) *Readings in Family Theory* has excellent examples of empirical extensions of this theory, especially Sprecher's (2001) paper using equity theory.

One of the major implications of the exchange-rational choice perspective on sexual behavior is its explanation of prostitution. Although this is still an area of academic disagreement, several authors have used the exchange-rational choice approach to explain prostitution. For example, Edlund and Korn's (2002) paper "A Theory of Prostitution" argues this perspective. These authors assert that

> prostitution has an unusual feature: it is well paid despite being
> low-skill, labor intensive and, one might add, female dominated.

Earnings even in the worst paid type, streetwalking, may be several multiples of full time earnings in professions with comparable skill requirements. (p. 182)

Most scholars recognize that this is not a simple sudden choice, and furthermore, it is a choice where the social and economic constraints are considerable. Nonetheless, the dominant perspective for voluntaristic economies is rational choice theory. Indeed, this theory has proven useful for even complex cases. For instance, Liu (2011) supplies a fascinating profile of this cascade of choices for women in China entering the sex trade and then becoming ensnarled in human trafficking.

Finally, following the original work by Becker (1964), several authors such as Levine (2000) and Paton (2002) have extended rational choice theory to explain adolescents' sexual choice of contraception and sexual behavior. The application of rational choice to such an area as adolescent sexual behavior is controversial for two reasons. First, adolescents, because of brain maturation, are not yet fully rational. Even the courts recognize this by assuming that adolescent criminal cases are tried in juvenile rather than adult court because the offenders cannot yet fully comprehend the consequences of their actions. The second reason this is controversial is that sexual behavior is thought to be one of the most emotional rather than rational forms of behavior. So on both counts, we would not expect rational choice theory to provide a very good explanation. Paton (2002), however, argues that adolescent behavior in a British sample is not random behavior but more likely to be a rational choice. Some studies in third world countries, such as Gurmu and Dejene's (2012), have argued that rational choice is explanatory as an individual level process, but it must be seen as rational within a context of poverty, low education, and restricted opportunity. Even though the application of rational choice to sexual behavior is still contested, the notion that individual rational choices are always to be interpreted within specific contexts appears to offer some explanatory utility.

Critiques and Discussion

Our focus in this section is on the criticisms commonly directed at microexchange theories. We recognize that each of the criticisms discussed is more applicable to some microsocial variants than others. Our central target must be the general notions presented above and principally derived from Nye (1979) and Coleman (1990). One caveat should be mentioned: No social theory solves all the problems we raise in our critiques. Our criticism is not aimed at convincing the theorist or the student that one theory is better than another. Rather, these critiques are intended to illuminate the choices we make in adopting a theoretical stance and to point out the areas that are in need of more creative thinking by the next generation of scholars.

As we mentioned at the beginning, microsocial exchange theories are usually based on *methodological individualism,* the assumption that the individual is the appropriate unit to study to gain an understanding of the family. As far as we know, there has never been a definition of the family as simply an aggregation of individuals. But when we take the individual's ratio of rewards and costs as the basis of our theory about families, we are assuming that the aggregation of individual members is the family. Theoretically, this would make the family no different from any other collection of actors. Yet the family has characteristics that seem unlike other social groups. For most of us, our families are lifelong social groups that we enter by birth and leave by death. Our families have roles that are unlike work group roles, such as filial obligations toward the parents. And our families have biological and social relations (blood and marriage) that are unlike those in any other social group. Thus, to assume that individual actors are interchangeable and that families as social groups can be explained by the motivation of individuals seems problematic.

Explaining social order poses a problem for all the forms of utilitarianism. If we view explanation as emanating from individual motivation, then it is usually difficult to demonstrate how we developed social norms and social institutions. Although most microsocial theorists include a discussion of the norm of reciprocity (you should help those who help you), it is much less clear how this norm is derived from individual self-interest. In addition, in analyzing costs and rewards, theorists readily accept the given nature of social norms and institutions without indicating how these are explained by the theory. For instance, in weighing the rewards and costs of not wearing clothing on a hot summer day, you automatically take into account formal norms (laws) and informal norms. Most of you recognize that no matter how rewarding you might find going without clothing, there are strong formal and informal norms that constrain your behavior. The major answer utilitarians have given this question regarding social order is known as the *social contract.* There are many variants of this idea, but basically it involves the assumption that individuals band together and form a social order so as to have security of person and property. This social contract implies that some individual freedom is relinquished so that order may be maintained. But this view, although admitting the importance and power of social institutions, largely begs the question of how these social institutions evolve and change. Clearly, most of you have no recollection of relinquishing some of your freedoms in exchange for order. Rather, you were socialized by institutions to be on time, to behave in certain ways, and to expect formal and informal sanctions if you transgressed the social order.

Another problematic area for microsocial exchange theory is altruistic behavior. Many times we see (and praise) behaviors that seem to be characterized by the individual giving up rewards and suffering costs so that others may prosper. Some simple examples are a soldier giving up his or her life in combat or a mother running into a burning house to save her child. Exchange theorists would point out that this is a problem of attribution or inference. All we have really observed is the behavior (not the motive), and we incorrectly attribute an other-directedness to an act that was actually calculated to yield profit. Thus, the mother is acting in the least costly way if she regards the death of her child as more costly than the personal risk she incurs by her attempt to save the child. The soldier who refuses to fight faces court martial, humiliation, and shame. On the other hand, critics might argue that these people are not acting rationally at all, but emotionally.

Rewards are even more problematic because they may not be stable. For an individual to make rational decisions about rewards and costs, the importance, or salience, of rewards and costs must be relatively stable. For example, if I am offered a reward for doing something and I get to choose a Snickers candy bar or Mars candy bar, the assumption is that my "taste" remains relatively stable. By the end of the task when I get the reward, the assumption is that I will not have changed my mind. The idea of *generalized rewards* assumes a societal level constancy. Dew (2009), however, has suggested gender differences in rewards. Sabatelli and Ripoll (2004) have suggested that reward saliences change by birth cohorts and historical period. Other researchers have indicated life course changes in reward saliences (South, 2001; White & Booth, 1991). Although there has not been a test of the stability hypothesis for rewards that incorporates all these dimensions, there is certainly the suggestion that reward saliences may not be stable; therefore, rational decisions would be all but impossible.

The assumption of a rational actor provides further difficulties, especially in the study of the family. The family is often considered a social group characterized by intense loyalty and emotions. Most police officers will tell you that domestic quarrels are often emotional and potentially explosive situations because of their irrational nature. Furthermore, the institution of marriage has long been viewed as 'til death do us part, which flies in the face of the exchange view until profitability declines. And of course, children do not choose their parents, nor is the family they enter representative of the voluntaristic ideal of unfettered choice needed for the optimization of profit. Thus, it seems natural to question whether the assumption of rational actors calculating their most profitable choice makes sense in the context of the family.

One of the most basic questions in the study of the family is, "Why do people have children?" Exchange theory should treat this choice as bearing profit for the parents. But as most economists and parents will attest, children are expensive. Although there are many ways to estimate the costs of raising one child (to age 17, without advanced education, etc.), inflation-adjusted estimates for raising a middle-class child today are usually above a quarter of a million dollars. Furthermore, the decline in the norms regarding filial care of the aged, coupled with social security and institutional care, make returns to the parents in old age unlikely. Nye (1979) attempts to answer this question by saying there is a form of intergenerational norm of reciprocity. You feel an obligation to pass on what your parents did for you to the succeeding generation. But people who are childless by choice can pocket the quarter of a million dollars and seemingly feel little remorse in not passing on the favor. It may be that having children is not a rational decision.

There is a problem of weighing costs and rewards. We have previously mentioned that the salience, or importance, of rewards and costs must be examined to understand a choice. Of course, theorists would like to believe that some costs and rewards have roughly similar value across actors. If this were not so, then it would be unlikely that we could develop successful microeconomics. Even the symbols and meaning associated with economic units may be unstable, however. In our society, there are symbols of wealth and success. Increasingly, both the wealthy and the indebted may attain these symbols. These symbols may vary across cohorts and periods. We know of a very wealthy man who insisted on driving himself in a 10-year-old vehicle. His offspring all had fancier new cars with chauffeurs. And the meaning of rewards and costs changes more drastically once we move our comparisons to other cultures. In Tikopia, a man's wealth was based on the number of wives he had. But number of wives did not just reflect material well-being. Daughters could be traded for wives; therefore daughters were a means to wealth and status.

Turner (1991) argues that exchange theory can be accused of tautological reasoning. In essence, a *tautology* exists when terms are all defined by one another and there is no possibility of disproving the statements. Turner argues that reward is defined as that which is valued by the person. The choice that a person makes is the maximization of profit. Thus, all actions are rewarding, and the reason we undertake an action is that it brings rewards. For example, we may ask, "Why did Tiffany get married?" Some exchange theorists would answer that Tiffany got married because it was a more profitable choice than remaining single. But we may ask, "How do the exchange theorists know that this maximized Tiffany's profits over remaining single?" If the exchange theorists responded that we know because people always choose those behaviors that maximize their profits, then we have just completed a tautological circle. Turner believes that this circular logic is often found in deductive theories. We do not disagree that deductive systems can be self-referential and closed systems of definitions, but we do disagree that deductive scientific theories are ever like this. Indeed, the hallmark of a scientific theory (as opposed to a theory in general) is that some of its concepts are tied to empirical measures. We may define force (f) as f:ma, but we have standard empirical measures for mass (m) and acceleration (a). A problem with utilitarian theories is that they often seem to lack this mooring to the concrete empirical measurement system.

Conclusion

Despite the criticisms, utilitarian, or exchange, theory is one of the most popular social science theories applied to the family. One reason for this popularity is that exchange theories typically have great scope and breadth. The notions of reward, cost, and profit are sufficiently abstract and content free that the researcher may fill in the content from any number of contexts. The assumptions of rational actors calculating profit provides some problems, as does the inadequacy of the theory for explaining how and why institutional and normative constraints operate on choices, but the more general approach provided by rational choice theorists promises to address this problem.

STUDY QUESTIONS

1. What is the difference between a purely individualistic rational choice approach and a social exchange approach? (Hint: Are there any individual goals that can be reached only with the assistance of others? If so, are others then valued as means to get what you want or as ends in themselves?)

2. If the rational choice approach to relationship intimacy is really about getting others to perceive that we offer lots of rewards and few costs, then how would you design an algorithm for a successful dating website? Would the dating site be aimed at short-term or long-term relationship success?

3. In a state of nature, I am hungry, and I see food on the other side of a raging river which I cannot cross. I do see that a fallen tree trunk could be used to cross the river, but it is too heavy for me to lift by myself. I see some people not far away. What would a rational choice theorist predict, and would it be any different from an exchange theorist's prediction?

4. I want to disprove the important assumption that *people act in their own self-interest*. Imagine that I can demonstrate cases where people act altruistically or for the benefit of others rather than their own self-interest. The rational choice theorist argues that either (1) the action really benefits the individual's self-interest (e.g., helping others makes them feel good) or (2) the person is *irrational* and therefore outside the boundary conditions of the theory. Can this assumption be disproved or is it tautologically true?

5. Methodological individualism argues that causes must be understood at the level of the individual actor. Let's think of some macro-level theories and see how this would work. Can you reduce evolutionary theory to the individual? How would you reduce the Great Depression to the individual level actor? Can you reduce social conformity to the individual level and still maintain that choices are *rational*?

6. Is it a rational choice to have children? (Hint: Consider the context of the decision.)

CHAPTER

4

The Symbolic Interaction Framework

Nicole, Michael, and their teenage son, James, have agreed to participate in a social survey about family life. Survey officials requested that all three of them participate in answering questions. The doorbell rings, and they meet the interviewer, a young woman named Kim. Kim asks that each of the family members fill out a section of the questionnaire independently of the others. James takes his questionnaire to his room, Michael fills his out in the kitchen, and Nicole completes hers in the living room, where Kim is waiting. After all three family members have completed their questionnaires, Kim briefly examines them. She pauses and then says, "Gosh, all three of you answered the question about how traditional or nontraditional your family is in very different ways. Would you folks mind discussing this with me for just a moment? We are supposed to discuss differences of opinion as part of the survey, and if you don't mind, I'll take notes occasionally." The family agrees.

It turns out that James believes that his family is fairly traditional. Nicole believes the family is very traditional. And her husband, Michael, thinks the family is extremely nontraditional. Nicole says that she thinks the family is traditional because she feels she has to do all the cleaning up after the "guys." Michael says he thinks they are nontraditional because his wife earns more money than he does. James believes they are fairly traditional because he has a mother and father who aren't divorced. Finally, Michael asks Kim, the researcher, what the survey means by "traditional." After the family is told the meaning, Kim asks if that information would change their answers. All three family members say that it would and that the survey meaning is not very close to what they think of as traditional.

Contemporary social science applied to the study of groups such as families is, for the most part, concerned with people's behavior. Within a society or even a family group, much of our varied forms of communication are taken for granted. For example, a researcher usually assumes that questions on a questionnaire hold the same meaning and will be interpreted in the same way by all respondents. The variation in answers to questions is supposed to reflect differences in behavior, not in the interpretation of a question. If we ask a husband and wife how many times they quarreled during the past week, we assume that they label the same events as quarrels. Yet even between husbands and wives who must both have been present for a quarrel to take place, we find differences in responses. We must conclude that differences in counting quarrels may be a difference of interpretation in what constitutes a quarrel, a difference of memory, or both. In an even broader perspective on diversity of meanings, we know some of the persons responding to our questions may have another mother tongue, the families in which they were raised are different, and they have diverse educational levels and abilities. How, then, can we assume that they will interpret and understand our questions in the same way? Maybe their responses are based not on different reactions to the question but on very different interpretations. Symbolic interactionism, more than any other of the family theories, calls for paying attention to how events and things are interpreted by social actors.

Some social scientists have divided the subject matter of human behavior into disciplines studying personality (psychology), culture (linguistics and anthropology), and social behavior (sociology, economics, family studies, and political science). At the base of these distinctions is the assumption that a culture is composed of commonly shared signs and symbols from which actors construct the meanings found in the culture. Many social scientists approach the meaning of symbols and signs in a culture as being relatively uniform; therefore, the words on the questionnaire are viewed as commonly and uniformly understood. But some social scientists have argued that we cannot understand a behavioral response (including answering a questionnaire) unless we know what meaning the situation and the stimulus have for an actor. In broader terms, these social scientists believe that to understand social behavior, the researcher must understand the meanings actors assign to the situation and action. This uniting of the study of cultural meanings with social behavior is the prime focus of theories of symbolic interaction.

Intellectual Traditions

The symbolic interaction approach has a rich and complex history. Today, the term *symbolic interactionism* represents a diverse set of family theories, and it can be difficult to detect what many of the variants now have in common that unites them under a single banner. The common threads that exist are perhaps best highlighted by understanding the common progenitors from which the current variants developed.

Without a doubt, the greatest single influence on social science thinking in the 20th century came from Charles Darwin. Darwin (1880) provided a concrete and biologically rooted approach that was in stark contrast to the more abstract *idealism* (e.g., Hegel) that was in philosophical favor in Europe at the time. To intellectuals in North America, the more concrete biological approach emphasizing the adaptation of organisms to their environment was much more attractive. Three North American scholars were particularly influential in generating ideas that would become incorporated in symbolic interactionism. Charles S. Peirce developed a theory of signs and symbols, William James (1975) developed a notion of self in relation to environment, and John Dewey (1925) developed the concept of mind. As Charles Morris points out in his preface to Mead's (1934) *Mind, Self, and Society,* pragmatists saw no sharp distinction or conflict between science and philosophy. Together, these scholars represent the foundation of the philosophical school called *pragmatism,* from which symbolic interactionism sprang.

The philosophical foundation for symbolic interactionism is complemented by advances in social science thinking that were occurring in the first two decades of the 20th century. Charles Horton Cooley (1902, 1909) expanded William James's (1983/1890) idea of the self into the more elaborate social science concept of the *looking glass self.* The importance of Cooley's (1909) notion is that it conceptualized part of the self as capable of reflection on its own behavior. This later became incorporated in Mead's (1934) conception of the self. W. I. Thomas and D. S. Thomas (1928) expanded on the pragmatic premise formulated by Peirce (1905) that the conception of an object is wholly given by the conception of all possible effects. Thomas and Thomas (1928) reinterpreted the pragmatic maxim as the important social-psychological principle "*What humans define as real has real consequences*" (p. 572). This has become known as the *definition of the situation* and provides a linkage between how we perceive our environment and how we act in it. Both of these notions guided the early formulations of symbolic interactionism.

Despite these important earlier influences, it is really the work of George Herbert Mead that most scholars identify as the start of symbolic interactionism. Mead's thinking is, for the most part, accessible only through the lecture notes of his students, compiled and edited by the linguist Charles Morris (e.g., Morris, 1934). Indeed, Morris (1934) points out that although Mead's students took notes, Mead never even used lecture notes, and his thinking was constantly evolving. Yet Mead's influence and contribution have been sufficiently strong to establish him as the paternal figurehead of symbolic interactionism.

Central to Mead's approach is the idea that by sharing common symbols, humans can adapt to and survive in their environment. He was especially interested in the process by which the flexibly adaptive infant came to share the conventional understandings in any society. His work incorporated the idea of stages of interactional learning through play and games, an especially important perspective for the study of socialization in the family.

Although Mead is an important starting point, numerous scholars have contributed to symbolic interactionism, and it would be misleading to portray its development as monotonic and united. In fact, scholars have quarreled bitterly about the relative emphases and interpretation of ideas. Most secondary sources record an original bifurcation of symbolic interactionism into the Chicago school (Blumer, 1962, 1969) and the Iowa school (Kuhn, 1964), but we see more variants than just these two. We discuss many of these in the variants section below. We believe it is also important for the student to first gain some notion of the unifying elements in this theoretical perspective before we turn to such variants.

It is easy to say that symbolic interaction theories focus on meaning but quite a different and more difficult task to explain what that means. To understand this complex issue, we must return to the seminal work of Peirce and later Morris. Humans have the ability to mentally form invariant associations. For example, when Event A is associated with Event B, we could say that A is a *sign* for B. Where there is smoke, there is fire. Smoke is thus a sign for fire. An octagonal traffic sign is a sign to stop. A sign is the necessary ingredient for the development of a *symbol*. A symbol is any sign that is agreed on by convention. Now, although there are several important aspects to these distinctions, the question that symbolic interactionism poses is, "How do we agree on (convention) the sign?" Let's apply this to language. We have words such as *dad* that stand as a sign for a particular person in our lives. Not only do you have a dad, but others understand the referent of that utterance, too. In addition, if you think about this issue for very long, you will note that many words (both written and spoken) refer not to things but to other clusters of symbols. The complexity of human symbolism and meaning as we now know it escapes any simple notion that every sign has a referent, because words can stand for other symbols as well as things.

To understand the term *meaning* in a social context, symbolic interactionists focus on the idea of how these complex systems of symbols are shared. Indeed, for communication to take place, symbols must be shared or commonly agreed on. Thus, the focus for Mead and many other interactionists is on the process by which the infant comes to acquire the symbol system of the society.

The symbolic content of any culture is constantly changing. Words such as *limn* leave our system through disuse and abuse, and new words, such as *LOL* or *sriracha,* come into use. Too, old words and symbols take on new meanings, such as # evolving to denote not only a number or pound sign, but more commonly a *Twitter hashtag* (another new term in and of itself) as well. Even though the symbol system must be relatively stable for the achievement of agreement and convention, it nonetheless changes. But it changes within the rules of the system. As Chomsky (1965) and other linguists point out, a key ingredient to understanding a symbol system, and therefore meaning, is that users of the system adopt rules that allow the generation of new and meaningful utterances based on these rules, or *syntax*. This insight is responsible for a second focus for interactionists. That focus is on the process by which meanings are constructed through interaction with both the environment and other people. In fact, most human symbol systems are so complex as to allow the generation of meanings for specific contexts and environments.

The general focus of symbolic interactionism can be summed up as being on the acquisition and generation of meaning. It should not be forgotten that in the study of the family and other social groups, we are assuming that actors think about and act according to the meanings they attribute to their actions and context. For example, a 3-year-old child may show no interest in a particular toy doll. But when an older sibling plays with the doll, it suddenly takes on new interactional and situational meaning. Now the doll is desired. The meaning of the toy is constructed by the situational interaction of the two siblings. Symbolic interactionism is not simply a motivational theory (as exchange); it is much broader. Certainly, symbolic interactionism posits that humans are motivated to create meanings to help them make sense of their world. In addition, it encompasses actors' motives as constructed from the meanings available to the actor and relevant to the situation in which the actor is located.

Another example is contained in the following story. A 5-year-old girl abruptly asked her mother, "How do babies get born?" Nervous as to what she should say about sex and reproduction, the mother paused and then responded, "Do you mean where do babies come from?" The young girl briskly replied, "No, are they born with clothes on or clothes off?"

Meaning emerges through the course of social interaction. Words have no communicative meaning at all unless they are mutually understood by conversing actors. Of course, as the above episode illustrates, we all may have private understandings that are not identical, so we must construct a common understanding of other words and expressions through an exchange of already meaningful symbols. When misunderstandings occur, we attempt to overcome them.

As focal points for intense interaction, families are crucial sites for creation and verification of meaning. When children are young, the meanings of things are usually simply acquired and taken for granted, based on exposure to usage by parents, other family members, and others in society (including Big Bird on *Sesame Street*). Parents, in turn, acquired many meanings from elders when they were younger so that at least some of our linguistic heritage is passed on from generation to generation. Still, in any specific encounter between humans, there must be a meeting of minds, with some assurance that a shared sensibility either preexists or is capable of being created through a new communicative process. Thus, effective relationships, both inside and outside of families, are dependent on nurturing a culture of shared meanings.

Focus and Scope Assumptions

Human behavior must be understood by the meanings of the actor. The most basic assumption in symbolic interactionism is that the explanation of human behavior is impossible without knowing the meaning such behavior holds for the actor. Interactionists believe that to be human is to use symbols. Indeed, they would say we live in a largely symbolic world. Our language structures the way we perceive and the way we think. Material objects, such as jeans and cars, not only perform functions (utility) but also have symbolic significance aesthetically, religiously, and socially. Humans live in a symbolic world, and our actions have both physical and symbolic import. If we were to attempt to understand behavior simply from the physical side of the equation, we would miss the mark of understanding. For example, if we were to describe to you a man in the woods cutting down a tree, you would not understand that behavior unless we discovered the actor's meaning (e.g., he is employed as a lumberjack, he is getting a Christmas tree, or he is a vandal). To understand behavior, we must understand the meaning that an action has for the actor. This has become a major assumption for many methodological approaches, such as "grounded theory" (see Glaser & Strauss, 1967; Corbin & Strauss, 1998), but these methodologies are beyond the scope of this theoretical chapter.

Actors define the meaning of context and situation. The assumption that actors define the meaning of the contexts and situations in which they find themselves is in some ways an extension of the previous assumption. If humans live in a symbolic world, then the context in which humans find themselves will be both physical and symbolic. This assumption is only fully understood, however, by returning to Thomas and Thomas's (1928) maxim that what humans define as real has real consequences. Imagine that a terribly inebriated person hallucinates a herd of pink elephants charging down the street toward where he or she is standing. In response to the hallucinated charging elephants, the person begins to run down the street. Regardless of the fact that no elephants exist, the fact that the person defines the situation as dangerous is important in understanding why the person runs down the street. How we define the situation in which we find ourselves explains what problems we define and what actions and solutions we undertake. The fact that some definitions may be entirely mental rather than physical constructions makes our understanding of the actors' definitions of the situation even more important.

Individuals have minds. Another basic assumption of symbolic interactionism is that humans have minds. This may seem a trivial assumption unless we examine it more closely. All of us recognize that we have an organ of the body that sends and receives electrochemical impulses. But the idea of an individual mind presupposes an individual self that perceives, reasons, senses, and imagines. The notion of mind includes memory and willing actions as retrospective and prospective operations. Whether there is one organ or a system of interconnected organs that gives rise to these complex operations is not totally resolved, even in the neurosciences. In addition, the discovery by the 2000 Nobel laureate Eric Kandel that synapses are modified by experience further complicates issues in that the organ of the brain may be changed and modified throughout our lives by experience. Indeed, it is the assumption in symbolic interactionism that the human mind acquires, integrates, and processes information. At the same time, the mind is capable of reflecting on its own processes so that the individual can develop a self as both actor (I) and object (me).

Society precedes the individual. When symbolic interactionists assume that humans live in a symbolic world and use their minds to manipulate and interpret these symbols, it is tempting to ask, "When did this all begin?" At some point in evolutionary time, we as a subhuman species lacked these talents. The problem with asking when we gained the abilities is that it was such a gradual process that there was no single point in time. Indeed, it might be considered a moot question whether symbols, social organization, or mind came first, because they are so strongly interdependent. But because we cannot conceptualize without symbols, and symbols are shared, society in rudimentary form must precede the individual mind and self. The single most important point to understand about Mead's conception of mind is that *individual minds are results of the society and not vice versa.* As Morris (1934) says,

> Instead of beginning with individual minds and working out
> to society, Mead starts with an objective social process and
> works inward through the importation of the social process of
> communication into the individual by the medium of the vocal
> gesture. The individual has taken the social act into himself.
> Mind remains social. (p. xxii)

Probably the best-known empirical cases illustrating Morris's point would be the two cases of infant isolation documented by Kingsley Davis (1947). In both cases, children lacked socialization and failed to develop language and social skills. The assumption that society precedes individuals leads interactionists to focus on the process of socialization.

Concepts

Self and Mind

The notion of self is pivotal in symbolic interactionism. But our understanding of this concept is not well served by translating Mead's (1934) concept of self as that which we commonly understand as our identity. For Mead, self, mind, and symbol developed concurrently. Our notion of self is founded on symbols and consciousness. The essence of symbolic interaction is that the self is a symbolic representation of that which did an act (I) and that which was acted on (me). In other words, we may represent ourselves as both subject and object. This means that humans can look at their own behavior as an object (me) and as such take "the role of the other." The concept of taking the role of the other is directly analogous to what Cooley (1902) called "the looking glass self." Mead (1934) extended this concept from looking at our actions as a specific other (How would my father see my action?) to looking at our actions as a "generalized other" (How would others in society look at my act?). The self, then, is constructed by our consciousness from the two perspectives of I and me. The self as object contains the perspective of specific others when we take on the role of particular persons to see ourselves as they might, and it is constructed from the perspective of generalization of roles, or generalized other.

Socialization

Socialization is the process by which we acquire the symbols, beliefs, and attitudes of our culture. Although the notion of socialization is central in symbolic interaction, Mead (1934) did not use it as a concept. Rather, Mead talked about this process as the "importation" of social symbols into the mind as part of the development of the generalized other: "Mind is nothing but the importation of this external process into the conduct of the individual so as to meet the problems that arise" (p. 188). For the child, the process of socialization is marked by two stages. First is the *play stage,* in which the child plays at being something such as a police officer or mother. The play stage incorporates Mead's notion of taking the role of the other. Second is the *game stage,* in which the child must be able to incorporate his or her self in an organized activity through the generalized other. As Mead says,

> If we contrast play with the situation in an organized game, we
> note the essential difference that the child who plays in a game
> must be ready to take the attitude of everyone else involved in
> that game, and that these different roles must have a definite
> relationship to each other. (p. 151)

Thus, the play stage assists in the learning and practice of *role taking,* whereas the game stage assists in the more complex task of learning the rules governing all social actors in the game. It is the game stage that is most similar to the complex social game we play as adults with our ability to "play a role" in society.

Role

Although the concept of role does not originate with symbolic interactionism, it is without a doubt one of the most basic concepts in symbolic interactionism. It is also the concept that has proved most problematic, because Mead (1934) uses the term throughout his work but seemingly takes its definition as self-evident. Probably the closest passage to a definition comes in a footnote in which Mead identifies social intelligence as depending on

> the given individual's ability to take the roles of, or "put himself in the place of," the other individuals implicated with him in given social situations; and upon his consequent sensitivity to their attitudes toward himself and toward one another. (p. 141n)

From this, we can clearly see that a role must be the "place of an actor." Mead also dealt with roles as rules to be learned in the game stage of a child's development. *Role taking,* then, is to put oneself in the place of the actor, and it includes the rules that the actor is expected to follow. The sketchiness of these references and lack of a clear definition has fueled bitter debates among later symbolic interactionists.

Several dimensions of the concept of role are significant in explaining family phenomena. If we assume that roles have the two characteristics alluded to above—rules of behavior for positions—then we can see how these rules also provide others with *expectations* for what someone in that position is to do. For example, the general norm, or rule, for a person who is "it" in the game of hide-and-seek is to close one's eyes and count to 10 while others hide. If the person who is *it* does not do this, he or she has not performed the role as others expected. Note that the others' behavior is predicated on the expectation of how *it* would behave. Thus, one important dimension of roles is the expectation that both the actor and others have about the performance of the role.

The *clarity* of the role expectations or rules of the role is another important dimension. Without clear expectations shared by both the actor and others, it is impossible for the actor to perform the role or for others to know how their behavior integrates with that of the actor. Returning to the game of hide-and-seek, if *it* counts only to five but others expect *it* to count to a higher number, their behavior cannot be successfully meshed nor the game carried on.

Role strain and *role overload* are additional important dimensions of roles. Role strain is where the actor does not have sufficient resources to enact a role or roles. Similarly, when there are multiple roles, the accumulation of expectations across roles may be so great as to create role overload. A corollary to role strain is the special case in which the expectations of one role contradict or conflict with the expectations of another role. This conflict usually produces role strain because the actor cannot enact the opposing roles simultaneously.

Definition of the Situation

The concept of the definition of the situation originated with W. I. Thomas (Thomas & Thomas, 1928) but is also implicit in Mead's (1934) work in his emphasis on the social situation and taking the role of the other and the generalized other. The definition of the situation refers to the dictum that what we define as real will have real consequences, and this sensitizes symbolic interactionists to the role of perception in forming our behavior. Mead, however, seemed wary about an approach that was too perceptually oriented and lacked focus on humans as problem solvers interacting with their environment. He stated,

> This process of thinking, which is the elaboration of our responses to the stimulus, is a process which also necessarily goes on in the organism. Yet it is a mistake to assume that all that we call thought can be located in the organism or can be put inside the head. The goodness or badness of the investments is in the investment, and the valuable or dangerous character of food is in the food, not in our heads. (p. 115)

Thus, Mead, in a manner consistent with Thomas and Thomas's (1928) dictum and Dewey's (1925) pragmatism, focuses us once again on the problem-solving interaction with the environment rather than on isolated internal mental processes.

Identity

Certainly, *identity* has been a core concept of symbolic interactionism, but it has been raised to the status of a mini theory within the symbolic interaction framework through the work of Sheldon Stryker (1968a, 1968b, 1994; Ervin & Stryker, 2001; Stryker & Burke, 2000). Stryker and Burke (2000) argue that the theory of identity has been developed on two fronts. First, Stryker and his colleagues have detailed the process by which the self is formed by the society. Much of this work has been focused on the many social statuses available to an actor (parent, friend, employee), the roles that might be enacted within each status (for the status of *parent*, roles might include disciplinarian, nurturer, financial provider, e.g.), and the hierarchies an actor uses in forming identities based on these multiple statuses and roles (Adamsons, O'Brien, & Pasley, 2007).

The second front for identity theory has been the investigation of the link between identity and behavior. Burke and his colleagues have argued that identity links to situational behavior through the meanings that actors carry for the identity (Stryker & Burke, 2000). Thus, the complete picture for identity is that society provides the social roles (and meanings of those roles) that an actor interprets and organizes into hierarchies of salience (how likely the identity is to be enacted in a particular situation, a subconscious process) and centrality (how important the identity is to the actor, a conscious designation). The actor then behaves in any situation according to the identity and meanings relevant to the situation. This perspective allows the actor to have agency and invoke different role identities based on salience of the identity and situational relevance. It also allows actors to have multiple roles both across the life span and at any given time point.

Burke, Swann, and others also have expanded on the ways in which important *others* influence the negotiation of identities through the process of *identity verification*. Burke's cybernetic model (1991) proposes that actors enact identity-relevant behaviors with the desired goal of receiving feedback from others that confirms that their behaviors (and therefore their identities) are appropriate and desired. Others then provide feedback to the actor, which either confirms or contradicts that the behavior (or identity) is desirable, and actors then adapt their behavior (or in some cases, their identities) in order to bring about congruence between identities and feedback. Swann further explored the concept of *self-enhancement*, which sometimes competes with the goal of *self-verification*. Swann and colleagues (Swann, 1987; Swann, De La Ronde, & Hixon, 1994; Swann & Read, 1981) found that individuals with negative self-perceptions will tolerate flattering (but disconfirming) feedback from casual acquaintances, but desire feedback that is unflattering (and confirming) from more intimate partners. For example, if a person believes that they are uncoordinated and not good at sports, receiving a compliment on their athleticism from a stranger would be a positive experience, but the compliment would be distressing if coming from a spouse, as from a spouse, it would seem to indicate either a lack of knowledge about the person or a lie, both undesirable options.

Recently, a number of identity researchers also have investigated the relationship between identity verification by an *other* and emotions produced in this interaction. Stets (2005) demonstrated that the relationship is not so simple as imagined; that is, actors do not simply experience positive emotions when the most salient or central roles are confirmed by others. Indeed, we see work in the area of emotions as critical to understanding family relationships. Although work in the area of identity and emotions is still multitheoretical at this time, symbolic interaction and the concept of identity remain central to many of these explorations (e.g., Burke, 2006; Stets, 2005; Stets & Turner, 2006; Turner & Stets, 2005).

Propositions

Numerous authors have employed a symbolic interaction approach in the empirical study of the family and relationships (e.g., LaRossa & LaRossa, 1981; LaRossa & Reitzes, 1993; Stets, 1992); however, none of the contributions to date has equaled the theoretical presentation by Burr and his colleagues (Burr, 1973; Burr, Leigh, Day, & Constantine, 1979). They focus on the general propositions that are directly relevant to understanding families and, in our opinion, provide the most elegant and systematic statement of symbolic interaction theory applied to families. For this reason, much of the clarity and power of the theory to explain family behavior and processes originates in the propositional inventory provided by Burr, Leigh et al. (1979). Here we discuss a few of the propositions that we regard as among the most useful for understanding families.

> *The quality of ego's role enactment in a relationship positively affects ego's satisfaction with the relationship.* (Burr, Leigh et al., 1979, p. 70)

Although most of us assume that our satisfaction in a relationship such as marriage is "made" by the other person, this proposition states that a person (ego) is more satisfied in a relationship when he or she is doing a good job of enacting the role in that relationship. For example, a wife would feel more satisfied about her marriage when she feels that she is doing a good job in the role of wife. Burr and colleagues also offer a proposition regarding the role performance of the other, but that would be more expected. The proposition regarding ego's role enactment is a little like the homilies "You like what you're good at" or "The more you put into something, the more you get out of it."

> *The greater the perceived clarity of role expectations, the higher the quality of role enactment.* (Burr, Leigh et al., 1979, p. 74)

A role is defined as the normative expectations attached to a specific position in a social structure. For example, the role of mother is defined by the social norms or expectations of nurturance and protection of her young. The more clearly defined these are to any person occupying the position of motherhood, the easier it is for that person to perform the role in a socially acceptable way. Obviously, a lack of clarity could result when nonbiological mothers receive unclear or no anticipatory socialization as to the expectations of social motherhood, or if the society lacks clear expectations of motherhood and this lack of clarity is passed on through socialization to mothers. In either instance, the result would be decrements in the role enactment of the young mother. For example, years ago, breast-feeding of infants was not as socially expected as it is today. Today, the normative expectations for breast-feeding are gaining increased force and clarity as role expectations for mothers.

The more individuals perceive consensus in the expectations about a role they occupy, the less their role strain. (Burr, Leigh et al., 1979, p. 79)

As Rossi and Berk (1985) point out, one critical aspect of a role is that expectations are shared or consensual. Indeed, Mead (1934) argued that all social symbols are the result of consensus. If a person perceives that there is a social consensus on a norm or expectation, then the role as an instruction for behavior is clearer. As we have seen with the second of our propositions, the clarity of such prescriptions facilitates enactment of the behaviors. Thus, if a young mother believes that there exists a broad social consensus that mothers should breast-feed their infants, she is less likely to feel that that expectation is vague or ambiguous. Vague and ambiguous role prescriptions cause people to feel uncertain about what the prescriptions are and whether they can meet those expectations. This is the experience of *role strain*. Burr, Leigh et al. (1979) defined role strain as the felt stress generated when a person has difficulty complying with the expectations of a role (see p. 57). The mother who is uncertain as to the socially approved pattern of infant feeding would undergo role strain.

The greater the diversification of a person's roles, the less consensus the person will perceive in the expectations about those roles. (Burr, Leigh et al., 1979, p. 80)

When a person plays multiple roles, there are multiple expectations. At the very minimum, the multitude of expectations may become murky, and at worst, contradictory expectations may lead to conflict between the expectations of roles. In both situations, it is difficult for the person to perceive clearly that there is a consensus about the expected behavior. For example, a working mother with an infant may feel that, among nonworking mothers and health care professionals, there is a consensus preferring breast milk for infants. Among fellow workers, she may feel that there is a consensus that expressing milk while at the office is unprofessional and shows a lack of commitment to work. Among working mothers, there may be no consensus, some siding with fellow workers and some with health care professionals. Conversely, the stay-at-home mothers (without role diversification) perceive greater consensus.

The greater the perceived role strain that results from performing a role, the less the ease in making a transition into the role and the greater the ease in making a transition out of the role. (Burr, Leigh et al., 1979, p. 86)

Naturally, most of us try to avoid feeling stressed, and it seems reasonable that roles that are perceived as producing stress are regarded as requiring a more difficult adjustment than roles perceived as carrying little stress. For example, the perceived role strain of motherhood suggests that although becoming a mother is a biological function, it is not an easy transition. As a result, we have developed elaborate rituals and forms of anticipatory socialization in attempts to clarify the role expectations and ease the transition. Prenatal classes for expectant parents are one example of such anticipatory socialization. Conversely, many such classes focus on expectant mothers rather than expectant fathers, leading to less socialization and greater role strain for fathers during the transition to parenthood.

The systematic propositions above are only a few examples of the many proposed by Burr, Leigh, and colleagues (1979). These authors presented these propositions as part of a deductive formalization of symbolic interactionism. As you may recall from the introductory chapter of this book, one of the strengths of a deductive theory is that propositions can be chained together to produce new and informative propositions. If we assume that the propositions are conceptually equivalent and transitive, we can put them into deductive chains. For example,

The greater the diversification of a person's roles, the less consensus the person will perceive in the expectations about those roles (Burr, Leigh et al., 1979, p. 80)

and

the more individuals perceive consensus in the expectations about a role they occupy, the less their role strain. (Burr, Leigh et al., 1979, p. 79)

Therefore,

the greater the diversification of roles, the greater the role strain.

This deduction provides an illustration of how the propositions developed in symbolic interaction theory may be used to produce theoretically derived propositions important in guiding empirical research on families. Let's now turn to some of the variants of symbolic interaction theory.

Variations

After Mead's death in 1931, two major schools of thought within symbolic interactionism emerged. One of these is known as the Iowa school and is associated with the work of Manfred Kuhn (1964). The other is known as the Chicago school and is identified with the position of Herbert Blumer (1962, 1969). Briefly, Kuhn's Iowa school is more positivistic and assumes more structural and normative causality and less interactional creativity than Blumer's Chicago school. Although many authors such as Turner (1991) continue to focus on the disagreements and intellectual battles between the two schools of thought, we see this as a useless emphasis. Indeed, although the warriors may still be fighting on the battlefield, the castle has quietly been occupied by noncombatants from elsewhere. Many contemporary family scholars spend no time on the metaphysical questions raised by Kuhn (1964) and Blumer (1962, 1969), such as the nature of causality, the truthfulness of observational versus quantitative methods, and the nature of sociological theory. Instead, many of today's family scholars have returned to the pragmatic roots of symbolic interactionism and use whatever methods are most appropriate to the research question they are asking.

A central issue that divides most symbolic interactionists is whether interactions between people are (a) a product of the expectations residing in the social structure or (b) created and negotiated by the actors in each interaction. We use this issue as a theme in exploring the unique contributions of four variants of symbolic interactionism. In the study of the family, three relatively recent major variants of symbolic interaction theory have evolved. We identify these three as the *structural* approach, the *interactional* approach, and the *microinteractional* approach. Although each could be related to the schools of thought represented by Kuhn and Blumer, we believe these variants are sufficiently well formulated to deserve to be considered on their own merits and that little clarity is gained by forcing them into the restrictive categories of belonging to either the Chicago or Iowa school.

Structural Approach

We begin by examining the structural approach. Although many family scholars align themselves with this approach, it is probably most identified with the work of Sheldon Stryker (1964, 1980). Others who have made significant contributions include Nye (1976), Burr, Leigh et al. (1979), Stryker and Burke (2000), and Stets and Turner (2006). We intend a general characterization that does not focus on any one scholar but on the scholars who assume that social roles are learned and then enacted by people when they occupy positions in a social structure. Sometimes, the focus of the structural approach is so much on one concept that scholars develop strong attachments to these mini-theoretical areas. For example, those focusing on the concept of *role* may label themselves *role theorists* rather than symbolic interactionists, and those who focus on *identity* may call themselves *identity theorists*.

The three most basic notions in this approach are position (or status), norm, and role. A position, or status, is seen as embedded in a social network of interrelated positions. Each position has associated social norms or expectations. In our society, as in most societies, a woman in the kinship position *mother* is expected to behave "nurturantly" toward her infant. A social role simply represents the complete cluster of the expectations or norms for any status or position. A person may occupy several positions and therefore roles at any one time or across the life span. For example, the young mother may also be a teacher. Much of the research emphasis of the structuralists derives from the fact that an individual may play multiple roles at any one time and thus be exposed to role strain and role conflict.

Jonathan Turner (1991) points out that the metaphor for the structuralists is clearly that of "actors on a stage." Indeed, one approach within symbolic interactionism in which this metaphor is emphasized is Goffman's (1974) "dramaturgical approach." In the most general terms, the structuralists think that the scripts for the roles are passed down to the actors from society, which *precedes the individual.* The actors' performance of the roles is largely a matter of how well they have learned their roles through primary and anticipatory socialization. And although the actors' role performances vary somewhat, the actual normative content of the roles changes little from actor to actor. According to this view, despite decades of talk about equal participation by both spouses in household chores, chores remain largely the province of wives rather than husbands because such norms are deeply embedded in the social structure and are not strongly affected by the whims of individual actors.

The structuralist perspective has produced an impressive array of theoretical propositions (Burr, Hill et al., 1979) as well as an impressive amount of empirical research on such topics as role strain and identity. Sheldon Stryker, one of the major theorists in this area, has pioneered work in the area of roles and an actor's identity (e.g., Stryker, 1968a, 1968b, 1987a, 1987b, 1989, 1991; Stryker & Burke, 2000; Stryker & Serpe, 1994). Indeed, the topic of roles and identity has been of great interest to family symbolic interactionists (e.g., Marks & MacDermid, 1996) because of the multiple roles (work and family) assumed by most of today's parents.

The structuralist perspective has garnered some rather severe criticisms, especially from the "interactionist" wing of symbolic interactionism. Most significant among these criticisms is the argument that the structural perspective provides a deterministic view of humans being poured into the molds of the social system. This "oversocialized" self has little freedom to adapt to or change the environment. However, Burke's recent work with the cybernetic model accounts for such adaptations. The problem-solving and adaptive nature of humans stressed by both Mead and Dewey seems lost within the structural symbolic interaction perspective. As a result, interactionists accuse the structuralists of viewing social change as, at best, slow and phlegmatic.

Interactional Approach

The interactional variant of symbolic interaction is most closely associated with the work of Ralph Turner. Turner (1970) focuses on individual families. His work is not concerned with aggregate patterns for families or cultural patterns. Instead, he focuses on the patterned processes within the family as a small group. Unlike the structuralists, Turner believes that many of these patterns are developed through interaction. Rather than seeing social structure as encompassing and monolithic, Turner believes social structure and culture provide a broad, vague, and often ambiguous outline for behavior. The individual's role taking is not simply the enacting of a well-defined role but is "making" the role through interaction with others and the context. Individuals have the freedom to make roles and communicate those roles to others. Thus, Turner emphasizes the creative and problem-solving dimension of roles that is neglected by the structuralist symbolic interactionists. Whereas the structuralists emphasize how humans are constructed by their culture and society, the interactionists emphasize how culture and society are created by interacting actors.

After Ralph Turner's (1970) work *Family Interaction,* he continued to refine and formalize his thinking on role theory. The formal propositions that Turner and his associates (Turner, 1980; Turner & Colomy, 1987) have developed have led them into more and more structural terrain. For example, Jonathan Turner (1991) describes Ralph Turner's deductive system as containing some laws: "Functionality is, therefore, one of Turner's 'laws' of social organization, at least among 'roles' as a basic property of all patterns of social organization" (p. 439). Although it would be inaccurate to describe Ralph Turner as straying far from interactionism, his program to develop a nomothetic deductive role theory is bound to lead to more general statements. He increasingly focuses on the explanation of more aggregate phenomena than any one family or situation (e.g., Turner & Colomy, 1987). It probably is not unfair to say that interactionists may have assumed too much power within the individual to "role-make," and they may have failed to adequately consider the constraints of the preexisting social structure and its tenacity in maintaining the status quo.

Microinteractional Approach

The microinteractional perspective is not so much a coherent school of thought as an extension of interactionism focused mainly on the individual and self. Certainly, the influence of the early work by Ralph Turner resides within this approach, but if we were forced to identify one major progenitor for this approach, it would be Erving Goffman. In his first major work, *Presentation of Self in Everyday Life,* Goffman (1959) elaborated the *dramaturgical* metaphor as central to his approach. This metaphor returns to the notion of role as it is found in stage productions. In contrast to the type of influence Goffman's work has exerted on structuralists, a different dimension of Goffman's work has affected the microinteractionists. Microinteractionists emphasize the fluidity and contingency of roles. Actors play roles with scripts and props; there is a backstage reality and an onstage reality. Roles are contingent on the interactions with other actors and thus are organized by systems of rules, such as rules about talk and rules of relevance. The self is relatively fluid and defined by the interactional context and the way in which the person frames or schematically understands the context and the rules. Microinteractionists view Goffman's work as focused exclusively on microinteraction and make no attempt to extend their explanations to a macroscopic level.

Although Goffman did not directly apply his work to the family, his influence is nonetheless present among family scholars studying family microprocesses, such as LaRossa and LaRossa (1981) in their study on the transition to parenthood and the ways in which parents formulate "accounts" of their parenting contributions. New fathers were found to have a greater number of socially available accounts to justify noninvolvement in child care duties than mothers had. LaRossa and LaRossa's work relies heavily on an analytic strategy centered on the way people frame their behavior. This strategy is closely aligned to the microinteractional approach with an emphasis on roles being contingent on other interactions and the context and the frame that the actor is using.

Empirical Applications

We examine two areas of study in which symbolic interactionists have contributed to an explanation. The first area entails research on the proposition we earlier derived: "The greater the diversification of roles, the greater the role strain." We examine this proposition as it applies to working parents' role strain. The second area of application is the study of aggression in dating.

Role Strain and Working Parents

As a research question, our derived proposition is of some interest. Indeed, it provides one of the two major perspectives on the role strain experienced by working mothers and fathers. In the study of working parents, two relatively simple conceptual hypotheses have been developed. One perspective is sometimes referred to as *enhancement theory* (Marks, 1977). The enhancement hypothesis is based on the assumption that multiple roles lead to an enhancement of role performance in any given role and to lower role strain. The logic behind this claim is that multiple roles allow the person to gain more skills, experience, and coping strategies. These greater skills can be transferred by a person from one role to another so that the ability to competently perform any role is enhanced. As people gain increased competency in their roles, role strain is decreased. The other conceptual hypothesis is derived from the symbolic interaction proposition that states that "role diversification is positively related to role strain," commonly called *role overload.* This theory is based on the assumption that the more roles one has, the greater the strain. Clearly, our deduction fits better with the role overload perspective. This is a clear illustration of how theory guides research to critical questions.

Research on role strain among working parents provides a less than clear resolution between the competing perspectives of enhancement and role overload, particularly when comparing mothers and fathers. The dominant finding seems to be that whether a mother perceives work strain or not is related to her reported feelings of well-being and the reports of other family members (Crouter, Bumpus, Maguire, & McHale, 1999) and by work, family, and child characteristics (Lee, Vernon-Feagans, Vazquez, & Kolak, 2003), whereas fathers' role strain was related only to family characteristics (Lee et al., 2003). Research reviewed by Menaghan and Parcel (1990) fails to resolve the conflicting hypotheses but does show us that there are more variables relevant to the question than are suggested in our initial derivation. Some of the most salient of these are whether the mother desires to enter the labor force, whether her husband supports her work and family intentions, and the amount of spousal support in household and family tasks. These variables are called *moderating* because they change' the effect of maternal employment on role strain. Other research further emphasizes the differences for working mothers and fathers. Radcliffe and Cassell (2015) found that women tend to have more flexible work hours and environments which leads them to take on the role of "organizer" and primary responsibility for balancing work and family responsibilities, and in such cases, their husbands were largely shielded from such role strain. However, when men had greater work flexibility, wives were not shielded from role strain in the same way and remained highly impacted by and aware of work-family conflict.

In addition to learning that more variables than simply the number of roles are necessary to explain role strain, researchers have created some valuable theoretical insights to add to our theory. Voydanoff (1987) proposed that a more processual and dynamic approach is useful for examining the relationship between employment and parents' roles. She argues that there are various paths by which families may articulate the relationship between work and family roles and that these change over time. For example, the demands of small children may be so great as to create role strain with most types of employment. As the children become more self-sufficient, maternal employment may have a salutary effect. Thus, Voydanoff argues that the time dimension should be incorporated. Menaghan (1989) correctly cautions that not all roles are equally demanding and that motherhood is especially demanding. Role diversification is affected by the differing strengths and extent of role demands. White (1999) showed that the balance between family and work roles is strongly related to satisfaction with the division of household labor, which further implicates concepts such as role performance and the literature on division of labor (e.g., Voydanoff & Donnelly, 1999). Other researchers caution us that both mini theories may apply. Tiedje et al. (1990) propose that every set of roles probably has some areas of enhancement and some areas of strain and overload.

Rothbard (2001), in a study regarding "enriching and depleting" roles (corresponding to enhancement versus role strain, respectively), reported continued differences between mothers and fathers:

> Specifically, depletion existed only for women and only in the work-to-family direction. Men experienced enrichment from work to family, while women experienced enrichment from family to work. Overall, more linkages were found between work and family for women than for men. (p. 655)

Other researchers such as Fischer, Zvonkovic, Juergens, Engler, and Frederick (2013) have also encountered gender differences in this regard. It is probably safe to state that although this is a continuously researched and theoretically developed area of academic concern, enhancement and role overload (or enriching and depleting work-family roles) remains an active and ongoing research question.

Fathers also might uniquely experience strain between work and fathering roles due to the historical association between fathering and breadwinning. Recently, societal expectations have been expanding to include expectations of nurturant and affectionate behavior as well as "being there" for children, which often conflicts with the goal of being a good financial provider (Gregory & Milner, 2011; LaRossa, 1997). The potential influence of such changes in societal expectations to incorporate additional roles and responsibilities, without absolving fathers of the responsibility for being the primary financial provider, is an area of research that symbolic interactionism is particularly well suited to address. In many dual-earner families, alleviating strain for one family member may simply shift it to another family member. No wonder the question is commonly asked, "If both parents feel like they have to work full-time, who will take care of young children?" You can begin to imagine all sorts of answers, some of which may reduce the total role strain in a family more than others.

The dynamic interchange between empirical research and symbolic interaction theory leads us to some wariness regarding our derivation, yet we are far from obtaining a definitive resolution to its truth or falsity at this time. This area of application provides a clear and important example of how theory guides research and research clarifies and extends theory. This interchange between theory and empirical research provides us with an illustration of the very heart of the process of rational-empirical social science.

Dating Aggression

The study of aggression in dating is one that is particularly salient for university and college students. It is easy to assume that such acts occur in groups less privileged than university students, but as recent research has shown, this would be an incorrect assumption. In addition, the notion of a hurtful act deliberately aimed at a dating partner, a person that is supposedly liked, seems almost a contradiction. How can we explain why such acts occur among university student couples?

Jan Stets (1992) attempts to explain dating aggression in university couples using concepts and propositions from symbolic interaction theory. Stets proposes that interactional rather than demographic variables can explain date aggression. She argues that taking the role of the other entails putting yourself in that person's place and feeling and understanding the other's emotions and actions. She states that role taking has been previously related to relationship satisfaction and to the use of less abrasive styles in interaction. It appears that as role taking increases by both partners in a relationship, the chances of conflict leading to aggressive acts would decline. Following this logic, Stets predicts that when at least one person is low in role-taking ability, there is a higher probability for aggressive acts in dating relationships.

The findings in Stets's study offer considerable support for this theoretical perspective. First, interactional variables explain more of the variance in dating aggression than do demographic variables. This leads Stets to conclude cautiously that interaction is probably more important in explaining and producing date aggression than background variables, such as age, race, gender, and socioeconomic status. Role taking is related not only to aggression in dating but also to the seriousness of the aggression. The less the role-taking ability of one partner, the greater the seriousness of aggression when it occurs. Although complete prediction of dating aggression would require additional variables (see Pirog-Good & Stets, 1989), this research supports the contention that symbolic interaction propositions and concepts must be part of any such explanation.

An important application from the research by Stets and others (e.g., Connolly & Friedlander, 2009; Josephson & Pepler, 2012) on dating aggression concerns role taking. Although Stets (1992) argued that role-taking ability is related to dating aggression, other researchers have broadened this to include a history of bullying (Josephson & Pepler, 2012) and the ways in which peer group attitudes and culture can support dating aggression (Connolly & Friedlander, 2009; Connolly, Friedlander, Pepler, Craig, & Laporte, 2010). Certainly, colleges and universities have responded to the continuing problem of dating aggression, with the most notable example being the formulation and adoption of rules of sexual conduct at Antioch College in 1991. The "Antioch Rules" have spawned a debate about how we can apply our knowledge in this sensitive and intimate area (see Humphreys & Herold, 2003).

Critiques and Discussion

Although symbolic interactionism enjoys great popularity among family scholars, it is not without its detractors and critics. Most interesting in this regard is that some of the more vicious attacks on parts of the theory have come from those whose work is included under the same theoretical umbrella. The critiques of structural interactionists offered by microinteractionists and vice versa contain some of the most devastating criticisms. We regard some of these as red herrings and begin this section by identifying those criticisms we believe are relatively baseless.

The branching of symbolic interactionism into the structural and interactional perspectives derived from profound differences, but with time and academic progress, we believe that at least some of the differences between these schools no longer represent valid criticisms. First, is social behavior mainly created by social structural norms or by interactional role making? To a large extent, the contemporary interactional theorists (e.g., Turner & Colomy, 1987) have moved to increasingly include macrostructural elements in their theories, and the macrotheorists have witnessed the interactional emergence of relatively new social structures, such as cohabitation. We think it is now clear to most scholars that there are some norms and roles in every society that are clear and strictly sanctioned and as a result provide little room for role making. There are many other roles and norms that are less clearly defined and are sanctionless (e.g., grandparental roles, mother-in-law role), providing room for individuals to make roles. Thus, we see both perspectives as valid and necessarily complementary for a truly useful analysis of social behavior. The two major critiques associated with this debate have been that the structuralists put forth an oversocialized conception of humans and that the interactionists overestimate the actor's influence in creating roles and downplay structural constraints. In our view, for any given social role, there are degrees of truth to each of these criticisms based on the clarity and strength of the norms for the role.

Although symbolic interactionists agree that perceived clarity of and consensus about roles have important consequences, they do not agree about how common clarity and consensus are. The structuralists believe that social meanings and behavioral expectations are clearer and more widely shared than do adherents to the other varieties of the theory. Perhaps people in relationships usually do have a pretty good idea about reciprocal roles and do not struggle to define situations. Other symbolic interactionists, however, place relatively more emphasis on the necessity of people to create meaning and order as situations and relationships unfold. And the enactment of roles may depend more on the coming together of unique personalities than on a single generalized formula or script for all actors. For example, suppose that you marry a spouse who has adolescent or young adult children from a previous marriage. To what extent would you feel like you know in advance how to play the stepparent role with these new children, in terms of power, emotion, or communication? How sure would they be about how to interact with you? It may very well be that some family circumstances are not clearly defined and that actors must therefore improvise. Therefore, one way to resolve this dispute among symbolic interactionists is to seek and specify the conditions under which each is correct.

The ongoing construction or reconstruction of meaning may be most important in times of rapid social change. When relationships of a particular kind are fairly new and uncommon in the collective historical experience of a population (or in the biographical experience of the actors themselves), the search for meaning and order is likely to be a process with some duration. One way that you might judge which aspects of family life are ill defined is to visit a major bookstore and explore titles in the family or relationships section. If there are a variety of self-help, or how-to, books on a particular topic, this suggests that social norms and meanings are somewhat ambiguous. After all, if almost everybody already knows how to act when the topic becomes relevant in their lives, there would be a small market for books that provide advice.

A second area of disagreement between these two perspectives that we believe fails as a valid criticism of either is the argument about qualitative versus quantitative methods of data collection. Again, we see this dispute as being resolved by the earlier pragmatists, such as William James (1975). Indeed, this argument is unresolvable only when it becomes a metaphysical argument about which method is "true," similar to asking how many angels fit on the head of a pin. Most researchers now agree that some research questions are best addressed by qualitative methods and others are best addressed by quantitative methods. If we are interested in how people in specific situations feel, perceive, and experience, then qualitative methods are appropriate; if we ask questions about how many people behave in a certain way or what "most" people do, then quantitative methods are appropriate. If we want to know why young people find cohabitation appealing as an added step toward marriage, we would start with in-depth observation and talk. But if we want to know what proportion of young people who finish university then cohabit, we would use quantitative methods. Many times, both methods can be used fruitfully in a multimethod approach to answer a research question. Thus, we see no critique of substance for either school of thought.

One of the principal criticisms of symbolic interactionism as a whole is that the concepts it offers are vague and poorly defined. Although this may be a problem in some cases, researchers such as Burr, Leigh et al. (1979) are careful to define and elaborate their terms. Still others such as Turner (e.g., 1970) have argued that some terms such as *role* should not be defined at the outset, but rather, one should allow definitions to arise from how the terms are used. Certainly, such a strategy has a long history in mathematics, in which certain terms are considered *primitive* or are defined as tautologies, such as "equals" and "identity."

The criticism that concepts are vague should mean that the theory is difficult to apply; however, there are an abundance of examples to the contrary. For example, a recent area of intervention employing symbolic interactionist principles has been in work with individuals with Asperger's syndrome. One of the hallmark indicators of Asperger's is difficulty interpreting social cues and "reading" and appropriately responding to others' words, expressions, and behaviors. In other words, Asperger's is, at core, difficulty with understanding the meanings of interactions. Applying Mead's concept of the "Me" can assist individuals with Asperberger's in considering how others might view them, what others' expectations of them might be, and, consequently, what behavior they should exhibit in response (Hughes, 2016). Individuals with Asperger's frequently think of and refer to themselves in the third person, and so using symbolic interactionism to "create a 'third person' persona that one can 'use' in real-life situations ... is something that can be worked through individually or can be developed by people who support the learner with Asperger's syndrome" (Hughes, 2016, p. 71).

Symbolic interactionists in the family field no doubt sometimes offer vague and ill-defined concepts. But the root of this criticism probably lies in the fact that symbolic interactionism is so fertile it has given birth to many variants. Critics would say that some of this richness is supplied by vagueness and ambiguity in the original concepts. There is some truth to that claim, but today's symbolic interactionists seem to be on the way to rectifying this shortcoming. Indeed, it may be that every theory starts out containing ambiguity and vagueness, and it is the task of future theorists to refine the efforts of the forebears. We must also remember that symbolic interactionism emphasizes the processes by which meaning is constructed. Groups of family scientists are meaning makers just as families are. Both sets of actors can be vague and ambiguous while the process unfolds. Ultimately, of course, what scientists say about families should bear some connection to what family members say about them.

Another major question about symbolic interaction theory is whether a symbol-specific theory can ever be nomothetic, or cross-culturally relevant. The interpretation of behavior in symbolic interactionism relies in large part on the meaning of symbols and context to the actors. Not only does the actor's interpretation depend on his or her culture and situation, but it is also subjective. If our explanations are always subjective and context and symbol specific, can symbolic interactionism ever amount to more than low-level interpretations constrained by the culture and time in which they occur? Another way of posing this question is to ask if symbolic interactionism can generate statements such as the general laws associated with scientific theory. This criticism is a fairly easy one for symbolic interactionists to answer, because the propositions provided by scholars such as Turner (e.g., Turner & Colomy, 1987) and Burr (e.g., Burr, Leigh et al., 1979) are clearly not culture or period specific. In addition, social psychology has a long history of scientific (and objective) study of the uniformities in subjective interpretations, such as attitudes and attributions.

The problems surrounding the concepts of mind and self are more serious. The concept of mind incorporates aspects of neurophysiology that are not rooted in the organ of the brain. Indeed, even Mead (1934) was aware of the reflex arc (muscle memory) and the problems it provided his concept. The fact is that the mind, like our notions of group and society, turns out not to be a "thing" or "organ" but a complex system for which we have a name. Most social scientists have not had to confront this conceptual problem, but when they do, they will find that it provides the same problems inherent in the question "Are families just a collection of individual members, or are families something more than just the individual members?" This is a very old question in philosophy and social science. The early pragmatists, especially William James, paid a great deal of attention to this question. We do not pretend that others or even that we have resolved this question to the satisfaction of those who believe that a function must be attached to an organ that performs that function.

The problems with the concept of mind carry over to the concept of self as a construction of the reflexive activity of the mind. Just because humans act (I) and are able to see themselves as actors (me) does not necessarily imply the existence of self. Because the mind is unidentified and self is a construct of mind, self raises the same problems as our concept of mind. Particularly when you add in the notion of developmental change and maturation, the notions of self and identity become difficult to pin down. At least one symbolic interactionist, Turner (1970), does not use the concept of self but prefers the concept of "self-conception," for it appears more fluid and less of an immutable structure than does the concept of the self.

LaRossa and Reitzes (1993) mention the criticism that symbolic interaction theory has failed to deal effectively with emotions. The absence of emotions, feelings, and affect as major concepts has in some ways limited the theory's conceptual utility. Symbolic interactionists invariably discuss an actor's feeling as part of the definition of the situation but leave the details of conceptualizing the type and degree of the actor's emotional experience to psychologists and psychotherapists. LaRossa and Reitzes expressed some optimism that this oversight is being addressed, but we do not share their opinion. Certainly, there has been noticeable theoretical activity in the area of emotions (Stets & Turner, 2006; Turner & Stets, 2005). However, family theorists have not yet integrated the recent work on emotions in symbolic interaction into their research on families. Nevertheless, the reason for theorizing about emotions in families is clear. Family members certainly look for cues about how other family members are feeling, and they communicate with each other as if those feelings matter. Indeed, mixed emotions may be common in families. What parent or adolescent has not worried about his or her feelings concerning independence, trust, and loss when the adolescent first leaves for college? Perhaps we will see in the future more family theories about ambivalent emotions and attitudes between spouses, across generations, and among siblings (e.g., Lüscher & Pillemer, 1998).

Some critics of symbolic interactionism see the theory as too focused on the individual and "self as agent," ignoring the causal efficacy of social institutions and social structure. Although some of these criticisms can be dismissed as more feuding between the structuralists and interactionists, some of the critiques apply to both schools of thought. For example, the notion of norms is central to both the structuralists and interactionists, but neither examines the development and change of institutional norms. The structuralists take institutional norms for granted with the axiom that "society preceded the individual." Interactionists see norms as emerging from interaction but fail to explain how it is that social institutions exist with relative permanence.

Additionally, we could accuse symbolic interactionists of losing their way. The early pragmatists and Mead (1934) took the interpretation of sign and gesture as central to their study of human behavior. Among today's symbolic interactionists, we seldom hear theoretical discussions about the nature of signs and gestures. Today, in discussions of interpretation and meaning, it might be needed to incorporate *schematic processing* from psychology into the concept of *framing* as well as the work of linguists and contemporary semiotics.

Finally, some have voiced concern about the continual emphasis by symbolic interactionists on the person's construction of meaning even in quantitative measures such as marital satisfaction. These critics worry that the *behavioral* sciences are forgetting that the observation of behavior may be significantly different from experiential reports by actors. Indeed, Gottman and Notarius (2000) voice such a concern in relation to the study of marriage: "Observational measures will always be [the] most informative data source we will ever get about process, which will be the richest source we will ever have for describing and building theory" (p. 942).

Conclusion

There can be little doubt that symbolic interactionism has had an influence on how we study families. Both role theorists and interactionists have contributed greatly to our understanding of families. Thus far, although interactionists' claims about the symbolic nature of human interaction have sensitized researchers, they have not tackled many critical questions, such as how patterns evolve as lasting rather than momentary and idiosyncratic. Within symbolic interactionism, role theory undoubtedly offers the most formal theoretical propositions and conceptual definitions. All four variants that we have discussed offer promise as we move away from dogmatic divisions toward a more systematic and thorough investigation of which and what type of family interactions lead to and sustain longer term social patterns of behavior within the family.

STUDY QUESTIONS

1. Why is this theory called symbolic interaction theory?

2. Although role is a central concept, it is often measured as a complex of variables such as *clarity*. What are the variables identified in this chapter?

3. The definition of the situation by an actor is seen as critical to understanding behavior. However, some critics have said that this emphasis on the actor's perspective neglects the importance of the actual reality and heightens the importance of a psychological investigation. What is the correct weight researchers should give individual perspective on context versus the actual context in understanding behavior? Do you believe that there is an "actual reality," or is it all just individual perceptions?

4. If you take a careful look at the propositions and pretend that you are the manager of a mid-sized company, what does each proposition suggest for how you structure the workplace environment? A university class?

5. Students often are intrigued by the different perspectives of their classmates, and certainly, symbolic interaction theory includes individual perspectives; however, the theory starts with a shared symbolic system that supplies symbols, concepts, numerals and so on. Do you believe that individuals can think without using these shared symbolic components?

The Family Life Course Development Framework

Raj was pretty upbeat about the number of Tinder matches he has been getting lately. The excitement of meeting potential hookups is hard to contain. In the back of his mind, thoughts about Shareev are also all consuming at times. After meeting her at his cousins wedding last month, they exchanged numbers, but she seems to be in no hurry to go out with him. She hardly returns his texts. She comes from a more traditional family, and the idea of dating doesn't seem to interest her all that much. Raj thought she was into him at the wedding, but now he is not so sure. Raj has dated a lot of women, some seriously. He actually moved in with one a few years ago, but that didn't really work out for either of them, so they both moved on. Shareev seems pretty set on only being with the man she marries, and Raj thinks that just doesn't make sense. "How will you know if you are compatible?" he thinks. Raj and Shareev have walked quite different relationship pathways during their young adult lives. Is it possible that those different pathways may lead to different futures, both individually and relationally? Does it matter, for example, to your future marital stability, how may partners you have, whether you have lived together before marriage with your spouse or someone else, had children from a previous relationship, or got married at a young age? The family life course development framework seeks to answer these and more questions about the individual and family life course.

Raj and Shareev are illustrating what family development and life course scholars study when they explore the impact of different sequences, durations, or frequency of life course events and stages on later life outcomes. In this case, scholars would be interested in information that may help better predict later union stability. They may look at Raj and see that he has had several relationships already. Scholars may be interested in the number of unions a person has entered prior to their current relationship. Scholars would also be interested in whether Raj or Shareev had cohabited with previous partners. They may also be interested in how long they lived with their partners and if they had children with any previous partners. Each piece of information that researchers gather about individual and family life courses helps them to better predict the future stability of people's future relationships. If any of this family life course development information increases the accuracy of predicting the future outcome of their relationship, then it is considered helpful and may provide information that leads to a better understanding of why certain outcomes occur more frequently than the probability of chance would suggest.

The family life course development framework contains three complementary theoretical approaches. Each approach comes from a different stream of social science. First among these is *individual life span theory*, which focuses mainly on ontogenetic development, or the changing form and structural development of the individual and the factors that affect that development. It is most commonly applied in the discipline of psychology. Many of the developmental factors affecting the individual are found in families, and as a result, this individual approach cannot avoid the family as the context of individual development. The reciprocal nature of this relationship would also point to family structural changes being initiated from the individual's change as well. The second theoretical approach within this framework is *family development theory*. This variant of the approach is mostly found in the disciplines of family studies and sociology of family. This theory focuses on the systematic and patterned changes experienced over time by families as they move through stages and events of their families' journey or experiences. Family development is distinct from theories about individual development, such as those offered by developmental psychologists (e.g., Erikson, Freud, and Piaget). Family development theorists acknowledge the importance of individual development, but the development of the family as a "group" of interacting individuals and organized by social norms is their major focus. The third major theoretical approach encompassed within this framework is the *life course theory*. It, like family development theory, is most often employed by family studies scholars and sociology researchers, although demographers, economists, educators, and health care professionals also employ this approach. Life course theory examines the event history of an individual and how earlier life events influence later life outcomes, such as divorce, fertility, or child achievement and adjustment levels. Although life course theory originally emerged from studies of the individual life course (e.g., Hogan, 1978), Bengtson and Allen (1993) suggested that this approach could be used on the family as a unit of analysis. Of the three theories within this framework, family development theory is the only one that emerged out of a specific interest in families. The other theories have broader applications to other social groups and social structures. Indeed, of all the theories in this entire book, family development theory is the only one developed expressly for understanding families rather than social groups or general patterns of social interaction.

As a framework, family life course development has several unique dimensions that characterize its focus. Family life course development incorporates time and history as major components. Although other theories may include time in the measurement of change, they do not involve discussion of the theoretical nuances of the conceptualization and measurement of time. Family development theorists have discussed time as measured by clocks, social processes, and event histories (Rodgers, 1973). A second unique dimension of family life course development framework is the focus on forms of family change and changing family forms. Family life course development deals with the changing content of social roles in the family as well as macroscopic changes in the membership structure of the family within the larger society. Of all the current theories about the family, family life course development framework is unique in emphasizing the interaction of time and change.

Although we will deal with the three theoretical variants later in this chapter, it is useful to point out the common ground that these three theories share as characteristics of the family life course development framework. First, all three theoretical schools within this framework are concerned with family factors affecting ontogenetic development of the individual. Second, all three of these theoretical schools focus on time and its role in individual and/or group change. Third, all three theoretical schools incorporate individual and family change within a larger framework of birth cohort, historical period, and individual age factors. Fourth, family change is understood to be the interplay of these macrosocial influences and the individual agency of the family members as they work to adapt and accommodate those changes. Although some scholars might argue that family development, life span, and life course are three unique frameworks, we argue that they represent slight variations on a singular theme of the groups' change and development over time. Life course theory has had only one major statement in regard to the family (Bengtson & Allen, 1993). On the other hand, both life span and family development theories have long and well-established histories. We represent all three as a common framework, choosing to discuss them individually as theoretical variants within this common framework.

Intellectual Traditions

There is little doubt that much of what we know today as developmental and life course theories about families actually originated from theoretical approaches to individual life span development. Certainly, the rudiments of these ideas were contained in early Western and Eastern writing, such as this biblical passage from Ecclesiastes 3:1–2 (King James Version):

> For everything there is a season, and a time for every purpose
> under heaven, a time to be born, and a time to die; a time to
> plant, and a time to pluck up that which is planted.

The modern playground song "K-I-S-S-I-N-G" also illustrates the importance of normative ordering of life events:

Sue and Bill

sitting in a tree

K-I-S-S-I-N-G.

First comes love,

then comes marriage,

then comes baby

in a baby carriage!

The tracing of changes in individual maturation were most immediately evident in the relatively rapid changes of child maturation. Child physical and cognitive development provided the focus for much of the early stages of the developmental framework. Freudian theory—with its emphasis on the age-graded, psychosexual stages of development—was one of the early progenitors of this approach. Most students are familiar with the anal, oral, and genital stages in Freudian development. The notions of development were soon generalized to other areas of individual development, such as cognitive (Piaget) and moral (Kohlberg). These approaches tended to view the child as acquiring competence at one stage of development in order to successfully transition to the next stage in the developmental sequence. Many students will be familiar with Piaget's version of cognitive stages of development, such as the sensorimotor (2–24 months), preoperational (2–7 years), concrete operational (7–11 years), and formal operational (11–15 years; see, e.g., Wadsworth, 1996). Piaget's system, like that of Freud and many other early developmentalists, is composed of discrete stages of development and a progression of biologically deterministic steps from one stage to the next higher stage of development (ontogenesis). The simplicity of this perspective is appealing, and it seemed that the only task for life span psychology was to add relevant stages for adult development to those that had been so well developed for children and adolescents.

It was the attempt by life span scholars to extend this model of ontogenetic development to adults that eventually led to the demise of this model. On the surface, adult development seemed more tied to the social context of the individual and less obviously tied to ontogenetic maturation than child development. A related problem was that the stages were neither readily discernible nor universal. Tied to this was the need to deal with the depletion, decay, and eventual death of the adult. These more "negative" processes contradicted the view in child development that the child was always growing and maturing, whereas adults eventually aged and died. These problems led scholars to a very different perspective of life span development. Baltes (1987) stated that life span developmental scholars must assume that development must deal with both loss and acquisition, social and historical context, and changes that are multidirectional (see Bengtson & Allen, 1993). More recently, scholars have noted that life course trajectories are seldom linear and often involve "U-turns, detours and yo-yo movements in and out of statuses" (Martin, Schoon, & Ross, 2008). The admission from life span scholars, such as Baltes (1987), that ontogenetic maturation is multidirectional and dependent on context not only challenged the simple stage approach of child developmentalists, such as Piaget, but also sparked a much more sociological approach to individual development. For example, Neugarten (Neugarten & Datan, 1973; Neugarten, Moore, & Lowe, 1965) argued that social timing norms exist so as to create life course events as being "on time" and "off time." Furthermore, these timing norms direct adult development. Elder (1974) demonstrated the effect of cohort normative culture in relation to events within a historical period, such as the economic Depression of the 1930s. These more sociological approaches were focused on the norms directing and constraining adult and child development and became known as the life course approach.

In the study of the family, a more sociological theoretical approach had enjoyed a long history. The theory was the dream of Reuben Hill and Evelyn Duvall who saw a unifying theory under the title of family development as the goal. Hill identified several streams of family research that combined would represent a more complete family theory. Life cycle categories, social system theories, human development theories, life span course theories, and life events-crisis theories made up Hill's list. Family development theory was initially characterized by the rise of the idea of the family life cycle. In this early phase, researchers viewed families as having a *life course*, or what in biological studies was commonly referred to as a "life cycle." Similar to a biological organism, the family group went through analogous processes of birth, growth, maintenance, shrinkage, and eventually death. The idea of the family life cycle appears in the work of rural sociologists, such as Lively (1932) and Loomis (1936), during the Great Depression. Through the work of Paul Glick (1947), the notion of family life cycle entered social demography as a descriptive tool. This *descriptive phase* represents an important step in the theory's maturation. Other important contributions came from social systems that captured functionalist thinking about the family with Parsons (1951) being the most recognizable. A human development stream encompasses the psychological works described in the first paragraph of this section. Theories on the life span and life course by Elder (1975, 1974, 1999) and theories by Bengtson (1977) placed the individual in the focus. The last stream of life events and life crises highlights perhaps the most recognizable work of Hill (1949,

1958) and his ABC-X model of family stress. Works by H. I. McCubbin (1979, 1980) and Klein, Borne, Jache, and Sederberg (1979), who build on the ABC-X model, are represented in this area. It was the chapter by Hill and Rodgers (1964) that provided the first systematic statement of the theory. In their statement, the family is composed of social roles and relationships that change with each stage of the family. Subsequently, Rodgers (1973) suggested abandoning the family life cycle concept in favor of a concept oriented toward the life course, the *family career*. Aldous (1978, 1996) further developed the notion of the family career. She conceptualized the family career as containing subcareers, such as the sibling career, the marital career, and the parental career, all influenced by careers external to the family, such as the educational and occupational careers. To differentiate family development from life course theory, Aldous (1990) stressed that the life course approach is focused on the individual, whereas the family development approach is focused on the family level of analysis. White (1991) coupled methodological distinctions in *event history analysis* (Allison, 1984; Tuma & Hannan, 1984) with an expanded conception of levels of analysis in his formalization of the family development theory. Rodgers and White (1993) argued that the "old" perspective of families moving through deterministic, invariant stages is moribund, much as are the deterministic stages in child development. They revise and simplify the concepts in the theory and produce formal propositions. Life course analysis evolved from a sociological concern about the contingent events experienced by individuals over the life course. For example, Hogan (1978) demonstrated that the sequential pattern of events, such as starting the first job and finishing one's education, are related to later life course events, such as divorce. Life course analysis received a major boost with the popularization of "event history analysis" (e.g., Allison, 1984). The weakness with this popularization is the overreliance on methodology unguided by theoretical principles. Event history analysis provides a tool for analyzing event-based data, but apart from solid theory-driven research, it contributes nothing to interpretation and prediction. Methodological and statistical advancements in areas of sequence analysis and optimal matching have begun to be applied to the testing of life course theory as well (Martin, 2009, 2015). This methodology complements event history by incorporating a whole sequence of life history data rather than a focus on just one event. Further discussion on these concepts follows later in the chapter. As mentioned, Aldous (1990) discussed the major difference between the family development and life course perspectives as family development being focused on the "family group" level of analysis, whereas life course focused on the individual. However, this distinction certainly does not necessarily distinguish life course from family development theories. For example, in the work by Cowan and Cowan (2000) on the transition to parenthood, the couple was the unit of analysis. Furthermore, the first formal theoretical statement of life course theory (Bengtson & Allen, 1993) related to the family features multiple levels of analysis, including both the individual level and family group level.

The status of these three approaches is that they are exceedingly similar in many ways. Certainly, life span theory emphasizes individual onto-genetic development but within the context of social norms and historical period. Family development theory has moved to a more dynamic perspective and focuses on the normative timing of life events and the transitions that families make in the life course. Life course theory, though still focused on the individual, increasingly uses the family context to examine the individual's life course. For the most part, these three theoretical approaches are complementary and share so much common ground as to be categorized as a common framework that seeks to explain family and individual change over time.

Focus and Scope Assumptions

Many theories require basic assumptions about the nature of individual motivation (exchange theory) or about human nature (conflict theory). Family development theory relies on basic assumptions about the family. These assumptions extend beyond the basic family unit to the broader fabric of the social institution of the family. The basic assumptions of family life course development theory are the assumptions of the inevitability of the developmental processes, the importance of incorporating multiple levels of analysis, and viewing time as a multidimensional entity.

The first assumption is that *developmental processes are inevitable and important in understanding families.* This assumes that individual family members, the interaction between family members, the structure of the family, and the norms composing expectations about family roles all change with the passage of time. Individuals age, relationships have duration, family stages are traversed, and family structure changes. The changing roles and expectations for different stages of family are viewed as essential to an understanding of the family.

A second major assumption that family development scholars make is that the *family group is affected by all the levels of analysis,* including the social norms of the larger society and the social norms of clusters such as social class (Bengtson & Allen, 1993). For example, the norms about techniques of child discipline are related to social class as well as to the codifications of the larger social system. Component lower levels such as the nature of a sibling relationship or an individual disability also affect the family group. Family developmentalists, from the first systematic statements (Aldous, 1978; Hill & Rodgers, 1964; Rodgers, 1973; White 1998), have suggested that families be analyzed on different levels of analysis (e.g., individual family member, group, institution). Most theorists start with the family as a *social group*. Below the family as a social group are subgroup *relationships* such as the husband-wife relationship and the sibling relationship. Below the relationship level is the *individual* family member, who experiences his or her family and the relationships in it. If we move up a level from the family group, we find relatively homogeneous *aggregate clusters* of families and social norms that are structured by social class and ethnicity. And moving up levels once again, we find that each social system maintains general *institutional* norms and conventions about the family. Some of these norms are codified as legal expectations, such as those found in child neglect or child abuse laws, but more often the norms are less formal. These general social norms represent the level of analysis of the family as a *social institution*. The institutional level of analysis is generally the one we refer to when we talk about *the family* and is the level on which we often conduct cross-cultural comparisons (the U.S. family compared with the Japanese family). Media reports about the family are frequently referring to this institutional or population level of data and as a result may convey findings that are not representative of minorities or subgroups of the population.

Time is multidimensional. To understand this third assumption, we need to examine our notion of time. Time is a monotonic process; once a moment in time is gone, it doesn't come back. Time is measured by the *periodicity* of some recurring event. In ancient Greece, time was measured by a sundial. During the Renaissance, time was measured by the dripping water in water clocks. During the Industrial Revolution, time was measured by gears turning in mechanical clocks. Today, time is measured by the entropy, or decay of an element, in an atomic clock. Several recent volumes on the family have understood and incorporate the concept of time. Jacobs and Gerson (2009) document family members' division of time while Bianchi, Robinson, and Milkie (2007) use detailed time diaries to analyze the changing time use patterns of American families. In *It's About Time*, Moen (2003) edits a series of articles on how time affects couples and their careers across time. The concepts of *age*, *period*, and *cohort*, which are foundational to the family life course development framework, also connote measurements of time. Time is an important variable in studying the family whether it is used to measure something at a point in time or something across time. Discrete time measures are important in studying the development of the family, but this is not the only way that time is used or understood. Discrete time measures attempts to make sure that there is an equal interval of time between each event on the clock. For example, the gears in your wristwatch are the same distance apart. The problem is that there is absolutely no guarantee that the experience of time is so orderly (Daly, 1996). Furthermore, because all our methods of measuring time rely on recurring discrete events, there is no guarantee that time is continuous. Even the assumption that time moves at a uniform rate, as measured by gears in your wristwatch, is counter to much of our experience. Most of you have experienced an hour spent in an enjoyable pursuit as "flying by" or an hour spent in a dull and boring pursuit as "dragging on." In other words, your experience of time is perhaps not as regimented as your wristwatch would lead you to believe. Not only does your experience of time deny the orderliness of your wristwatch, but most of us use our family experiences as a separate way to divide up time as well. Thus, we might discuss with our family what we did in 1990 and 1991. More likely, we might abandon the calendar notion of time in favor of listing events, such as "when we first married," "before your sister was born," or "just after your father died." Interestingly, these events lack periodicity for any one family (you only expect your sister to be born once), but these experiences are commonly understood "markers" on the family life course calendar because they happen to most families over time.

This alternative conception of time is called *social process time* (Rodgers, 1973). Social, or family, process time is an important dimension of our conception of time for family scholars because social norms are tied more closely to this social process dimension of time than to calendar or wristwatch time. For instance, "when you get married" is tied to "finishing school" more closely than to any given calendar date. Other social and biological dimensions of time are age and historical period. It should come as no surprise that social networking sites, such as Facebook, have an integrated time line approach to organizing member profiles and uploaded data. Fortunately, because we conceptualize time as monotonic and flowing only in one direction, all the different ways of conceptualizing time can be organized into temporal maps of our life course and that of our family. A socially important stage can be identified by the events, such as "after our father's death" but "before our sister got married." Because family members usually recall the calendar dates of such major events, we can trace the multiple time lines of calendar and family process time. For family life course development theory, the family process dimension of time is critical to understanding and explaining family change because it provides the marker events (birth, wedding, death, etc.) for analyses.

It is interesting to note that of all the family theories, family life course development theory makes few, if any, basic assumptions about the individual. Rather, family development theory is true to its focus on the family group. Individuals are viewed as subcomponents of the family group, which is not merely the aggregate of individual members. The family group is affected by institutional norms that, along with the characteristics of individual family members and their relationships, determine the social organization of the family group.

Concepts

Family

It is interesting to note that earlier versions of this text have not contained a definition of the family. This edition will be no different, but it will acknowledge the vacancy and provide an example of a definition and suggestions for moving the discussion forward. Rodgers (1964) listed *family* as his first concept when he wrote a journal article attempting to move the theory of family development forward. He quotes a definition from Burgess (1926) of the family as a "unity of interacting personalities." This definition, although thin, may be more helpful than one might think at first glance. White, Martin, and Sayre (2016) argue that although family structure is one of the most common terms used in sociology and family scholarship, it is also an ambiguous concept. Burgess errs on the ambiguous side but does provide a clean canvas to work on socially constructed norms and variations about the family. Perhaps future editions of this text will explore potential definitions of the family.

Family Change and Development

Early family developmentalists were not clear about the distinction between change and development. Indeed, some seem to have used the two terms interchangeably. But with the rise of child development theory in the 1940s and 1950s came a new concern among family developmentalists that development meant more than just family change. Child developmentalists, such as Piaget, brought the notion of *ontogenetic* change to the forefront of their discipline and likewise raised the issue for family development scholars. Although the exact nature of family development has been a longstanding issue, the notion of developmental change has received significant scholarly attention (e.g., Baltes & Nesselroade, 1984; Dannefer, 1984; Dannefer & Perlmutter, 1991; Featherman & Lerner, 1985; Mattessich & Hill, 1987), although other scholars feel this has been a neglected area (McGoldrick, Carter, & Garcia-Preto, 2011) in current research. The outcome of all this attention is that two distinct versions of development have emerged. Child development focuses on ontogenetic development, which is founded on the genetic capacity of the species to progressively learn language and thought. A second, sociological meaning of development is focused on the traversing of normatively expected family events. Although there have been some attempts to unite these two versions, such as the definition of development proposed by Mattessich and Hill (1987), most developmental scholars shy away from the teleological and moralistic overtones inherent in an ontogenetic view of family development. Proscriptive discussions of the family development process have been problematic even among therapists (Falicov, 2012) due to the heterogeneity in family forms. As society moves further toward individualism, it would be expected that this trend will continue.

Both White (1991) and Rodgers and White (1993) argued for the sociological view of development. Although Bengtson and Allen (1993) clearly acknowledge ontogenetic development of the individual (rather than group) in their propositions, the great bulk of their propositions are either interactional (ontogenetic development combined with social-environmental factors) or sociological. Rodgers and White (1993) incorporate the proposal by Featherman (1985) that development is linked to the stage of the family and the duration of time the family has been in a certain family stage. White (1991) defines development similarly, arguing that family transitions are dependent on the stage a family is in and the duration of time it has been in that stage. According to the sociological approach, family development is a process following age- and stage-graded social norms. Unlike the rigid stage sequencing of ontogeneticists, such as Piaget, family developmental stages may be sequenced in a variety of ways, and family developmental change is only one type of many possible changes a family may experience. Family development theorists believe that developmental change is an important form of family change.

Positions, Norms, and Roles

Families are embedded in kinship structures. The positions in the kinship structure are what determines relatives or family relations. A *position* in the kinship structure is defined by gender, marriage or blood relations, and generational relations. The basic positions within the family are husband, wife, father, mother, son, daughter, brother, and sister. From these basic positions, other society-specific positions can be defined. For example, the North American term *uncle* usually refers to brothers of either your father or mother (father's brother, mother's brother).

Norms are socially constructed rules that govern group and individual behavior. For example, the incest taboo is a strong and pervasive social rule forbidding mating between certain family members. Norms may be rules about the way something is to be accomplished at various stages of the family and at various ages for an individual. Thus, many norms are age and stage graded. For instance, you do not apply the same rules to a toddler that you do to a teenager. The concept of norms may be proscriptive as in indicating what we should do or what a family should be, but norms are also descriptive or indicative of how families are. The distinction is important in the family life course development framework because proscriptive norms tend to carry moral implications, whereas descriptive norms may influence behavior but without the good or bad label. If everyone is "doing it," then that is going to influence others' behavior whether it is healthy or unhealthy. Corporal punishment is a good illustration. The detrimental effects of corporal punishment found in children who were raised in a social context that discouraged spanking were not found in children who received the same types of punishment in a social context where spanking was viewed as normative (Ellison & Bradshaw, 2009). White, Martin, and Bartolic (2013) suggest that within cultural communities where spanking is more common or normative, the effects decline or even disappear. White (1998) points out that norms will vary with levels of analysis. Although later propositions will focus on the general population level of norms, it is important to be aware of the differences a norm at one level of analysis may have from another (Table 5.1.)

A family *role* is defined as "all the norms attached to one of the kinship positions." In most societies, the role of mother, for example, entails the norm of nurturance of the young. Because positions are defined structurally, however, the content of a role (the norms) may change from society to society or ethnic subculture to ethnic subculture. And like the norms that compose them, social roles may be age- and stage-graded. For example, the nurturant role for a mother with an infant is quite different from that for a mother with adolescent children. The use of role concepts in family development theories is virtually the same as it is in symbolic interactionism, and as we will see later in this chapter, developmental theorists differ among themselves in their emphasis on structural versus interactional views of roles just as symbolic interactionists differ among themselves on this point.

Table 5.1 Major Levels of Analysis for Norms

Level	Construct	Process	Sanctions
Individual	morals	internalization	guilt
Group	rules	socialization	approval
Institution (aggregate)	modal frequency	institutionalization	life chances, stress

White (1998) p. 230. Used with permission.

Events

Family life events are typically discrete significant occurrences, such as births, deaths, weddings, relocations, or divorces. The event has a chronological date attached, but that date carries little significance apart from the event. To remember September 11, 2001, is to remember the events of New York, Washington, D.C., and Pennsylvania, not that it was a Tuesday in September near the turn of the century. It makes little sense to talk about October 7, 1984, in a conversation since saying the day I got married would carry so much more meaning.

Events are discrete or relatively short in duration. The birth of a child is usually noted by the minute the child fully leaves the birth canal, but to the parents and especially the mother, that birth was eventful for more than a minute. Events that last a period of time are referred to as stages and discussed below. These life events are important because they mark the end of a previous state such as being single and the beginning of a new state such as being married. The timing, frequency, and sequencing of events can be helpful in explaining diverse life course pathways and life course outcomes.

The *normative* nature of life events is what makes them useful in the discussion of the life course development framework. Birth is a universal experience of being human, as is death. The significant life events that populate the time in between these two are of great importance to understanding the heterogeneity and homogeneity of the life and family course. Death at old age is not experienced the same by close relatives as the unexpected death of a child. The first marriage is not experienced the same as higher order or subsequent marriages.

Family Stage

A *family stage* is an interval of time in which the structure and interactions of role relationships in the family are noticeably and qualitatively distinct from other periods of time (Aldous, 1996). Stages are characterized by three defining elements. First, all stages have a beginning defined by a transitional event; second, they have an ending defined by a concluding transitional event; and finally, they have duration defined by the period of time between the two transitional marking events. A stage is made up of the continuous state entered into at the first transitional event. For example, a couple may be cohabiting for a period of time and then choose to get married. The marriage event changes the state of their relationship from unmarried to married. The duration of time in that marriage state is the marriage stage. A stage at the group level represents a pattern of role interaction between family members distinct from those stages that precede and follow it. The stage is usually inferred from events that indicate a change in the membership of the family or the way in which members are spatially and interactionally organized. For example, launching a child into adulthood does not mean the end of the parental role but a change based on the spatial and interactional organization of members. Even divorce can mark stage changes in parenting interactions (Adamsons & Pasley, 2006).

Transitions

Transitions are shifts from one family stage to another. A family's career is composed of many such transitions between stages. Magrabi and Marshall (1965) were the first to conceptualize family transitions as a branching process; others such as Klein et al. (1979) and White (2004) have further developed the notion. The concept that has emerged is that family transitions viewed over time consist of paths taken and not taken. For example, at any one time, a married couple may stay married or get divorced, one of the spouses may die, or they might have a child. Each of the possible events would move the family to a new series of possible alternative transitions. The process charted over time would look like a tree with many branches; the path that any one family takes would be one series of branches.

Transitions from one family stage to another are indicated by the events between stages. Family stages and events are experienced as on time or off time with the expected timing for these events. For instance, giving birth to a child when your postadolescent children are leaving home would be off time. In general, the age- and stage-graded social norms supply timing expectations. Not only might events be off time, but sequences of events and stages might be "disorganized" also. For example, the sequence of getting married before the birth of your first child is normatively organized, whereas a premarital birth would be a departure from the normative expectations for sequencing marriage and births.

Pathways

As indicated in the section on transitions, the cumulative charted branching resulting from movement across events and stages produces a life course or a pathway. The life course can be conceptualized as a pathway line drawn from earlier life events through later life events, based on the new events entered. For example, everyone's life course begins with the state of being single. As time goes on, a person may choose to remain single, get married, cohabit, or enter some other alternative union arrangement. If that person chose to cohabit, then the choices at the next time point would be to remain cohabiting, end the cohabitation, get married to his or her partner, or enter some alternative union form. Each time point presents the available options that the previous selection opens up. For example, if at time point one a person was single and at time point two he or she was married, at time point three he or she can now get divorced. Had they remained single or chosen to cohabit at time point two, then divorce would not be a possibility nor be included in that person's pathway.

The movement between states across time is often conceived as being the result of individual agency. But many transitions and pathway histories are not just the result of choices we make. The death of a spouse or a child is not something we normally choose. An unexpected pregnancy or the birth of triplets is seldom the result of choice. Larger institutional influences such as economic collapse, natural disaster, and war will undoubtedly influence individual and family pathways as well.

Developmental Tasks

Early developmentalists thought transitions were linked to developmental tasks that arise in the life course of individuals and families. The successful achievement of these tasks was thought to lead to happiness and success with later tasks (Havighurst, 1948). The notion of developmental tasks was an attempt to integrate age- and stage-graded social norms with the ontogenetic maturation of individual family members. However well-intentioned the concept, it has fallen into a myriad of difficulties. The notion of developmental tasks has been criticized as making nonscientific value judgments about what constitutes "success." In addition, the notion of developmental tasks is tied to a preformational, ontogenetic view of child development that has largely been rejected by those studying the social group of the family. As a result, researchers early on redefined the concept as a set of norms (role expectations) arising at a particular stage of the family career (Hill & Rodgers, 1964; Rodgers, 1973, p. 51). Rodgers and White (1993) posited that the task concept is redundant with the age- and stage-graded notions of norm and role and no longer include it among the core concepts of the theory; the concept also is not central in the work of Bengtson and Allen (1993).

Family Life Course (Family Career, Family Life Cycle)

For most developmentalists, the concept of the *family life course* has replaced the earlier concept of *family life cycle*. Some theorists (Aldous, 1996; Rodgers, 1973) have attempted to replace the notion of life cycle of the family with the concept of *family career*. This "replacement" has so far failed to become popular with scholars and students, although it does still appear periodically in current literature (Goldberg, 2010; Hosegood, 2009). The original concept of family life cycle contained the connotation that family life somehow "cycled." This was not the meaning that life course theorists meant to convey. Rather, development as a process is viewed more like a career, in which current stages are affected by the past, but there is no teleological end to the process that would bring it full circle. The family's life course is composed of all the events and periods of time (stages) between events traversed by a family. For families in any one society, such as North American, we find that stage-graded norms are indicated by the sequence of events followed by most families (Marks & Lambert, 1998; White, 1987, 1998). For example, the great majority of people get married before having a child, and for most people, a premarital birth is considered out of the normative sequence. Every culture and society has a range of both variations and deviations from the normative expectations.

Normative Variations and Deviations

The extent of accepted *variations* in the family life course indicates the strength of the norms within any given birth cohort and historical period. The stronger and more rigid the norms regarding how families are to live their life course, the less accepted are variations. Conversely, the greater distribution of acceptance, the less likelihood of social sanctions. For example, the Chinese government's one-child policy represented an official institutional norm regulating how many children families may have and was buttressed by strong negative sanctions. On the other hand, the general acceptance of more permissive sexual mores among single adults today versus the 1950s means there would be less impact of that behavior on later outcomes such as marital stability. The one-child policy example would be illustrated by a leptokurtic distribution of the number of children a couple has. That variation would be very limited, and the mean, mode, and median would all be closely gathered around one with a very small standard deviation. The second example would be illustrated by a platykurtic distribution in which the variation of prevalence of sexual activity prior to marriage would be quite wide. Some people would be sexually active young and often, and others would not be, with the bulk of the population distributed between these two. The difference between variation and deviation at the aggregate level of analysis is that variation about a measure of central tendency (mode or median) is random, whereas deviation is nonrandom and systematic. *Deviation* by large numbers of families from a normative career sequence is viewed as a source of social change. Clearly, people deviate from the normative path only when they perceive that the deviation produces greater net rewards (perceived benefits from the action minus the expected costs associated with the action) than adhering to the normative path. Once an individual or family is out of sequence or off time with the expectations in a society, it is often difficult to resume a normative course. Sometimes, such situations arise from individual mistakes; these would be random. Other times, large numbers of families seem to deviate from social norms, such as at present with the popularity of premarital cohabitation. If such deviation becomes systematic (it is one as opposed to many alternatives to marriage) and larger and larger numbers of people follow this "new" path, at some point the social norms shift so that it becomes deviant *not* to live together before marriage as part of mate selection (Hewitt & de Vaus, 2009; Liefbroer & Dourleijn, 2006).

One of the reasons such deviance comes about is the attempt to align family timing and sequencing norms with those of other institutions, such as education and work. In the past few decades, there has been increased pressure from the labor force for higher skills and more education. This pressure to get more education coupled with the sequencing norm of "finish your education before you get married" has resulted in the delay of marriage for younger people. But with the delay in marriage, another problem arises. A dominant norm in mate selection is that women seek mates who are the same age or older, and men seek mates the same age or younger. As a result, older men have a higher probability of marriage, and as they marry, there are fewer of them available for younger women. If women delay relationship formation until age 27 or later, then there are fewer available men their same age or older. Cohabitation becomes a way to establish a residential intimate relationship without entering marriage. As both genders delay marriage to finish school and start careers, cohabitation represents a way to enter an intimate relationship with a potential spouse but without the constricting roles of husband and wife and without pressure to have children. The norms would suggest that before people would ask, "When are you two going to have a child?" they would ask, "When are you two going to get married?" Thus, social change comes about because individuals seek to align their sequencing of family stages with the sequencing and timing norms of nonfamily institutions (such as education and the labor force). These cross-institutional norms, such as "finish your education before you get married," encourage systematic deviation in family careers and ultimately social change.

Age, Period, and Cohort

Life course theory, a subcomponent of the framework under discussion, contributes clarity to the study of the family in its discussion of the concepts of age, period, and cohort. Karl Mannheim (1956) wrote in the early 20th century, "Even if the rest of one's life consisted of one long process of negation and destruction of the natural world view acquired in youth, the determining influence of those early impressions would still be predominant" (p. 298). Ortega y Gasset (1933) also discussed the importance of one's birth on a person's worldview. To him, the concept of generation was the most important in human history. Life course theory explores the influencing agents on change across the life of individuals. The age of a person and the sociohistorical context in which he or she is raised and lives shape clusters of people in unique and patterned ways. Life course differs from the concept of life cycle. The life cycle assumed a patterned teleologic progression and reproduction of life and family courses (Elder, 1975).

An age effect is the understanding that the age at which individuals or members of a family experience a sociohistorical event will have differing effects on that person or family. The impact of 9/11 is different for children than for young adults and for families who experienced the loss of a loved one versus those who didn't. A cohort effect can be defined as a distinctive formative experience or event that members of a cohort or cohorts share and that shapes their collective identity for the rest of their lives. A period effect is similar to a cohort effect in that an event shapes a group of people over their life course, but a period effect tends to be defined by a geopolitical or sociohistorical event that has influence across all ages and cohorts.

Elder's study of the influence of the Great Depression on the lives of children is a seminal study in life course research. It is valuable in that he illustrates statistically and graphically the distinctive nature of the influence of age, period, and cohort on the development of these children. Older children and younger children were not affected in a uniform fashion by the Great Depression. This led to his conclusion that a cohort effect exists when historical context differentiates the way an age-grouped set of the population experiences historical events (Elder, 1999). Or in the words of Riley (1998), "Because society changes, members of different cohorts cannot age the same way" (p. 42). Experiencing a divorce in 1955 would not be the same as experiencing a divorce in 2013 because society's view of divorce is not the same. Another example would be cohabitation. The reason young people cohabited in the 1950s is seldom the same reason the majority of young people do today.

According to life course theory, how people think about the social world around them is heavily dependent on what the world was like when they were growing up (Alwin & McCammon, 2007). An example of this can be traced through the life course of baby boomers, who became a political force during their later adolescence and early adulthood. This statement does not suggest that identity development becomes set at this age or that it can't continue to change and develop over time. It is a statement that points to a time period in an individual's life that is particularly important in the life course. Alwin and McCammon (2007) point to research that supports the idea that many of our most important life events are self-described to have occurred in this stage of the life course (Schuman & Scott, 1989; Scott & Zac, 1993).

Cohort size is also an important concept to consider in understanding difference across time. Cohort replacement is understood to play an important role in social change. Cohort size is generally equated with cohort influence. The larger the cohort, the more influence they will have across the life span. As mentioned above, the baby boom generation or baby boom cohort(s) have continued to be influential in many aspects of society, including economic and social variations.

Propositions

Rodgers and White (1993) caution that propositions that might be reasonable for one level of analysis might not be as accurate for other levels of analysis. (See Table 5.1, this volume, reprinted from White, 1998, p. 230.) For example, we can reasonably talk about an individual's "motivation," but it might be unreasonable to assume that groups or social institutions are motivated in the same way as individuals. It is usually more appropriate to move propositions from higher to lower levels of analysis than the reverse. Thus, we focus our examples of propositions from family development theory on the more general institutional and group levels of analysis.

> *Family development is a group process regulated by societal timing and sequencing norms. Although social norms vary culturally and across time, when societal timing and sequencing norms are out of sync, it is more likely that disruption will occur.*

This proposition asserts that family development is a process defined by social norms. Because norms are different from culture to culture, the process of family development may be different from culture to culture. We have used the North American norm regarding premarital births as an illustration of a sequencing norm. In many cultures such as the Polynesian culture, a premarital birth was expected before marriage and considered a necessary step in mate selection. How could a prospective husband discern the reproductive capacity of a woman if she had not demonstrated her fertility? This proposition also asserts that because family development is regulated by social norms, the central focus for understanding this process must be on the institution of the family. The institution of the family is composed of all those norms that regulate and define family life within a culture or social system. The assertion that the process is governed by social norms involves the assumption that family development is not a form of biological preformationism or ontogenesis. Rather, social systems are viewed as defining the norms of family development, and like all social norms, those regulating the process of family development change over historical time.

Although timing and sequencing norms are interrelated, research suggests that the sequence (order) of stages or events is more strongly regulated than the timing of stages or events (Hogan, 1978; Modell, 1980; White, 1987). People appear more likely to attempt to maintain the order of events than they are to maintain a set number of years between these events. What this suggests is that the family career as a sequence of stages or events is probably more important in explaining family behavior than is the timing. Indeed, military men returning after World War II were conscious of needing to compress the timing of family events but did not change the order of events or subtract events. Those pursuing advanced education, such as a medical degree, may also delay family events and then compress the time between events without changing the order.

If a family or individual is "out of sequence" or "off time" with the normative societal patterns, the probability of later life disruptions is negatively correlated to the degree of variance around the norm. The greater the concentration around the norm, the greater the likelihood of later life disruption for deviation from the norm.

Like it or not, every society must be organized. A significant part of social organization is the age and stage grading of various institutions. An often overlooked dimension of the social fabric is that timing and sequencing norms, such as those regarding education, must be synchronized with norms in other institutions, such as work and family. If a person or family gets out of sequence within one institution, the result is that they are more likely to be thrown out of synchrony with other institutions (Donnelly, Burgess, Anderson, Davis, & Dillard, 2001). Most of the research in this area has suggested negative outcomes for families and individuals, such as higher rates for marital disruption. There is, however, the argument that when the norms are changing, successive cohorts pursuing what is originally deviant behavior and suffering the consequences of being out of sequence or off time gradually come to represent the new dominant norm (normative succession). This new dominant norm gradually synchronizes with other institutions as they realign. The institutional lag or change between one institution and the adaptation of other institutions is often a time of social unrest. A useful example of this process of normative succession is premarital cohabitation. During the 1980s, researchers invariably demonstrated negative effects for premarital cohabitation on later marital stability (e.g., Teachman & Polonko, 1990) Gwartney-Gibbs (1986). This suggested that premarital cohabitation was on its way to becoming a normative stage in family development. By 1992, evidence surfaced that the most recent cohorts of cohabitants seemed to have less probability for marital disruption than their non-cohabiting counterparts (Schoen, 1992).

As the cohabitation literature continues to mature, there is evidence for a correlation between social acceptance of cohabitation and the likelihood of negative outcomes resulting from cohabitation (Hewitt & de Vaus, 2009; Liefbroer & Dourleijn, 2006), indicating that changing social norms influence life course outcomes.

The concept of normative succession does not preclude the widening or narrowing of acceptable life choices. For example, there has never been a specific number of children that any couple should have in America, so we cannot speak of one best number replacing another best number. Because social norms often allow a range of acceptable behaviors, we cannot say in this example that the childbearing stage has a definite acceptable duration. In some cultures, the norm is that you should have as many children as you can afford to raise, and affordability is the situation variable. The concern over the perception of increased disorder in the life course (Rindfuss, Swicegood, & Rosenfeld, 1987) or de-standardization of the life course (Brückner & Mayer, 2005) has some researchers questioning the importance of the order and timing of life events. These researchers found that disorder does have heterogeneous effects, but when it came to the transition to parenthood, a simple measure of disorder did not uniformly affect this transition.

Within the family group, family members create internal family norms. Family disruption is positively related to the degree internal family norms are held and deviate from institutional family norms.

Within the family group, each family creates social rules, such as bedtimes, rules about how much television can be watched, and rules about staying out late. The institution of the family provides the broad parameters within which families can interactively create their internal rules. For example, in North America, few parents would suggest to their children that they have multiple premarital births. The internal family norms or rules are further circumscribed by the institution of the family in that internal rules must not overly threaten institutional functions of the family. For example, parents who do not want to educate their children would probably find their children declared wards of the state. Although many of the internal family norms are not developmental in the sense of timing and sequencing norms, some clearly are. For instance, when a parent says to a child, "You can go in the canoe when you can swim," the parent is stating a sequencing rule. Or more relevant to family relations, "You can babysit your brother after you demonstrate that you can responsibly stay at home by yourself." Many such norms in the family rest on the stage of individual development of the members, such as, "When you can accomplish this" or "Your grandmother can't do that for herself anymore." Thus, some of these internal norms are developmental. There are, of course, a great number of internal family norms that are not developmental, and many of these could be said to be universal because they are neither age- nor stage-graded, such as "Always tell your parents the truth." A fruitful exploration in this area would be to explore the impact of dissonance between family norms and institutional norms. For example, what if it was socially normative to cohabit with a partner prior to marriage yet one or both partners come from traditional family environments that do not approve of the behavior? Martin (2014) proposed that it is conformity with the meso level of social influence that may be more predictive of disruption. In the example provided, a family or socially conservative community may make life difficult for a couple cohabiting even though it is social acceptable at a population level.

Interactions within the family group are regulated by the social norms constructing family roles.

Family interactions are predictable and uniform across families because of the institutional norms and expectations regarding family roles. As we indicated previously, these norms provide the parameters within which family members can create rules unique to their family. The parameters for roles such as mother and father of young children are especially restrictive because the society at large has a tremendous stake in the reproduction and socialization of new members of society. Indeed, when mothers and fathers fail to meet these roles, emissaries of the state step in to supervise or seize the children from the parents. For example, mothers are expected to be nurturant of the young. Failure in this regard can show up in behavior disorders in the children and more seriously in an infant's failure to thrive. Less codified norms exist about parental disciplinary techniques, such as spanking and control of the children. Even the method of infant feeding—breast or bottle—has become the focus for normative pressures and informal sanctions from health care professionals and resource groups.

In addition to the regulation of parent-child relationships, there are general social expectations regarding other family relationships, such as the sibling relationship. Siblings are expected to care for and watch out for each other. The norms constructing this sibling relationship extend into old age, when siblings rely on each other for support.

Transitions from one family stage to another are predicted by the current stage and the duration of time spent in that stage.

Although families move through their life course, making what seem to be individual decisions about when to move in together, get married, have a child, and so on, there is a high degree of predictability for families in general. This is not surprising, because this process is largely formed by social timing and sequencing norms. Couples who are recently married have a high probability of having a child, whereas the longer the couple stays in the childless stage, the lower the probability that they will have a child. These patterns of family development vary from culture to culture. Even within one culture, there may be variation. The variation within one culture demonstrates the strength of family timing and sequencing norms. For example, in at least one totalitarian state, the government has attempted rather successfully to control family size. The norms are formal and enforced with strict sanctions. In North America, our norms are less formal, and people respond more strongly to the need to be articulated with the timing and sequencing of educational and work careers.

It is useful to keep in mind that the effect of duration in a stage depends on the topic and on the stages involved. For example, it is rather obvious that the longer you have been in the child-rearing stage, the more likely you are to begin launching children into adulthood. In contrast, after the third wedding anniversary, the longer you are married, the less likely you are to divorce. So the direction of the effect of duration in a stage on entering another stage may be positive, negative, or curvilinear.

Beyond the proposition here about one stage influencing another, developmentalists often argue that stage placement, duration in a stage, and the transition to another stage help predict or explain other things about families such as how they function or the likelihood of problems. The empirical applications later in this chapter deal with such propositions.

Individuals and families systematically deviate from institutional family norms to adjust their behavior to other institutional norms, such as work and education.

The timing and sequencing norms for family transitions do not stand in isolation from other major social institutions. In fact, one of the important issues brought up through this institutional interaction is the flexibility to adapt to other institutional changes. Indeed, in the past, religious institutions reinforced and strongly sanctioned norms about family life, and religious organizations organized their own normative content to be in conjunction with family norms. Today, the family is less buttressed by institutional religious norms but strongly forced to articulate family sequencing with sequencing in work and education. Indeed, the conjunction of timing and sequencing norms from various institutions constructs the normative life course for individuals and families. For example, an educational norm, such as "Get more education," in conjunction with a cross-institutional sequencing norm, such as "Finish your education before you get married" and "Get a job before you get married," all conjoin to form the normative life sequence of "Finish your education, then get a job, then get married." Although there are no formal sanctions for not following this sequence, there are informal ones. The informal sanctions are subtle; they derive from the fact that all social institutions are age- and stage-graded. In work, as in family, there are stages of development, such as "formative" and "consolidation" stages of career development (Drobnic & Blossfeld, 2004; Moen, Kelly, & Huang, 2008; Voydanoff, 1987). If an individual or family becomes off time or out of sequence within one institution, its members find it increasingly difficult to meet the timing and sequencing expectations in other institutions. For example, it has been demonstrated that collegiate women without families are far more advantaged than young mothers regardless of the union status of the mother (Amato et al., 2008). An early entry into motherhood has distinct ramifications for meeting the timing and sequencing norms in education and work. The resulting modifications in the family, work, and educational careers make for difficulties and hardships associated with being out of synchrony with the social fabric of society and its reward systems. Of course, deviance is necessary as part of social change and adaptation to a changing society. As with premarital cohabitation, however, those in the vanguard of such adaptive deviance suffer to bring in the new normative order.

Variations

There are three major variants of the life course development framework: family development theory, life course theory, and individual life span theory.

Family Development

Although family development theory has evolved to have greater similarities to life course theory, there are some significant aspects to family development theory that suggest its uniqueness. One of these differences is that among family developmentalists, there are two distinct perspectives on change. The structural perspective represented in the work of White (1991) and Rodgers and White (1993) is focused on the institutional and cross-institutional processes affecting family development. The interactional perspective represented in the work of Aldous (1978, 1994, 1990, 1996) is focused on the relationships within the group and the construction of unique family norms and roles. The sociological dilemma of harmonizing institutional level influences and individual agency are clearly at work in these two approaches.

In the structural approach, commonly shared social timing and sequencing norms in a social system are emphasized. Although the structuralists admit that norms internal to the family can emerge through the interaction of family members, they emphasize the societal timing and sequencing norms that constrain any idiosyncratic emergent norms or roles. They argue that what family social scientists should be concerned with are the aggregate patterns and variations of family development within societies. Furthermore, the structuralists argue that a focus on the aggregate patterns also provides a way of addressing social change within the institution of the family as well as other institutions. The principal concept that structuralists use to explain social change is cross-institutional adaptation of the timing and sequencing norms of one institution with the norms of other institutions. In their view, the institution of the family is continually adapting to align and synchronize with other institutions. Deviance from the timing and sequencing norms of one institution (often to conform to the norms in another institution) is the mechanism by which social change occurs.

On the other hand, the interactional approach to family development theory is identified with symbolic interaction, especially the approach proposed by Turner (1970). Essentially, those adopting the interactional perspective maintain that the norms constructing social roles in the family in large part can be created by the individual family members and their interactions. Contrary to the structuralists, interactionists maintain that emergent norms and roles are not just idiosyncrasies of one family within the constraints of the larger society's timing and sequencing norms. The interactionists argue that family members can construct social roles (role making) and thereby set the course for social change. For example, there are many ways in which a mother may nurture children. Some mothers may take their infants to work, other mothers may stay home, and still others may judiciously select a warm and nurturant caregiver. The interactionists argue that all these behaviors fit within the broad framework of being a nurturant mother, but there is sufficient scope for the individual to construct her own norms and rules about *mothering*. Furthermore, the interactionists argue that such role making and norm making is how social change comes about. First, the individual family constructs its norms and roles to adapt to the social and economic situation. As larger numbers of people join in similar adaptations, the norms and roles become more common and acceptable until these norms eventually become the new norm.

In the interactional perspective, the internal dynamics of the family are emphasized. The consensus that family members reach on norms and roles provides an understanding of family behavior and possible directions of normative change. The interactionists view family development as a process governed by the interactions of family members. The family developmental stage is defined similarly to the structuralists' definition, but the emphasis is somewhat different. The interactionists argue that each stage of family development represents a qualitatively distinct pattern of interaction between family members. Whereas the structuralists define stages mainly by the more cross-culturally relevant dimension of group membership, the interactionists use more qualitative assessments of interaction. For example, in North America, the age of the oldest child's entry into school has been used to demarcate a change in family interaction because the child is now away from home for extended periods of time and integrated into the community (e.g., Aldous, 1978; Rodgers, 1973).

The interactionists' perspective on family development remains a vital part of family development theory, and it supports research more sensitive to the definitions and processes used within each family (Klein et al., 1979). Recently, White (2005) unified these two approaches, structural and interactional, in a new theoretical model he labeled "transition theory." In transition theory, the interactional components are used to provide impetus to transitions from one family stage to another. Probably the greatest strength that family development has over other approaches is its interactional component. Indeed, throughout the history of family development theory, the family development interactionists have provided the most popular North American formulations of the theory (e.g., Aldous, 1978; Duvall, 1957).

Individual Life Course Analysis

The past three decades have witnessed the emergence of a type of analysis of individual event histories referred to as "life course analysis." Although this form of analysis has been developed largely independent of family development theory, much of life course analysis is focused on family events. Family development theory has both contributed to these formulations and received impetus from this approach to expand developmental theory by incorporating some of the methods used in life course analysis. Indeed, Mattessich and Hill (1987) criticized family development theorists for not incorporating the effects of the timing of nonfamily life events on family development. Rodgers and White (1993) and White (1991) expanded family development theory to incorporate these other institutional events (e.g., education and work) in the developmental paradigm as "cross-institutional" timing and sequencing norms. Bengtson and Allen (1993) argued that life course analysis is a theory in its own right. They endeavored to produce a set of propositions unique to life course analysis.

Life course analysis, like family development, incorporates the historical dimensions of change: period, age, and birth cohort. Besides the recognition that timing and sequencing norms are affected by and change with a historical period, the age of the individual experiencing events, and the norms carried by the birth cohort, life course analysis appears to rely mainly on methodological innovations in studying the sequencing and timing of events (e.g., Allison, 1984). Similar historical dimensions and event history methods also show up in the work of family developmentalists as early as Glick

(1947). More recent methodological advancements in sequence analysis have led to a more family-based life course research agenda for researchers from various fields. European research is benefiting from the wealth of strong nationally representative longitudinal data sets, such as the British Household Panel Survey and the Integrative Council of European Social Science Data Archives. This emphasis on population-based life history data has led to an increase in the use of life course theory in the study of the family (Huinink & Feldhaus, 2009). Sequence analysis allows for the study of whole career sequences rather than just the examination of one isolated life event. Optimal matching analysis (OMA), a sequence analysis strategy, was initially developed by Abbott (1995) with the idea that it would be of value in studying family interaction issues. Initial concerns regarding the subjective nature of some aspects of OMA are being addressed (Martin, 2015). Aisenbrey and Fasang (2010) feel that the second wave of sequence analysis addresses these concerns and makes it even more of a suitable complementary approach to event history analysis. They state that the primary advantage of sequence analysis is its ability to study trajectories. In addition, they write:

> New developments in sequence analysis foster conceptual as well as empirical precision in the analysis of life course patterns. Methodologically, sequence analysis provides the possibility to approach data without any distributional assumptions, and its exploratory potential is particularly well suited to analyzing nonstandard and "outlier" life courses. Given the focus on single transitions with event history methods, we argued that sequence analysis can play a fundamental role in bringing the much neglected trajectory concept, the actual "course," back into the life course. (p. 450)

Aldous (1990) argues that because family development theory is focused on the family group and life course analysis is focused on the individual, the two approaches are not the same. But other contributions such as Bengtson and Allen's (1993) suggest that life course incorporates the family as one of several levels of analysis. What little difference there is can be attributed to the emphasis on individual units of analysis rather than on the family group. As we have seen, that emphasis is a matter of the level of analysis selected by the researcher rather than a substantive theoretical difference. Two examples of the approach used in life course studies are provided first in the study by Crosnoe and Elder (2002). These researchers found that a transition life course event, such as gaining higher education, had effects on the interaction between grandparents and their grandchildren. Second, Thornton, Axinn, and Xie (2007) found that if grandparents grew up in a rural environment, their grandchildren were much more likely to marry straight away rather than cohabit first. Thus, in these cases, an individual life course event has ramifications for the intergenerational transmission of specific outcomes within the family.

Individual Life Span

As Bengtson and Allen (1993) point out, the life span approach is rooted firmly within the discipline of psychology. From the outset, the emphasis on ontogenetic development over sociogenic factors in development was evident in the work of child developmentalists and subsequently in the theoretical work of Piaget, Erickson, and others. This emphasis on ontogenetic development was linked to the project aimed at finding universals in human psychology that would demarcate human development across time and place. It was thought that the human species had specific stages of development that all human organisms would necessarily traverse in order to be "human." Piaget's (1952) stages of cognitive development or Erikson's (1950) stages of adult development are examples of such attempts.

This emphasis on species-specific, biologically determined stage progressions failed to take into account the considerable impact that social norms and context have on individual development. Certainly, this more deterministic perspective of ontogenetic development was bound to reawaken the nature-nurture debate in regard to developmental processes. Indeed, in 1984, sociologist Dannefer (1984) and life span developmentalists Baltes and Nesselroade (1984) embarked on a series of exchanges that elaborated this debate (see Bengtson & Allen, 1993, pp. 477–480). The end product of such criticisms of life span ontogenetic development is that developmentalists more broadly acknowledged the social and historical context of development and that development might proceed along different lines in different contexts (Baltes, 1987). Although life span developmentalists continue to examine developmental processes, the current research is much more context sensitive and less deterministic in its approach. For example, Schoon et al. (2002) concluded that "the impact of risk factors depends on characteristics of the individual but also on the context, including the proximal family environment as well as the wider sociohistorical context that dictates opportunities and possibilities" (p. 1501).

Empirical Applications

There exists such a myriad of applications of family life course development theory that it is difficult to select only a couple of examples to demonstrate the great strength and richness of this framework. This theoretical perspective continues to inform family historians and demographers (e.g., Elman, 1998) and guide researchers into new areas of study (Price, McKenry, & Murphy, 2000; Watt & White, 1999), and the sequencing of events continues as a major focus in marital dyads (Marks & Lambert, 1998). Martin (2018) provides a detailed assessment in Box 5.1 of current trends in the research.

Box 5.1   A Summary of Recent Research Informed by Family Development Theory

More recently, FDT has been used to research a wide variety of family topics. Some of the more popular topics utilizing FDT over the past 30 years have been in the area of life course stages or events like adoption (Bejenaru & Roth, 2012; Fitzpatrick & Kostina-Ritchey, 2013), parenting (Anderson, 1988; Brotherson, 2007; Crawford & Fischer, 1993; Moore, 1989; Seiffge-Krenke & Pakalniskiene, 2011), marriage (Hall & Adams, 2011; Moen, Bradford, Lee, Harris, & Stewart, 2015; Storaasli & Markman, 1990; Willoughby, Hall, & Goff, 2015), grandparenting (Waldrop et al., 1999), retirement (O'Rand & Farkas, 2002), and death (Maxymiv & Blankemeyer, 2001). Topics such as health issues (Cavanagh, Compton, Tluczek, Brown, & Farrell, 2010; McCubbin, 1999), nursing (Flanagan, Holmes, & MacInnes, 2002), pets (Albert & Bulcroft, 1988), computer use (Watt & White, 1999), children's use of media (Davies & Gentile, 2012) and work, business, and family finance (Chaulk, Johnson, & Bulcroft, 2003; Minola, Brumana, Campopiano, Garrett, & Cassia, 2016; Shams & Björnberg, 2006; White, 1999) have also used FDT to guide their research. Research attempting to be more inclusive has focused on same sex couples or the family from a feminist perspective (Demo & Allen, 1996; Gravenhorst, 1988; Hostetler & Cohler, 1997) in addition to non-white populations, such as African American (Littlejohn-Blake & Darling, 1993) and Japanese American families (Krause, Ingersoll-Dayton, Liang, & Sugisawa, 1999). South African (Maconachie, 1989) and Vietnamese (Ha, 2014) populations are examples of cross-cultural studies using FDT.

Martin (2018) pp. 54–55. Used with Permission.

We have selected four areas to illustrate the empirical application of this approach. Two of the areas we focus on have a long history of study within the family life course framework: family stress and the transition to parenthood.

The other two areas we look at, cohabitation and work-family interaction, have received more recent attention in family life course literature.

Resiliency and Stress in Families

One of the major empirical applications of family development theory has been in the area of stress. One of the early architects of family development theory, Reuben Hill (1958, 1971), was responsible for the original theoretical formulation in this area. Boss (1988) argues that although individuals experience stress as a felt inability to cope with change, families are organized units that also demonstrate group symptoms of stress. She defines family stress as a disturbance in the organization and process of family life. Although individuals perceive and react to stresses, it may be the resources of the family that explain the successful management of stress. Furthermore, individuals' perceptions of a stressor are guided by their understanding of timing and sequencing norms for family development. For example,

> The event of pregnancy is viewed more positively by the families
> of a couple in their thirties than by the families of a couple still
> in their teens. The different levels of family stress caused by
> the same event (in this case pregnancy) can be explained by
> developmental context. (Boss, 1988, p. 32)

Accordingly, family stress and individual stress must be explained by using multiple levels of analysis focusing on both the individual and family resources and coping skills. Furthermore, family life course researchers are examining the effects of sequencing family stages along with work stages. For example, White (1999), following Voydanoff (1987), showed that simultaneous sequencing of certain combined *formative* stages of work and family resulted in increases in stress.

The study of stress and therapeutic applications of family development theory (e.g., Carter & McGoldrick, 1988; Falicov, 1988; Klein & Aldous, 1988; Walsh, 2015; Weber, 2011) have emphasized significant events and "pileup" of events in the individual and family history. For example, we all appreciate that a recent event such as a divorce places family members under significant stress by requiring emotionally intense adjustments. In recent analyses, researchers have examined not just such events but also where the event falls in the family's event history. A family may have moved to a new house then experienced a prolonged illness of a family member and then undergone a separation and finally a divorce. Clearly, each event alone would be considered stressful, but the compression of the events in a brief time span also must be considered in an analysis of stress on individuals and family members.

Over the past three decades, McCubbin and his colleagues have produced a developmental model of how families adapt to stress that incorporates the pileup of stressors as an integral mechanism. This model was first developed by Hill (1949) as the ABC-X model of family stress. The Hill model has been iteratively expanded to the family resiliency model. This model focuses on the dynamic process by which a family deals with stressors (McCubbin & Patterson, 1983). McCubbin and colleagues (McCubbin & McCubbin, 1987, 1989; McCubbin, Thompson, Thompson, & Futrell, 1999) have argued that resilient families adapt much more successfully to stressors than do nonresilient families. Patterson (2002a) has united the resiliency and stress models into a more encompassing model she labels the "family adjustment and adaptation model." The fact that all these models conceptualize family adaptation and adjustment to stressors as a dynamic and developmental process tacitly acknowledges that Hill, the originator, was one of the major intellectual progenitors of family development theory as well as the ABC-X model. Further discussion on the ABC-X model, as well as the family resiliency model, is presented in the Systems Theory chapter.

Transition to Parenthood

Family life course development scholars have also turned their attention to the stress attached to particular transitions in the family life course. Hill and Rodgers (1964) argued that particular transitions from one family stage to another might be stressful. Menaghan (1983) examined the stress associated with the transition to parenthood. She argued that the stress on individuals of assuming the roles and norms of parenthood was mitigated by anticipatory socialization and coping skills. Belsky and Rovine (1990) documented that many families suffered declines in marital role relationships during the transition to parenthood. The transition to parenthood continues to occupy developmental researchers as they incorporate events such as prenatal preparation, infant feeding practices, and the timing of work-related events in their analyses. For example, Bulcroft, Forste, and White (1993) argued that the decision to breast-feed an infant must be studied as part of the transition to parenthood because the choice of infant feeding technique is linked to strains on the marital relationship that are elevated by breast-feeding. An important part of the strain put on the marital relationship by the entry of the first child is due to changes in the content of the roles. Cowan and Cowan (2000) observed that they become much more traditional and gender based. Levy-Schiff and Israelashvili (1988) found that when fathers are involved in caregiving, there is a positive effect on marital satisfaction for both husbands and wives. Demo and Cox (2000) suggest that there is general agreement that the degree of stress experienced in the transition to parenthood is related to the level of marital adjustment before the birth of the child (e.g., Cox, Paley, Burchinal, &

Payne, 1999). Researchers in other countries (e.g., Feeney, Hohaus, Noller, & Alexander, 2001) have corroborated the stressfulness of this transition.

Although we do not as yet know whether all family transitions are stressful for family members, we do have an indication that the birth of the first child and transition to parenthood is fraught with potential strains for individuals and relationships in the family. As family life course researchers study the factors in this family transition, we find not just the details of how and why couples experience such stress but also how intervention strategies may assist families with such a transition. For example, Cowan and Cowan's (2000) study titled *When Partners Become Parents: The Big Life Change for Couples* demonstrates the stress that couples feel during this transition and also develops an effective intervention strategy to reduce the stress that couples experience.

Cohabitation

The rise in cohabitation levels in the latter half of the 20th century caught most demographers and family scientists by surprise. A majority of Western-based relationships now include some spell of cohabitation. What was considered deviant and reserved for mostly marginalized members of society has now become the norm. Early cohabitation research focused on the negative consequences on later marriages and as a result narrowed in on the sequencing of union states. That was followed up with an emphasis on the duration of cohabitation. Research demonstrated that shorter spells of cohabitation did not have the same negative effect on later marital stability that longer spells did (Teachman & Polonko, 1990), but that trend seems to have reversed in later research in which longer spells of cohabitation appear to enhance later marital stability (Hewitt & de Vaus, 2009). As cohabitation becomes more normative, the incidence of negative outcomes is diminishing. Societal expectation for the life course to include cohabitation may have become the norm, but higher order or multiple cohabitations continue to have strong negative implications for later marital stability (Lichter & Qian, 2008). This finding provides support for the addition of frequency of an event in influencing the life course in addition to sequencing and duration variations. The influence of social norms on the life course has been previously stated. Research on the level of adoption of cohabitation on later marital stability by Liefbroer and Dourleijn (2006) demonstrates that when the level of adoption is low, there is a greater penalty for cohabitation on later marital stability. When the level of adoption is near its nadir or when half the population does and half does not, then the difference of dissolution rates of those who cohabit prior to marriage and those who don't is at its minimum. Interestingly, they go on to show that when a minority of people do not cohabit, then the penalty for premarital cohabitation on later marital stability increases again. The interpretation is that as diffusion of adoption increases across the population, the population that does not cohabit represents a selective group that highly values marriage and is probably motivated by strong religious convictions. Cohabitation provides a current and relevant example of the value of the life course development framework guiding family research.

Work-Family Interaction

Early work-family interaction research focused on the dysfunctional aspects of the interaction. Coser (1974) referred to work-family interaction as the tension between two "greedy institutions." Hogan (1978) looked at the importance of the temporal order of significant life events. He demonstrated that negative consequences were associated with nonnormative life event patterns. Marital instability was higher in those cases that did not follow the normative pattern of completing one's education, followed by gaining employment and then beginning a family. More recent work has framed the interaction as more normative and having the potential for positive outcomes and enhancing one's life (Carlson, Kacmar, Wayne, & Grzywacz, 2006). The dynamic nature of work-family interaction has been addressed through longitudinal research. Longitudinal studies have looked at transitions from school to work (Schoon, McCulloch, Joshi, Wiggins, & Bynner, 2001); career pathways (Blair-Loy, 1999; Huang, El-Khouri, Johansson, Lindroth, & Sverke, 2007); job stability and interruptions (Fuller, 2008); and employment, housing, and marital status (Pollock, 2007); and studies to gain a better understanding of the importance of time in the work-family interface in general (Han & Moen, 1999). Voydanoff (1987) and White (1999), in their research on the staging of work and family careers, see the importance of studying work-family interaction from a developmental perspective. Finally, when work-family research sees the impact of this interaction influencing not just individuals but work environments and families as well, the institutional dimension is again highlighted for its importance in the life course development framework. Grzywacz, Almeida, and McDonald (2002) look at the bidirectional effect of positive and negative spillover in both families and the workplace. Drobnic, Blossfeld, and Rowher (1999) look at the cross-cultural difference in women's employment patterns across the family life course. The rapidly changing nature of the economy, educational expectation, and government legislation mean family pathways will continue to adapt to the new realities.

Critiques and Discussion

A central problem area for life course family developmental theory is the identification of the process of development. Mattessich and Hill (1987) offered a definition of family development that was influenced by the thinking of scholars in child development. As a result, their definition contained elements such as "progressive structural differentiation." The more ontogenetic versions of life span theory have a similar problem in regard to the invariant stage conceptions in some ontogenetic developmental perspectives. But family groups are more social and less biological in their development than are individuals. For individuals, developmental scholars argue that there are ontogenetic, or biologically based, stages of development. But for the family, the argument about a biological basis doesn't stand up. The only established biological parameters are fertility and mortality, and with the onslaught of fertilization technology, fertility may not last long as a parameter of family life.

White (1991) suggested that family life course development theory should explain the transition from one family stage to another. As a result of this emphasis, White's definition of development is that it is a process in which the probabilities of a transition change according to the family's current stage and how long it has been in that stage. For example, usually newlyweds allow themselves a period of adjustment before having a first child. The probability for a first child peaks during the early years of marriage; after 5 years, the probability of a birth rapidly declines. The developmental process is where a transition to a family stage, such as parenthood, is dependent on the current stage (childless marriage) and the duration of time in that stage (less than or greater than 5 years). This view of family development relies on the behavior of individuals and families as being guided by social norms rather than ontogenetic causes.

The ontogenetic-sociogenic argument will continue to plague this theory until there is a clear link with ontogenetic child development theories. There can be little doubt that the maturation of children makes for large changes in interaction in families, but family developmentalists have not studied these interactions longitudinally to discover which norms and patterns change and which do not. On the other hand, child developmentalists have largely ignored the family context of ontogenetic development, and we have little idea of the interactions between a child's development and family norms and patterns. White (2004) suggests an interactional approach following the work of Breunlin (1988) to model the interaction between parents and their children. Although such efforts are in the correct direction, the goal of a theoretical linkage between individual and family development remains elusive.

A substantial problem for the family life course framework is using behavior to infer norms (Hogan, 1978; Neugarten, Moore, & Lowe, 1965; White, 1987). Marini (1984) argues that norms cannot be inferred from behavior. She states that norms always carry sanctions and are part of a group. The aggregate patterns of family development cannot be used to infer social norms because there is no demonstration that these norms are carried by group members and have sanctions. White's (1991, 1998) response to Marini's (1984) argument is that she fails to incorporate the many levels of analysis appropriate for analyzing norms. He argues that Marini's definition is suitable only for the group level of analysis, not for the institutional level of analysis. Marini's argument, however, raises important questions about the conditions under which scholars may validly infer norms from patterns of family behavior. Claiming that there are institutional norms does not relieve us of the duty to provide independent empirical evidence for their existence. If institutional norms cause behaviors, we do not want to infer institutional norms from behaviors. No cause can be inferred from its presumed effect.

A longstanding critique of the stage concept is that it cannot incorporate the myriad family forms and is not cross-culturally relevant. Today, we must wonder whether there is so much diversity of family forms that the stage concept cannot work. We believe that although this criticism might have been appropriate for earlier versions of the theory in which stages were given culture-specific content, it is no longer appropriate for the recent versions of the theory in which stages are based on either possible membership structure or patterns of families. Indeed, family development stages are appropriate as long as there are patterns of family life.

A more serious criticism of the theory is that many of the changes viewed in family development theory as discrete jumps associated with changing family stages are more realistically conceptualized as gradual, continuous changes. For example, critics would argue that the preparation for a first child is more continuous than discrete. Even among family developmentalists, there is the view that transitions are not a point in time but a process (e.g., Aldous, 1978; Bohannan, 1970; Klein et al., 1979). A possible rebuttal is that no matter what the preparation, if the relatively discrete event of the birth of the first child does not take place, then we cannot say that a transition has taken place. This rebuttal relies on the fact that transitions are usually tied to a relatively discrete event and that such events are turning points for the family. Contrary instances can be noted, however. For example, when does an American child become an adult, such that we can identify when families enter and exit the launching stage? Given how often young adults leave home and return again for periods of partial dependency on parents, it seems clear that the transition to adulthood is now a rather complicated and extended process (Goldscheider & Goldscheider, 1999), and it could occur repeatedly for one or more children in the family.

Another problem we see for family development theory is its scope. Family development theorists attempt to explain the uniform and patterned ways in which families develop not only within a society but also from society to society. Much of family development theory, however, has been focused on family development during the decade of the 1960s within middle-class U.S. families. Although older versions of the theory appear to lack cross-cultural applicability, there is some cause for optimism with the newer theoretical versions. For example, research by both Kumagai (1984) and Rodgers and Witney (1981) demonstrated the utility of family life course development in cross-cultural comparisons. The generality of the newer theoretical propositions and the specification of events hold greater promise for cross-cultural researchers than did the older culture-specific stages.

The single most important contribution of developmental perspectives on the family is that they alert us to the importance of changes over the course of a family's existence. So whenever it is asserted that families with a particular characteristic have a certain outcome, we are alerted to ask when the characteristic emerged in the family and when the outcome changed. And we want to find out the reason why the change happens when it does rather than assuming that changes are random in families.

Conclusion

Family life course development theory provides a broad theory to explain the patterns of family formation and dissolution (e.g., Bengtson & Allen, 1993; Rodgers & White, 1993). Family development theory grew and matured throughout the second half of the 20th century. In this chapter, we have conjoined life span development, family development, and life course analysis as a single framework. These three approaches have great similarities. Where they do diverge to emphasize ontogenetic or sociogenic development, they actually complement each other. We have little doubt that a conjoined theory of family life course development will provide both students and scholars insight into the ways families grow and change over time. Indeed, recent evidence suggests that this framework is used by a great number of family researchers (e.g., Hill, Erickson, Fellows, Martinengo, & Allen, 2012; Kamp Dush & Taylor, 2012; Sassler, 2010; Thomson, Winkler-Dworak, & Kennedy, 2013).

STUDY QUESTIONS

1. The family life course development framework is the synthesis of three complementary theoretical approaches: individual life span theory, family development theory, and life course theory. Which of these three

contributes the most to the theories value and which contributes the least? Substantiate your response by demonstrating what predictive value may be gained or lost as a result of your decision. (Hint: Think levels of analysis.)

2. In chemistry, hydrogen shrinks when cooled. Oxygen also shrinks when cooled. When you fill an ice tray with water (H_2O) and put it in the fridge, what happens? Relate this to the individual and family levels of analysis in this theory.

3. The life course of an individual or a family is made up of events, stages, transitions, timing, duration, and sequencing. Discuss how each of these may affect outcomes later in the life course. Work on both an individual in a family and the family as a unit.

4. Using family life course development theory, can you provide an explanation why cohabitation may be considered socially acceptable, even normal, but still lead to higher marital instability when it (cohabitation) precedes marriage?

5. Use the concepts of age, period, cohort to provide a partial explanation for (a) The sexual revolution of the 1960s; (b) The rapid rise of divorce rates in the 1970s and 1980s.

6. Some scholars have questioned the future relevancy of family life course development theory. Reflect on the propositions provided in the chapter and make an argument for or against the future relevancy of the theory.

6

The Systems Framework

Today is Jack and Jan's 10th wedding anniversary. For the past 10 years, Jack has always presented Jan with a dozen yellow roses. When he gives her the roses this year, Jan makes a funny face. She says thanks and puts the roses aside while she finishes reading a newspaper article. Jack is disappointed that Jan did not respond more positively to his gift. He asks Jan what is wrong. She informs him that she has an allergy to roses. Jack says that he remembered her liking them even before they were married. She says she has always been allergic but received them enthusiastically because of the "thought." Jack responds that the thought is still there. Jan counters that after 10 years of marriage, she had hoped his knowledge about her would grow deeper. Jan says that she has sent a number of messages that not only does she not like roses but some variety would show more thought on Jack's part as well. Instead, all she receives is the message that their marriage has sunk into thoughtless routine. After all, says Jan, variety is the spice of life. Let's take a closer look at this example, for it illustrates some general principles about a communications system. First, Jack inferred from Jan's premarital behavior that she liked roses. He has incorporated this into his understanding of his wife for the past 10 years. Jan is disappointed that Jack does not know her better, but unless Jack asked Jan about her flower preferences, or had occasion to observe Jan being disappointed previously, he would have no reason to doubt the validity of his premarital inference. Indeed, the only reason Jack would change his inference would be if he received new information. Jan, on the other hand, thinks Jack's perceptions are shallow. She thinks he should have been sensitive to her subtle cues that she liked the thought but not the flowers without her having to say it. She feels she provided sufficient nonverbal cues to alert her husband and that he is simply insensitive to the information she sends (e.g., Gottman & Porterfield, 1981).

In general, then, we can see both spouses as being linked in a system in which one person's behavior becomes the other person's information. In turn, this person's information provides the beliefs and basis on which future actions are taken. Those actions become evidence that the other spouse doesn't understand him or her and has not received the more subtle messages. Jan is thus disappointed in what she believes is her husband's insensitivity to her behavioral cues. In a distilled sense, this interactional spiral, composed of behaviors between the spouses and each one's perception and reception of the information carried by those behaviors, captures the notion of a marital interaction system.

In this chapter, we address the question "What is a system?" rather than examine marital communication. Through defining and discussing the properties of a system, we become more adept at analyzing cases such as that of Jack and Jan. Indeed, the study of marital and family interaction has been an important component in the recent development of systems theory in the social sciences. What we now call *general systems theory* does not have a simple pedigree or lineage, however. Originally, systems theory evolved from a set of diverse influences such as biology, robotics, and mathematics. Of all the theories we consider in this book, systems theory is among the most recent, following only family development theory. Most, if not all, of its evolution took place within the 20th century.

Intellectual Traditions

Before the beginning of the 20th century, there were two major influences that were to prove foundational for systems theory. One of these was the *organic* and *evolutionary* perspective on society launched by Herbert Spencer (1880). Spencer's belief that the same basic processes operated throughout the universe led him to assume a set of principles that would apply within biology, psychology, and sociology. He viewed the universe as a continual process that forms and dissipates structures. Spencer's work is one of the major contemporary sources for the idea of *emergence,* that is, the notion that aggregations may come together in an organized form that is "more than the sum of its parts." Of course, this notion was voiced by the ancient Greek philosopher Democritus (460–360 BC) and after the turn of the 20th century was tied up with the notion of *vitalism* in biology and the process cosmology of Alfred North Whitehead (1929). Spencer's work also rekindled the age-old quest for unity among the sciences. This quest for universal principles common to all domains of study reached an apex during the 1950s and 1960s as evidenced by the publication of the *International Encyclopedia of Unified Science*, with such illustrious contributors as Charles Morris (see Chapter 4), Rudolph Carnap, Niels Bohr, and Carl Hempel.

The second major influence came from the emerging science of information and *automata*. Along with the invention of the telegraph and telephone, new ways of conceptualizing and measuring the flow of information developed. This was the start of communications theory. The digital codes that could be sent on telegraphs were the subject of early research that culminated in the invention of digital computers. At the same time that the study of these message systems was evolving, new technologies for control and guidance were being developed. For example, the servomechanism used on ships' rudders incorporated the ideas of error detection and feedback. But the greatest single impetus for the growth of information theory came from technological demands during World War II. For example, with the increase in the ability of aircraft to fly faster came a need for antiaircraft guns to anticipate the position of such fast moving targets. Probably one of the more familiar examples is that of the early rockets developed by Germany. The first V1 rockets were notorious for having a guidance system as rudimentary as a skyrocket's "point and ignite." Although these rockets were aimed at London, they probably terrorized more cows in rural Britain than Londoners. The subsequent version of the rocket, the V2, incorporated an error detection and trajectory correction feedback loop that increased the accuracy. Fortunately, these advances occurred only as the war was coming to a close.

The technological developments during the war created a need for theory to unite areas such as guidance systems and information flows. This need culminated in a series of academic developments. Soon after the war, Norbert Wiener (1948) published what became acknowledged as the seminal work on cybernetics and control systems. At about the same time, C. E. Shannon, a research scientist with Bell Laboratories, developed a mathematical theory of information and coding that he subsequently published with W. Weaver as *The Mathematical Theory of Communication* (1949). This theory consolidated the measurement of information (bits and bytes) in a way that we still use and offered several propositions regarding coding and error detection. From Shannon and Weaver's (1949) work, we find that the amount of information carried on a channel is inversely related to the amount of redundancy used for error detection. Another important postwar development was the founding of the Society for General Systems Research in 1954 by such notable social scientists as James Miller and Margaret Mead. It was at this point that systems theory started to gain a particular focus among those using it to study families.

The way in which systems theory evolved in the study of the family is especially interesting because its application to families preceded its entry into more established domains such as sociology (Buckley, 1967). This was principally due to the influence of a small group of researchers in San Francisco. Gregory Bateson, an anthropologist, had explored both psychiatry and systems theory during his postwar years at Harvard University. Don Jackson was a psychiatrist who, along with Bateson, forged the early entry of systems theory into the study of the family. These scholars founded the Mental Research Institute (MRI) in 1958 after Bateson, Jackson, Haley, and Weakland (1956) published their influential paper "Toward a Theory of Schizophrenia."

In this and subsequent papers, Bateson and his colleagues argued that the family represents a communications system in which, if double binds occur, one member may show signs of schizophrenia. The notion that the schizophrenic individual is a symptom of a family system pathology rather than an individual pathology gave rise to terms such as *dysfunctional family*. This view is seductive to many even though decades of research have failed to produce any substantial empirical support for the double-bind hypothesis (e.g., Mishler & Waxler, 1968; Olson, 1972; Schuham, 1967). The view of the family as a system, however, continues to operate as a strong metaphor within family therapy circles. For example, Kantor and Lehr's (1975) book *Inside the Family: Toward a Theory of Family Process* typified the family as being a self-regulating system in which members control each other's access to meaning, power, and affect. The applications of systems-type thinking in the realm of family therapy has become identified as one of the major variants of general systems theory and is commonly known as "family process theory" (see Broderick, 1993).

The initial entry of systems theory into the subject area of family through practitioners and therapists was closely followed by more formal statements from disciplinary scholars. The impact of von Bertalanffy (1968) in biology and Buckley (1967) in sociology was complemented in the social sciences by the more traditional *functionalist* approach used in anthropology, biology, and sociology. In all three of these disciplines, researchers had made arguments that, when we observe an existent structure, it must exist because either currently or at one time it performed functions for the organism or society. Thus, when we examine what seem to be nonfunctional organs in the human body, such as the appendix, we argue that the structure (the appendix) must have served some function at a previous time or it wouldn't exist. These *structural-functional* arguments reached a theoretical zenith in the work of Talcott Parsons (1951). Parsons used the systems metaphor and even incorporated many systems notions, such as "hierarchy of control," yet most scholars would not classify him as a general systems theorist. In spite of his lack of acceptance as a general systems theorist, Parsons's intellectual contribution to systems theory is kept alive today primarily through the neofunctionalist variant discussed later in this chapter. General systems theory is sufficiently abstract and general to be applied to both animate and inanimate objects. We can speak coherently about *planetary systems* and *family systems* even though the two subject matters differ dramatically in many regards. Indeed, this great generality is one of the compelling points of the theory and is tied to the unification of science movement. Yet several systems theorists (e.g., Buckley, 1967) have noted that although nonliving systems tend to follow the second law of thermodynamics and exhibit increased states of randomness (*entropy*), living systems tend to increase in order and differentiation (*negentropy*). Because all physical matter emits radiation, it loses energy used to organize its structure. This loss of energy creates the dissipative process of entropy. But as Toffler pointed out in his foreword to Prigogine and Stenger's (1984) book, biological systems do not seem to follow the same pattern as physical systems:

> Evolution proceeds from the simple to complex, from "lower" to "higher" forms of life, from undifferentiated to differentiated structures. And, from a human point of view, all this is quite optimistic. The universe gets "better" organized as it ages, continually advancing to a higher level as time sweeps by. (p. xx)

The diametrical opposition of these processes gave rise to the suggestion that the processes of living systems must be studied separately from nonliving systems. This view is most thoroughly explored by James G. Miller (1978) in his book *Living Systems*. Miller provides a classificatory view of living systems based on subsystem functions, such as "reproduction," that are necessary for living structures. Each subsystem function is examined at various levels of analysis. For example, the subsystem function of "reproducer" at the cellular level is performed by the chromosome and at the group level by the "mating dyad." The taxonomic approach used by Miller bears some resemblance to functionalist theory in sociology and has led at least one scholar (Turner, 1991) to discuss systems theory as "general systems functionalism." Regardless of Miller's (1978) similarities to Parsons and other functionalists, one critical dissimilarity is that he presents some general theoretical propositions that go beyond mere class inclusion. Also, Miller represents the currently dominant view that living, as opposed to nonliving, systems are driven by different *negentropic* and organizing processes.

This dominant view of living systems—one of which would be the family—as characterized by processes atypical of nonliving things has recently been challenged within biology. Researchers in the natural science of biology assume some continuity with other physical sciences, such as chemistry and physics, and this has perhaps made the disjunction with the physical science perspective more sharply felt. The idea that there are two distinct processes at work, one for living and another for nonliving systems, threatens the continuity of science as well as the unification of science envisioned by Spencer and others. Two biologists, Brooks and Wiley (1986), argued that the contradiction between nonliving systems being entropic and living systems being negentropic can be resolved by sorting out the level of analysis. Brooks and Wiley proposed that the problem is largely resolved by clarifying levels of analysis. Their argument is too detailed to present here in full, but the essence is that what might seem "organizational" (negentropic) at an aggregate level of analysis may be entropic at a micro level of analysis. The importance of their claim for us is that we are cautioned that the division in systems theory between living and nonliving systems may not be as clear and obviously acceptable as many authors in the social sciences have claimed. This caution leads us to present the concepts and propositions of general systems theory rather than only those deemed appropriate only for living systems.

Focus and Scope Assumptions

All parts of the system are interconnected. Although the assumption of interconnectedness in a system seems obvious, it is far from trivial. Burr, Leigh, Day, and Constantine (1979) stated, "The discovery by the family process group that changes in one part of a system influence all other parts of the system should be greeted with as much enthusiasm as the observation that people talk and think" (p. 98). We would agree with this comment if this assumption were to be treated as a claim to knowledge rather than as a basic orienting assumption. But this assumption is a basic *epistemological* statement announcing that systems theory is not concerned with isolating Cause A and Effect B from the environment in which they occur. In this sense, the assumption is a statement about the ecological validity and inclusivity of systems theory.

Understanding is only possible by viewing the whole. The assumption that one must consider a system in its entirety serves a similar epistemological function to our first assumption. This assumption in systems theory largely resulted from the "vitalism" tied to the discovery that when some animals, such as the paramecium, were sliced in two, they grew a new half. Clearly, these animals were "greater than the sum of their parts" because when you divided them, they replicated. This assumption was immediately relevant to sociology and family studies. Indeed, the argument that social groups, such as families, were "real" and greater than just a collection of individuals has raged in these fields for a considerable time (White, 1984).

A system's behavior affects its environment, and in turn the environment affects the system. Some of the output of a system becomes input of the system (feedback). The notion of feedback is twofold: It is both a concept and an epistemological assumption. The most simple of systems may not incorporate direct feedback loops, but this assumption serves to sensitize us to the fact that even the most simple systems affect and are, in turn, affected by their environment. In this sense, all systems have some form of feedback. This is the epistemological assumption, and it coheres nicely with the previous two assumptions of wholeness and connectedness. In the study of the family, we are usually concerned with the type of feedback whereby some of the output of a system becomes input to the system. In this sense, feedback represents a particular type of system operation that can be specified and measured. This second meaning of feedback does not refer to the assumption but to the concept.

"Systems" are heuristics, not real things. Systems theory is not reality but a way of knowing. This fourth and last major assumption is one that has more recently been formally recognized in systems theory. The assumption is that defining an object as a system composed of subsystems, inputs, and outputs is just one among many possible ways we might study the object. The systems perspective offers no special claim to veracity. But most of all, to say something behaves like a system is a model or metaphor, not the thing itself. Ernst von Glasersfeld (1987) summed up this "constructivist" perspective as the "view that knowledge must not be taken to be a picture of objective reality but rather as a particular way of organizing experience" (p. 10). It follows from this perspective that we should not consider the "model" to be the "thing." Indeed, the systems model becomes a heuristic for understanding our world. If we attribute reality to a family system rather than see it as a heuristic device, we make the mistake commonly called *reification,* or what the philosopher Alfred North Whitehead (1929, p. 11) called "the fallacy of misplaced concreteness."

In summary, there are four basic assumptions underlying the systems perspective: (a) System elements are interconnected, (b) systems can be understood only as wholes, (c) all systems affect themselves through environmental feedback, and (d) systems are not reality. These four assumptions are necessarily broad but represent the foundation on which the architecture of concepts and propositions rest.

Concepts

System

Hall and Fagan (1956) defined a system as a set of objects and relations between these objects and their attributes. This definition is useful for those who understand the formal set theory behind the definition, but for many students, this definition doesn't seem to say much. For this reason, we characterize systems in a more familiar and, we hope, approachable manner. At minimum, a *system* is a unit that can be distinguished from and that affects its environment. We regard this as a "minimalist" definition, and usually we would say additional things such as that a system has exchanges with its environment and has internal elements. But the major characteristic needed to identify something as a system is that it is separable from its environment and has an effect on its environment. That effect may only be that the system requires energy as input from the environment, such as a black hole, or it may only be that the system has output that affects the environment, such as a perpetual motion machine. In both cases, the system is a system because it affects its environment and can be distinguished from its environment.

Boundaries

All systems have some form of *boundaries*. A boundary is a border between the system and its environment that affects the flow of information and energy between the environment and the system. Boundaries can be measured on the dimension of permeability to the environment as running from closed boundaries, through which nothing goes in or out, to completely open boundaries, in which there is no impediment to energy and information transfers of any kind. Clearly, a completely closed system can only be imagined (as in mathematics), and a completely open system would lose most of its identity as a system because the system would be difficult to distinguish as separate from its environment. Fortunately, most systems occupy a position between these two ideal types. This means that the great majority of systems can be categorized by their *degree of permeability*. So, families usually live in households on plots of land, with fences, doors, walls, and so forth. Still, families differ in their openness to outsiders and in their ability to maintain privacy. This "privacy" is both physical and symbolic, as in the case of knowledge about what goes on within the family.

Rules of Transformation

All systems have internal *rules of transformation*. A rule of transformation represents a relationship between two elements of the system. For example, a husband and wife are both elements of the marital system. A rule of transformation for the marital system would be the quid pro quo rule that whenever the husband is nasty to the wife, the wife is nasty in return. One of the major functions of a rule of transformation is to transform inputs to the system from the environment into outputs from the system. For example, if a family's house is on fire and the smoke alarm goes off late at night, this information is transformed by the family into output as behavior that may doom or save them. If the family has a rule that on hearing the smoke alarm they are to exit the house according to a "fire plan," then they might be saved. On the other hand, if the family's rule is a less organized response—some members want to "shut the damn thing up" and others pull their pillows over their heads— they might be in considerable danger.

Feedback

Previously, we developed the idea of *feedback* as an epistemological assumption. Now we turn to feedback as a concept in systems theory. Feedback refers to the circular loop that brings some of the system's output back to the system as input. Feedback can be of two types. On one hand, it may be *positive,* or *deviation amplifying.* Do not confuse positive feedback with the concept of positive reinforcement from psychology; the two are very different. Positive reinforcement makes the goal behavior more likely, whereas positive feedback (deviation amplifying) may make reaching the goal less likely. On the other hand, negative feedback is deviation dampening. To make this categorization of feedback, we must rely on the identification of either the past output or the goals of the system. With higher order systems that monitor error from their goals, feedback is invaluable in error correction, as when you get a poor grade on an exam. In lower level systems that lack error correction or monitoring, feedback can either increase the amplitude of output or decrease the amplitude. In families, we are mainly concerned with goal-oriented systems, so negative feedback dampens deviations from the goal, and positive feedback amplifies deviations for the goal.

Variety

All systems have degrees of *variety.* Variety in a system refers to the extent to which the system has the resources to meet new environmental demands or adapt to changes. A system that has a large array of diverse resources would have more options (variety) available to meet the diverse adaptations required by a dynamically changing environment. Some systems may lack the requisite variety to adapt to changes. For example, a family with rigid rules may lack the flexibility to adapt to changes such as a daughter wanting to marry someone from another religion or race. The lack of variety in such a rigid family might result in a rupture to the family system because it is unable to adapt to this change.

Equilibrium

Equilibrium refers to a balance of inputs and outputs. For example, most families require a balance of income and expenditures. A family system can also be described as *homeostatic*. A homeostatic system dynamically maintains equilibrium by feedback and control. A physical example of a homeostatic device is a thermostat; an organic example is the dynamic maintenance of your body temperature within fairly limited parameters. A family may maintain its dynamic equilibrium by using its resources to maintain its rules. For example, a family that goes camping in Alaska might purchase sleeping shades so it can maintain the rule that everyone is to go to sleep by 8:30 p.m. even in the land of the midnight sun. As you can see, homeostasis is neither inherently good nor bad but describes the manner in which equilibrium is maintained over time.

System Levels

Systems have *levels*. A first-order system is simply composed of environmental input filtered through the system's rules of transformation and exiting as output into the environment. There is no method of control or error correction within the system. Feedback is from the output of the system as it affects the environment and then reenters the system as input. A second-order system (and all higher order systems) has a *comparator* that monitors the output and compares the output to the goals of the system. If the comparator computes an error, it then corrects the first-order (level) rules of transformation. A simple example of a comparator is a thermostat. A thermostat set at 70 °F that senses that the ambient air temperature is 60 °F should attempt to correct by turning on the furnace. We will provide a family-oriented example of these second-order control systems shortly.

Subsystems

Not only do systems have various levels but they may also contain subsystems. For example, one way of viewing the family system is that it contains sibling subsystems, marital subsystems, and parent-child subsystems. Each of these subsystems could be further analyzed in terms of subsystems. In general, a subsystem is a part of a system that is analyzed separately as to its exchanges with the system and other subsystems. Some system characteristics, such as the control system discussed earlier, can emerge only with a system that has two subsystems, one containing rules of transformation and the other comparing output with the goal of the system. For example, a thermostatic system can be broken into one subsystem that performs heating, including elements such as the furnace and ducts, and another subsystem that senses the air temperature and turns the heater on if the temperature is not within the goal parameters. In a family system, we might see the parental subsystem as the control subsystem. It must be kept in mind, however, that subsystems, like systems, are intellectual ways of understanding and analyzing our world. There are many ways to conceptualize subsystems and systems in families, and some serve one purpose better than others, but none is "true." They have heuristic value but no "ontological" reality.

Propositions

Systems theorists, such as Mesarovic (1970) and Miller (1978), have offered general propositions regarding the behavior of systems. These propositions, because of their necessary abstractness and generality, are less immediately applicable to the study of the family than are several applications of systems theory to the family, such as Kantor and Lehr's (1975); Wilkinson's (1977); Burr, Day, and Bahr's (1993); and Broderick's (1993). In this section, we incorporate some of the more abstract propositions but especially concentrate on examples of propositions that are directly applicable to the study of the family.

As far as we know, all family systems theorists conceptualize the family as a goal-oriented system with a control subsystem (comparator). Broderick and Smith (1979) talked about this as a Level 2, or cybernetic, system. Most scholars conceptualize the family as having many more levels of control than just one. Perhaps an example will make this clear.

Jack and Jan now have a 3-year-old who is in the process of developmentally "dropping" her afternoon nap. This has made the family rule of a 7 p.m. bedtime even more important for both Jack and Jan. Jack is putting his overtired and cranky daughter to bed when she rebels and begins to throw a screaming tantrum about not going to bed. Jack first tries to manage the rule breaking by increasing the level of threats and punishments, threatening to close the door if she doesn't settle down. The tantrum continues until Jack realizes that by continuing to "follow the rule," he is escalating the conflict. He is getting farther from the important goal of making sure his daughter gets some sleep. He takes his daughter out of bed. Holding his daughter in his arms, he rocks and sings to her, and the exhausted little girl is asleep in a few seconds.

This example illustrates several important concepts in systems theory, such as variety, goals, and control. The initial rule of the system was set by the first-order goal of "7 p.m. bedtime." But this first-order goal was actually deduced from a higher order goal of "ensuring their daughter gets sufficient rest." Likewise, ensuring their daughter gets sufficient rest is deduced from a much higher order goal of "being good parents." What happened in the example is that Jack attempted to correct the negative feedback (error from the initial 7 p.m. bedtime), but his correction by enforcing the rules produced positive feedback (amplified the deviation from the goal) and more error. As a result, Jack changed control levels to "check" what was wrong. What was wrong was that with an overly tired child, tantrums are positive feedback loops, and the way to break those loops is less enforcement of the Level 1 rule. In other words, the way you achieve the goal of rest for the child is by not enforcing the Level 1 goal of the 7 p.m. bedtime. This example also shows that if Jack lacked the requisite variety to change behaviors in midstream, he would have been trapped in his daughter's positive feedback loop.

What theoretical propositions does systems theory supply to help us understand our example? Miller (1978) suggested that the greater the number of channels for processing information in a structurally differentiated living system, the less the strains and tensions among subsystems. Miller's proposition would seem to illustrate just one advantage to variety in a system, however. Wilkinson (1977) stated a similar proposition using the concept of variety:

The adaptability and therefore viability of a (family) system (as contrasted to rigidity and vulnerability) is positively related to the amount of variety in the system.

In addition,

The adaptability and therefore viability of a (family) system (as contrasted to rigidity and vulnerability) is related negatively to conflict and tension in the system.

These two general propositions help us identify that in Jack's family system, variety is related to the dampening of tension. This general proposition does not, however, entirely capture the process in our example whereby Jack reassessed and corrected his behavior in relation to his daughter by reference to higher order goals. Both Mesarovic (1970) for general systems and Broderick (1993) for family systems clarified this point, and Broderick added a further proposition that is useful in this regard. Broderick proposed that family goals are organized into hierarchies:

Higher level goals define the priorities among lower level goals and are intrinsically less likely to be revised and abandoned. (p. 43)

According to this proposition, the variety of a system is positively related to the number of levels of the system. This explains why Jack was guided by one set of goals over another and suggests how he could reassess the utility of lower level goals by comparing them and the output with the higher level system goal of sleep for his daughter.

It would be somewhat misleading to portray most of the explanatory work by systems theorists as being incorporated in theoretical propositions such as the ones we have identified above. Much of the "explanation" provided by systems theorists is by means of flow charts or diagrams. Despite the often-heard claim that systems theory provides an approach that is nonlinear, most of the diagrams and the solutions to systems equations are by means of either linear algebra or linear programming.

Figure 6.1 represents a simplified comparator or Level 2 control system. In this figure, information is expressed as signal quantities, and these signals are transformed by transformation functions (in boxes). We could also express what is going on in this system as a series of functional transformations of the initial signal entering the system from the environment. When the environmental signal (I_{e1}) enters the system, it is transformed by the receiver (r). After the receiver function, the signal becomes system input (I_s) rather than environmental input (I_{e1}). The system input enters the rules of transformation and then becomes system output (O_s) until it is transformed by the sender function (s) to be sent into the environment (O_{e1}). The system output is also sent to the comparator for monitoring against the goals (g) of the system. The comparator compares the goals against the output. This output would be Jack's escalation of his punishments and thus keeping his daughter awake by trying to put her to bed. This is then subtracted from the goal signal (g) of a good rest for the child. A positive or negative result from the comparator is error (e). The error message is then used to change or modify the input into the system or to modify the rules of transformation. The resulting message is then transformed by the sender function (s) for certain channels and enters the environment as output (O_{e1}) from the system. At this point, Jack decided to enforce the bedtime by threats and punishments. The environment transforms the output (O_{e1}) so that it is changed to another quantity (I_{e1}), and the sequence is reiterated. The child, already in an irrational state, saw Jack's behavior as further reason to be upset. The environmentally transformed output of the system is joined with other systematic signals from the environment and random noise to compose the totality of the environmental input back into the system (I_{e1}). The example of Jack and his daughter did not contain a lot of other systematic signals (such as visitors in the house), and other sorts of random interferences were not a question. Therefore, most of the environmental input (I_{e1}) was from the daughter's tantrum.

To use a diagram such as the one in Figure 6.1 to explain higher order goals, we would have to add a linkage where the error signal (e) becomes input to an even higher level comparator containing a higher order goal that is not included in the simplified version in Figure 6.1. In our example, the higher order goal was getting sufficient rest for the child. The Level 1 rule of transformation was a 7 p.m. bedtime. When a higher level comparator compares the error with its goal, it may send an error message to change the lower order rule of transformation or even a lower order goal. This is commonly called recalibration. Every time you turn the heat up on

Figure 6.1   A Level II Comparator System

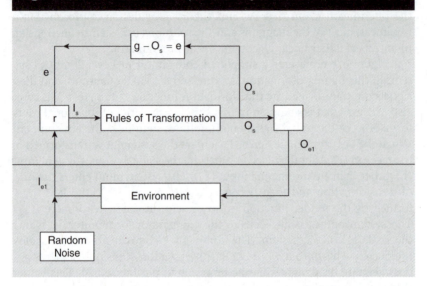

the thermostat in your house, you (a higher order goal system) recalibrate the goal in the lower order thermostat in a way similar to what Jack did.

The model in Figure 6.1 seems very appealing. We can follow a sequence of events and paths and feel we "understand" what is happening. Furthermore, if we could identify all the mathematical functions indicated by the boxes, we could know exactly how any message or signal (indicated by the lines) would be produced. Indeed, any system could be represented by a group of linear or dynamic equations. This approach, first suggested by Rapoport (1960, as cited in Broderick & Smith, 1979), has been used to investigate marital inter-action (Cook et al., 1995).

There are differences in the type of explanation afforded by using systems diagrams rather than systems propositions. Although much of the thinking and analysis are similar, the two provide very different explanations because the questions each addresses are distinctively different. The systems diagrams address the question of *how* the process works, whereas the systems theory propositions address *why* the system works as it does. In general, this is the distinction between *modeling,* which supplies an analog of how things operate, and *theory,* which explains why things work in this way. Systems diagrams have proven popular because they allow us to visualize and simplify complex processes. According to one theory of knowledge (epistemology), the operations (or how) question is all we need to know, and the *why* question represents a very limited "billiard ball" understanding of causation. As we shall see, von Glasersfeld's (1987) catholic, constructivist view of knowledge as multiple models fits this operationalist epistemology. This basic distinction, however, gives rise to some significant variation among systems theorists as to the type and form of the explanation. Furthermore, as we will find later, this constructivist epistemology is a prime target for critics of systems theory who say that systems theory is not a theory at all but simply a general model.

Variations

This section covers three of the major variants in family systems theory. There are many variants of systems theory, but we limit our discussion to what we regard as the three dominant approaches. The first of these is a general systems approach to the family. This approach tends to include use of the full arsenal of systems concepts and tools. Second, we examine family communications theory. And last, we examine family process theory, in which unique constructs for extending and modifying the systems approach have been developed, particularly for the use of family therapists. Although there are many other ways to cluster the theoretical variants in family systems, such as those using mechanical, organic, or cybernetic analogs, we feel that these other approaches would less accurately represent the true nature of the variation in family systems theory.

General Systems Theory

Broderick and Smith (1979) provided a sound introduction to the ways that systems thinking might be applied to the study of the family. Their presentation can be characterized as "cautiously optimistic." These authors suggested that family systems are minimally cybernetic, or control, systems with at least two levels. For example, they provide an introductory analysis of a family system as a four-level system in which the first level has an environmental feedback loop, the second level (cybernetic) has a comparator for error detection and correction, the third level (morphogenesis) has a higher level comparator allowing for control of lower levels, and the fourth level (conversion) is the highest level goal system; if goals are changed at this level, all lower level systems are changed. More detailed models might have six or seven levels, as William Powers (1974) found necessary in his application of systems theory to individual psychological systems. Broderick and Smith (1979) were cautious to make limited claims for the application of general systems theory. They call it an "approach" rather than a "theory," responding to the perception that it largely offers models rather than theoretical propositions. They viewed attempts to produce propositions from systems theory, such as by Wilkinson (1977), as "premature." In part, their caution and judgment are due to the point in time at which they authored their contribution, but subsequent developments have not provided much more than was available in 1979 (e.g., Miller, 1978; Wilkinson, 1977). Moreover, Broderick and Smith (1979) seemed to approach systems theory with the positivistic, axiomatic notion of theory rather than the operationalist view currently touted by most systems theorists. This undoubtedly adds to their caution in regard to the promise of systems theory. Yet to date, Broderick and Smith's (1979) statement remains one of the better outlines for the application of general systems theory to the family.

Neo-Functional Systems

A general system theory application to the family developed out of the waning influence of a functionalist perspective that dominated the literature during the mid 20th century. A functional approach to the family also saw the family as a system but a more simplistic mechanical or organic system that was value laden by the existing cultural norms around the gendered division of labor in the home and marketplace. Talcott Parsons was a major proponent using functionalism to explain family behavior. Attempts to integrate general systems theory concepts with functional is refereed to as neo-functionalism.

Parsons pursued his early studies in both Great Britain and Germany. He was clearly influenced by the classical theorists in sociological theory, such as Weber and Durkheim (see Parsons, 1937). This influence was both substantive and methodological. Substantively, Parsons was concerned with incorporating individual meaning (Weber) with the need for social systems to maintain order (Durkheim). Methodologically, Parsons believed in the desirability and possibility of a "grand theory" of social systems that would be encompassing and explanatory. Most of Parsons's work was produced while he was at Harvard University's Social Relations department from 1927 until his death. During this time, Parsons's work became the most widely read and accepted theoretical framework in the social sciences, and later the most criticized. There is no doubt whatsoever that Parsons's work has had a profound, deep, and continuing influence on the thinking of contemporary social scientists. It is also interesting that Parsons produced numerous essays and one book (*Family, Socialization and Interactional Process*, with Robert Bales, 1955) on the family. Although one could argue that many of the classical grand theorists paid scant attention to the family, Parsons would not be counted among these.

Parsons's perspective on the family is best understood within the architecture of his larger theory of social systems. Parsons divided up the social world into three systems. The cultural system is composed of shared symbols and meanings. The social system is composed of organized social groups and institutions. Finally, the personality system is composed of the species generic types of personalities. For Parsons, much of the personality system was drawn from Freudian psychoanalysis. The great bulk of Parsons's thinking was devoted to the social system. His work on family, however, also encompassed the socialization processes needed for the social system and the ways in which the integration of adult individuals into the group or social system maintained the institutional social system (see Parsons & Bales, 1955; Turner, 1991, p. 61).

Parsons (1937, 1951) argued that every social system needed to achieve a state of order or system equilibrium. Subsystems such as institutions functioned to assist in achieving this system order. He posited four "functional imperatives" that all systems require: adaptation, goal attainment, integration, and latency (or maintenance of morale and motivation). This system of functions is commonly referred to by the acronym A-G-I-L. Every system must have subsystems that function for the adaptation of the system. Every system must satisfy the goals of the system and must integrate its members. Finally, every system must ensure that motivation for action (latency) remains above a certain level.

Parsons's major work on the family resides in his essays in the Parsons and Bales (1955) book on the family. Parsons suggests that the basic and irreducible functions of the family are two: the primary socialization of children so that they can truly become members of the society into which they have been born; and second, the stabilization of the adult personalities of the population of the society.

Although much of functional thinking lay dormant during the decade of the 1970s, the 1980s began to see a resurgence of interest in functionalism. Jeffrey Alexander (1985) was one of those who helped create the perception that functional explanations had acquired new life in the form of neofunctionalism. There is some debate as to how well the moniker of "functionalism" actually fits this movement. For example, Turner (1991) observes that the notion that functions are to have consequences for system needs is lacking in these statements. But notions of system needs and requisites are what make functional analysis unique and distinctive; if one simply removes them from analysis, then the approach is no longer functional. Thus, to some extent, neofunctionalism is nonfunctionalism.

Neofunctionalists seemed largely unperturbed by such criticisms. In the area of family studies, Kingsbury and Scanzoni (1993) resurrected the functionalist paradigm. Their approach was to outline the many areas in which functionalism had made significant contributions to our thinking about families and larger social systems. They did not directly confront critiques of functionalist thinking as tautological and circular, nor did they resurrect debates over the logic of functionalism and functional alternatives. Rather, in their overview, Kingsbury and Scanzoni attempted to reacquaint family scholars with the rich potential for functionalist approaches to the family.

The success of this reawakening is most obvious in the recent work by Don Swenson (2004). Swenson attempts to unite the diverse family theoretical frameworks, as found in the work of White and Klein (2002), through the unifying lens of functionalism. Although Swenson uses Parsons's body of work as his major source for functionalism, there are some major omissions of what some scholars might regard as critical elements of Parsonian thinking. For example, there is virtually no discussion of Parsons's functional imperatives and the A-G-I-L categories. On the other hand, Swenson does not shy away from the notion that families provide functions both for the social system and for individual needs. However, these needs are only partially discussed in Parsonian terms. Swenson adds to the functionalist view of the family and the 50 years of empirical research and middle-range theory development that have taken place since Parsons first elaborated his functional theory of the family. In addition to the traditional Parsonian role structure of the family, we also find that Swenson has incorporated middle-range theories, such as attachment theory, to enhance the explanatory value of the functional argument. There is little doubt that Swenson would not fit the Turner (1991) accusation of being a "nonfunctionalist" because he clearly deals with functional explanations within the family and between the family and larger systems. Swenson builds on the systemic aspects of neofunctionalism in his integrative work on religion and family (Swenson, 2008). He makes the argument that systems theory is a part of neofunctionalism that is consistent with Parsons's later work (1977). Indeed, Swenson states that systems theory is more central to his theory than all other features. Currently, there is no doubt that Swenson provides the clearest statement and application of neofunctionalist explanations available to family scholars and researchers.

Communications Theory

Communications theory originates with the work by Shannon and Weaver (1949) titled *The Mathematical Theory of Communication*. The mathematical theory of signal communications is complemented and extended by work in the area of automata and cybernetics. The particular path on which this work entered family studies was mainly from the concerns about family communications raised by Bateson, Jackson, and others at the Mental Research Institute (MRI) in Palo Alto, California, during the late 1950s (Bateson et al., 1956). Family process theory, our third variant, shares this common ancestry with family communications. Unlike family process theory, the study of family communications largely became the focus of those in the then-emerging academic field of communications studies.

The field of communications uses a basic sender-receiver model of communications. Although there are many variants of the model, the basic elements are contained in Figure 6.2.

Figure 6.2   Sender-Receiver Communications Model

Sender	Message	Receiver
Meaning ——→ Encoding ——→	Verbal & ——→ Nonverbal Channels	Decoding ——→ Meaning
Selection		Selection

To understand Figure 6.2, let's follow a simple message through the model. Jack wants to tell Jan that he loves her. Of all the possible messages he could send to Jan, the meaning he selects to send is "I love you." The next step is that Jack must select the type of encoding most appropriate for the message. There are two types of codes, *digital* and *analog*. An analog message bears a resemblance to that for which it stands. Thus, analog codes have a degree of *isomorphy*, or similarity, to the object, idea, or feeling they represent. For example, in many film or theater productions, actors fool you by making their behavior similar to a person in love. A "picture of an apple" is an analog code for an actual apple. Digital codes, on the other hand, are arbitrary assignments that receive their communications effectiveness by consensus or agreement. For example, children often play games with the arbitrary character of language by getting everyone to agree that no means yes and yes means no, and "Now, let's ask Dad for ice cream cones." Arabic numerals provide another example: 2 bears no resemblance to *two* things, nor does the sound have any inherent "twoness" to it.

Returning to our example, if Jack selects a digital code, it will most likely carry accurate, commonly agreed-on information but will probably not carry much of the affect intended in his sentiment of I love you. Indeed, imagine a completely digital message, such as Morse code, carrying the message *I love you*—not much affect there! If Jack is an effective communicator, he will select either both types of encoding or the more affectual analog codes.

The selection of the code directly affects Jack's choice of channels. Nonverbal channels are most appropriate for analog codes (Gottman, 1979; Mehrabian, 1972). Verbal and written channels are most appropriate for digital codes. If Jack is going to write Jan a letter saying "I love you," he will most likely embellish it with metaphor and other techniques to carry more affect or rely on Hallmark to come up with the correctly packaged digital communication. On the other hand, if Jack sees Jan face-to-face, he will probably use analog and digital codes carried on nonverbal and verbal channels simultaneously. Not only do multiple channels carry both affective and cognitive dimensions of a message, but they provide message *redundancy* as well so that if noise interferes with one channel, the message will get through on another. For example, if Jack is holding Jan's hand, gazing lovingly into her eyes, and smiling, the fact that an airplane flying overhead obliterates the sound of his words, I love you, may not result in loss of the message.

Jan must have the appropriate sense receptors to receive the channels on which the message is sent (Figure 6.2). For example, if Jan hears a noise and is distracted from Jack's nonverbal message and if, in addition, the noise drowns out Jack's verbal message, then much of the message is lost because of poor reception. Once the channels are accurately received, to get the message as Jack sent it, Jan must decode in the same way in which Jack encoded. A far-fetched example of decoding error would be if Jack meant his eye gaze to carry the analog affect of "love" but Jan decoded his "blinking" as something caught in his eye. Once the decoding occurs, then Jan must select from among the repertoire of possible "meanings" of messages she expects from Jack. If Jack and Jan had been married only a short time, the probability of decoding and selecting the message I love you might be fairly high. Finally, feedback in this model is simply where Jan becomes the sender and Jack the receiver. Perhaps in response to Jack's message of love, Jan will send Jack the digital message "ditto."

The complexity of the processes in the basic communications diagram is enormous. Most scholars focus on the most directly measurable and observable part of the process, which is the message. Great strides in the study of marital interaction have been made by studying gender differences in decoding verbal and nonverbal messages. For example, Gottman and Porterfield (1981) reported that dissatisfied husbands are poor decoders of their wives' nonverbal messages. Many researchers have also worked on the sequential dependencies between husband and wife messages (Gottman, 1979). The research in this area has reached such magnitude that there are several excellent reviews of the marital interaction literature, such as Noller and Fitzpatrick (1993) and, most recently, Gottman and Notarius (2000). This area continues to be one of the most active and encouraging areas of scientific research of all the variants of systems theory.

Family Process Theory

For the most part, family process theory can be identified with the more applied practitioners and therapists studying the family. As we have previously noted, scholars such as Bateson and Jackson had very tangible concerns, such as the treatment of schizophrenia (Bateson et al., 1956). The tangible interests giving impetus to such scholars should, however, in no way demean their theoretical contributions. After all, before a therapist can effectively treat a psychopathology, he or she must have some idea of the causative factors. Recent contributions (e.g., Day, 2005; Day, Gavazzi, & Acock, 2001) have been more concerned with family stress and how families cope with stressors.

Several theorists such as Broderick (1993) have contributed to family process theory. This work built on earlier contributions from family process theorists, such as Kantor and Lehr (1975). All this work views the family as a goal-seeking system. Much of the family process system, however, is devoted to maintaining social and spatial relationships within the family and between the family and the environment. Within the family, social and spatial relationships between dyads must be managed so that individuals are protected from each other's demands (buffering) and individuals are linked to each other (bonding). The relations between the family and its environment are composed of transactions that bridge and link the family to external systems while maintaining the boundaries of the family system. Broderick's (1993) view of the family system is one of the most ambitious to date because he sought to identify both internal and external relationships.

Another influential process theorist has been Pauline Boss (1999, 2002), who explored ambiguity in family system boundaries as a crucial concept. Her work links systems theory to family stress, which we noted in Chapter 5 has also been an important idea in developmental theories. In systems theories, stress on a family may be random or situationally induced, whereas in developmental theory, the stress is always experienced in connection with socially based life course expectations with which families are off time or on time. Recent examples of family process theory to guide research have been in the areas of child trauma within the context of parental incarceration and maternal incarceration's effect on child well-being (Arditti, 2012, 2015).

Because many family process theorists are also immersed in the treatment of psychopathology, in some senses, the theories they have constructed are more theories of family therapy than of the family. The emphasis to scientifically test claims may seem less important than if the theory "works" in the therapeutic situation. This has led to family process theory being considered metaphorical. Because so much of family process theory is concerned with applications, much of it strays from the precision we would seek in scientific theory and is more focused on guiding metaphors. For example, Minuchin (1974) developed the notion that boundaries are critical in distinguishing pathologies in families. He pioneered aspects of family process theory linked to distance regulation and closeness and coined the term *enmeshment* to describe these processes. Nowhere, however, did Minuchin provide a systematic definition of his concept of boundaries. Indeed, terms such as *enmeshment, bounding,* and *buffering* offer sensitizing metaphors for the clinician (e.g., Rosenblatt, 1994). These metaphors are similar to the ones offered by psychotherapists, such as Carl Rogers, Jung, and Freud. They may prove useful in the formulation of more rigorous scientific and theoretical concepts, but this development will never happen if family process scholars are content to view these collections of metaphors as "theory."

Social Network Analysis

Social network analysis provides an example of the structural functionalist connection to systems theory. The historical roots of this theoretical-methodological approach can be traced back to Simmel, Le Play, and Durkheim as each attempted to understand and explain the social interaction they studied in a broader context. Scott (2013) suggests there are three main traditions that converged into contemporary social analysis: the sociometric analysts whose study of small groups developed advanced methods, using their graph theory; the 1930s researchers who focused on the formation of cliques and studied interpersonal interaction; and the social anthropologists who synthesized the previous two positions in order to study human interaction at the tribal and village level. From the structural functionalist line came Canadian psychologist Elizabeth Bott. Her doctoral work examined the family and social networks of British families (1957). It is important to see that although she focused heavily on the idea of gender roles and norms, she understood the family to be influenced at several social levels as well as referring to the family as "a social system." She understood that her small homogeneous sample of mainly English urban working-class Protestants did not represent all families, but they did represent some families and provide a foundation for further family-based network analysis research by highlighting the importance of physical proximity, type of family relationship, and the connectedness of the kinship network in determining the impact of those networks. That research was built upon by Milardo, who applied network analysis to a variety of family-centered topics, including the implication to social networks after divorce (1987) and a general discussion of the theory as it applies to families (1988), as well as several works discussing the implication of networks on union formation (1982, 1987, 2005). Application has been made to the study of extended kinship networks (2005, 2010). Others have attempted to integrate social network analysis with attachment theory (Gillath & Karantzas, 2015; Gillath, Karantzas, & Selecuk, 2017).

The use of social network analysis seems well suited for the study of both extended kinship networks and the influence of social connection on nuclear families. Despite this apparent fit, the application of this approach to the family is still limited but active. Some recent areas of research have focused on mental health recovery (Pernice-Duca, 2010), parenting (Cochran & Niego, 2002), and marital and family satisfaction (Hostetler, Desrochers, Kopko, & Moen, 2012).

Empirical Applications

Marital and Family Communications

Systems theory has proven to be the major conceptual framework used by both practitioners and researchers. As we have seen, the systems approach first entered family studies through the work of therapists such as Don Jackson, who was very concerned with the family system of communications. This impetus later bifurcated into the two variants of communications theory and family process theory. A chronological thread will be used to present relevant application of systems theory first from the research perspective followed by an intervention overview. It should be noted that both utilize the theory in a symbiotic way. Much of the family-based systems theory research has its roots in therapy-based applications. Academic research based on family systems theory is then applied in therapeutic settings. This is evident in the three areas discussed below: marital and family communication, family adjustment, and the adaptation and response model, as well as the circumplex model.

From the outset, systems ideas and ideas from communications theory were fused because a communications system is simply one type of general system. Researchers in the 1960s had been guided by the early work of Bateson et al. (1956). Following in this tradition is the work by the MRI group of Watzlawick, Beavin, and Jackson (1967). This book goes far beyond earlier explorations into systems theory by Jackson (e.g., 1974). Its major contribution is to introduce family scholars to communications theory and to establish a systematic approach to the encoding and decoding of both nonverbal and verbal messages. Many of the suggestions in this work regarding nonverbal communications were simultaneously developed by an independent group of scholars in psychology led by Mehrabian and Wiener (1968).

In 1968, Mishler and Waxler published their now classic study on family processes, *Interaction in Families*. In their research, they examined patterns of marital and family communications and the possible linkage to schizophrenia. Their empirical work raised significant doubts about the double-bind hypothesis (Bateson et al., 1956) but at the same time demonstrated how complex questions about family communications patterns could be scientifically studied. Indeed, their finding—that families containing a schizophrenic child showed more orderly patterns of interaction than the chaotic patterns of interruption and lack of rule following demonstrated by "normal" families—turned previous suppositions on their head. Mishler and Waxler's conclusions exemplified scientific caution; they pointed out that they could not determine from their research whether the interaction patterns in the families with a schizophrenic child were the cause of the child's problem or the effect of the family's adjustment to the child's problem.

Building on the contributions of Watzlawick and colleagues (1967) as well as Mishler and Waxler (1968), in *Communication, Conflict, and Marriage,* Raush, Barry, Hertel, and Swain (1974) developed the sender-receiver model as a system of contingencies. These authors proposed that marital interaction was a system in which the next action of the husband toward the wife was contingent on the previous message the wife sent to the husband. Because messages are behavior, this model could be examined as a time series of spousal behavioral contingencies. A simplistic example of this process is if a husband is nasty to a wife, the "reciprocity" model of contingencies would predict that she would be nasty in return.

Although this notion seems somewhat obvious common sense, it turns out to be largely untrue. It is addressed in a much more sophisticated formulation by Gottman, Markman, and Notarius (1977) and later by Gottman (1979). Their approach was to test the contingencies between spousal verbal and nonverbal messages over time using a series of contingent probabilities (a discrete-state Markov chain). Their findings are important. They found that the emotional affect carried in nonverbal messages is a better discriminator of distressed from nondistressed couples than more traditional verbal measures, such as spousal agreement. Second, they found little support for a simple quid pro quo, or spousal reciprocity, hypothesis. The patterns of marital interaction over a series of time points showed that research in this area is both complex and worthwhile. For John Gottman, this has become a programmatic theme in his research, culminating in the identification of specific patterns of interaction that lead to couple disintegration and to the specification of causes for these patterns (e.g., Gottman, 1979, 1993, 1994; Gottman & Krokoff, 1989; Gottman & Levenson, 1992; Gottman et al., 1977; Gottman & Notarius, 2000; Gottman & Porterfield, 1981; Levenson & Gottman, 1983). This program of research has certainly resulted in a much better understanding of the behavioral contingencies between marital partners. Indeed, Gottman claimed that researchers can now predict with great accuracy whether or not relationships will fail (see Gottman, Coan, Carrere, & Sawnason, 1998; Gottman & Levenson, 1992).

Gottman's work remains strongly moored to the measurement of behavior rather than attitudes and beliefs. As a result of this focus, he has largely ignored questions about message reception and perception. Mary Ann Fitzpatrick (1988), in her book *Between Husbands and Wives,* studied some of the verbal and nonverbal codes tied to disclosure and intimacy for traditional and nontraditional marriage. Her work and that of her colleague, Patricia Noller (1984), culminated in a joint project providing a systematic overview of communication in the family (Noller & Fitzpatrick, 1993). More recently, Koerner and Fitzpatrick (2002) have developed a two-dimensional conceptual typology to assess family communication. This model categorizes families on the dimensions of communication frequency and behavioral conformity. Such typologies are not new to family communications since David Olson (e.g., Olson, 1995) developed his now classic and well-accepted circumplex model. Although there remain significant unresolved theoretical problems in family communications, there can be little doubt that scholars studying communications systems have provided clear examples of the force and utility of a systems approach for the scientific study of the family. Researchers such as Olson, McCubbin, and Patterson have incorporated the communication literature into their own family systems models.

Circumplex Model

The circumplex model of family system mapping was developed by David Olson. The examination of multiple family health research findings led Olson to identify three dimensions of family functioning: cohesion, flexibility (adaptability), and communication (Olson, Sprenkle, & Russell, 1979). Cohesion and flexibility are the two dimensions that, when overlaid on each other, form the basis of the model. Each dimension is made up of five levels that intersect one another to form three main family types: balanced, midrange, and unbalanced. The intersection of these two dimensions creates 25 potential classifications. The cohesion scale, placed on the x-axis, begins with the label *of disconnected, somewhat connected, connected, very connected*, and last, *overly connected.* The flexibility dimension is located on the y-axis and is labeled *inflexible, somewhat flexible, flexible, very flexible*, and finally, *overflexible.* The center nine values form the balanced family types, the extreme four corners represent the unbalanced types, and the remaining 12 types represented around the perimeter are the midrange families. The cohesion dimension is a measure of physical and emotional closeness demonstrated by the family at the time of assessment. The flexibility dimension measures the ability of the family to adjust and adapt to different roles and changing family norms. Communication, the third dimension, facilitates change across time and incorporates much of the communication research discussed in the previous section. The circumplex model is more focused on avoiding extremes of family behavior than it is in establishing an ideal type. The model incorporates changing needs of flexibility and closeness across the life course of the family. It is also ideally suited to address divergent ethnic norms regarding family behavior. The main hypothesis of the circumplex model according to Olson is that balanced levels of cohesion and flexibility are most conducive to healthy family functioning. Conversely, unbalanced levels of cohesion and flexibility (very low or very high levels) are associated with problematic family functioning (2011).

The work of David Olson and his circumplex model provides an excellent example of how research and practice come together. A widely used application of a family systems approach, PREPARE/ENRICH, will be used to illustrate this fact. This tool uses the circumplex model to help couples explore relationship strength as well as areas for growth. Imbedded in the tool are aids to help strengthen communication skills via enhanced listening and conflict resolution training. It is available through a wide variety of delivery sources. The tool is often administered by certified family life educators, family therapists, and social service agencies as well as a broad cross section of religious representatives. The research findings that utilize the circumplex model show that the model is able to accurately predict distressed couples. The model has also produced findings that correlate elevated risks of domestic family violence among poorer functioning couples (Asai & Olson, 2003) and has been shown to adapt to cultural differences as well (Asai & Olson, 2004; Rada & Olson, 2016). The therapist addresses imbalances in the system by helping couples or families move to more balanced levels of cohesion and adaptability. For some families, this might entail learning to regard family rules as less important. In other families, it might entail helping the family to become more organized. Olson's systemic approach has a broad range of life course applications, from dating to elderly families, including families of orientation as well as procreation. His work stands as one of the most popular of the systems approaches and one of the better examples of the fusion of science with therapy.

FAAR, Resiliency, and Stress

The family adjustment and adaptation model builds on Hill's ABC-X model discussed in the previous chapter. McCubbin and Patterson (1982, 1983) expanded Hill's model to include the systemic concept of feedback in their double ABC-X model. Their model is multivariate, incorporating various levels of analysis, including the individual, family, and society. The model makes the assumption that families go through a cyclical process of adjustment, crisis, and adaptation. Cyclical models typically assume linear progression from one stage to the next. McCubbin and Patterson feel that this may not always be the case for families dealing with crisis. They suggest that families may stagnate or regress before successfully dealing with the stressors. The family adjustment and adaptation response model (FAAR) shifted the focus of family stress from family weaknesses to family strengths. This change in emphasis to positive qualities, such as coping skills, led to a focus on family interaction and shared meaning as the basis for family health. The FAAR model was a direct result of this change in focus (Patterson, 1988, 1989, 1993, 2002; Patterson & Garwick, 1994). McCubbin and McCubbin (1987) extended the double ABC-X model to develop the typology model of family adjustment and adaptation. Weber (2011) sees this model as a synthesis of the double ABC-X model and the two phases of adjustment and adaptation from the original FAAR model. Patterns of family functioning were identified and classified as typologies. These typologies included the regenerative, resilient, and rhythmatic.

Constructs of cohesion, hardiness, bonding, and flexibility are jointly reflected in the FAAR and circumplex models described below and pay tribute to the joint work of David Olson and the McCubbins (Olson & McCubbin, 1982; Olson, Russell, & Sprenkle, 1983)

The resiliency model of family stress, adjustment, and adaptation was a further iteration of the FAAR model (McCubbin & McCubbin, 1993). The concept of family resiliency resulted from a change in focus on negative aspects of family dysfunction to positive qualities of healthy family functioning. Positive coping skills were identified as playing a role in buffering the negative implication of change and stress while contributing to healthy adaptation and adjustment at the same time. Why some families were better able to weather the storms of stress and crisis motivated both practitioners and researchers to explore the concepts of resilience and resiliency. McCubbin and McCubbin (1988) define family resiliency as "characteristics, dimensions, and properties of families which help families be resistant to disruptions in the face of change and adaptive in the face of crisis situations" (p. 247). Walsh (2016) defined it as "the ability of a family, as a functional system, to withstand and rebound from adversity" (p. 14). Resiliency and stress research continued to build momentum in the new century. Boss (2002) felt she had traversed the gap to a postmodern approach to family stress and resiliency while Patterson (2002) helped integrate the research and practitioner's conceptual understanding of resiliency. Walsh has developed a tool to operationalize family stress (2016). The Walsh Family Stress Questionnaire is made up of nine processes clustered into three dimensions. The three dimensions are composed of belief systems, organizational processes, and communication processes. Belief systems measure the way families make sense of adversity, how positive an outlook they have in life, and the family's approach to higher powers or transcendence. The organizational process theme measures family flexibility, connectedness, and levels of social and financial capital. The final theme, communication processes, accesses clarity of communication, emotional expression, and problem-solving skills and approaches. The questionnaire has demonstrated validity and reliability in a number of studies including a family's dealing with breast cancer (e.g., Lane, Meszaros, & Savla, 2016). Family resilience literature continues to proliferate in major family journals with research represented by diverse disciplines. Comparative and cross-cultural studies of family resiliency help expand the application and understanding of the role of resiliency beyond the North American context.

In summary, systems theory is a broad concept that is conceptualized and operationalized in a variety of ways. Systems theory as applied to the family has been used to study family and marital communication as well as stress and resiliency. The family systems concept continues to be used to guide research from a variety of disciplines. Recently, it has been applied to the study of communication with cancer-affected families (Harris et al.,

2010); youth obesity (Kitzman-Ulrich et al., 2010); and the role of families in critical nursing care (Leon & Knapp, 2008), just to name a few. The challenge for current family systems theory research remains the same as always. Researchers need to move beyond the heuristic aspect of the systems model and develop propositions and hypotheses that can be tested. In this way, the theoretical value of family systems theory will be advanced.

Critiques and Discussion

Without a doubt, the criticism of systems theory that has the potential to be the most damaging is that it is, in truth, a "model" or "flow chart approach" rather than a theory. Critics charge that even the concepts in systems theory, such as variety and feedback, are more heuristic than theoretical. These concepts lack any real substantive content, compared with concepts such as power and consensus in other theories. Critics also argue that systems approaches using mathematical models (e.g., Markov models in Gottman, 1979, and Raush et al., 1974) may seem to provide prediction, but they do not succeed. The critics make a distinction between *forecasting*, which, as in weather forecasting, is simply based on past records, and *prediction*, which is a deduction from a set of substantive theoretical propositions. Even Gottman's work would not be immune from such criticisms because there are few, if any, theoretical propositions from which to deduce marital outcomes.

Systems advocates argue that the accusation that the systems approach is a model and not a theory is tenable only if one adopts a specific view (epistemology) of how science works. The traditional model of science is called the *hypothetico-deductive* model in that a set of propositions is logically linked to produce a deduction that can then be empirically tested. In this view of science, whichever theory produces the most efficient explanation is the best theory. In this sense, theories are in competition with one another. This hypothetico-deductive perspective is based on a viewpoint (epistemology) that is counterpoised to the *constructivist* position. You may recall that according to the constructivist position, different models may be useful for different purposes. Even models intended to explain the same phenomena may illuminate different aspects, as in the parable about the blind men feeling the elephant, in which no one description was an accurate description of the whole elephant, yet all the descriptions were true. Thus, systems theorists do not see themselves as playing by the same competitive rules as traditional science. This is not to say that systems theory is less scientific in the broad sense, but it does adopt a less competitive view of scientific theory.

A second criticism that has plagued systems theory is that it is too abstract and global to be of much use. The ideas in systems theory are so general as to be almost meaningless. In their quest to unify the sciences, systems theorists have abstracted to a level in which there is little meaning.

Critics claim that when systems theory is applied to concrete empirical situations, the generality of its concepts trivializes and glosses over important distinctions. Turner (1991) gave the example that notions of "information" do not communicate the properties denoted by more traditional concepts such as norms, values, beliefs, ideology, and so forth.

Systems theorists say that what most of these critics miss is that it is always easier to apply general ideas across diverse contexts than to apply specific ideas. For example, the "information processing" of crustaceans provided a basic analog for Gottman's (1979) work on marital communication. Although no one doubts that discipline-specific concepts and theories are important, it is increasingly difficult to see parts of the natural and social world as not being tied together. Naturally, systems theorists would argue that the only way we can move between diverse contexts and species is by using a common set of concepts that will help us see the connections and similarity of processes.

Another criticism is that family systems theorists tend to reify the idea of system. This criticism is perhaps aimed more at the family process variant of systems theory. For example, family therapists who claim they are using systems theory in simply calling a family a system of interrelated parts or interacting personalities are attributing reality to a heuristic model for understanding. Family process theorists, like many other scientists, would like to see their knowledge benefit humankind. But in their attempts to apply systems theory to the family, they seem prone to slip from viewing the family as a system to the view that the family *is* a system. This slippage from an epistemology favoring knowledge as possible heuristic models to a way of knowing that clearly makes ontological claims about the nature of family reality is a prime example of reification, or what we have already seen Whitehead (1929, p. 11) refer to as "the fallacy of misplaced concreteness." In the social sciences, this is always a threat. Hard on the heels of this threat of mistaking knowledge claims for ontological claims are the arguments that what is ontologically given represents the correct moral order. This argument from "what is in reality" to "what should be reality" is typical of 17th-century "natural law" arguments. The following quote provides a vivid example of how clinicians, scholars, and practitioners may get caught in reification and moralism:

> In reviewing this attempt to summarize how family systems *do* operate, I am struck by how clinicians spend a good deal of energy trying to get families to operate as they believe a good family system *should* operate; that is, by establishing joint goals and monitoring progress toward them. These clinicians work hard to make family members more aware of the dynamics of their previously unmediated escalating cycles so that they can bring these cycles into line with their intentions. In short, such

clinicians do all they can in their power to make families more cybernetic, less reflexive, and less opportunistic. (Broderick, 1993, pp. 85–86)

Clinicians and systems theorists might respond that this criticism can be substantiated by an ample number of instances in which scholars make such incautious claims in almost every area of science. Systems theorists might argue that every field contains its proportion of naive participants and outrageous claims. The rejoinder that systems theorists offer is that reification is totally inconsistent with the constructivist epistemology according to which systems models are not models of reality so much as heuristics for different purposes. Therefore, systems theorists feel that their area is no more prone to reification than any other theory. Furthermore, systems theorists would argue that the constructivist epistemology militates against such abuses more than is the case in the traditional theoretical approaches.

Conclusion

Family systems theory has proved useful in two areas of family studies. One of these areas is family therapy. Family process scholars have found systems theory to be a useful metaphor in guiding intervention and interpreting the complex relationships between individuals and their families. The second area in which family systems theory has proved useful is that of marital and family communications and interaction. Communications theory is properly a form of systems theory because it incorporates many of the basic concepts such as feedback and variety (see Shannon & Weaver, 1949). It has proven a most useful approach for the scientific study of the family. The conflict, if any, between these two variants is whether systems theory is both metaphor and science. A clear understanding of the constructivist epistemology behind systems theory allows both interpretations. The same model may be used for different purposes and in different ways.

Is the future of systems theory in the study of the family a bright one? Turner (1991) was pessimistic because he felt the concepts and models in systems theory do not fit well with social phenomena. For example, efforts to adopt decision theory, game theory, information theory, analysis of servomechanisms, and similar bodies of precise concepts have never proven very useful. The experience of family scholars appears to differ with this assessment. Furthermore, Turner's view of what has "proven very useful" may be at odds with the more open perspective assumed by systems theorists. In the final analysis, optimism or pessimism about systems theory may largely depend on how scholars view the noncompetitive epistemology of constructivism. Von Glasersfeld (1987) ended his essay with the warning of a true believer: "Looking at the world today, one must conclude that this way of thinking rather than fostering competition, may be the only way to maintain human life on this planet" (p. 11).

STUDY QUESTIONS

1. Family systems have boundaries; those boundaries can be physical like houses, plots of land, and geographic territory, or they can be social constructs like affinal and consanguineal relationships. If understanding a system is possible only by understanding the whole, where do you draw the boundaries on what makes up the whole?

2. Let's return to Jack and Jan. Use communication theory to discuss the reason why Jack doesn't seem to be getting what Jan is saying. Do not blame but explain the role each plays in the interchange.

3. Discuss the differences between individual resiliency and family resiliency.

4. Is system theory really a theory or just a model or flowchart? Evaluate each criticism of the system's framework in light of the Criteria for Evaluating Family Theories as presented in Chapter 1, Table 1.1.

5. Systems theory is used extensively in family therapy contexts. How do you feel about a holistic approach to better understanding something detrimental like domestic violence? How do you make sense of abused members of a dysfunctional family system being included in the discussion about the dysfunction?

6. Would you say that the term *holistic analysis* is an oxymoron? Why or why not?

CHAPTER

7

The Conflict and Critical Theories Framework

Bill and Mariel have been living together for about a year. They have decided to get married. They both wanted to have a church wedding. The minister they contacted told them that the church requires all those wanting to be married to attend a marriage preparation course offered by the church. Tonight, they are attending the first of the marriage preparation classes. Bill is quite sceptical of the course. He believes that because he and Mariel have lived together for almost a year, they should know a lot about what to expect in marriage. Bill and Mariel complete their answers to an inventory of questions regarding expectations for marriage before they sit down with their counselor. The counselor's first question is, "The two of you have answered the question 'How many arguments and fights do you expect per month?' in very different ways. Mariel expects about four per month and Bill envisions only one per month. Can you each explain to me how you view fights and why you have such different expectations about the number of fights?" Bill answers that perhaps he and Mariel have a different definition of what a fight is. He defines a fight as not just a disagreement but also as one person being angry toward the other person. To his surprise, Mariel agrees with his definition. Bill then asks Mariel, "So if there is no difference between our definitions, why do you think we will fight that much?" Mariel responds that her parents have been happily married for 30 years and that is about how much they fight. Bill says, "Fighting that much isn't healthy for a relationship," but Mariel counters that fighting is normal in a marriage as long as it doesn't get out of hand. The counselor then asks, "If a couple were always harmonious, what would spark them to grow and change?"

Bill and Mariel have encountered some differences in their basic expectations about marriage. Bill appears to believe that happy marriages are harmonious, with few disagreements or fights. Mariel seems to be more accepting of conflict as being "natural" in marriage. The counselor's final question about growth and change would appear to support the view that conflict in marriage might even play an important dynamic role. Bill and Mariel are faced with an important task. They are being asked to identify what they see as the role of conflict in marriage. Are good marriages free of conflict? Is conflict always destructive, or can it be a source of growth and nourishment for a relationship? And how do partners in a marriage keep conflict from getting out of hand?

These questions are part of what we address in this chapter. This chapter is concerned with the way conflict theory explains family behavior. In every theory, there reside assumptions about the nature of humans and the constraints under which humans operate. In addition, we all carry around our own assumptions and expectations, such as assumptions about what our marriage will be like and what is "normal" and "not normal" in marriage. In a sense, then, this chapter on conflict theory will not answer the questions posed above. But perhaps more than any other of the theoretical frameworks in this book, conflict theory allows us to fully discuss and examine these important questions and assumptions about conflict.

Intellectual Traditions

The central question for conflict theory was first and perhaps most simply stated by the social philosopher Thomas Hobbes (1651/1947) as "How is social order possible?" Without an understanding of the perspective Hobbes and later conflict theorists have about human nature, the question regarding social order might appear naive. Like utilitarian theorists, Hobbes believed that the first law of all organisms is self-preservation and self-assertion. He emphasized that among humans, this law is elevated to a natural right. As a result of the natural right of the human self to survive and assert itself, the first law presents us with a natural order in which people's self-interest collides with the self-interest of others. The basic state of nature, then, is a "war of all against all." Hobbes acknowledges that such an existence would be short, brutish, and largely intolerable. This leads Hobbes to his second law, according to which humans form a social contract whereby all humans give up some of their rights of self-interest to live in a stable and secure society of laws. Unlike the utilitarian perspective, once a society of laws is established, much of human self-interest is regulated and governed by laws rather than negotiated. Hobbes did not see all rights of self-interest being relinquished to the state, however. Human self-interest continues to provide the impetus for collision and conflict but within the framework of the laws of the state.

It may be helpful to note that both conflict and exchange theorists assume that humans act out of self-interest. They both recognize the importance of human disagreements, disputes, and hostilities. A difference between the two major perspectives, however, is that exchange theorists assume a basic similarity in the resources of social actors so that there is potential for freely bargained agreements that are fair to all negotiating parties and with a willingness to renegotiate when the net profits to involved actors become misaligned. Conflict theory, however, becomes especially relevant when resources are decidedly unequal. In such cases, relatively dramatic and temporarily disruptive actions on the part of deprived and powerless persons and groups may be necessary to restore or create a social order that is fair to all participants.

Hobbes and other social contract theorists set the stage for much of the evolution of conflict theory. The assumptions of human self-interest and the need for a social contract are ideas held by most conflict theorists in one form or another. But it was Karl Marx and Friedrich Engels who not only developed a more thorough and sophisticated view of conflict but also directly applied their perspective to the family. Marx and Engels developed a theory of history (*historiography*) in which they envisioned social and historical change occurring by means of class conflict. Marx and Engels, like most of their cohort in Europe, were influenced by the German idealist Friedrich Hegel (1770–1831). Hegel viewed history as ruled by a dialectic of ideas (thus the moniker *idealism*). According to Hegel's dialectical logic, each idea (thesis) automatically presupposed its opposite (antithesis), and out of the tension between the idea and its opposite, the mind would seek to unify the opposition, doing so by creatively moving to a more encompassing idea (synthesis). This synthesis would form a new thesis and presuppose another antithesis, followed by an even more encompassing synthesis, and so it would continue as a process.

Marx and Engels vehemently attacked the Hegelian notions (e.g., Marx & Engels, 1845/1932). They argued that history was ruled not by ideas but by material production. Using Hegel's dialectic, they explained that there were, in fact, only two relations to production. People could either control the means of production or labor for those who controlled production. Marx and Engels then proposed a *dialectic material* explanation of history from primitive to modern times. For example, in feudal times, the opposition was between the lords who owned the land and the serfs who worked the land. In the industrial era, the opposition was between the new industrialists (bourgeoisie) and those who labored in their plants (proletariat). Marx and Engels envisioned an end to the dialectic of class opposition only with the development of automation and communal society.

The family occupies a unique niche in the conflict theory of Marx and Engels. They recognized that the family was rooted in biological self-interest (sex and reproduction) and yet is also a form of social organization. Engels (1884/1946), in his book *The Origin of the Family, Private Property, and the State,* attributes the move from matrilineage (mistakenly termed "mother right" because of the inaccuracies of ethnographies in the mid-1800s) to patrilineage, patriarchy, and monogamy (father right) as being the result of the first division of labor, based on gender. Out of this biologically rooted division of labor came the first class conflict: The first class opposition that appears in history coincides with the development of the antagonism between man and woman in monogamous marriage, and the first class oppression coincides with that of the female sex by the male (Engels, 1884/1946, p. 58). Although Engels did not see the family as a causal influence, he did see it as a microcosm of the conflict in the larger culture: It is the cellular form of civilized society in which the nature of the oppositions and contradictions fully active in that society can already be studied). Thus, for Engels, the family provided a microcosm of the class conflict in the larger society rather than having its own independent microsystem process of conflict. This introduces a basic question in conflict theory, which is, "Does conflict in marriage and the family simply mirror a macrosocial process, or is the conflict in the family of a different kind?"

At the core of the conflict theory of Hobbes, Marx, and Engels lies a basic assumption about scarcity of resources. If there were a surplus of resources, then even if humans act out of self-interest, there would be no reason for them to pursue conflict. Indeed, Marx made this scarcity a key to the last phase of his dialectical materialist view of history in switching from resources being distributed "to each according to his work" to "to each according to his need." Later, family conflict theorists (e.g., Scanzoni, 1972; Sprey, 1979) became more conscious of this assumption as being the basic factor underlying the notion of conflict. The ideas of resources and power have become central to what many consider to be the true nature of conflict in the family.

Although some conflict scholars undoubtedly see resources as the key to understanding conflict, others may argue that social status processes are central; still others believe that conflict has a structural dimension. Georg Simmel (1904) viewed conflict as being embedded in the structure of groups. Moreover, he emphasized the positive role of conflict in achieving greater unity for the group. Sprey (1979) has a more concrete perspective on the structural characteristics of the dialectic within families. He envisions "a perpetual confrontation between the quest for 'autonomy and jointness' as characteristic of all groups but especially small intimate ones, such as marriages and families" (p. 141). Indeed, Sprey sees this form of structural conflict as so endemic that "issues involving individual autonomy and the competition between privacy and jointness cannot be 'solved' except through the termination of the relationship" (p. 147). One of the implications of the structuralist perspective on conflict is that because conflict is endemic in the group, the only alternative is to *manage* conflict so that it does not escalate to damaging levels or reduce the group to totally separate individuals.

In the century that has passed since Marx and Engels, conflict theory has developed as one of the theories in the pantheon of social science theories. The writings of Marx and Engels contained both a theory of history and what Turner (1991) calls an emancipatory call to action (e.g., Marx & Engels, 1867/1971). This emancipatory element has led some scholars to view conflict theory as essentially nonscientific:

> Conflict theory tends to be only a step away from ideology, which may be defined as the organization of ideas for the promotion of social movements or for the defense of social institutions. An ideology is a system of ideas intended to serve practice rather than to promote the aims of understanding. (Martindale, 1960, p. 151)

On the other side, some proponents of the emancipatory vision of conflict theory argue that all social science theories are ideologies because they all defend one institution or another. Marx and Engels argued that understanding is emancipatory and that knowledge and political action are always tied together (praxis). Without pretending to resolve this argument, we should nonetheless point out that some family conflict theorists (especially critical theorists) view the theory as providing both understanding and political direction.

Although Marxian thinking was expressed in political action (praxis) by socialism, some scholars were critical of the *selective* interpretation of Marx, which seemed to emphasize *The Communist Manifesto* and *Das Kapital* to the exclusion of works such as *The German Ideology*. These neo-Marxist dissidents converged their dissatisfaction and founded what has become known as the *critical theory*. Originally, this intellectual movement began to coalesce in Frankfurt's (Germany) Institute for Social Research. Eventually, many of the best known of these scholars, such as Marcuse (1964), Adorno (1973), and Horkheimer (e.g., 1947), immigrated to North America. It was Horkheimer (1982), however, who succinctly defined critical theory as that which "seeks to liberate human beings from the circumstances that enslave them" (p. 244). In this statement, he clearly indicated that social theory is about understanding, practice, and action. Thus, critical theory is a practical critique of our world aimed at emancipation from the conditions of oppression.

In the 20th century, one of the major challenges to the Marxian view of conflict over material resources has been the conflict theory of Bourdieu. The influences of Marx, critical theory, and French structuralism were fused in the work of Bourdieu (e.g., 1984). Bourdieu, similar to Marx, viewed inequality as an outcome of social conflict and competition between social classes. Unlike Marx, however, Bourdieu sought to balance the effects of social structure with the individual actor's "agency." His perspective is that individual agency can change the structural determinations and that structure necessarily is dynamic and fluid rather than statically determined. Bourdieu argues that conflict is endemic to social groups because they seek not just material resources but status distinction from other groups as well. His book *Distinction* (1984) was cited as among the top 10 most influential books of the last century by the International Sociological Association. Bourdieu's ideas have gained purchase as scholars interpret his work for different cultural contexts (see Weininger & Lareau, 2003). His work, as we shall see later in this chapter, is especially germane to understanding the family as a key agent in the transmission of social class.

Summing up, the focus of conflict theory is on both conflict within groups (e.g., family interaction) and conflict between groups (e.g., class conflict). Some conflict theorists of the family view internal family interactions as being part of the larger social process, and others view conflict in the family as being unique because of the affectual nature of the resources (Scanzoni, 1970). Most conflict theorists accept the assumptions from Hobbes that humans act out of self-interest and that social order needs to be negotiated and ritualized. The existence of social order in the form of the state and laws does not mean that conflict is absent. Rather, conflict continues between interest groups and between self-interested individuals, and these conflicts must be managed to keep the group from the extremes of social breakup on one hand and war on the other hand.

Focus and Scope Assumptions

Humans are motivated principally by self-interest. Individuals' self-interest is rooted in the will to survive and persevere. By extension, humans generalize this orientation of self-interest from mere survival to a more general mode of operating in the world. Thus, if one desires something owned by another who has more power or force, the solution is to band together with like-minded persons to gain sufficient force to realize your desires. This is the state of nature. In contrast to utilitarian theories, this self-interest is not necessarily tied to an ability to be rational. This rather unbridled, primitive self-interest is the source of Hobbes's "war of all against all."

Conflict is endemic in social groups. People who join together to attain a goal of common interest such as having children nonetheless have conflict because of disagreements on other issues and the structural opposition between autonomy and *togetherness*. Indeed, we can imagine that in those social groups (family) in which we spend the most time and have the greatest expectations for togetherness, we might also find the greatest conflict.

Conflict is inevitable between social groups. We expect to find conflict within small, intimate social groups but also *between* social groups. Individuals have *interests*, but in any society, those interests must be pursued by means of group affiliation. All social groups have interests, even if only for survival. Usually, these interests are far-reaching such as for wealth, status, or land. Because not all groups can simultaneously achieve their goals (resource scarcity), there is conflict. The assumption is that groups and individuals must compete for scarce resources. Many times, the interests of a group might be quite distinct from the interests of an individual, as we see in the relationship between political parties and those individuals who would like to run for office. Indeed, resource scarcity, whether it be wealth or political power, is the necessary condition for competition.

As a result of both structural conflict and competition, we find that *the normal state of society is to be in conflict rather than harmony.* Harmony is an achieved rather than a natural state. This assumption is crucial to our understanding of families through the perspective of conflict theory. Accordingly, when you get married, you should expect to be entering an arrangement more prone to conflict than to harmony.

As a result of competition and conflict, *some individuals and groups find that they are oppressed and need to be empowered because of inequalities and oppression.*

Because conflict is both endemic and inevitable, the primary concern in the study of social groups, such as the family, is how they manage conflict. If conflict is the rule, then the Hobbesian question "How is order possible?" makes sense even in the study of such close and intimate groups as the family. Indeed, much of family conflict theory involves examination of the techniques used in marriages and families to keep these groups from either separation or war.

Concepts

Conflict

Of course, the most basic concept in conflict theory is that of *conflict.* Conflict has been variously defined as disagreement, clashes, and discordance in interests or ideas. The definition Sprey (1979) offers is exceptional in its clarity. He says that conflict *as a process* "is defined as a confrontation between individuals, or groups, over scarce resources, controversial means, incompatible goals, or combinations of these" (p. 134). Sprey's emphasis that conflict is a process rather than a behavior is consistent with Marx and other theorists who emphasize the dialectical nature of conflict. Thus, behavior might be used to infer this process, but the process itself is not necessarily observable. For example, your parents might want you to visit on the weekend, but this clashes with your plans for a fishing trip. This particular example of parent-child conflict of goals may not be obvious to an external observer and represents a more covert conflict. The same might be true of a clash in ideas. But the conflict between runners at a track meet attempting to be first across the finish line is readily observable and overt.

Norms of the Situation

Any situation can be defined by individuals or groups as governed by social rules. We all know that we have social rules for *cooperation* and *competition*. *Cooperation* refers to the process by which members interact, whereas competition does not refer to a process but to an observable organization or structure of scarce resources. Competition is the way in which a situation is organized or structured. For example, if we tell students that we will "fit" their grades to a "normal" curve so that only 5% will receive an A, then we are structuring the learning situation in a competitive way. In this case, it makes sense for students not to assist one another because they lessen their own probability of getting an A in the course. If we tell all students what the standard is for attaining an A and that all may get As if they attain these standards, then we structure the learning situation in a noncompetitive way, a way that emphasizes cooperation. In this situation, the free exchange of ideas and assistance makes sense. Competition and cooperation, then, are set by the social rules, or norms, that organize an activity or social system. These rules, or norms, structure the situation so that not all parties interested in the goal can achieve it (competition) or so that potentially all parties interested in the goal can achieve it (cooperation).

Structure of the Group

The *structure of the group* is a micro-level interpretation. At the micro or group level, there are several dimensions that conflict theorists view as salient. First, and most obvious, is the number of members in the group. Conflict theorists from Simmel (1904) to the present recognize that group size affects the techniques with which the group can manage conflict. For example, a two-person group cannot be democratic; a dyad can only argue and negotiate. Groups of three or more can form power coalitions to get their way (e.g., Caplow, 1968). A second dimension of group structure is the age of the members. Marx and Engels (1867/1971) pointed out in *The Communist Manifesto* that children and women were subjugated to the male bourgeoisie. Later, Caplow (1968) argued that resources and power accrue with the aging of children in the family. He supposed that as children developed social skills and resources, their power in the family increased.

Likewise, becoming elderly may involve some loss of resources and power. The third dimension of the structure of the group is gender. Marx and Engels viewed gender as important in the internal dialectic of the family in the first division of labor. Some later theorists concentrate on gender and the family (see Chapter 8 of this volume; see also Firestone, 1970). Thus, most conflict theorists analyze the structure of the group by the number of members, the age structure, the gender structure, or a combination thereof.

Social Structure

The macro-level view of structure is the social structure. Certainly, some readings of Marx would suggest that the dialectics of historical materialism will simply overpower individuals as though they were "leaves in the wind." Leaving aside the accuracy of this interpretation of Marx, there is little doubt that Bourdieu's perspective challenges such determinism. Bourdieu's (1984) perspective on social structure is that while all societies have inequalities, there is a continuing struggle for the redistribution of resources (capitals) and even what is defined as a resource. In this perspective, families socialize children with resources (capitals) that may or may not be useful in continuing inequalities. So the current perspective on social structure is that it does structure inequalities (capitals) but that it is also dynamically driven by conflict (and symbolic violence).

Resources and Capitals

The notion of *resources* is a pivotal concept for conflict theory. Marx and Engels viewed the basic resource as the "control of the means of production." Their focus on the material economy has proved too narrow for most current conflict theorists. The concept of resources is a broader concept, closely aligned to the notion of *power.* There exists considerable scholarly debate over the exact relationship between power, resources, and authority (e.g., Brinkerhoff & Lupri, 1989; Cromwell & Olson, 1975; Szinovacz, 1987). We present what we believe is a coherent picture of the relationship between authority, power, and resources. The notion of resources is the broadest of the three concepts and includes the other two (power and authority) as subsets. Resources include all the knowledge, skills, techniques, and materials that are at the ready disposal of a person or group. Clearly, resources provide a potential base for the exercise of power. Power, according to Sprey (1979), is the ability of an individual or group to exercise effective control over others and things. By this definition, power can be measured only by its outcome, which is control, whereas resources provide the potential for power and control. Authority is a type of resource that is constructed by the normative system of a specific culture (Rodman,

1967). Thus, for example, a woman in Greece might have more resources (potential) than her unemployed husband, but if there is a strong cultural norm for patriarchy, then the husband may have greater control (power) in the family. Under more egalitarian or democratic authority norms, the greater resources of the female would give her greater control (power; Scanzoni, 1972). Thus, the relationship between authority and power is that the normative system (authority) can serve as one among many resources. Resources that are relevant in a situation can be used to exert control or exercise power.

Bourdieu (1984, 1986) developed the idea that resources in the broad sense can be categorized as "capital." Capital is not narrowly defined as in economics but is generically defined as that which allows for the appropriation of social energy or its own reproduction. Although this is similar to economic capital, Bourdieu distances himself from purely economic treatments, such as Becker (1964). Bourdieu lists cultural, social, and economic capital and the "conversions" between these capitals. It is the notions of social and cultural capital that have served to awaken family researchers to the noneconomic dimension of family resources.

Negotiation

Negotiation is one of the major techniques used in families to manage conflict. Negotiation is restricted, however, to those situations in which each person or group desires a goal that cannot be attained without the assistance of other parties. A simple example of this is playing a board game, such as Monopoly. Although winning may be one person's goal, without the cooperation of at least one other family member—that is, his or her willingness to participate—winning is impossible. Another example is when a mother wants to take the family on a picnic, but the father prefers taking the family to the swimming pool. Behind both options is the notion of "doing something with the family," which means that willing cooperation is needed to reach the goal. Negotiation happens when both parties state their goals and then each uses his or her resources to induce or coerce the other to move closer to his or her goal. Argument, bribery, and deceit may all be involved in negotiations.

Consensus

Consensus means agreement. It is the preferable outcome of negotiation. Consensus is achieved when parties to a negotiation agree. For example, many family members enter into temporary coalitions with a sibling or parent to achieve an end. Such coalitions rely on agreement between the coalition partners. Agreement or consensus can also be achieved in mate selection by selecting mates with the same values and orientation and by socialization of mate or children to accept the same view one holds. The opposite of consensus is disagreement. Dissension is discord arising from a disagreement. It is an interesting trademark of close relationships that we spend enormous amounts of time focused on areas of disagreement but seldom feel a need to focus on areas of agreement because these areas have been successfully managed.

Propositions

Conflict theorists have often concentrated on macrosystem analysis of society and global confrontations. Some conflict theorists believe that the family is simply a microcosm of these larger processes and that what is said of the larger society is naturally also true for the family. A significant number of family conflict theorists have claimed, however, that the family (and some other small groups) is sufficiently unlike larger social units and that it must be analyzed separately. Sprey (1979), for example, argues that the autonomy-togetherness issue is atypical of macro-level analyses and yet important in analyzing the family. Caplow (1968) argues that there are distinct and important structural differences between even two- and three-person groups. The propositions we include below focus principally on the family.

Social groups, such as the family, are structurally disposed to conflict both within and between groups. This supposition implies that variables subsumed under structure of the group (membership, age, gender) and structure of the situation (competition and cooperation) are related to the degree of conflict. Even the most homogeneous group (two women of the same age) in the most cooperative normative situation would still be predisposed to conflict, because in a dyad there is the structural issue of autonomy-togetherness, and in dyads all issues can be resolved only by direct negotiation.

Conflict between groups is based on resource allocation and competitive social structure.

There exists no known society in which resources are allocated equally to all. This is not to say that resource allocation is unfair. Indeed, even Marx was not egalitarian in this regard but said "to each according to his need," and needs are not distributed equally. Thus, the mere fact that some families have more than others ensures competition. Families may participate in larger interest group clusters such as Children First or other pro-family or pro-child groups. Regardless of the validity of the perceptions involved, the recent uproar over *family values* attests to the fact that many families see themselves competing for scarce benefits against what they perceive as "nonfamily" groups such as gays, singles, and even single-parent families. As a corollary to the above,

Conflict within the group (e.g., family) is due to the inequity of resources between individuals.

Resources are differentially allocated in a social system, often by group membership, age, and gender. As a result, resource differentials exist in the family so that some members have more resources than other members. This resource inequity leads to conflict to the degree that the norms internal to the family are competitive rather than cooperative. For example, women generally make less money than men, ensuring that they have fewer resources; therefore, even in egalitarian authority structures, they have, on average, less power in relation to their husbands.

Conflict within marriages and families is minimally structural. Regardless of gender and age, dyads and larger groups are faced with the conflict of individual members over autonomy versus togetherness. This issue is especially salient for the dyad in two regards. First, togetherness necessarily involves the only other member. A family group offers several levels of togetherness (sibling, mother-child, etc.), but togetherness in the dyad always involves the other person. The second reason the issue of conflict is especially salient for the dyad is that negotiations are always against the same adversary. In families, coalitions can be formed to overpower the resources of any one individual. One implicit strength of family coalitions is that your coalition partners on today's issue might well be your adversaries on tomorrow's issue, and today's enemy might be tomorrow's coalition partner. The dyad lacks this dynamic; today's adversary is also tomorrow's adversary in negotiations (Caplow, 1968).

Negotiation, as a form of conflict management, is more likely in egalitarian authority structures.

And,

The outcome of negotiation is more likely to favor the person with the greatest resources in the family.

The authority pattern in the culture sets up the norms or rules as to who has authority based on age and gender. The more unilateral the authority pattern (matriarchy, patriarchy), the less room there is for negotiation. Indeed, negotiation is most likely in democratic or egalitarian families.

Negotiation involves resources; whoever has the greatest resources can negotiate the greatest rewards in a compromise.

This proposition is somewhat akin to the old saying "Them that's got, gets." It must be remembered, however, that there are many forms of resources in addition to money and occupation. Indeed, personal abilities to manipulate, lie, and cajole must be counted among the resources of relevance in negotiations. Negotiations are almost invariably used in egalitarian marriages, whereas once children are present, coalition formation might play a larger role than negotiation.

Coalition formation is most likely in groups (families) with democratic authority patterns.

And,

In democratic groups, material resources alone do not necessarily predict family coalitions and outcomes.

In most North American families, one person does not make all the decisions. Decision making is a complex matter of consultation, coalition formation, and lobbying. Caplow (1968) points out that as children grow and mature, they gain increased interpersonal competence, knowledge, and material resources. The power that they have is not so great as to countermand the father's residual patriarchal authority and greater material resources, but coupled with the mother and other siblings, children might have significant influence over decision making. Indeed, even before the children are old enough to participate in such coalitions, they are assumed to be coalesced with the mother and constitute a resource for the mother in that she might voice what is best for the children as part of negotiations.

These few propositions represent a small subset of the many that have been developed in conflict theory. These few should be sufficient to demonstrate how conflict theorists deal with the sources of conflict and the management of conflict in families. Most scholars would agree that the family is the central building block of social systems, and we might propose that the techniques of conflict management and authority patterns learned in the family influence the directions to be taken by the entire social system. In this sense, it could easily be argued that Marx's view that the family is a microcosm reflecting processes in the larger society could be turned on its head. It is equally defensible to propose that family structure and conflict resolution techniques are imitated by larger social institutions to maintain balance and resolve disputes.

Variations

There are many variants of conflict theory. Some variants involve latching onto one dimension of conflict, such as gender, and elevating it as the major explanatory variable of all conflict, much as Marx elevated the "means of material production" to such explanatory status. The four variants we focus on below represent the most conspicuous schools of thought on family conflict and the most productive to date. Although these variants do not exhaust the varieties of conflict theory in general, we feel that they represent the range of work on family conflict theory.

Structural Conflict

One of the acknowledged fathers of sociology is Georg Simmel. Simmel's sociology was *formal* and theoretical, following the style of the formal philosophy of nature of the German philosopher Immanuel Kant. Simmel viewed conflict as a constant process of associative and dissociative forces that brought unity and coherence to society. Simmel did not identify one underlying cause of conflict, such as Marx's relation to the means of production, nor did he view the processes in the family as simply a microcosm of larger scale processes. In regard to the family, Simmel focused his attention on the formal properties of small group structure and interaction. He viewed marriage and family as distinctly different social structures with different social properties. Marriage, because it is a two-person, or dyadic, structure, involves one individual being totally dependent on the other:

> This dependence of the dyad on its two individual members causes the thought of its existence to be accompanied by the thought of its termination much more closely and impressively than in any group, where every member knows that even after his or her retirement or death, the group can continue to exist. (Simmel, 1950, pp. 123–124)

Simmel (1950) argues that marriage is unlike most dyads in one regard: "namely, absence of a super-personal unit" (p. 129). He argues that the institution of marriage seems to transcend the two individuals involved, in part because it is socially regulated. Even though marriage is different from other dyads, it lacks the structural dimensions of three-person and larger groups. Indeed, Simmel says, "a marriage with one child has a character which is completely different from that of a childless marriage" (p. 138). The critical difference for Simmel is that once the group grows beyond the dyad, "parties of interest" may form alliances. Simmel sought to characterize the types of triads that are universal to this social group. The task of fully formalizing and applying the notions of "ties" and "coalitions" to the family fell to later sociologists, however.

Caplow (1968) calls the mother-father-child triad the "primary triad." He acknowledges that there are other significant family triads, such as sibling triads, but views this parent-child triad as most basic. In Caplow's view, family members form coalitions based on each person's relative power. If the father had greater power than either the mother or child, a winning coalition between the child and mother might be possible. Caplow suggested that over the family's life cycle, the relative power of family members changes, and potential coalitions also change. One of the strengths this has for families is that today's coalition partner might be tomorrow's opponent, and today's opponent might be tomorrow's partner. Caplow (1968) suggests that the typical family evolves from a dyad in which the husband (father to be) usually has more power than the wife (mother to be) (F > M). As a child grows, the mother-child coalition tends to equal the individual power of the father (F = M + C). This might increasingly force the father into a coalition with the mother (F + M > C). Eventually, the mother-child coalition surpasses the relative power of the father (F < M + C). Because the mother would be the dominant member of the mother-child coalition, she would effectively have the greatest power in families with one adolescent child. Of course, Caplow recognizes that coalition strategies become more complex when there is more than one child or a parental member is absent. His theory is a direct extension of Simmel (1950). It adds the ingredient of the ordinal (<, >, =) computation of individual power and graph theory to the prediction of coalition formation. Caplow acknowledges that social norms of authority and the compatibility of coalition partners play a role in coalition formations, but the initial step in the theory is to outline the logically possible coalitions. In the end, Caplow (1968) provides a systematic and scientifically measurable approach to the resolution of family conflict through coalitions.

Caplow (1968) is sensitive to criticism that he might be ignoring the emotional context of family life. He argues like Simmel (1904), Coser (1956), and many other conflict theorists that the "function" of conflict is "solidarity." Caplow argues that emotions are tied to coalitions because coalition partners attempt to reinforce and protect one another. Out of this coalition partner interaction comes the emotions that we associate with being in a family: "Love is an intense preference for a particular coalition partner. Hate is an intense reaction against an opponent" (Caplow, 1968, p. 78). For Caplow, then, conflict and coalitions are not a sideshow in family life but compose the very essence of being in a family:

> Family life is fraught with the tension of conflicting emotions
> precisely because it is based on coalitions and every coalition
> involves an opponent. Begun with a husband-wife coalition,
> continued by a mother-child coalition, a family is sustained by
> the interlocking forces of love and hate in somewhat the same
> way that buildings are held up by opposing forces of tension and
> compression. (p. 78)

In their structural conflict approach, Simmel (1904) and Caplow (1968) attempt to provide a scholarly and scientific approach to conflict in families in which love, partnership, hate, and solidarity emerge from conflict.

Microresource Conflict Theory

Microresource theory is unique in incorporating the giving and receiving of affection in an accounting of resources. Macroresource theory tends to be focused on larger social structures rather than the interpersonal dimension of *affect* or *expressiveness*. As a result of this interpersonal emphasis, microresource theorists are more prone to stress "negotiations" as a technique of conflict management, whereas macroresource theorists are more prone to see the need for more revolutionary forms of conflict to bring about structural social change.

Scanzoni's (1972) microresource theory eclectically draws from a diversity of theories such as exchange theory, conflict theory, and even functionalist theory. It is somewhat difficult, not to mention risky, to identify Scanzoni's (1972) theory with any one framework. But because the basic focus is on marital conflict and its resolution through negotiations, it appears to us to best fit as a variant of conflict theory.

Although Scanzoni (1972) accepts Simmel's (1904) argument that conflict may lead to solidarity, he also shares with Coser (1956) the suspicion that this glosses over "what tears families apart." Following Coser, Scanzoni (1972) distinguishes two forms of conflict: basic conflict, which brings into question the most basic "rules of the game," and nonbasic conflict, which is played out according to the rules of the game. He provides a tidy analogy. Imagine a game of football. The two teams can conflict and yet build solidarity as long as they follow the rules of the game. But if they lack agreement on these rules, then we have basic conflict. Scanzoni then portrays the basic rules of the family or marital game.

Scanzoni views the rules (norms) of the family as governing the exchange of the husband's instrumental duties for expressive rights and likewise the wife's expressive duties for instrumental rights. The husband's right is the reciprocal of the wife's duty, and the husband's duty is the reciprocal of the wife's right. An instrumental activity is a means to some end, whereas an expressive activity tends to be an end in itself and carries affect or emotion. For example, the father holding a baby while the mother searches for a diaper is instrumental in the sense that a playpen might also do the job. On the other hand, holding, cuddling, and playing with a baby enjoying the simple affectual expression of love is an expressive activity. Scanzoni argues that the traditional rules for family are that the husband has instrumental duties, mainly as a provider, and the wife has mainly expressive duties, such as tension reduction, child care, and sexual services. The wife has the right to expect the husband to adequately provide for the family, and the husband has a right to expect expressive services from the wife. Nonbasic conflict may occur within these marriages over the discipline of children, economic matters, division of labor, and so on, but such conflict does not bring into question the basic rules of the game. Indeed, Scanzoni, following Simmel (1904), says this nonbasic conflict may enhance the stability of the marriage and the family and bring about change and growth.

Basic conflict, on the other hand, challenges the rules of the game. According to Scanzoni (1972), there are several ways that basic conflict emerges. One is if one partner fails to live up to role expectations, such as provider or sexual partner. This is a key to feelings of inequity in the marriage. Other sources are exogenous, or outside of any one marriage, such as the change away from patriarchy and the increased accessibility for women to their own resources such as education and work. As these changes come about and women have greater instrumental resources, they would want to renegotiate the basic rules, because those rules are now a source of inequity for them. Wives now have instrumental resources of their own, devaluing the contribution of husbands' resources. When women have approximately equal instrumental resources to those of the man in a relationship, they may renegotiate the expressive roles they have fulfilled in traditional marriages by demanding more expressive duties from the husband as their right or reducing the expressive duties they perform, because the value of the man's provider role (resources) has been reduced.

Although Scanzoni's (1970, 1972) analysis began more than three decades ago, it continues to be refined (Scanzoni & Szinovacz, 1980) and remains one of the more cogent analyses of changing gender roles in the family and the resulting conflict that surrounds such basic redesignation of family roles. Today, we can see that there are a number of forces exogenous to the family that might also be responsible for the decline in male ability to fulfill the provider role. For example, the rate of increase for male earnings relative to female earnings has decreased. Furthermore, the purchasing power of families has been eroded to such a degree that most families require two incomes simply to maintain living standards equivalent to one-earner families in 1970. Female participation rates in education and the labor force have increased dramatically. Women have tended to seek work in the growing service sector (tertiary) of the economy rather than the downsizing production sectors (primary and secondary). As a result, women find themselves increasingly to be the more stable provider in a marriage. Of course, women still do the lion's share of the housework, or "second shift," compared with men. Thus, women have increased their instrumental duties for the family but with no corresponding reduction in their expressive duties. Two decades later, this inequity in the family's rules and roles seems to have become greater and still provides the foundation for the basic conflict predicted by Scanzoni (1972).

Dialectical Historiography

There are few attempts in the area of family theory to follow the grand historical mapping and dialectical interpretation of scholars such as Hegel and Marx. Ogburn and Nimkoff (1955) offer a modest version in their analysis of the relationship between the loss of family functions and technological change. Without doubt, the most ambitious historical perspective on family change has been that of Carle Zimmerman in his book *Family and Civilization* (1947). Zimmerman's analysis is seldom cited by today's family researchers intent on testing hypotheses with immediate practical implications and rooted to a specific time and place. When we ask "big" questions, however, such as "Where is society headed?" and "Will the family survive?" we find Zimmerman's theory of great relevance.

Zimmerman views social change as a dialectical process based on authority and power. The history of the human family can be understood by examining the *dialectic* between the family being the major site of authority over individuals and other institutions such as church and state being the major authority over individuals. Zimmerman argues that the family and the state struggle for dominant authority over the individual. Failure to grasp this major struggle may be why others who have discussed theories of the family treat Zimmerman as an "institutional" theorist (e.g., Nye & Berardo, 1966/1981) rather than a conflict theorist.

In Zimmerman's perspective, human history goes through cycles. At the beginning of a historical cycle, family authority evolves as paramount and unchallenged. This first of three phases is marked by the *trustee family*. Because family descent is a way of passing on wealth and status, the head of the family wields enormous power over the well-being of individuals. State and church control are limited because the trustee family controls the behavior of its members and transmits its values and systems of control from generation to generation. In this phase, the individual family member is subordinate to and dependent on the decisions of the head of the family. The family name and estate are ultimate in the trustee family.

The second phase of the cycle is marked first by the gradual increase in the abuse of authority by the unquestioned and uncontrolled head of the trustee family. Because there are no checks and balances to the head of the trustee family, church and state slowly evolve to offer some relief to the consolidation of authority and control in the trustee family. The type of family that is indicative of this second phase is called the *domestic family*. The domestic family represents a balance between the authority of the head of the family and the authority of church and state. Although the individual is buffered from the abuses of family authority by the state's increasing recognition of individual rights, the state and church also support and condone the family as an institution of social control because it passes on the values and discipline needed for civil society.

In the last phase of the historical cycle, the state wields most of the power and authority over individuals. Individual rights are supreme, and the family group has little authority or control over its members. This phase is marked by what Zimmerman calls the *atomistic family*. The atomistic family is a loose social group, and individual members are fully protected by the state from the authority of the family. Zimmerman stresses that this last phase is doomed to destruction because, to maintain a disciplined and civil society, the state is dependent on the family's socialization of the individual but has supplanted the family's authority so that adequate socialization and training can no longer occur. Once family authority is undermined and individuals are no longer trained, social control breaks down, as does the civilization. In the vacuum of authority, the trustee family once again takes over control and discipline, and the cycle begins anew.

Zimmerman argues that civilization is now nearing the end of its second historical cycle through the three family types. Currently, we have evolved atomistic families and view the individual's rights and privileges as preeminent. Zimmerman's interpretation of history is, of course, not the only plausible analysis. There can be little doubt, however, that Zimmerman's work is one of the best examples of family historiography in the 20th century.

Critical Theory of the Family

Critical theory certainly has its roots in the Marxian perspective on the family and, hence, tends to see the family as either a mirror of larger economic relations or as being determined by larger economic relations. For example, recall that Marx and Engels (1867/1971) declared in *The Communist Manifesto* that the bourgeoisie saw wives as an economic utility rather than as participants in an affectionate relationship. This observation led to the inflammatory conclusion that wives were little more than the prostitutes of the bourgeoisie. Critical theorists, however, added a more psychological dimension to Marxian analysis by incorporating the insights of psychoanalytic theory into their historical and social analyses. Although the exact progenitors of the school of thought may be argued, there is little doubt that the so-called Frankfurt school is usually identified with the emergence of this school. The Institute for Social Research in Frankfurt, Germany, brought together many of the thinkers who were to develop the direction of critical theory. Some notable names involved in the early

Frankfurt school are Theodor Adorno, Erich Fromm, Max Horkheimer, Herbert Marcuse, and Jürgen Habermas (Osmond, 1987).

Max Horkheimer was the original director of the Institute for Social Research (Osmond, 1987). Although Horkheimer did not develop a focused theory of the family, he nonetheless emphasized that social relationships are inextricably tied to sociohistorical developments. In his *Dialectic of Enlightenment* (1947/2002), Horkheimer and his coauthor Adorno focused on the robotic mind necessary for the Nazi pogroms. They believed that the root of this psychological manifestation was tied to the "self-destruction of the Enlightenment" (1947/2002, p. xiii). The Enlightenment had laid the foundation for a faith in human rationality, but within this faith in human reason lay the seductive trap of unreflective acceptance of technology and pragmatic thinking as opposed to reflection. As such, humans might be turned from the reflective thinking of the Enlightenment to a robotic reliance on technology and pragmatism. The family participated in this change toward technology by systematizing and establishing relatively fixed roles for parents and children.

Although Horkheimer and the early critical theorists did not pursue a detailed theory of the family, many of the scholars in North America were more inclined to do so. The fact that the writings of Horkheimer, Adorno, Fromm, Marcuse, and Habermas have all been available and influential in North America to academics assisted in the continuation of critical theory in North America. Furthermore, writers in North America have focused more on the family than did the early progenitors, especially Eli Zaretsky and Mark Poster.

Eli Zaretsky's *Capitalism, the Family, and Personal Life* (1973) is an attempt to formulate a critical theory of the family. Zaretsky argues that it is only in the capitalist system of relations that we find the development of sex-divided public and private spheres concealing the economic contributions of women. He states, "It is only under capitalism that material production organized as wage labor and the forms of production taking place within the family have been separated so that the 'economic' function of the family is obscured" (pp. 26–27). This point is illustrated using several of the early feminist critiques, especially that of Firestone (1970). Indeed, a central theme in Zaretsky's work is to explain how and why the feminist movement developed independently of the socialist movement rather than as part of the socialist movement. To explain the social and emotional relations in the family, he argues that a Freudian perspective is necessary but not without problems. For example, Zaretsky ends up with a Freudian view that is largely biological, yet he fully realizes that the socialist view is largely historical. It is the melding of these two that he leaves to others (p. 133). Zaretsky does, however, implore socialist thinkers to "catch up" with many of the insights offered by the substantial theoretical work of feminists in the early 1970s.

Mark Poster's *Critical Theory of the Family* (1978) is certainly the most central application of critical theory to understanding the family. Poster reviews various conceptions of the family from areas such as Freudian psychotherapy, ego psychology, communications, French structuralism, functionalism, and family therapy. From this review, Poster suggests that there are key elements that any critical theory of the family must address. Among these elements are the development of the child and the development of the family. He proposes that a theory of the family would use age and sex hierarchies to understand families across developmental and historical time frames. His final analysis is more diachronic and historical, suggesting that there have been four models of family: "The four models are the bourgeois family in the mid-19th century, the aristocratic family of the 16th and 17th centuries, the peasant family of the 16th and 17th centuries, and the working-class family of the early industrial revolution" (Poster, 1978, pp. 166–167). Although Poster defends these "models" as expressions of particular age and sex hierarchies, he also admits that there may be other plausible models. In each of his four models, the nature of social relationships is different. For instance, he notes that in the contemporary family, romantic love is very demanding and an onerous responsibility for its participants. Poster's synthesis and integration of various psychodynamic contributions into the sociohistorical paradigm offered by Marx and Engels offers a broad perspective on the family. It remains for a new generation of critical theorists to pursue the course that Poster has envisioned.

Bourdieu's Capitals and the Family

Whereas Marx's followers view class conflict as being tied to economic materialism, Bourdieu (1984) views conflict as being more diverse and broadens the analysis of conflict to other forms of capital. Much of the direct application of Bourdieu's forms of *capitals* to family scholarship in North America has been through such work as Coleman (1988, 1990), Teachman, Paasch, and Carver (1996, 1997), Lareau (2000, 2003), Weininger and Lareau (2003), and Lareau and Goyette (2014). Here we sketch the broad picture that Bourdieu affords of the family.

Bourdieu begins his work on *Distinction* (1984) with the question "What is taste?" His answer to this question is complex. Bourdieu sees taste as being an expression of our cultural capital. Cultural symbols are used to maintain differences between groups. The symbolic differences are attached to status. For example, in today's society, one could choose to go to a rock concert or to the opera. The decision would not be an economic decision because often these are about equally expensive. Rather, the decision is based on one's taste. That taste is translated into consumption, and that consumption has symbolic significance for status. Many people would assume that the person choosing the opera has "high-brow" taste and that the rock concert choice shows more "common," or lower status, taste. Bourdieu argues that such cultural symbols create differences between groups so that stratification can take place. Bourdieu, however, acknowledges economic capital as important, but as we have pointed out with the example of the rock concert versus the opera, consumption of high cultural versus low cultural symbols often relies less on money than on values and education. Indeed, Bourdieu argues that the correlation between cultural and economic capital is less than perfect. He states that those with the highest cultural capital do not have the highest economic capital. Thus, we have the disconnect noted by Veblen where the *nouveau riche* are relatively low in culture, leading to a host of TV shows such as *The Beverly Hillbillies*.

The mechanism by which values and education are transmitted to children at an early age is principally the family. Bourdieu argues that those who acquire cultural symbols associated with high status groups will optimally have learned the values and be educated by their families in what he calls their *habitus*. Although habitus is broadly defined as one's habits, these are deeply ingrained in children by their families at an early age so that these habits seem almost inherited or inborn. Bourdieu argues that you can acquire upper-class habits through education, but these will always be less complete because the individual will lack the confidence and natural attitude acquired by those raised with such habits at an early age. One example of this is simply saying "please and thank you." Even preschool teachers respond more positively to polite than impolite children, and these responses are part of the child's success.

The early learning of habits of life may include table settings, trying different foods, seeing parents read, being surrounded by art and classical music, and having conversations. Bourdieu believes that those raised in such families will be comfortable and at ease with the rules of the game. Persons not raised in such settings may acquire the symbols through education but will fail to master the "comfort zone" of those raised with the symbols. For instance, imagine entering a conversation with classmates about baseball. Certainly, some people will have grown up with family members discussing baseball rules, players, and teams. For them this is comfortable territory. But if you had grown up discussing palette knife techniques in oil paintings or Ravel's orchestration cheapening the simple beauty of Mussorgsky's *Pictures at an Exhibition*, then you might be uncomfortable with the baseball discussions yet at home with discussions of art and music. This illustrates the distinction that Bourdieu makes between authentic acquisition of class symbols through the family and acquisition that occurs through the educational system (*autodidact*).

All the various cultural symbols, high, low, and in between, are in a dynamic process. As lower classes try to imitate and acquire the symbols of upper classes, the upper classes continually change and modify the symbols. One can stay in touch with changes in the symbol system of one's group by regularly interacting within the group and reinventing those symbols. This is a dynamic process so that symbols cannot be easily copied and the upper classes can still practice *symbolic violence* on those who do not understand the deep rules of the game. Thus, each generation modifies the symbols and to some extent the rules of the game. The *modifications* in the symbols of class help explain upward mobility as persons who learn and successfully practice the *rules of the game* and downward mobility as those from the upper class that lose contact with the changing rules of the game. Although the social class system is dynamic,, certain practices prevail among the upper classes such as not being ostentatious (showing off one's wealth or status) and the importance of art, music, and literature.

Bourdieu's contribution to the study of families is to see the family as an integral mechanism in the social class structure of society. Families replicate social class not only by economic advantage but also by cultural advantage. Indeed, the cultural symbols are used to identify the people who would be "appropriate" for the economic positions. Of course, this would be most true in societies where stratification is more rigid and there is less intergenerational social mobility. Surprisingly, the United States ranks last of 10 countries in an article in *Forbes* magazine drawn from an OECD report: The three most mobile societies are Denmark, Australia, and Norway, while the last three were Spain, France, and the United States (Serchuk, 2011). That would mean that these last three, including the United States, are more structured and pass on social and economic advantage intergenerationally. Although Peterson and Kern (1996) have argued that elites in developed countries, such as the United States, are more "cultural omnivores" and favoring a more diversified and diffuse elitism, other researchers such as Warde, Wright, and Gayo-Cal (2007) argue that the idea of cultural omnivore is largely mythical. Indeed, such a myth would assist in drawing attention away from the increasing intergenerational stratification of inequality in the United States.

Empirical Applications

Wife Assault

One of the major empirical areas for the application of conflict theory has been family violence (see Johnson & Ferraro, 2000). The very nature of the subject matter, family violence, immediately implies that some variants of conflict theory rather than others will be more relevant. For example, because we are attempting to explain why some husbands assault their wives, theoretical variants of conflict theory that assist in predicting conflict seem more relevant than those variants that deal with negotiating, conflict management, and the unifying function of conflict (Caplow, 1968; Simmel, 1904). In general, conflict theory predicts that clashes and confrontations occur when there is competition for scarce resources. One way we can determine the potential for conflict is when one person or group does not have the same resources as another person or group. For Marx, the proletariat did not have the same resources as the bourgeoisie. For feminist theorists, patriarchy helped ensure that men and women did not have the same resources. Thus, conflict theorists view social inequity as indicating the necessary conditions for conflict to arise.

Wife assault is difficult to observe and study. In North America, there is no uniform method for reporting and recording such incidents. Self-reports by both victims and perpetrators may be biased. Gelles and Straus designed and conducted the 1985 National Family Violence Survey, which probably represents the most complete data we have on wife assault and family violence. Wife assault can be measured as one of the following: pushed, grabbed, shoved; threw something at her; slapped her; kicked, hit, or punched; hit or tried to hit; beat her up; choked; threatened with knife or gun; used a knife or gun (Straus, 1994). Large studies are necessary because of the low incidence of family violence. As Gelles (1994) points out,

> Despite the fact that individuals are more likely to be hit, hurt,
> and even killed in the privacy of their homes and in intimate,
> as opposed to non-intimate relationships, the actual annual
> base rate of such victimization is still about 3 or 4 per 1,000
> individuals. (p. 1)

Even though the number of victims adds up over the years, the annual rate of incidence is relatively low.

One version of conflict theory relevant here is based on gender inequality. Some feminist conflict theorists suggest that where gender inequalities exist, there is a *patriarchal* social system that justifies and condones wife assault as one of many forms of the subjugation of women to men. Men basically are defending their greater resources from an underclass. Many of those resources are predicated on women "staying in their place." Yllö and Straus (1990) investigated this proposition using the National Family Violence Survey. They reported that the relationship between structural gender inequality (measured by each state's legal, political, and economic equality status) and wife assault is curvilinear. Those states with both the lowest and highest gender inequality showed the highest rates of wife assault. This suggests that feminists might be accurate in their interpretation but only for states in which there is great gender inequality. On the other hand, for states in which there is relatively high gender equality, perhaps Scanzoni's (1972; Scanzoni & Szinovacz, 1980) theory of sexual bargaining and the resulting social disorganization to traditional family roles would supply an explanation for the high rates of spousal abuse.

Straus (1994) tests three versions of conflict theory in an attempt to explain wife assault. The three versions of conflict theory he uses are gender inequality, income inequality, and social disorganization. His measures for gender inequality are the same as those used by Yllö and Straus (1990). He uses a single measure of each state's income equality and a composite measure of each state's social disorganization, composed of items such as divorce rates, geographical mobility, and lack of religious affiliation. Straus (1994) reports that both gender inequality and social disorganization measures are significantly related to rates of wife assault. Income inequality, when age is controlled, is not directly related to wife assault. And although the proportion of the variance explained in wife assault is relatively modest (7%–13%), his findings suggest that these theories might be explaining different aspects of wife assault and might interact with income inequities.

Straus's (1994) research supplies an example of how conflict theory may be applied in research. His results should caution theorists about becoming too focused on a single, universal, explanatory source of conflict, such as gender inequality. It may well be that there are different, independent, but complementary explanations of phenomena such as wife assault. In the end, it may be that a broader, more abstract, and inclusive theoretical perspective such as provided by Simmel (1904, 1950) would provide a unitary theoretical framework for these diverse sources of inequality and conflict.

Social Inequality

Certainly the Occupy Wall Street movement of 2011 targeted inequality. For example, Xiao (2013) reports that in the United States in 2009 the top 20% of households received over 50% of the income, whereas the bottom 20% received under 4% of the income. McCall and Percheskie (2010) argue that income inequality in the United States is greater than at any point in the last 40 years of history (Xiao, 2013). Economic deprivation and poverty are associated with parental depression, poor marital outcomes, and poor child developmental outcomes (see Conger, Conger, & Martin, 2010; Saxeby, Rodriguez, & Margolin, 2013).

There are many factors influencing the intergenerational transmission of income inequality such as biological inheritance, inheritance of capital, and education (Bowles & Gintis, 2002). Of the many factors, Cristina d'Addio, in her 2007 OECD report "Intergenerational Transmission of Disadvantage," sees differentials in education related to early family experiences. As Bourdieu (1984) argues, these early advantages are exposure not just to books or computers but also to the adult response to children who have manners, such as saying "please and thank you." Lareau, in her two books *Home Advantage* (2000) and *Unequal Childhoods* (2003), demonstrates not only that middle and upper-class parents are more proactive in their children's education but also that these parental activities, whether attending parent teacher meetings or assisting with homework, supply a continuing demonstration and reinforcement of the value and importance of education. Interestingly, Lareau's fieldwork with 88 families suggests that social class culture is more influential than race in determining children's school success. These children are culturally and socially prepared by their social class background to attain the education and professional positions that would replicate a social status similar to their parents. The macroscopic effect for these social class differences in parenting is a country's relatively low intergenerational occupational and status mobility.

Cristina d'Addio (2007) concludes her OECD report with some recommendations for changing intergenerational inequality. Prominently, she argues that "there seems to be a relation between cross-sectional income inequality and intergenerational earnings mobility. To promote equality of opportunity might then require reducing current income inequality" (p. 47). In addition, she argues that family structures (lone parenting) and educational attainment need to be addressed as contributing factors.

From the perspective of Bourdieu (1984) and Lareau (2000, 2003), these macroscopic interventions do not deal with the more subtle transmission of cultural habitus. The fact that habits of mind and action predispose children to success in school is not necessarily treated by income equality. As both of these authors point out, the middle and upper classes train their children in behaviors that when enacted in cultural situations will be rewarded with long-term success. For example, middle-class children are encouraged to express themselves in dinner table conversations at home, resulting in more confidence and verbal skills at school, which are rewarded by the educational system that values these behaviors. The obvious intervention point would be for the educational system not to reward these behaviors but to reward other forms. This, however, is unlikely unless we change occupational demands and the economic system. Bourdieu (1984) saw the middle and upper classes as constantly changing the habitus to accommodate changes in their class values and interests. As a result, interventions at the level of habitus are extremely difficult.

Critiques and Discussion

One of the major hurdles for conflict theory continues to be its emphasis on explaining conflict rather than order. This emphasis was undoubtedly justified in reaction to the stasis inherent in sociological structural-functionalism. Today, however, the emphasis on conflict often appears to highlight the sensational or negative rather than the dialectical process of conflict. For example, some scholars focus on gender or social class inequities without a clear picture of the dynamic process in which these inequities represent either a thesis or an antithesis. A very real danger for conflict theory is becoming focused on conflict as an existing social inequity rather than as a dynamic process. It must be said, however, that Bourdieu (1984) and Lareau (2000, 2003) both address the dynamics of inequality.

Another challenge for conflict theory lies in explaining the relative permanence and stability of the social order. It is probably an understatement that norms, roles, and social structure appear to change slowly. Even conflict theorists, such as Caplow, Bahr, Chadwick, Hill, and Williamson (1983), report that in the decades since the original Middletown study in the 1920s and subsequent return of the researchers in the 1980s, the hallmark comparative finding is that not much of importance has changed. If conflict is a dialectical process, it may be that it must be studied over fairly sizable units of time as envisioned by Marx. The challenge, then, is for conflict theorists to demonstrate the applicability of conflict theory to more limited units of time, such as decades or years.

This challenge might be partially overcome by a greater emphasis on the details of the process of the dialectic. Between thesis, antithesis, and synthesis comes a lot of social interaction. For example, Scanzoni's (1972) work on renegotiating gender roles in the family is the type of detail work that fills in the gaps in the dialectical process. It is this more detailed work that may aspire to be more concrete and scientific than the more emancipatory view of the sweep of history.

What Turner (1998) has labeled the emancipatory viewpoint of some conflict theorists provokes some fairly hostile criticism. This criticism, however, is more subtle than it initially seems. Certainly, no scientist would assert that scientific knowledge might not have an emancipatory aspect to it; there is no disagreement on the issue of whether knowledge can be emancipatory. The issue is whether emancipation is the central aim of a theory (ideology) or whether the central aim is the production of knowledge (science). If the central role of theory is knowledge, then clearly knowledge claims must be judged by a set of criteria that is universally and equally applied to all such claims. In science, claims are subjected to the rules of logic, experiment, and replication. The fear of scientists is that if claims support the ideology (alternative facts), then they will be judged true because they are consistent with the ideology. One of the basic canons of science is that mere consistency of a finding with previous beliefs is insufficient to justify a claim. If such were the case, then findings would only need to support the prevailing ideology or common sense. Indeed, the history of science is the history of the downfall of systems of thought, such as the heliocentric universe, Newton's mechanics, Maxwell's daemon, and the eventual fall of Einstein's relativity theory.

On the other hand, historiography represents a particular form of analysis that lends itself to "seeing into the future." Hegel, Feuerbach, and Marx all believed that the historical processes they identified are inevitable. Furthermore, they believed that an actor's consciousness and knowledge of the process is part of the process. For example, class consciousness and conflict is a necessary and inevitable part of the process of extinguishing class conflict itself. Thus, our knowledge is viewed as a necessary part of the process. What scientists seem to be saying is, "Let scientific knowledge claims be subjected to scientific criteria; then if the knowledge is emancipatory within any historiography or ideology, so be it." "But," they would continue, "don't expect science to conform to the canon of consistency with the beliefs of ideology or even consistency with previous findings as the sole arbiter of the adequacy of a knowledge claim." In brief, knowledge may be emancipatory, but one of the criteria of knowledge should not be whether or not it is emancipatory.

One of the most difficult challenges confronting conflict theory is, as Zaretsky (1973) observed, to explain why and how feminism developed outside of socialist theory. Indeed, the fact that many types of social relationships cannot be explained by economic structures has propelled critical theorists to move toward psychodynamics and feminist theorists to move away from economic determinism to the broader motif of sex and gender. It remains to be seen if and when a unifying sociohistorical theory can reintegrate these disparate and diverging schools of thought.

Another criticism of conflict theory is the tendency to find one underlying theme or causal relation and then use that one cause to explain all family and human behavior. Single-cause theories are suspect in this day and age of multivariate analyses and ecological consciousness. In defense of conflict theory, it must be pointed out that although there may be only one underlying cause, it keeps changing manifestations throughout history. For instance, although Marx viewed the "relation to the means of production" as being causal, the way it manifested conflict during various historical eras changed. Nonetheless, as we found in the research on wife assault, it may be that a more inclusive conceptualization of conflict that allows for multiple sources of conflict, such as gender and production, provides both inclusiveness and explanatory power.

Conclusion

Conflict theory is diverse. It has both macrosocial and microsocial variants. But we cannot agree with the assessment by Farrington and Chertok (1993) that such diversity has contributed to the near demise of family conflict theory. Rather, what has contributed to that impression is a too narrow focus on *conflict* rather than the process of conflict and management of conflict. There are several themes that allow us to see family conflict theory as a coherent and unified theory spanning time and history, micro and macro levels. Conflict is a process. The process is dialectical and must be studied over time. The way conflict is managed is part of the dialectical process of reaching a new synthesis. Of all the social groups we might study, the family provides the "laboratory" in which there is intense conflict and resolution, hate and love, and violence and support.

Conflict theory stands out in the pantheon of family theories as incorporating both time and history as a common process (the dialectic). As part of a historical process, conflict theory connects the study of contemporary families to families of the past. As grand and sweeping a vision as it provides, it nonetheless can be focused on the specific processes of negotiation and conflict management so that we can understand our day-to-day existence. Conflict theory, as Caplow (1968), Scanzoni (1970), and Straus (1994) have demonstrated, can be explicitly scientific. We believe the strengths of conflict theory far outweigh the criticisms launched against it. There is only one element that could destroy the potential of conflict theory to offer family researchers a vital, process-oriented theory that links family studies with the larger social system and historical processes. That one destructive element is if the theory is dragged into the quagmire of ideology and findings judged by *political correctness* rather than the canons of science. We are optimistic that this will not be the case.

STUDY QUESTIONS

1. Is economic inequality the same as social inequality? (Hint: See section on Bourdieu.)

2. How much of your family life could be described as *harmonious* and how much could be described as *managing conflict*?

3. Both rational choice and conflict frameworks assume that individuals are motivated by self-interests. Is there a difference in what these two frameworks construe as self-interests? If the assumption is the same, why do we end up with two different theoretical frameworks?

4. The economist Thomas Piketty (2014) in his book *Capital in the Twenty-First Century* argues that as long as the rate of growth of capital increases

faster than the rate for wage income, inequality will increase (e.g., the rich will get richer, and the poor will get poorer). He does cite the Bourdieu argument that educational inequality is part of this process. How did your parents support your education? Is there a difference in education between those who want it to lead to a job and those who just want to be an educated person? What kind of college or university would you choose if your goal was to be an educated person versus getting a job? If your wealth is inherited, do you need a job?

5. Marx argued that as the modes of production change, class conflict changes. During your lifetime, how have the modes of production changed (hint: hard currency to mining bit coins). Do the same people control the old and new modes of production? Will this change the way you educate your children?

The Feminist Framework

Jennifer and Heather hadn't seen each other since their university days. After bumping into each other in the grocery store, the two college chums decided to go catch up on what had transpired in each other's lives. "What are you doing now? Are you still painting?" asked Jennifer. "I'm a stay-at-home mom of three little ones," responded Heather. She continued that between meals, homework, laundry, and her volunteer work at her children's elementary school, she has little time to paint. "What about you?"

Jennifer paused for a second and then responded to Heather that after university, she did get a law degree and is about to finally become a partner in a law firm downtown. "What about marriage, kids, family, any of that stuff?" Heather inquired. "Oh yes!" said Jennifer, "We have quite a household: My daughter Maggie is 4, my husband, Cody, is also a lawyer, and we have a live-in nanny, Isabella, who makes it all possible."

Heather was impressed. "Gosh, you're amazing to 'do it all'! I thought about staying at work, but when my first child was 6 months, I just couldn't leave him in someone else's care. Since that time, my family has become the most important thing in my life. Being a mom has become my central identity in life, and the other 'stay-at-homes' I know have all sacrificed a lot for their families."

Jennifer replied that she, too, was heavily invested in parenting. She had gone to great lengths to get their daughter into a very expensive day care only to find that her daughter didn't get the attention she felt she should get. "So we were delighted when we found Isabella. Her English is very good, and she is in the process of getting a driver's license, so she can take Maggie to school and pick her up. Our only problem is that her work visa expires this summer, and we are not sure about renewal. She may have to return to her village in Guatemala."

(Continued)

Heather glanced at her watch and said, "Wow, I have to go soon to take the girls to ballet; it's my turn." Jennifer said, "Your turn?" "Yes," said Heather. "We moms organize car pooling so that we get some respite from the continual barrage of delivering to baseball, soccer, ballet, Olympics of the Mind, chess tournaments, and on and on. I am so grateful for the camaraderie and female culture that goes with the moms who volunteer at school."

Jennifer said, "I guess I haven't experienced that sort of thing since I'm at work and don't have the time. I guess these are all 'stay-at-homes'?" "Yes they are," said Heather as she gathered her purse and packages to go.

Jennifer and Heather may both be feminists, but they represent different perspectives on feminism because of the choices, decisions, and directions their lives have taken. Jennifer represents a feminism that espouses equality and emphasizes work roles. On the other hand, Heather represents a feminism that emphasizes the nurturing mother role and the sharing culture of women. And in between these two is the nanny, Isabella, who represents an immigrant laborer and woman of color. All three of these women represent positions within feminist thought: egalitarianism, cultural feminism, and racial-ethnic feminism. One purpose of this chapter is to identify the diversity within feminist thought.

On the other hand, these diverse positions are united in the feminist framework. Although feminist thought has, overtime, become more diverse, the recent Me Too movement has served to remind us that there are issues that unite and bind feminists despite the diversity and variations. The other purpose of this chapter is to highlight the continuing unity of feminism and its many variations within this framework. The understanding of the theoretical unity of the feminist framework entails an examination of basic assumptions, epistemological, and cultural arguments that have been used to buttress many of the central positions in feminism.

Intellectual Traditions

Feminism

Identifying the dimensions that unite the various approaches to feminist theories is more problematic than it may appear. This is due in large part to the particular way feminist social thought has developed. Feminist thought originated within a social movement for change.

Theory in feminism can be described as both evaluative and empirical. The fact that feminist theories are empirical does not distinguish them from many other theories found in this book; the fact that they are evaluative and ideological does.

Turner (1991, 1998) discusses this type of theorizing as "ideological" or "emancipatory." The role of such theory is not simply to establish explanation but to use theory as a tool in changing the world. Some theories contain a strong moral or evaluative element of what is right and wrong, fair and unjust. Needless to say, such evaluative approaches either implicitly or explicitly suggest how things should be changed. Furthermore, if theoreticians know how things "should be," they are in some ways utopian in their viewpoint. That is, they know what kind of society would be ideal and will work toward that ideal society. This *emancipatory* role of theory is shared by some of the frameworks we discuss, such as conflict theories, but is anathema to others because it brings into question the assumptions of neutrality and objectivity often claimed by scientific realists.

Feminist theory originates from a social movement, and this fact helps us understand the number of variations. Over time, feminism has focused its attention on many different, although related, areas. For example, at the end of the 19th century, feminists concentrated on equal rights. As the social movement and its proponents shifted focus throughout the 20th century, attention turned to such diverse areas as female psychology, the culture of femininity, the basis for female nurturance, and mothering. Not all these analyses necessarily agreed with one another. The outcome of this complex history is that there is a rich tapestry of perspectives that is difficult to paint with a single canvas.

In this section, we offer a brief overview of the intellectual history that has been tied to this social movement. Many scholars studying feminism discuss the movement as historically divided into two phases. The first was from the 1880s to around the early 1920s, when many governments recognized universal suffrage. The Depression of the 1930s, followed by the war and later reconstruction of the 1940s, represented a hiatus in the activities of the women's movement.

The second phase is usually identified with the 1960s to the end of the 20th century. Even though these phases may be adequate descriptions of the social movement, they do not seem to help us understand the intellectual contributions throughout this time period.

Any intellectual history of feminism must begin with Mary Wollstonecraft's *A Vindication of the Rights of Woman* (1792/1975). Although Wollstonecraft was not the only voice to speak out for women's rights, her voice represents what has become the most significant statement of what Donovan (1985) labels "Enlightenment liberal feminism" (p. 1). This early feminism was rooted in the rationalist thought of the Enlightenment.

Among its tenets were a faith in rationality and a belief in natural rights. But Wollstonecraft's critique goes much further than merely subscribing to inalienable rights of individuals. She argued that women failed to develop their minds because the only avenue of obtaining power for a woman was through marriage. As a result, she explained, women were forced to "prostitute" themselves even though it was through the legal mechanism of marriage. This same sentiment was expressed by Marx and Engels in their communist manifesto almost 60 years later.

Another early intellectual contribution was Friedrich Engels's *The Origin of the Family, Private Property, and the State* (1884/1946). Engels argued that the family was originally matriarchal and communal. Domestication of animals allowed for the rise of commodity exchanges and placed more economic power in the hands of men, thus destroying the equality of labor and rights that had existed previously. Engels described this evolution toward commodity exchange and eventually capitalism as the overthrow of the female sex. Female work became undervalued and patriarchy the rule. Although Engels's argument is based on a limited and dated ethnography of one tribal group, the arguments nonetheless represent one of the first analyses to openly identify female subordination as neither natural nor necessary. Much of Engels's writing was to inform later feminist scholars in both Marxist feminism and radical feminism (Donovan, 1985, pp. 65–90).

Charlotte Gilman's (1898) *Women and Economics* and *The Home* (1910) both assumed a social evolutionary perspective, as was common in the social Darwinism of that period. The ideas contained in *The Home* are perhaps the most radical. She argued that women are subjugated and kept in a state of arrested development in the home (Donovan, 1985, p. 48). She described the roles women filled—cook, nutritionist, provider of child care, and so on—and proposed that they should become trained professionals and be paid for their services. Such professionalization would allow for services to be offered at a community rather than family level. As a result, Gilman argues, women would be freed from the tasks of the home to develop and enter the public world. Gilman was one of the first scholars to identify the private versus public roles in the family. She believed that women would unite around feminism, and a truly cooperative social movement would evolve from this consensus.

After the attainment of universal suffrage, the onslaught of the Great Depression followed by World War II dampened much of the social movement's momentum. The intellectual contributions during this hiatus are important, however. Probably the most significant intellectual contribution during this period originated in the anthropological writings of Margaret Mead. The significance of Mead's work in such books as *Coming of Age in Samoa* (1928), *Growing Up in New Guinea* (1930), *Sex and Temperament in Three Primitive Societies* (1935), and later, *Male and Female* (1955) is that she argued strongly that gender behaviors were largely cultural formations and definitions rather than any form of natural or genetic endowment. Her work clearly suggested that gender practices are relative to the cultural context and that often when we compare cultures, we find male behavior in one culture that shares similarities with female behavior in another culture.

Both Gilman and Mead had been social scientists. The next major intellectual influence came from a philosopher and literary figure, Simone de Beauvoir, in her work *The Second Sex* (1949/1953). Simone de Beauvoir was influenced by the French existentialists, most notably Albert Camus and Jean-Paul Sartre (de Beauvoir's companion for many years). Concepts such as the *subject-object dichotomy* and *authenticity* guided her analysis of gender relations. Donovan (1985) states that de Beauvoir

> realized that a dialectic obtains within a culture as well as within an individual: In a patriarchal culture the male or masculine is set up as the positive or the norm, where the female or the feminine is set up as the negative, the unessential, the abnormal, as in short, the Other. (p. 122)

Her analysis of the root of this "otherness" for women lies in the reproductive capacities of women and the division of labor tied to those capacities. Although de Beauvoir rejects the acceptance of this otherness as "bad faith," she nonetheless recognizes the difficulty in rejecting what seems a biological imperative. Her solution is to charge women with becoming more "transcendent," for example, to engage in a career and education.

Critics of de Beauvoir, such as Rabuzzi (1982), have suggested that she simply took the male model of work and career as "transcendent" and denigrated the female model in the very way she criticized in her analysis. Rabuzzi and other critics are quick to point out that the culture around traditional women's work should not be so denigrated and can be seen in a much more positive light than that which de Beauvoir used. It is, however, virtually uncontested that de Beauvoir's analysis occupies a central role in the reemergence of the women's movement after suffrage.

Although some intellectual historians of feminist theory might dismiss Betty Friedan's (1963) popular work *The Feminine Mystique* as modest, there can be little doubt that this *New York Times* best seller refueled the feminist social movement and prepared the ground for other intellectual contributions to follow. Friedan struck a chord among American middle-class women living in the suburbs, who by all appearances had obtained the "American Dream" yet still suffered feelings of dissatisfaction. Friedan challenged the notions that the American Dream nuclear family in the suburbs was the most "functional" (Osmond & Thorne, 1993) and the most psychologically fulfilling. The dissatisfaction of women living this *dream* had previously been labeled as neurotic from the perspective of Freudian psychology. Friedan, however, challenged the Freudian perspective that a well-adjusted woman was a passive object. Indeed, she saw this as labeling as neurotic any role for women other than one of inferiority. Friedan saw the situation as one in which women are oppressed by the male-dominated institutions surrounding them.

Shortly after Friedan, a host of feminist scholarship emerged. Three related works are Shulamith Firestone's *The Dialectic of Sex* (1970), Kate Millet's *Sexual Politics* (1970), and Juliet Mitchell's *Woman's Estate* (1972). All three criticize Freudian psychology's construction of women, but they diverge in important ways. Firestone sees a woman's biology as being one of the primary problems in that reproduction and ownership of children produced a division of labor that subjugated women. Millet argues that contrary to Freudian psychology, biology is not destiny. Her analysis, however, raises questions for Firestone in that Firestone views female liberation as being achieved by freeing oneself from reproduction—that is, from the biological determinism of "motherhood." Mitchell (1972) focuses more on economic and social factors and somewhat chides Firestone for her emphasis on biology. All three of these authors agree that women's subjugation and oppression is closely tied to the family and its ideology.

Not all feminist theorists have so robustly rejected Freudian psychology. Indeed, the significant contribution of Nancy Chodorow in her book *The Reproduction of Mothering* (1978) relies heavily on the psychodynamics of "object-relations." Chodorow argues that the social roles of mother and father that are respectively characterized by nurturant affect and instrumentalism are not due just to patterns of socialization but to the psychodynamics of early childhood as well. In early childhood, the girl's identification with an affectionate mother and the boy's rejection of his mother's power over him provide the roots for both women's subjugation and men's misogyny. Female adults seeking affectively charged relationships are forced to turn from the affectively neutral male to the intimate bonding inherent in the mother-child relationship, thus *reproducing motherhood* from generation to generation. The reproduction of motherhood, because it demands nurturant affect rather than the rational, *affective neutrality* of the male workplace, reproduces the subjugation of women. Chodorow's work should not be interpreted as simply a diatribe against the role of mother, because she also pointed out the positive emotional dimension this role plays for women in an affectively neutral society. This was, in fact, a significant step for some feminists in realizing the importance of some aspects of traditional roles that might even be tied to female oppression.

In retrospect, the decade of the 1970s could be seen as one in which feminist theory was largely of one mind and a single voice. Although there was some variation, feminist thinking of the 1970s was to provide the foundation for the development of great diversity and variation in feminist theories in the decade of the 1980s. One starting point for this developing diversity sprang from the new work of one of the founders of the 1960s' movement, Betty Friedan.

Chodorow's insight regarding the importance of some traditional roles was not lost on Friedan. In 1981, Friedan sparked great controversy with the publication of her book *The Second Stage*. In this work, she clearly praises and acknowledges the many successes of the feminist movement since the initial publication of *The Feminine Mystique* (1963). Friedan argues, however, that in the fight to achieve equality of opportunity, there lies an inherent danger of losing or even willingly giving up many of the positive aspects of traditional roles. Friedan does not argue that traditional roles shouldn't be changed but that we don't want to be caught "throwing the baby out with the bathwater." She especially focuses on the affective rewards of parenting and of intimate relationships found in the family. She argues that the second stage of the women's movement should be aimed at finding ways to successfully articulate the instrumental world of work with the affective world of family. She cautions that if feminists are forced to give up the very values and orientation that have made them different from men in order to fit into the male-fashioned work world, then success will be defined by some very great losses for women.

Friedan's position raised great controversy and also gave momentum to one variation of feminist thinking, *cultural feminism*. This variation is distinguished by the position that what women value most may be intrinsically tied to and originate from traditional women's culture (Donovan, 1985, p. 62). This was just one of the variants to arise in the 1980s, however (e.g., Kourany, Sterba, & Tong, 1999). Various authors distinguish different variations of feminism. For example, Donovan (1985) identifies seven variations, Tuana and Tong (1995) identify nine variations, and Osmond and Thorne (1993) point to six variations. These variations have led to clashes of perspectives on such issues as the liberal feminist position on equality, such as in military service, clashing with the cultural feminist position that an integral component of female culture is the value of life and the pacific character of women as nurturers, not destroyers (see Donovan, 1985, p. 62). As we shall see in our discussion of these theoretical variants, issues of ethnicity and culture have also been the subject of disputes between variant feminist theories.

The many voices that arose during the 1980s provided the impetus for the new developments in feminist theory that were to mark the decade of the 1990s. With many voices and theories that sometimes clash, the question for feminist theorists became "How can we include this diverse and sometimes contrary group of perspectives under the common umbrella of feminist theory?" This question has prompted scholars to address whether multiple and contradictory knowledge claims can simultaneously be held. Interestingly, in this regard, one theoretical school of feminism appears to answer affirmatively and another one negatively. We discuss this question of the many voices of feminism in considerable detail in the next section, which deals with the assumptions of feminist theories.

First-, Second-, and Third-Wave Feminism

Heywood and Drake (1997) have argued that there have been three historically distinct epochs of feminism, which they call "waves" of feminism. The first wave was led by the suffrage movement in the late 1800s and early 1900s. The second wave began in the 1960s with emphasis on both equality and personal liberation. The most recent, third wave is identified with today's younger cohort of women and poststructuralism. Certainly, it is this third wave that usually identifies with postmodern ideas of relativism and antiessentialism. Many of these ideas were embedded in the feminist assumptions of the second wave and have only become more fully elaborated by third-wave scholars. So although there is a distinction regarding the waves, we see many of the basic concepts of feminism to be relatively consistent over time.

Focus and Scope Assumptions

Although we have previously left the term *feminist theory* undefined, it is useful at this juncture to define it. Gordon (1979) defines feminist theory as "an analysis of women's subordination for the purpose of figuring out how to change it" (p. 107). Although there are definitions such as that by Wood (1995), emphasizing similarity between males and females, such definitions tend to be identified with only the *liberal* school of feminism. Gordon's definition is extremely useful. As Osmond and Thorne (1993) point out, Gordon's definition presents three themes that are common to feminist theory. These themes are the "emphasis on women's experience, the identification of oppression, and the emancipatory purpose of feminist theory" (Osmond & Thorne, 1993, p. 592). These themes also express the basic scope and focus assumptions of feminist theories.

Women's experience is central. One of the core assumptions of feminist theory is that women's experience is real and provides the foundation for knowledge claims in feminist theory. This assumption does not rule out other forms of evidence or data but provides a strong epistemological statement as to how such claims will be judged. Tuana and Tong (1995) state that in the history of philosophy, there have often been serious reservations raised about women's capacity to think and reason "rationally" (p. 1). The emphasis on women's *experience* is in part a way of legitimizing and empowering the insights that women have. However, this assumption goes much further to a deep distrust of the kind of thinking, both rationalistic and positivistic, that has systematically excluded the experiences and claims of women, especially in such realms as children, violence, and moral decisions. As Tuana and Tong (1995) point out,

> This emphasis on women's experience—on women's ways of knowing and making moral decisions as well as perceiving reality and controlling their destiny—builds on the understanding that from time to time, what women feel, think, or do will differ from what men feel, think, or do. (p. 1)

Feminist theory has many voices. If women's experience is central, then there is probably more than one way of looking at any given problem, issue, or knowledge claim. It is the centrality of women's experience that partially offers a foundation for the diversity we find in feminist theorizing. Women from different cultures, places, and times may have vastly different experiences that are accorded the same status and respect.

> "Women's experience" is not shorthand for some sort of monolithic "groupthink" but for a vast array of thoughts, feelings, and activities mediated through the lenses of each individual woman's race, class, sexual preference, ethnicity, religion, age, physical condition, and states of mind. (Tuana & Tong, 1995, p. 2)

As we have already alluded, the first assumption—that we can judge the adequacy of a statement by referring it to "women's experience"—is seemingly at odds with the second assumption that women's experience is diverse. This problem has not gone unnoticed by feminist theorists. For example, Harding (1986) says,

> It is a vast overgeneralization to presume that all Africans, let alone all colonized peoples, share distinctive personalities, ontologies, ethics, epistemologies, or worldviews. But is it any worse than the presumption that there are commonalities to be detected in all women's social experiences or worldviews? (p. 659)

Harding (1986) points out that the argument that feminist theory has many voices is problematic for the development of stable concepts and a theoretical structure. Other feminists, such as Smith (1992), have argued that women's experience does provide a strong epistemological foundation, yet others argue that the many voices notion throws feminist thinking into the intellectual flux of *relativism*. On the other hand, categorizations such as those used in positivism are seen as a form of *essentialism,* where diversity is concealed by lumping every member of a group such as African Americans or women into generalizations. This argument, between relativist and essentialist, raises the question of whether or not feminist knowledge claims could have any more privileged authority in challenging patriarchal or biased knowledge than any other group based on one characteristic, such as class, race, ethnicity, or age (Harding, 1986, p. 659). Indeed, this quandary is nicely summarized by the feminist philosopher Duran (1998):

> Without some kind of notion of empirical confirmation, claims
> to have had any kind of experience—including an experience of
> victimization—cannot be confirmed. The contemporary efforts
> on the part of many reactionary political forces to delegitimize
> a great deal of what has transpired in the history of various
> minority groups should disabuse us of any notions we may have
> that confirmation is not important. (p. 181)

Duran continues that the underrepresentation or trivialization of such events as the Holocaust as only one among many possible constructions, all of which are equally valid, suggests the need for a notion of knowledge claims and evidence that goes beyond postmodern relativism. Although there is no simple resolution to this debate, it is useful to acknowledge that the resolution of it is critical to the continued credibility and growth of feminist theory.

Feminist theory is emancipatory (praxis). Feminist theory is closely linked to the feminist movement. This movement has identified patriarchy as being one of the major sources of oppression and inequality in the lives of women. Turner (1991) describes theories that describe, evaluate, and prescribe social action as emancipatory theories. He states that in this perspective,

> theoretical knowledge cannot, therefore, merely describe events.
> It must expose exploitive social arrangements and, at the same
> time, suggest alternative ways to organize humans in less
> oppressive ways. Social theory cannot be neutral; rather, it must
> be emancipatory. (p. 182)

Feminist theory, then, does not simply have to meet criteria about validity but also is judged by whether it is emancipatory. Although this might seem a somewhat foreign assumption to some, to others, this third assumption is not that different from the demand that theoretical knowledge should be useful; only with this meaning, *useful* theory is that which liberates women from patriarchal oppression. Indeed, one way out of the relativism inherent in allowing many voices within a theory is to raise this emancipatory criterion as a pragmatic test of a theory's empirical adequacy.

Concepts

Gender and Sex

Feminist scholars have routinely made the distinctions that *sex* refers to the biologically determined component and *gender* to the cultural and learned component (e.g., Fox & Murry, 2000). This distinction has carried with it the tacit assumption that much of what we identify as gender because of its social nature is more malleable than sex. Osmond and Thorne (1993, pp. 604–606), following Harding (1986) and Scott (1988), discuss three dimensions of gender. First, there is individual gender or gender identity. This dimension of gender focuses on the ways by which we acquire our personal construct of gender—what is masculine and feminine. Second, there is structural gender or gender as a social status. This is gender as a class or category that is part of a hierarchical organization. So, for example, to say that women are second-class citizens would be using this meaning of structural gender. Finally, there is cultural gender that focuses on the symbols attached to social gender and their construction, such as the religious symbols around Eve the Temptress versus the Virgin Mary or the adage that "cowboys don't cry." It is in this cultural realm that scholars have examined the way our language constructs gender.

The discussion of sex and gender has proved to be complicated. First, there is some doubt that any meaningful nature-nurture distinction can be made in this regard. The acquisition of social constructs is so interactively tied to biological maturation that we may not be able to tease these processes apart nor correctly label which effects are due to which processes. A second problem is that one's gender identity probably interacts in complex ways with the other dimensions of gender, structure, and culture so that these distinctions may lack clarity.

Despite criticisms, gender has remained one of the most popular concepts in feminist scholarship. It has been used as the basic dimension for identifying differences, gender relations, culture, and language. It represents the basic dimension for feminist analysis.

Family and Household

Many feminist scholars do not define the family as most other social scientists would—as an empirical entity with members and kin relationships between those members. Rather, the family is more often treated as an *ideology* or as a conceptual fabrication used to justify and maintain certain patterns of privilege. Ferree (1990) states that examining the family from a gender perspective "requires distinguishing between household, which are the coresidential units in which people empirically can be found, and family, the ideology of relatedness that explains who should live together, share income, and perform certain common tasks (Andersen, 1991; Rapp, 1982" [as cited in Ferree, 1990, p. 870]). In this perspective, family is defined neither by its membership nor by the fact of coresidence but by the prevailing ideology that suggests that a certain division of labor or type of coresidence is normal or natural. Thus, part of family would be the understandings that in family, certain work is "women's work" or in custody disputes that mother custody is preferred because of some inherent maternal ability. Family, then, is an ideology and normative set that is ripe for the analysis of gender-based distinctions and inequalities.

Public and Private

The idea that women's and men's experience is divided into fairly distinct sectors is viewed by feminists as a means to organize people into social classes based on gender. During the Industrial Revolution, women were increasingly "protected" from the exploitation of capitalism and poor working conditions by eliminating them from any role in the paid labor force and relegating their work and industry to the private sphere of the home. The private sphere of the home was removed from public accountability not only in terms of work but also in terms of public social norms. What was illegal or nonnormative in terms of public behavior could be tolerated in private. Thus, the exploitation of women and children continued in an even less regulated environment where men could escape public sanction for beating, violence, and even rape because it was in the private sphere of the family. Indeed, in the 20th century, the family became the dominant ideology tied to the private sphere. For example, what might be a criminal assault in public could be concealed and even forgiven in private. Hence, the dichotomy of private and public spheres is seen by feminists as being an ideology that supports and maintains a gender-based class system (see Osmond & Thorne, 1993, pp. 608–612).

Sexism

This concept shares similarities with concepts about age and race, ageism and racism. In fact, we can adapt the definition of racism by Pierre van den Berghe for our definition of sexism.

Sexism is any set of beliefs that organic, genetically transmitted differences (whether real or imagined) between human groups are intrinsically associated with the presence or absence of certain socially relevant abilities or characteristics and, hence, that such differences are a legitimate basis of invidious distinctions between groups socially defined as sexes (adapted from van den Berghe, 1979, p. 11).

This definition clearly states that when someone believes a trait such as sex is genetically determined and relatively immutable and then makes harmful or damaging attributions about all individuals with that trait, such beliefs would be labeled *sexist* and behavior guided by such beliefs would be *sexism*. It should be noted that the veracity of the beliefs is not the determinant, only the harm or damage associated with the class distinction. Thus, to say that all girls cannot play in a soccer league is to make a potentially harmful distinction based on class inclusion and would be an example of sexism. It would also be sexist by this definition to say "All women are nurturing" or "All women are peace loving."

Intersectionality

Over the last two decades, third-wave feminist scholarship has increasingly employed the concept of *intersectionality*. This concept has emerged as a new theoretical construct used across a broad spectrum of feminist theories (e.g., Allen, Walker, & McCann, 2013; De Reus et al., 2005). Intersectionality is broadly defined as the multiple ways that characteristics, socially defined and constructed by structural systems (e.g., age, sex, sexual orientation, race, gender, and social class), converge in a particular time and location for a group or individual to structure outcomes of privilege and oppression (Allen et al., 2013, pp. 141–142). Some feminists believe that the concept of intersectionality broadens the theoretical approach and is the hallmark of third-wave feminist scholarship (Allen et al., 2013, p. 141).

Other key terms are *inequality* and *oppression*. In fact, they are usually the major dependent or outcome variables in feminist theories. These ideas are important in order to appreciate that it is not enough to simply understand gender differences. The differences that matter are those that subordinate women to men, and such inequality is not natural or inevitable but the result of social forces that "push down," or subjugate, women relative to men.

Propositions

Feminist theory has been inclusive of women's differing experiences and perspectives. As a result, some theoretical statements that we include below express the perspective of one group of feminist scholars but not others. Indeed, some of the propositions listed below would spark controversy among these groups. We highlight the differences in perspectives in the Variations section, which follows this section. For this section, we attempt to present a reasonably consistent and coherent theory that we believe captures the major propositions and logic in this area of discourse.

Gender structures our experience.

Although biological sex may account for some differences between males and females, every culture raises these few differences to a heightened status in the social construction of gender. For example, in North American culture, women stereotypically have had longer hair than men. The sex difference is that females' hair on average grows faster than males' and that females do not inherit alopecia. Yet from this rather simple difference, entire industries are spawned to highlight, manage, and accentuate this difference in cosmetology, hairdressing, and fashion. Thus, the experience of females and males is socially constructed to be different in all cultures.

Gender structures all societies.

Gender is used as a basic class distinction in all societies. Looking around at the world in which we live, we see babies wrapped in pink or blue blankets, we see washrooms designated by gender, and we see girls' soccer teams and boys' soccer teams. Gender, like age, represents one of the most basic social class distinctions. Although some might argue that the division is sex and not gender, we would simply point out that being in the appropriate washroom is more a function of attire and deportment than it is related to biology, as any transvestite can attest. Thus, it is cultural symbols and meaning that construct this social class.

Women as a class are devalued and oppressed.

Andreas (1971), as well as many other feminists, has pointed out that gender as a class distinction is not simply an organizational principle but also represents invidious distinctions that privilege one class (men) while oppressing another (women). The basic structure of all societies seems organized by the principle that females are inferior—physically, mentally, or both—to males. As a result of such distinctions, referring back to the definition of sexism, all societies are sexist to some degree. Some feminists state this fact as being the dominance of *patriarchy*. Sexism could occur even in the absence of patriarchy and be aimed at either gender, however.

As a result of sex, gender beliefs, and historical and continuing sexism and oppression, there exists a "female culture."

Centuries of patriarchy and sexism have resulted in female identity being formulated in opposition and as an antidote to oppression. The result has been the development of a "female culture" founded on a much different vision of the world than usually supplied by patriarchy. For example, Donovan (1985) lists some attributes of this vision as being "pacifism, cooperation, nonviolent settlement of differences, and harmonious regulation of public life" (p. 32). In this perspective, the social construction of gender combined with gender class distinctions has given rise to a culture that represents an alternative to the patriarchal, bellicose, and competitive worldview that seems to dominate the world today.

The family is not monolithic.

Feminists such as Eichler (1988) have pointed out that, in large part, the ideology of the public and private spheres has been buttressed by the vision of the family as unitary and monolithic. By portraying the family as a monolithic single type of organization governed by unchanging social norms, scholars in sociology and other disciplines have established the status quo as a moral norm. Young women and men are led to believe that to be a "family," certain norms and timetables must be followed; otherwise, one will not have a family as we now know it—that is, the reconstruction of their own family of orientation in their family of procreation (see Chodorow, 1978). This view is often couched in language that would assign particular immutable social functions to the organization of the family and imply that if the family changes, society, as we know it, would founder. Feminist scholars have been at the leading edge of research on family diversity in terms of sexual preference, organization of family roles and labor, and culture and ethnic variability.

The family is a central institution for the reproduction of oppression.

Feminists view the concealment of diversity within and between families as part of the construction of gender because it allows a portrayal of gender roles as fixed and immutably defined by the tradition of patriarchy. As a result, the family as an institution is often viewed as one of the central organizations responsible for the reproduction of oppression through socialization and social expectations (Taylor, 1997). As Ferree (1990) notes, feminists recognize both the need for changing constraining sex roles and that "families are also institutions of support and resistance for women as they confront other forms of social oppression" (p. 868). Thus, feminists carefully examine the institution of the family with an eye to not throwing the baby out with the bathwater.

One last caveat in regard to these propositions is required. Such propositions are not laid out in many other feminist works. The reason for this is twofold. First, as we have already noted, there exist some disagreements between different theoretical variants. Second, much of feminist scholarship has either rejected positivist approaches or viewed such approaches with suspicion. One of the suspicions has been that in the search for nomothetic general laws, not only have women been poorly represented but diversity and variation have been seen as standing in the way of generalizations—and hence poorly represented too. Although we believe that both of these reasons bear consideration, we also believe that feminist theory is sufficiently well developed that some general propositional inventory is appropriate and assists students and scholars in more fully understanding this theoretical framework. One example of a more propositional approach to feminism is Lorber (1998).

Variations

The feminist framework is very complex. There are many variants of feminist theory. Like other theoretical frameworks, these variants have developed for numerous reasons over the last 40 years. Probably the largest change in the way we conceptualize this array of feminist theories is the distinction of second- and third-wave theories (Heywood and Drake, 1997). In this section of variants, we organize the theoretical diversity by those theories that would be second wave (1960–2000) and those that would be third wave (2001–present). It should be noted that because a theory might be second wave, such as liberal feminism, does not mean that it is not currently popular or useful for researchers but just that it was developed during the second-wave historical period (1960–2000).

Second Wave (1960–2000)

Second-wave variants tend to have sprung from the major first-wave theory of human rights from the Enlightenment (Wollstonecraft, 1792/1975). Certainly, there is a direct connection to the variant of liberal feminism. Some of the second-wave variants latch onto one substantive dimension of feminist theory, such as mothering or patriarchy. Macroscopic and microscopic analyses also explain some of the variants. And finally, some of the variants are tied to broader theories such as psychoanalysis or Marxist theory. In the following section, we review what we believe are the most significant of the variations for the study of the family. Our discussion follows the distinctions made by feminist scholars, such as Fox and Murry (2000), Osmond and Thorne (1993), Tuana and Tong (1995), and Donovan (1985).

Liberal Feminism

Liberal feminism is tied to the Enlightenment philosophy of rationalism and human rights (Donovan, 1985). The rationalist belief that "all men are created as equal" was easily envisaged as extending to both genders. The major thrust of this perspective is on achieving gender equality. Barriers to gender equality are viewed as any law, institution, or person that discriminates on the basis of gender. Thus, most of the efforts of liberal feminism have been directed at equality of opportunity and the removal of barriers that would work against such equality.

Although this variant does not directly appear in any particular feminist theory of the family per se, it nevertheless informs many research perspectives. For example, much of the research on the division of labor in the household has taken as an implicit assumption that equality of labor is desirable (Hochschild & Machung, 1989; Scanzoni, 1972). When researchers report inequitable hours of labor in the home for working wives and husbands, they immediately assume that this is far from desirable (Acock & Demo, 1994). This perspective has a firm basis in Enlightenment rationalism and informs our views of fairness and justice.

Although many would find the tenets of liberal feminism appealing, these same tenets have contributed to various contentious debates. One example is the break between liberal feminists, who support the inclusion of women in the armed forces, and cultural feminists, who have opposed this move on the grounds that women's pacific nature and culture are at odds with the militarism of this traditional male bastion. Another example of the contentiousness of the liberal feminist stance is that it ignores any true biological differences between sexes. Most liberal feminists tend to see few, if any, real differences between males and females. Most differences are viewed not as fixed but rather as malleable by socialization. Other variants question these assumptions, however. They are perhaps most strongly questioned by cultural and psychoanalytic schools of feminism, where biological differences, such as breast-feeding, are viewed as interactively creating roles and identities that are universal for females. This debate really ignites when we discuss whether "extra" rights are required for maternity leave as opposed to paternity leave or other workplace benefits.

Many of these issues have led some liberal feminists to become more radical in their thinking. Gender is a long-term, historical construction. It is a more complex issue than simply one caused by a denial of equal rights, and it will not be cured by equality of opportunity alone. One need only point to the failure to ratify the Equal Rights Amendment in the United States, where female voters were a major factor in the defeat. Clearly, identities, social roles, and social structure are deeply embedded in our world.

Radical Marxist/Socialist Feminism

One of the most cogent and impressive analyses in this area is contained in the work *The Dialectic of Sex* by Shulamith Firestone (1970). Firestone (1970) begins her analysis with an acknowledgment of her debt to Engels's (1884/1946) analysis in *The Origin of the Family, Private Property, and the State,* and her evaluation that Engels and Marx failed to go deep enough in their analyses:

> Engels did observe that the original division of labor was between man and woman for the purposes of childbreeding; that within the family the husband was the owner, the wife the means of production, the children the labor; and that reproduction of the human species was an important economic system distinct from the means of production. (p. 5)

Where Marx and Engels went wrong, according to Firestone, is that they did not plumb the depths of the nature of reproduction and sex but instead envisioned these as part of the underlying economic class conflict. Firestone proposes a view of history based on sex rather than economic relations. She supposes that, unlike economic class, "sex class" sprang directly from a biological reality: Men and women were created differently and not equally privileged (p. 8). She argues that for most of human history, the family (and women) has been characterized by four fundamental points. First, before the relatively recent development of birth control, women were at the mercy of their biology in terms of pregnancy, lactation, and care of infants and thus were dependent on others for survival. Second, human infants take a long time to become self-sufficient and are dependent on adults for their survival. Third, basic mother-child interdependency has shaped the psychology of every woman and child. Fourth, and last, the basic reproductive division of labor provides for the most fundamental class distinction—that of sex. From these four points, Firestone (1970) argues that sex class underlies other social divisions by economic class or race. She suggests that male patriarchy as well as female socialization in the family have encouraged the social partitioning of labor so as to justify not only social inequality but also inequality of opportunity. Her argument does not lack for either historical, cross-cultural, or contemporary examples of inequity based on gender.

Firestone (1970) notes that the root source of the inequity is biological in origin. As long as women get pregnant, bear children, and breast-feed, they are tied to the very elements that justify the division of labor:

> Nature produced the fundamental inequality—half the human race must bear and rear the children of all of them—which was later consolidated, institutionalized, in the interests of men. Reproduction of the species cost women dearly. (p. 232)

Firestone (1970) suggests a program to correct the damage that has been done to both males and females by the excessive sexual division of labor. The central point in her program is that females should be freed of the tyranny of biological reproduction. She argues that only when we use reproductive technology to free women from biological reproduction will the division into sex classes cease. She goes even further and argues that removing biological reproduction and creating economic independence of both women and children "would be enough to destroy the family, which breeds the power psychology" (p. 236). Firestone's program thus envisions the reorganization of reproduction in addition to the more traditional Marxian focus on the reorganization of production. She believes that the changes she envisions are already under way as technology slowly replaces the functions of the family and care of infants becomes increasingly performed by "professional caregivers." In the end, she believes that "revolt against the family could bring on the first successful revolution" (p. 274).

Firestone (1970) probably represents the more radical wing of Marxist feminism, but other scholars have followed up on various aspects of these ideas. For example, Berk (1985) deals with the family as the major component in the reproduction of gender relations and the division of labor. Ferree (1990), in her review of feminists' contributions to the family literature, cites the family ideology that can be used to legitimate appeals for female self-sacrifice. Osmond and Thorne (1993) point out that feminist scholars have been critical of what constitutes "family" because they are "critical of that ideology and alert to contemporary disputes . . . (i.e., over surrogate mothering, the control of reproduction, child custody, and legal provisions for domestic partnerships)" (p. 618). Although all feminist scholars are not necessarily Marxist-feminist or as radical as Firestone (1970), the issues that she raises are indeed central.

Cultural Feminism

Linda Alcoff (1995) defines cultural feminism in the following passage:

> Cultural feminism is the ideology of a female nature or female essence reappropriated by feminists themselves in an effort to

revalidate undervalued female attributes. For cultural feminists, the enemy is not merely a social system or economic institution or a set of backward beliefs but masculinity itself and in some cases male biology. (pp. 435–436)

Although this quote serves to orient us toward cultural feminism, it does not identify the characteristics that are most often seen as essentially female. Different positions exist within this framework, yet the traits of pacifism, nurturance, and expressiveness are often listed. Aggressiveness is often identified as a male trait, linked to testosterone—that is, the antipathy of femaleness.

Donovan (1985) traces the history of cultural feminism back to 1923 and documents the dispute between liberal and cultural feminists as a component in the failure to ratify the Equal Rights Amendment. Indeed, it is a centerpiece of cultural feminism that equality may be a hindrance and threat to preserving female culture and its values. If equality means becoming like males in terms of power, politics, and war, then most cultural feminists would reject it. Furthermore, the strong vein of pacifism and environmental concerns that runs in cultural feminism would favor not equality but protection and special attention.

Cultural feminists are not exactly clear about whether the origins of female culture are biologically or socially constructed. The work of psychoanalytic feminists, such as Nancy Chodorow (1978), has suggested that it is a complex weave of culture and genes that interact to create the femaleness that cultural feminists treat as central. Although many women are leery of claiming "differences" that deserve special treatment, there are certainly new calls for this in regard to female education and relationship development (Gilligan, 1982).

Other Variations

There are numerous other variations that could be considered, such as psychoanalytic feminism, anarchist feminism, lesbian feminism, and so on. Several of these variants could be joined with the ones above. For example, environmental feminism (e.g., Gaard, 1993) might be best linked to cultural feminism. The realization that the North American family is not a monolithic institution but contains great diversity of family types and structures can in part be credited to feminist scholars (e.g., Eichler, 1988). Accompanying this idea is the insight that ethnic, religious, and racial identities help create much of this diversity in form and structure. For example, Dilworth-Anderson, Burton, and Johnson (1993) argue that most of the existing theories about families need to be reframed to predict and understand minority families. More recently, Allen (2000) has argued that family scholarship needs to direct research toward diversity and be more sensitive to the presence of diversity in families.

Third Wave (2001–Present)

The third wave of feminism, while diverse, is more easily systemized than second-wave feminism. This may be in part because proponents are more sensitive to the academic audience and less driven by the social movement. We see three ways in which feminist scholarship sees the theoretical contribution to family studies as deriving from the social movement of feminism. For example, Allen, Walker, and McCann (2013) summarize such contributions as follows: "Investigating families from feminist perspectives has invigorated the field of family studies by challenging taken-for-granted assumptions about the dynamics and structures of family relationships in social contexts" (p. 139). This position sees the feminist movement as supplying critical feminist and deconstructionist dialogues for the study of the family. In large part, this is an important critical voice that is independent but complementary to family scholarship. However, some feminist theorists and family scholars share an emphasis on the constructs of sex and gender as central to social science and family research.

Gender Theories

The study of gender and sex continues to occupy significant scholarly attention. Some of this interest is from areas outside of family studies as varied as sports physiology and brain differences. Among family scholars, gendering, or the social construction and social learning of gender, continues to be a major area of academic study. Wood (2013) cites four broad theoretical perspectives on gendering: social learning theory, cognitive developmental theory, performance theory, and standpoint theory. All these theories focus on the role of parenting, schooling, and early childhood experiences in defining and structuring gender. Indeed, in many areas of family scholarship, gender remains a central concern. For example, Bianchi and Milkie's (2010) decade review of work-family research was organized with headings reflecting this focus (e.g., gender, time and division of labor, maternal employment). Even in Wood's (2013) review, the author examines academic theories explaining either gender differences or the process of gendering. There is little or no attention to the concept of intersectionality that has been so identified with third-wave feminism.

Intersectionality

Using the concept of intersectionality does not imply that the concepts of gender and sex are not important. However, sex and gender become conjoined with other characteristics that are pinpointed in one position. For example, we might be interested in the interactions of age, gender, race, and ethnicity for 20-year-old, black African women living in Los Angeles. The interactions of these four variables (age, gender, race, and ethnicity) would be different for Boston, Milan, or Mumbai. One of the often cited applications of intersectionality is in an area that has become known as critical race feminism.

Critical Race Feminism

The rise of third-wave feminist theory is probably most associated with critical race feminism. Several basic tenets set this school apart from some of the previous second-wave schools of feminist scholars. Most notably, the very nature of seeing constructs such as *female* or *women* as meaningful is questioned. For example, De Reus, Few, and Blume (2005) argue that "poststructural feminists have challenged the unified category of 'woman' as the basis for a general theory of oppression of *all* women because it obfuscates within-group variation" (p. 449). Their perspective is that women have multiple identities and that these identities are concealed and lost with essentializing constructs, such as "woman." As a result, they propose that feminist scholars should study the way women's multiple identities intersect in their everyday lived experiences. They argue that poststructural theories are different from even the standpoint theories in that "standpoint theories, including multicultural feminism, are essentialist and lead to false generalizations, whereas poststructural theories are antiessentialist and deconstructive to a fault" (p. 450).

De Reus et al. (2005) prefer the fluidity of deconstructionism to what they see as the false generalizations of essentialist theories. This means that a multicultural theory or research about African American women would be, in their view, making false generalizations because the category of African American women contains women who are far from the mode and may have distinct combinations of identities where "African American woman" is only one among many of these identities. De Reus et al. argue that the way these women construct the intersections of their multiple identities is what critical race feminists really should be studying. The poststructural theoretical assumptions they make constrain their methodological approaches to qualitative case study techniques.

Multicultural feminism raises issues such as the exploitation of immigrant women from underdeveloped countries who labor as nannies and caregivers for dual-career families in North America. These women may relinquish many personal freedoms as they enter a semivoluntary legal arrangement between their sponsor family and immigration officials. Furthermore, many women from other cultures may desire to continue what they regard as their cultural practices, whereas other North American feminists may see these as "sexist" practices. Perhaps the most volatile example of this has been the "right" of women in parts of Africa to practice clitorectomy as a religious and cultural symbol of devoutness. Such examples raise the serious issue of feminist ideology versus respect and tolerance for religious and cultural diversity.

Empirical Applications

Gendered Division of Labor

One of the most obvious applications for feminist theory has been in the area of the division of household labor between husbands and wives. Thompson and Walker (1995) conclude that feminist scholarship has moved to the center of research in this particular domain. The context of much of the study of division of labor is the 40 or more years of feminist action resulting in initiating reforms in the areas of work and education. Historically, there appears a clear departure from these advances when we examine the private sphere of the division of labor in the household. Indeed, some authors have characterized this as a "stalled revolution" (Hochschild & Machung, 1989).

Hochschild and Machung (1989), as well as other researchers (e.g., Acock & Demo, 1994), have documented the fact that when researchers use hours of housework as a measure of the division of labor within the household, we find some estimates that wives spend almost double the time that husbands spend on household chores and child care (see Coltrane, 2000; Perry-Jenkins, Newkirk & Ghuney, 2013; Perry-Jenkins, Repetti, & Crouter, 2000). In addition, satisfaction with the division of labor in the household has proven to be a strong predictor of overall satisfaction with the balance between work and family (White, 1999). Attitudes about giving and receiving support in the household are also strongly correlated with marital quality (Vannoy & Phillber, 1992). Pyke and Coltrane (1996) found that husbands with an egalitarian gender role were more likely to share household chores.

A persistent anomalous finding in regard to the unequal number of hours spent by spouses on home labor is in regard to the perception of fairness. According to Acock and Demo (1994), wives typically report that they are satisfied with the fairness of the division of labor in the household. Acock and Demo argue that this may be due to the comparison with others where any assistance is viewed as a bonus. Other researchers such as Hawkins, Marshall, and Allen (1998) have argued that a sense of fairness is linked to the wives feeling appreciated by husbands. Finally, several researchers have demonstrated that among wives who sense unfairness in the division of labor, there is lower marital quality (e.g., Blair & Johnson, 1992; Greenstein, 1996; Voydanoff & Donnelly, 1999). Recently, the estimates of inequality have been changing. Bianchi and Milkie (2010) report that the gender gap in both household tasks and child care is becoming increasingly similar for both men and women. Increasingly, research is focused on the correlates of participation in these activities such as male employment and its positive association with fathering (Coley & Morris, 2002).

There is little doubt that sharing in the household labor is an egalitarian ideology (Pyke & Coltrane, 1996). Even early feminist scholars pointed out that equality of opportunity in the world of work and education can be stalled by the organization of the private sphere of the household. Indeed, feminists have argued that patriarchy is sustained by the household division of labor. Not only do males benefit from the inequality of work but this inequality in the private sphere helps guarantee as well the perpetuation of gendered class structure in the public sphere. Female ascension in the work world is short-circuited as a result of added labor in the private sphere (see Shelton & John, 1996). In addition, Thompson (1992) argues that ideology determines perceptions of fairness in that women who expect less than equal arrangements in domestic labor would tend to view inequality as fair. Certainly, research in the area of the division of labor in the household supports this suspicion, and theory in this area has focused on the gendered nature of the housework (Davis & Greenstein, 2013). However, it should be acknowledged that there are other competing theories, such as social exchange, that may offer an equal or superior explanation of these data (Shelton & John, 1996).

Ehrenreich (2000) speculates that housework is moving from the private sphere to the public in what she calls the "capitalization" of housework. She explains that more dual-earner families are hiring maid services to do the previously contested housework. The hidden dimension of this is that it represents a traditional class, gender, and ethnic division of labor. For example, she reports that between 14% and 18% of households employed an outside service for cleaning in 1999, but a recent report cites a 53% increase in demand between 1995 and 1999 (Ehrenreich, 2000). She cites a 1998 Bureau of Labor Statistics report that 37% of private cleaners and servants were Hispanic, and another 19% were Black or Asian. Furthermore, Ehrenreich (2000) reports that one study found that the median earnings for household cleaners and servants was "$12,220 in 1998, which is $1,092 below the poverty level for a family of three" (p. 64). If nanny and household cleaning services are added together, this area of the "private sphere" seems increasingly within the sphere of the "public" capitalistic exploitation of women of color. If this is so, then the suggestions by liberal feminists, such as Gilman (1910), that women be freed from home-based tasks by professionals trained in homemaker roles may be at the expense of an underclass of women of color.

Critiques and Discussion

Any theoretical perspective that is critical of the status quo is likely to garner reactions and critiques from those who might feel threatened by change. It is useful to avoid such simple reactions. Furthermore, it is somewhat difficult to address criticisms to such a diverse grouping of schools of thought. The discussion here addresses only issues that the schools of feminism tend to share and that are relevant to the nature and purpose of theory.

The first criticism often raised is that feminist theory is not a theory at all but an ideology. This criticism is often founded on the assumption that the sole purpose of "theory" is to explain phenomena. Calls to action and advocacy of values, such as those inherent in much of feminist theory, are viewed as a moral or valued perspective rather than an attempt to explain phenomena. Thus, critics argue that feminism is not a theory at all but a political ideology.

Undoubtedly, there is some evidence for this criticism when we find unsupported claims made because they are deemed morally justified. However, the same accusation could be made about other emancipatory theories, such as Marxian conflict theory. Furthermore, if ungrounded comments from some theoreticians were prima facie evidence that a theory did not exist, most existing theoretical frameworks would be equally tainted. It seems to us that the more valid question is not whether values or morals are interwoven with the theoretical perspective but whether this theory offers theoretical propositions that can be empirically disproved. To put it another way, we would focus not on where the theory comes from (context of discovery) but solely on whether it supplies disconfirmable propositions about family phenomena (context of justification).

In many ways, feminism falls short of this criterion of providing clear propositions for testing. This fact alone would suggest that it is not yet a theory in the traditional scientific sense. Nonetheless, it joins many of the other theoretical frameworks in this book in having concepts and some suggestive propositions that are not yet clearly specified. Indeed, our assessment is that feminism is a theoretical framework with great potential. The obstacles to developing this potential, however, are not inconsequential. First and foremost is the rejection of the traditional model of the justification of knowledge claims by empirical testing. As long as feminists reject the methods and goals of theoretical propositions, it is doubtful that they will produce a theory that is disconfirmable. The caveat here is that successive generations of feminist scholars may be more receptive to producing knowledge claims that are subjected to empirical testing. As Duran (1998) points out, the success of feminists has been due in part to their ability to produce empirical evidence to support claims of discrimination and inequities. This same strength can be used to develop empirically testable theory.

Closely aligned to this problem is the problem inherent in the feminist epistemology of *experience* (e.g., Haack, 1998). The claim that experience provides the basis for knowledge is not controversial. It should be noted that science should not care where good ideas come from but should focus on whether the ideas can be subjected to disconfirmation. It is at this point that some feminists might argue that subjective experience should count in the disconfirmation of statements. If this were so, we would not be teaching evolution in many school systems where subjective religious beliefs would hold sway over propositions that have been subjected to empirical tests. Indeed, this is a danger for the progress of feminism because it would make popularity and political sway the arbiters of fact rather than science. It can be argued that with all its frailties, science has proved useful for feminist goals and arguments.

Standpoint and poststructural epistemology both confront us with the impossibility of resolving disputed claims. This is another area of criticism. For example, standpoint epistemology argues that each group's or person's standpoint is valid (e.g., Smith, 1992). To adopt this position, however, it is necessary to assume a relativistic perspective on knowledge. The relativistic perspective then fails to provide a way to resolve contradictory knowledge claims other than by "might makes right," where might is determined by popularity, money, or power.

As we have seen from the diversity of the feminist schools of thought, the notion that feminists are defined by a value commitment to knowledge that liberates women from patriarchal oppression provides further difficulties. We are left asking whose values determine "true" liberation. For example, the cultural feminists opposed women entering the armed services because such integration was seen as undermining the pacifist values of feminism. On the other hand, liberal and radical feminists supported this move as following their value on equality of opportunity. More clashes will occur over issues such as universal day care as opposed to maternal care. With fertility falling in most of the developed world, a potential area for conflict will be whether women in the labor force should be treated as equal in all regards to males in the labor force or whether special concessions should be made for women because of childbirth and lactation. Again, we must ask every value-driven theorist how to decide whose values are the correct ones.

To make a theory of gender inequality useful as a family theory, ideas about the family must be included. One possibility is to attend to the familial aspects of the inequality itself. So we might focus on the power and division of labor among wives and husbands, mothers and fathers, or daughters and sons instead of all women and all men. The other major possibility is to locate at least some of the causes of gender inequality within family variables or processes.

Finally, the core concepts of feminism need to be developed more fully. Notions of psychological (identity) and structural gender need to be linked together. For example, Straus (1994) found support for the link between spousal abuse rates and the status of women for each state in the United States. There is the need for careful theoretical exposition moving from this structural level of patriarchy to individual family violence. The need for such exposition is not exclusive to feminism but is a critique that could be addressed to many social theories. However, feminist scholars have proved themselves particularly adept at producing insights linking different levels of analyses. Once feminism takes as one of its goals the production of knowledge claims that are logically coherent and empirically testable, much progress should be made. It is this potential that should excite scholars in family studies.

Conclusion

Is feminism dead? Russo's (1998) analysis of survey data reported that of the women in her sample who self-identified as feminist, 33% agreed with a statement saying that pushing equal rights has gone too far and 38% agreed that the United States would be better off if people worried less about how equal people are. Of the sample, only 27% of the females identified themselves as feminists!

Although in the critique section we argued that the major threat to the theoretical framework of feminism is its lack of investment in the goals of science and the production of empirically testable knowledge claims, overall there may be an even larger threat: becoming irrelevant as a social movement. Many authors have cataloged the successes of the feminist movement in winning legislated workplace equality and equality of opportunity (e.g., Friedan, 1981). Yet in many ways the rhetoric of the movement seems mired in the 1970s. When the movement is relevant, it is often because special interest groups focus on very specific goals (women of color). So on one hand, the movement is both increasingly diverse and specialized, and on the other hand, when it is univocal, it seems out of date. As one of our students expressed it, feminism is a movement unaware of its success. Indeed, the current and successive cohorts of students take for granted these successes and cannot comprehend a time when males and females were less equal.

The answer to this critique of irrelevance is in the form of the Me Too movement. Although the Me Too movement began in 2006 by New York activist Tarana Burke to help victims of sexual harassment and assault, it certainly reached a zenith after Hollywood film mogul Harvey Weinstein was accused by numerous female film stars of using his position of power to harass and coerce women. This revelation was just the beginning of a cascade of similar claims throughout North America and other countries. It became obvious that the widespread use of male power to sexually harass and coerce female employees is an issue that united feminists from almost all varieties of feminism.

Despite the unity that was shared, many voices were raised to caution the movement's excesses. For example, Margaret Atwood, Canadian author of *The Handmaid's Tale*, reflected on whether she is a "bad feminist" for advocating that due process be observed in the treatment of an accused professor of creative writing (see Atwood, 2018, "Am I a Bad Feminist?"). Catherine Deneuve and 100 other French women signed an open letter denouncing the Me Too movement as going too far (see CNN, 2018, update). Her position was subsequently softened after criticism. As well, the lawyer J. H. Grey argued that the movement should be careful about "ending careers based on unproven accusations," the confusion of serious criminal claims of assault and rape with lewd comments or looks, and judging behavior by today's normative environment rather than what was historically normative (Julius S. Grey, 2018, "Reign of Terror in Matters," p. A11). Despite these warnings, the Me Too movement has rejuvenated and unified feminists from all varieties.

Although the social movement seems to have coalesced and unified around the Me Too movement, the intellectual contribution from feminist scholars has consistently remained strong and vibrant even when the social movement was thought to be moribund. Wills and Risman (2006) reviewed the frequency of articles using at least some feminist content in three major family journals. They report that "there was an increase in feminist visibility from 1972 to 1992, at which point the growth of visibility stalled. From 1992 to 2002, almost 1 out of 4 articles appeared to be influenced, at least minimally, by feminist scholarship" (p. 690). The intellectual contribution, however, is not isolated to feminist theory but participates in the way other theories are developed and applied. For example, Foschi and colleagues (Foschi, 1996, 2000; Foschi, Lai, & Sigerson, 1994) have extended the social psychological theory of "expectation states" into the realm of the application of double standards of competence for men and women. She and her colleagues experimentally investigated how lower status based on characteristics such as ethnicity, social class, and gender contributes to stricter levels of competence being applied to these individuals. Foschi's work shows a concern with *feminist issues*, but her intellectual contributions are buttressed by strong theoretical and empirical science.

As Wills and Risman (2006) discuss, some might see 25% of the journal articles as having some modest feminist content as a great advance for the legitimacy and usefulness of feminist theories, whereas others might point out that 75% of the articles had no such content. Given the great number of theories and frameworks we cover in this book, we might tend to see the 25% as a significant portion of the articles in these three journals. Although we do not expect to see this framework as making future gains in this regard, it does seem that feminism has had a powerful and significant effect on family scholarship. So although the third-wave social movement of feminism may not have the numerical force and popular appeal of the second wave, we do see the intellectual contributions of feminist theory as consistently strong and productive. Feminist theory has an open and vibrant intellectual future.

STUDY QUESTIONS

1. Describe the ways that feminism has evolved over time from its start with universal suffrage. Do you think that different countries require different forms of feminism?

2. Feminist theory as an intellectual enterprise has struggled with the dual requirement to be both analytically refined and anti-oppressive. Although some critics see this as an inherent contradiction, do you think it is?

3. Since several males have reported assaults by other males as part of the Me Too movement, is this a feminist movement or a human rights movement?

4. How would you define *female liberation*? Would the others in your class agree?

5. Feminist scholarship has long struggled with the problem of differences between males and females. This has run the gamut from positions in liberal feminism arguing that most differences between males and females are socialized and therefore flexible, to arguments such as Firestone's argument that true liberation means getting rid of physical differences (e.g., pregnancy and lactation). There are many other varieties of these arguments. Do you think there are inherent unchangeable differences between men and women? Should these guide theory?

The Ecological Framework

"Mom, why does Dad take us to school and pick us up when all the other kids' mothers do that?" Katrina's mother answers that their father lost his job, and it's easier for her, the mother, to find work. Hidden in the mother's response to Katrina is a complex explanation. Recently, most of the growth in jobs has been in the service sector of the economy. Traditionally, men have been employed in the primary-extractive and secondary-manufacturing sectors of the economy. In North America, both of these traditional male employment sectors have been automated and streamlined to cut costs and compete in the global economic market. Katrina's dad, a civil engineer, was one of the victims of this realignment. At the same time, Katrina's mom, who also has a good education and had worked in banking previously, easily got a job in the growing service sector of the economy. This family is adapting to economic and social changes that are creating a realignment of family roles and responsibilities.

In 2005, Bronfenbrenner, one of the great ecological developmentalists, pointedly subtitled a book "Bioecological Perspectives." Over time, the various branches of the ecological approach have grown more similar as they rediscover the biological roots of this theory. The most basic notion in the ecological approach continues to be *adaptation*. The family in the example above is adapting to changing social and economic conditions, but there are other forms of adaptation such as changes in family structure (Adamsons, O'Brien, & Pasley, 2007). The notion of adaptation in ecology is far-reaching. This concept reaches down to our biological roots and up to large-scale interactive processes at the level of populations of organisms. The concept of adaptation can be applied to an individual organism's successful adaptation to a specific environmental niche or to global changes, such as increases in ultraviolet radiation. Indeed, adaptation is the central concept of ecology.

Some of you may ask what this has to do with families. A concern with families and the environment is at the heart of what ecology means and of the ecological social movement that became so active during the latter part of the 20th century. The term *ecology* was coined in 1873 by Ernst Haeckel, a German biologist (see Clarke, 1973). It was developed from the Greek root *oik,* which means "place of residence." Haeckel used the German *oekologie* in which the prefatory *oe* makes the term universal as "everyman's house or environment" (Clarke, 1973). As Clarke points out, although "Haeckel, a male biologist, saw that a science of everyone's house environment needed to be developed, the female chemist, Ellen Swallow Richards, slowly began to take up residency in the structure" (p. 40).

Ellen Swallow Richards was the first female student at Massachusetts Institute of Technology (MIT) and one of the pioneers of water purity analysis. Her many published books include studies in the areas of water analysis, minerals, and sanitation, and she also published works on the cost of food and shelter and the chemistry of cooking. Indeed, it was Richards who founded and served as first president of the American Home Economics Association. She believed that the family and home were central to the ecological movement: "Science has to apply its knowledge to [improve] that unit of the community, the home; for upon the welfare of the home depends the welfare of the commonwealth" (Clarke, 1973, p. 141). Although Richards's hard-nosed scientific empiricism has been challenged and rejected by some prominent "home economists" (e.g., Brown, 1984; Bubolz & Sontag, 1993), there can be little doubt that her viewpoint favored the development of interdisciplinary ecological and environmental sciences in the broadest of senses.

Richards lived in an era (1842–1911) when unbridled industrialization triumphed, but her keen scientific eye saw the hidden costs. She documented the loss in water quality in studies that were instrumental in leading to the first U.S. water quality standards. Although the 19th century was intellectually illuminated by Darwin, day-to-day life was governed more by corporate greed. For example, in the early 1870s, the Boston Milk War was fought between milk businesses and an embryonic consumer movement. The businesses routinely diluted milk with water, and when a group of citizens organized a consumer protection association to deliver untainted milk to Boston, their drivers were beaten, their horses crippled, and the milk tainted (Clarke, 1973). Increasingly, industry claimed areas of production that had previously been the principal role of women in the home. As a result, many women felt a loss of purpose, and the "manufacture" of previously "homemade" products was fertile ground for avaricious interests. Richards documented to the Massachusetts State Board of Health, Lunacy, and Charity in the first-ever scientific survey of the state's food supply that many common foods contained additives that were harmful. She reported that out of 33 samples of baking soda, 9 contained alum, 5 contained ammonia, and others contained large quantities of starch (Clarke,

1973). Rather than tight legislative controls, Richards favored the education of the major group of consumers—women:

> It is because I believe in the possibility of control of [the environment] and even economic conditions that I urge so strongly the dissemination of what knowledge we have. . . . [Otherwise] a cry for state interference will come in that day when it is clear that the carelessness of men threatens to extinguish the race. (quoted in Clarke, 1973, p. 211)

To further our education about our environment, Richards, in 1907, reiterated her proposal for a new science:

> Human Ecology is the study of the surroundings of human beings in the effects they produce on [other] lives. . . . The features of the environment are natural, as climate; and artificial, produced by human activity such as noise, [dirt], poisonous vapors, vitiated air, dirty water and unclean food. (quoted in Clarke, 1973, pp. 215–216)

Shortly after Richards died, Robert Wollcott and C. V. Shreve founded the Ecological Society of America in 1916 (Clarke, 1973). By 1919, the society had acquired *Ecology* as a journal outlet for its publications. By 1917, the society's membership was 307, and by 1973, the membership had swollen to 5,148 (Hinckley, 1976). Although the membership includes scholars from almost every field of science, in 1920, the president of the society, Barrington Moore, urged that human ecology be taken to represent an especially important aspect of ecology. Since this time, human ecology has developed mainly in association with the academic discipline of sociology (e.g., Burgess, 1925; Hannan & Freeman, 1984; Hawley, 1986; Park, 1925).

Intellectual Traditions

The early studies in human ecology (e.g., Burgess, 1925; McKenzie, 1924; Park, 1925; Park & Burgess, 1921) derived much of their intellectual and conceptual foundation from the work of plant ecologists. In contrast to the notion that the United States was a *melting pot*, these sociologists detected homogeneous spatial ordering and change that could readily be described in the language of plant ecology, especially ecological succession and species dominance. These early scholars were preoccupied with the spatial arrangement of the urban setting, particularly Chicago, and this explains why some students identify human ecology with this spatial approach and what has become known as the Chicago school of human ecology. But as Hawley (1986) points out, this spatial approach was superseded by a concern with population ecology. Population ecology united social demography with the bioecological study of populations so that spatial orderings became one of a myriad of ways a population adapts to a particular environment. To understand why and how human ecology became generally linked to population ecology, it is necessary to trace some of the historical currents that came together only in the mid-20th century.

Although the field of ecology is relatively new, significant scholarly work in the area of humans and their environment preceded the nomenclature identifying the field. Most notable in this regard is the work of Thomas Malthus (1766–1834). Malthus lived in a time when the prevailing notion was that a growing population increased the power of a country. Surplus population could be used to feed mercantilism and populate colonies. Before Malthus's (1798/1872) *An Essay on the Principle of Population*, the folk wisdom regarding food sources might be summed up as a reliance on nature to provide "no more children than teats" (Peterson, 1969, p. 146). Malthus (1798/1872) proposed that in an unconstrained situation, population would increase at a geometric rate (2, 4, 8, 16 . . .) and food production at an arithmetic rate (1, 2, 3, 4, 5 . . .). He pointed out that in reality, the relationship between food and population was always constrained by either preventative checks (e.g., moral restraint) or positive checks (e.g., wars, famine). Clearly, preventative checks tend to focus on fertility, whereas positive checks tend to focus on mortality. Regardless of the controversial nature of the predictions of overpopulation that can be derived from Malthus, his work served to bring an ecological focus to the emerging studies of economics, sociology, and demography by highlighting the interaction of environmental and biological variables with social and human variables.

Ecology, as a science, must trace its paternity to Charles Darwin (1809–1882). The early focus by Malthus on the interaction of biological and social variables was given broad substance and theoretical form in the work of Darwin. He published his most famous work, *On the Origin of Species by Means of Natural Selection*, in 1859. It was in this work that his ideas of natural selection and evolution first appeared, only slightly ahead of the exposition of these ideas by Alfred Wallace. Basically, Darwin argued that a species or population evolved principally by the process of natural selection or elimination of those members of the population who were less adapted to survive in their environment. Although evolution is a population process, elimination or selection takes place at the individual level.

The rudimentary understanding of this process led both Darwin and later social Darwinists to maintain arguments favoring eugenics and bordering on biological determinism. For example, Darwin argued that many times, we

> do our utmost to check the process of elimination; we build asylums for the imbecile, the maimed, and the sick; we institute poor laws; and our medical men exert their utmost skill to save the life of everyone to the last moment. . . . Thus, the weak members of civilized societies propagate their kind. . . . It is not surprising how soon a want of care, or care wrongly directed, leads to the degeneration of a domestic race; but excepting in the case of man himself, hardly anyone is so ignorant as to allow his worst animals to breed. (Darwin, 1880, pp. 130–134, quoted in Martindale, 1960, pp. 163–164)

Statements that confused acquired characteristics, such as being maimed (in the above passage), poor, or uneducated, with traits that are inheritable is a disturbing characteristic of early social evolutionists. Much of this confusion arose because the exact mechanisms by which traits were passed to later generations were not identified until the publication of Mendel's (1865/1965) work on genetics at the turn of the century.

If ecology traces its paternity to Darwin and his central notion of adaptation, then human ecology must trace its kinship through Gregor Mendel. This is especially true for those forms of family ecological theory that unite ontogenetic development with environmental interaction (e.g., Bronfenbrenner, 1979) and those family theorists who believe that much of family behavior is explained by biological factors (van den Berghe, 1979). Mendel first presented his ideas in two lectures in 1865, but his ideas were not "discovered" by the scientific community until the turn of the century (e.g., Brannigan, Wanner, & White, 1981). When Mendel's work was finally understood, it provided a theoretical understanding for the genetic mechanisms that drive evolution. Mendel proposed that genes attached to chromosomes transmit the genetic information to offspring. Attached to the chromosome were two alleles, one of which might be dominant and therefore expressed in the offspring's phenotype (visible physical characteristics); the other might be recessive but nonetheless remain part of the offspring's genotype (genes that are potentially transmittable). From his experiments, Mendel could show that although it was impossible to predict an individual-level genetic outcome, it was possible to predict the proportions or probabilities for a reproducing population. Mendel's work was seminal for both laboratory genetics and population genetics, but it was population genetics that carried the greatest implications for evolutionary theory and ecological theory.

Population genetics received its early impetus from the simultaneous work of Hardy (1908) and Weinberg (1908). They developed an equation for predicting allele frequencies for subsequent generations of a population based on the assumption that the only factor operating in the population is the initial distribution of alleles. Thus, their model assumed no evolution. The degree to which their predictions were inaccurate could be used as a measure of evolution. The discrepancy between their prediction and the actual observed allele frequencies could be explained by four evolutionary factors: natural selection, mutation, gene drift, and gene flow. In relatively large and immobile populations, the principal factors are natural selection and mutation (see Turner, 1991).

The mathematical nature of population genetics attracted statisticians and demographers. For example, Karl Pearson (1857–1936) served as editor of both *Biometrika* and *The Annals of Eugenics* and, like Galton (1869/1952) before him, felt that human progress and development were largely related to natural selection (Martindale, 1960). Another famous statistician, Ronald Fisher (1958), mathematically demonstrated that natural selection and not mutation is the major explanatory factor in evolution. He argued that variation in a gene pool was inextricably linked to natural selection and adaptation. Without sufficient variation in the gene pool, there is insufficient range from which to select an adaptation. Despite the fact that both Fisher and Pearson favored eugenics as a way to ensure the promulgation of the "fittest" genes, their statistical contributions confirmed that natural selection and adaptation are the central mechanisms in the process of evolution (Turner, 1991).

The genetic emphasis in human ecology found natural extensions into the area of human development. The first genetically based theories about human development were simple extensions from evolutionary theory summarized as "ontogeny recapitulates phylogeny." It did not take long to disprove the simple notion that human development followed the evolutionary tree as a progression of phylogenetic evolution. But this early approach launched the developmentalists' early concern with two basic dimensions of development. First, they were concerned with the development of the organism that was genetically transmitted and universal to the human species (ontogenetic). Second, they were concerned with clearly demarcating the "stages" they assumed all development would traverse. For example, theorists such as Piaget (1952) proposed invariant developmental stages through which all humans would progress in the development of their cognitive capacity. Such approaches, however, failed to acknowledge the contribution of the social and physical contexts in which the organism was developing. At roughly the same time, a more contextual approach developed from the work of Lewin (1935) that emphasized the interaction of the developing person with the environment. Lewin's work greatly influenced the development of an ecological theory of human development by Bronfenbrenner (1979). His ecological approach then greatly influenced family researchers, such as Belsky (1990), and family theorists (e.g., Bubolz & Sontag, 1993; Garbarino, 1992). Today, the ecological approach that originated from developmentalists is one of the most influential models in regard to theorizing about the family and the development of its members.

The human ecology framework brings together these diverse influences. From evolutionary theory and genetics comes the view that humans develop as individual biological organisms with capacities limited by genetic endowment (ontogenetic development). From population genetics comes the perspective that populations change mainly by means of natural selection. At the individual level, this implies that individuals demonstrate their fitness by adapting to their changing environment (family adaptation). From ecological theories of human development come *contextualized* and *interactional* theories of human development that emphasize the family. From the human ecology of Ellen Richards comes the notion that humans can, through education, understand their interactions with the environment and can direct their consumption (and production) to the benefit of the overall environment (family resource management). And most important for the scientist and scholar is the startling idea from evolutionary theory that a phenomenon needs to be examined at different levels of analysis. What we see as failure and death for an individual organism may be linked to success and adaptive fitness for the population (sociobiology). It is this idea that often leads ecologists and conservationists to suggest solutions that seem counterintuitive, such as killing some deer in a herd so that the population will survive. And lurking just under the surface of this view that we can control natural selection and thus evolution are the proposals favoring eugenics that are far too often driven by sexism and racism.

Focus and Scope Assumptions

Individuals and groups are both biological and social in nature. Like systems theory, ecological theory is a relative newcomer on the social science scene. Ecological theory is distinguished from other theories such as systems theory in its emphasis on the biophysical environment and especially the concept of adaptation. In systems theory, environment may be a heuristic device, whereas in ecological theory, environment is both spatial and biophysical. This basic assumption leads ecological theory to a more biological and geographic orientation and a less mechanistic perspective on human groups.

This first assumption links the dual nature of humans as constructions of both biology and culture. This dual nature of humans has given rise to some of the world's greatest literature, such as Goethe's *Faust*, and has also occupied generations of academics in the fruitless debate over whether human characteristics are due to biology (nature) or environmental influences (nurture). Today, we have not so much resolved this debate as moved beyond it. We now recognize that even an embryo in the mother's womb is affected by environmental factors, such as sounds from the environment and the health status of the mother. Furthermore, a supposed genetic trait, such as intelligence, requires the interaction of a nurturing environment as shown in the example of kwashiorkor (infant protein deficiency) and cognitive development (IQ). The particular nature of human development ensures that the development of most human traits depends on a nature-nurture interaction rather than on one or the other. Although some academics persist in attempts to identify the additive amounts of contribution made by the nature side and the exact amount made by the environment, most now readily admit that the entire multiplicative process, beginning with the formation of a DNA strand, depends on interactions with the environment. As van den Berghe (1979) puts it, our behavior can be understood "as the product of an extraordinary complex of interaction between genotype and environment" (p. 5).

Humans are dependent on their environment for sustenance (air, water, food, etc.). The assumption of dependency follows from the first assumption in that humans can survive only in environments in which their biological needs can be met. Of course, human culture has developed so that we can survive in fairly inhospitable environments with the assistance of technology. But even technology has its limits, as in the case of water supply.

Human beings are social and thus are dependent on other human beings. Another way to state this assumption is to say that most of what we think of as truly "human" seems social in nature—for example, language.

Humans are finite, and their life cycle coupled with their biological needs for sustenance impose time as both a constraint and a resource. This assumption points most directly to the fact that over any individual's life, there is species-common change and development (ontogenetic development). In addition, we must remember that time is a factor in the evolution of a population. Furthermore, because we are finite, time becomes a crucial resource for understanding social organization and individual behavior.

Human interactions are spatially organized. Populations of humans organize their interactions within their environments. The organized interactions show up as distinct spatial arrangements. Anyone who has ever looked down on the Earth from an airplane is struck by the spatial organization of human activities. But we are not dissimilar from the many other social animals that demonstrate distinct spatial organization as a way of channeling interactions with the environment (e.g., ants, baboons, wolves). The spatial nature of family is just beginning to be developed by theorists (see Perry-Jenkins, Newkirk, & Ghunney, 2013).

Human behavior can be understood on several levels. The two levels that are most often used in human ecology are the *population* and *individual*. For example, populations of organisms show spatial organization and represent particular frequency distributions of genes. Individual organisms may adapt or fail to adapt to their environment. Changing the level of analysis can radically alter our perspective, however. The failure of an organism to successfully adapt, leading to that individual organism's death, may seem a negative outcome at the individual level, but for the population, this same outcome might represent the evolution of a healthier gene pool or the survival of the group faced with food scarcity.

Concepts

Ecosystem

Although there are many varieties of ecological theory, most of these would identify the concept of *ecosystem* as central to ecology. Hawley (1986) defines ecosystem as "an arrangement of mutual dependencies in a population by which the whole operates as a unit and thereby maintains a viable environmental relationship" (p. 26). In Hawley's view, an ecosystem is necessarily a subset of the larger environment. The notion of ecosystem contains the elements of wholeness and the interdependency of parts. For example, we might talk of an urban ecosystem, a desert ecosystem, or a polar ecosystem. Each ecosystem, although attached to other ecosystems, has a set of characteristics that demarcates it as a whole. Bubolz and Sontag (1993) suggest that "a family ecosystem consists of a given family system in interaction with its environment" (p. 431).

Ecological Levels

One of the levels of analysis commonly used in evolutionary theory is *population*. Hawley (1986) argues convincingly that a population is not simply an aggregation of all those people or units sharing a common characteristic. If population referred to such simple aggregations, we might be tempted to talk meaningfully of the population sharing the characteristic of "wearing blue jeans." Hawley defines a population as an aggregate having unit character by virtue of internal organization. In his sense of the term, we could discuss the population of Canada but not the population of wearers of blue jeans. Hawley's definition of population moves the term away from the identification of a mere statistical aggregation and imbues it with theoretical meaning. Population processes are dissimilar to individual-level processes, as seen in the example that a population may have a death rate yet continue over time, whereas an individual who dies fails to continue over time.

There are perhaps many ways to view the levels of an ecosystem (see Bulcroft & White, 1997; White & Teachman, 2005); however, one of the most popular formulations is that offered by Bronfenbrenner (1979). His formulation suggests that the family is one among many "nested" ecosystems in which the individual develops and interacts. He examines these nested systems on four levels of analysis: the *microsystem,* the *mesosystem,* the *exosystem,* and the *macrosystem.* The microsystem involves the direct and concrete interactions of the developing person with significant others (p. 22). The mesosystem is defined by the interrelations of two or more microsystems, such as work and family (p. 25). The exosystem refers to systems that are not in direct interaction with the developing person but have indirect effects on the person's micro- or mesosystem. Finally, the macrosystem provides the general cultural context in which lower order systems are environed (p. 26). These distinctions have become widely accepted in the ecological theory of the family.

Niche

Every ecosystem contains *niches.* The interdependencies in an ecosystem are not between specific individuals but between specific niches occupied by individuals or even a species. Associated with each niche is a patterned and relatively stable set of activities. These activities provide *functions* for the maintenance or adaptation of units in the environment or those occupying a specific niche. For example, in a marsh environment, the activity of beavers serves the function of water regulation. In the human family, the role of father often has been tied to the function of provider. According to Hawley (1986), these niches represent functions for the ecosystem. Thus, "the mutual dependencies comprising a system (ecosystem) are seen to be linkages among recurring activities" (p. 32). The idea of niche is similar to Bronfenbrenner's (1979) notion of molar activity and to the social-psychological construct of social roles.

Adaptive Range

An organism that occupies a niche in an ecosystem can be characterized as having an *adaptive range.* The organism's ontogenetic development gives it a range of behavior, but the organism cannot adapt outside of this range. For example, a 2-year-old is not going to be able to understand the principle of conservation of matter because of his or her developmental stage (e.g., Piaget, 1952). Human intelligence represents a broad adaptive range because we apply technology (culture) to problems we would be hard-pressed to adapt to organically (e.g., space travel, underwater exploration).

Ontogenetic Development

Every unit within an ecosystem may undergo change that comes about from its own internal structure. Change that is a result of the internal organization and dependencies of parts is called development. For humans, the most important biological part of such developmental change is aging and *ontogenetic development* (see Chapter 5, Concepts). The most important social part of this internal development is experience or maturation. As Piaget (1952) and others have noted, ontogenetic development and social development are inextricably linked. Indeed, Bronfenbrenner (1979) challenges the very assumption that development can be discussed meaningfully as just occurring within the organism. He argues that development is always a relationship between the organism and its immediate environment.

Natural Selection and Adaptation

Before Fisher's (1958) proof that mutation could not possibly be a major factor in evolution, there were thought to be two major sources of evolutionary change: mutation and natural selection. Now we usually consider only natural selection and its correlate, adaptation. Indeed, the concepts of natural selection and adaptation are simply different sides of the same process. Natural selection is a concept about the outcome of adaptation. If an organism or population successfully adapts to (survives) changes in its ecosystem (interrelations among niches), then it has not been "selected." If the organism does not adapt, then it has been *selected*. If a population undergoes changes, it is because some poorly adapted organisms were *selected out*, and the remaining organisms represent a more adaptive set of alleles for the population. The classic example here is that of the species of white moths in late-19th-century coal-dependent Britain. The few dark-colored moths in this population survived the change to a coal-blackened environment, whereas their white relatives became readily visible against the gray, coal-covered environment to every hungry bird.

In ecological theory, natural selection is often treated as a population process and adaptation as an individual-level process. But natural selection and adaptation, population and individual, gene pool and gene can all be viewed as components of evolution and ontogenetic development. An organism's development over time is constrained by its genetic endowment. Whether a particular organism can adapt to changes in its environment depends on the adaptive range provided by its genetic endowment. If one type of organism is selected out of the population, then the gene pool changes. Thus, the adaptive range provided in the ontogenetic development of the organism interacts with the changing environment to produce the outcome of selection and adaptation.

Propositions

Human ecological theory has not produced one uniform and consensual set of theoretical propositions. At the most abstract level are the general propositions developed by Emlen (1995) and Hawley (1986), which are sometimes difficult to apply to human families. Some family ecologists, such as Bubolz and Sontag (1993), do not cite propositions and seem to advocate goals that might not be conducive to developing propositional theory in science. Bronfenbrenner (1979) has suggested several sensitizing concepts and highlighted many possible propositions. He focuses on the forces that propel and impede human development rather than focusing exclusively on the family. In this view, the family is one of the most important microsystems for the developing individual. The propositions we list here are principally drawn from this ecological developmental school of thought.

The family is a social organization embedded in a larger kinship network (Hawley, 1986, p. 73). The family occupies a niche in all social systems by providing for the sustenance and nurturance of its internal members while providing the larger society with the reproduction of economic and social organization. It is Bronfenbrenner (1979) who most clearly envisions the individual's development within the ecosystem:

> *The individual grows and adapts through interchanges with its immediate ecosystem (the family) and more distant environments such as school.* (Bronfenbrenner, 1979)

The individual child is always in a relationship with another person from conception onward. The above quote implies that in the study of development, the dyad is the smallest unit of analysis. Although the child develops ontogenetically, this development is always in the context of these relationships. Thus, the child's development is interactional. However, any point of development can be measured by the developmental status of the individual.

> *The developmental status of the individual is reflected in the ability of the individual to initiate and maintain a new level of adaptive range and to maintain these behaviors in the absence of directions from others.* (Bronfenbrenner, 1979, p. 55)

As Hawley (1986, p. 60) points out, when individuals or populations adapt and develop, they change their interactions with their environment. Thus, the developing organism changes the relationships in the ecosystem.

> *When one member of a dyad undergoes developmental change, the other member of the dyad will also be likely to undergo change.* (Bronfenbrenner, 1979, p. 65)

As the child develops, his or her functions in the family change from being mainly supported and maintained to increasingly symbiotic and interdependent functions, such as household production and consumption. The family as a production and consumption unit provides individual services and relates to other units as a social and economic household unit. In this process, the child takes on increasingly specialized roles according to his or her developmental maturation and age-graded norms.

> *Different settings have different distinctive patterns of roles, activities, and relationships for persons in those settings.* (Bronfenbrenner, 1979, p. 109)

For example, husband and wife dyads become increasingly specialized in the roles (niches) of mother and father with the arrival of a child. These roles are commensalistic (sharing) rather than corporate (role segmented). As the child matures and becomes increasingly specialized as a consumer and producer (corporate), the parents become less specialized in the commensalistic arena and more specialized in the corporate area of consumption and production.

> *Family organization is the processing system through which energy and information are transformed into life-supporting (consumption or commensalistic) activities and life-enhancing (socializing and corporate) activities.* (Bubolz & Sontag, 1993, p. 431)

As children mature in their corporate roles and become more interdependent, they tend to follow the normative system that gave rise to their parental ecosystem. Thus, children tend to reproduce the family organization of their family of orientation but under the new constraints of an ecosystem that has changed with the passage of time.

Hawley states that "closure" of a niche is a relative concept but that when a unit is involved in the biophysical environment, such as with the more commensalistic or family-oriented tasks of raising small children, closure is maximized and helps ensure the stability of the system. Thus, we would expect more resistance to information regarding role change in families with young children.

We have presented only a few of the many propositions in human ecology. Indeed, we have not presented the more abstract, population-level propositions developed by Hawley. The propositions we cite above reveal a picture of human ecology theory as driven by the realization that human ecological systems are different mainly in that human ecology "finds its fullest expression in the commitment to organization as the adaptive mechanism" (p. 126). In the sense that the family is the central social organization, we can see that human ecologists must view the family as a core adaptive mechanism, whether examining the ecosystem from the perspective of individual development (Bronfenbrenner) or from the perspective of macro-organization (Hawley).

Let's apply these propositions by returning to our initial example of Katrina's dad taking her to school. Recall that Katrina wanted her mother to take her to school as the other kids' mothers did. The family is reorganizing roles because of complex social and economic changes, yet these changes do not in themselves predict the particular direction and form of the reorganization. For example, Katrina's parents could decide that roles should be discontinued by sending Katrina off to other relatives. Katrina is responding to the fact that her family is reorganizing its roles because "changes in specialization involve changes in relationships among functions" (Hawley, 1986, p. 60). Katrina's mother and father have had to adapt to a complex economic environment. Part of this adaptation is that the father's role is being redefined to occupy some of the niche vacated by the now-employed mother (see Adamsons et al., 2007). But rather than eliminate these roles, the family preserves its functions because the family corporate unit "tends to replicate the structural properties of the parent ecosystem" (Hawley, 1986, p. 86).

Furthermore, the family unit tends toward closure regardless of the openness of the ecosystem (see Hawley, 1986), testifying to the inherent conservative nature or inertia of family organization. Part of this inertia comes from the commensalistic nature of the organization. As Katrina matures, however, she will have to do more to assist the family because her dad will also be looking for a job in addition to his expanded household role, and her working mother will not be free from aspects of her mother role. In Bronfenbrenner's (1979) formulation, "Different settings have different distinctive patterns of roles, activities and relationships for persons in those settings" (p. 109). And Hawley (1986) might say, "Increases in intensity of specialization of any given function are accompanied by increases in intensity of specialization of all complementary functions" (p. 85). In this regard, we can also see the school system changing, in that neither mom nor dad may be available to help with supervision and transportation on field trips and so on. Indeed, "ecosystem change occurs as new information is converted to new functions (specialization) or increased specialization of old functions" (Hawley, 1986, p. 60). Thus, the changes that Katrina's family and other families are experiencing may have ramifications for the educational system. And in the longer run, the demonstration that such "adaptation" is necessary may lead Katrina's generation to reduce the number of children they have so that reorganization is more easily accomplished. Such curtailing of fertility would lead to population-level changes.

In the final analysis, we cannot completely explain what is happening to Katrina's family without examining the complex causes in the higher order systems. Yet the rudiments of the ecological approach can be seen in this example. Basic principles are the connectedness and embeddedness of various ecological levels and the continual need for adaptation to the constant currents of change.

Variations

Family Demography and Ecology

Peterson (1969) defines demography as "the systematic analysis of population phenomena" (p. 1). He goes on to point out a basic distinction among classes of demographers. On one hand, there is "formal" demography, the study of population as a self-contained process using sophisticated mathematical models. On the other hand, there is "population analysis," which includes variables from the social setting such as norms, natural resources, and economic growth as both independent and dependent variables (Peterson, 1969, p. 3). Population analysis is a theoretical variant of human ecology.

Since its inception, demography has been necessarily concerned with the study of many "family" variables such as nuptuality and fertility. Demographers from the time of Malthus recognized that variables such as fertility were influenced by social custom and organization and that differences in the rules of organization would affect fertility patterns. But a concern with family variables does not necessarily suggest that demography occupies a niche in the human ecology of families.

The claim that demography occupies a theoretical role in the human ecology of the family would strike many demographers as unusual or questionable. The case for this theoretical contribution is quite strong, however. From the turn of the century, sociologists and demographers of rural life have been concerned with the life cycle of the family. Paul Glick (1947), a family demographer, formalized this life cycle approach to data on families in his article titled "The Family Cycle" (see Chapter 5). Demographers have also been interested in how families are integrated with other organized sectors of society, such as work and education. Hogan (1978) examined the effects of event sequences, including finishing education, starting a first job, and marriage. Oppenheimer (1988) examined family change and economic change. Sweet, Bumpass, Call, and others from the University of Wisconsin, Center for Demography and Ecology, launched a longitudinal panel study, the National Survey of Families and Households, focused on families and family forms in the United States (Sweet, Bumpass, & Call, 1988). Teachman, Tedrow, and Crowder (2000) focus on changes to the structure of American families during the past decade. Demographers study macroscopic levels of analysis, such as social organizations, institutions, and populations. The principal theoretical orientation they have provided is their focus on how these social groupings are interwoven in time and space for any given society. Some demographers have moved to global levels of analysis in their attempt to understand social phenomena such as the connection between fertility and rates of female labor force participation (e.g., Westoff, 1978). Demography, then, occupies the niche in ecology that is focused on population characteristics and population change.

Most recently, demographic ecological theory has been expanding to encompass the ways in which social groups adapt and react to environmental changes. McAdoo, Martinez, and Hughes (2005) argue that ethnic families adapt to tensions associated with acculturation while resisting the dominant cultural values that might undermine parenting styles. Furthermore, these authors ask if family theorists and researchers are ready to adapt to the demographic changes that will soon occur with the majority of American families being ethnic families of color by the year 2050.

One particular vibrant area of research and theory from a "new demography" perspective involves the incorporation of demography, geography, ethnography and sociology—in such works as Ellard's (2015) *Places of the Heart*, Valverde's (2012) *Everyday Law on the Street*, and Lauster's (2016) *The Death and Life of the Single Family House*. The Lauster work is especially useful in demonstrating the ways that the old numerical demography can be integrated with geography, ethnography, and sociology. Although the new demography is not quite theoretically conscious as yet, it does produce useful insights for ecological theorists and provides a richer vision of demography than in the past.

Human Developmental Ecology

Bronfenbrenner (1979, 1989) was the Jacob Gould Schurman Professor in Human Development at Cornell University. He tied together ideas from ecological theory and Kurt Lewin's (1935) field theory to formulate the ideas in his book *The Ecology of Human Development*. Bronfenbrenner argues that the child always develops in the context of family-type relationships and that development is the outcome not simply of the ontogenetic factors but of the interaction of the person's genetic endowment with the immediate family and eventually with other components of the environment. Although this central argument does not originate with Bronfenbrenner, his work represents one of the more detailed and systematic statements of this perspective. As a result, the ecological approach to human development has proven influential in guiding research by family scholars, developmental psychologists, and researchers in education.

Bronfenbrenner's (1979) work stands in sharp contrast to those psychologists who would explain individual behavior solely by examining individual traits or abilities. Bronfenbrenner argues that a person's behavior is a function of the interaction of the person's traits and abilities with the environment ($B = f \{PE\}$). This view supposes that a person's traits interact with the environment to create individual behavior that cannot be explained by simply adding the effects of the person's traits to the effects of the environment. The classic example of this is early toilet training. The child does not gain voluntary muscular control in this regard until about 18 months of age. Socialization before this time is likely to frustrate both the child and parent. It is only when the physical, ontological development and the environmental socialization coincide that the desired outcome is reached. The causes of the behavior, toilet training, cannot be seen as additive, because socialization before muscular control will have little effect, and muscular control without proper socialization will also have little effect in attaining the target behavior. It is the interaction of these two components (PE) that produces the behavior. And it is this interactionist perspective that distinguishes Bronfenbrenner's (1979) view of human development from the more ontological individual approaches. He defines his position as follows:

> The ecology of human development involves the scientific study of the progressive, mutual accommodation between an active, growing human being and the changing properties of the immediate environment in which the developing person lives, as this process is affected by relations between these settings, and by the larger contexts in which the settings are embedded. (p. 21)

Bronfenbrenner views the individual as being embedded in a microsystem (role and relations), a mesosystem (interrelations between two or more microsystems), an exosystem (external settings that do not include the person), and a macrosystem (culture). His idea of ecological change is very similar to Hawley's (1986) notion linking changes in niche specialization to changes in relationships among functions. In Bronfenbrenner's

(1979) definition of an "ecological transition," a "person's position in the ecological environment is altered as the result of a change in role, setting, or both" (p. 26). Later, Bronfenbrenner (1989) expanded this notion and discussed a model in which there are "differences in developmental processes and outcomes associated with different ecological niches" (p. 200). For example, as a child develops, he or she is brought into roles with caregivers other than the mother: day care, preschool, peers, and eventually the school system. All these interactions may represent significant *ecological transitions* for the developing child in that there are new roles (niches) and interactions with the immediate environment and increasingly distant environments. The child-school mesosystem is further affected by other exosystems and the macrosystem by forces such as economic pressures and political decisions. Bronfenbrenner's (1979, 1989) approach encompasses the entire environment of the developing person while maintaining a focus on the microsystem (roles and relations) and mesosystem interactions as having the greatest direct effects on the child.

The most important refinement Bronfenbrenner (1989) has made is to include *time* as a more integral part of his theory. This incorporation of time has led to two major additions to the theory. First, Bronfenbrenner now views his ecological theory as applying "throughout the life course" of the individual (p. 188). Second, he has added the notion of the *chronosystem*, which incorporates time as the developmental history of the individual (events and experiences) and its effect on development. The need for the addition of time 10 years after the original statement of the theory might be due in part to changes that occurred during the 1980s. The decade of the 1980s witnessed some significant theoretical and methodological innovations in regard to the occurrence and timing of life course events (see Chapter 5). These refinements also give Bronfenbrenner's (1979, 1989) theory a greater similarity to other life course theories covered in Chapter 5 and may suggest a gradual merging into more of an emphasis on development than ecology. For example, followers of Bronfenbrenner such as Moen, Elder, and Lüscher (1995) clearly move to a more life course perspective. On the other hand, Garbarino (1992) focuses more on families and the context in which they exist. Because these may be seen as complementary levels of analysis within ecological theory, such diversity may only increase the already powerful influence of Bronfenbrenner's developmental ecological approach on family scholarship.

Two relatively new developments have given new impetus to Bronfenbrenner's ecological theory. First, the development of a statistical approach commonly called hierarchical linear modeling (HLM) has supplied researchers with a way to estimate effects of independent variables from various levels of analysis (see Teachman & Crowder, 2002; White & Teachman, 2005). For example, researchers can now examine the effects of community organization (community level), family structure (group), and sibling relationship (dyad) on a developmental outcome such as the target child's prosocial behavior. Furthermore, as Bronfenbrenner suggested, HLM allows researchers to examine the interaction effects between diverse levels on the outcome variable. This powerful tool will undoubtedly propel both theory and research within the ecological model.

The second development originated directly from Bronfenbrenner before his death in 2005. Bronfenbrenner titled his last work *Making Human Beings Human: Bioecological Perspectives on Human Development* (2005). The move from the term *ecology* to *bioecology* seems to signal two developments for this theory. It reemphasizes the interaction between the biological and ontological character of development with the social character of development. This is important because ecology could be moved more toward *social* ecology, which would de-emphasize the nurture side of the equation. The other signal we take from this is that bioecology is a growing field within biology and is commonly defined as the study of plants and animals and their interactions between themselves and with their environment. Bronfenbrenner might well have been signaling a more encompassing perspective that included the work of these biologists and sociobiologists.

Completely consistent with Bronfenbrenner's emphasis of the dyad (especially mother-child) as the smallest unit on which we can analyze development is the more focused theory of attachment between mother and child. Ethologists, such as Lorenz, first hypothesized that humans might "imprint" on their parents similar to some subhuman species. Although data did not support the imprinting notion, they nonetheless gave impetus to Bowlby's developmental ecological theory of attachment.

Bowlby (1953) originally developed the developmental ecological theory of attachment. Bowlby suggests that infants develop a strong affectional bond with one significant caregiver, usually the mother. Bowlby's attachment theory was refined and empirically measured by Ainsworth (1967). The proponents of this theory suggest that infants need to form secure, affective attachments to one significant and consistent caregiver. The developing child will explore his or her environment when he or she feels there is a stable and secure relationship with the significant caregiver. Based on Ainsworth's (1978) laboratory observations of children 12 to 18 months, Ainsworth and her colleagues (Ainsworth, Blehar, Waters, & Wall, 1978) hypothesized three attachment styles. Later, Main and Solomon (1986) proposed a fourth attachment style. These four attachment styles are as follows: secure-firmly attached, anxious-resistant, disturbed, anxious-avoidant, and disorganized. Research suggests that the first, secure-firmly attached, has the best developmental outcomes for the developing child. Indeed, this theory is so established as to appear in the fourth edition of the *Diagnostic and Statistical Manual of Mental Disorders* (American Psychiatric

Association [APA], 1994). There have also been hypothesized extensions of the consequences of early childhood attachment styles to later adult attachment behaviors and problems (see Hazan & Shaver, 1987).

Attachment theory is not without detractors. For example, Hays (1996, 1998) suggests that much of the attachment literature overstates the case for the theory and expounds an ideology that would see women leave the labor force in order to be considered "good mothers" with securely attached infants. As we shall see later in this chapter's empirical applications section, this contention has been the subject of considerable debate.

Sociobiology and Bioecology of the Family

Since the writings of Darwin, various attempts have been made to explain social behavior as a consequence of evolution. Recently, most such attempts for a biological explanation of social behavior have been labeled *sociobiology,* following E. O. Wilson (1975). Sociobiology was preceded by the eugenics of Pearson (1909) and Fisher (1958) and early ethologists, such as Konrad Lorenz (1966). Pierre van den Berghe (1979) and Thomas Emlen are responsible for the most systematic applications of sociobiology to the family.

Sociobiologists of the family accept that human behavior is a complex interaction of genes and environment (van den Berghe, 1979). They do not offer a simplistic biological determinism of social behavior; rather, the key concept used in sociobiology is *inclusive fitness*, or kin selection. Inclusive fitness refers to individuals behaving in ways to maximize their own or their relatives' reproductive success (van den Berghe, 1979). This means that the individual attempts to maximize the transmission of his or her genes to the succeeding generation. Because a sibling carries 50% of one's own genes, the success of a sibling in reproduction is related to one's own success. The principle of inclusive fitness is used to explain much of human family behavior within the constraints of natural selection on the gene pool and the configuration of the environment. For example, van den Berghe discusses two parental strategies for maximizing reproductive success. One strategy is to have few children and invest a lot in the care and socialization of these few. The other strategy is to have many children but with the necessary reduction in the parental investment of time and energy per child. He points out that the two strategies have different strengths and weaknesses depending on the environment. In an unstable and hostile environment, high fertility might prove more successful, whereas lower fertility with high parental investment is more appropriate for stable populations close to the carrying capacity of the environment (van den Berghe, 1979, p. 26). Thus, the explanatory biological principle of inclusive fitness is always used within a particular environment.

An interesting example of how sociobiologists attempt to explain family phenomena is the application of inclusive fitness to pair bonding and marriage. Humans do not practice random mating or mating driven by female estrus. Rather, in most human societies, we find that relatively permanent heterosexual couples are the rule. To explain why this is so offers some difficulty for sociobiology. Van den Berghe (1979) argues, "Females invest more in offspring, have less of an incentive to be promiscuous, and have a greater concern to bind a male to themselves than vice versa" (p. 46). Males, on the other hand, have less at stake in the nurturance of individual children and more to gain by maximizing the contribution of genes to a larger number of females. Thus, according to van den Berghe (1979),

> Courtship (the rituals preceding the formation of a pair-bond) is primarily a method by which females assess and choose males and whereby males woo females. A woman subjects her suitors to tests that enable her to make the best possible choice of a provider—a mate likely to contribute maximally to her fitness. A man seeks to convince his prospective mates that he qualifies, but since he can also increase his fitness by being fickle, he will seek to deceive women. (p. 46)

For van den Berghe, females ultimately invest in their offspring because they carry the child, and the results of any promiscuousness are borne by them. Males may pursue a different strategy for maximizing their inclusive fitness in part because they may not have to directly bear the responsibility of care and nurturance. Indeed, until the recent development of DNA testing, paternity was difficult to prove compared with maternity. The so-called double standard for the sexual conduct for males and females is founded on this difference in reproductive strategy.

Sociobiology raises questions about social change. For example, in the explanation of pair bonding, we may ask about the effect of easily available and effective birth control for women. Would this lead to promiscuity? According to van den Berghe's argument, birth control would not lead to promiscuity as an inclusive fitness strategy for females because it would allow sex but not reproduction. Women would continue to bear the responsibility of childbirth. From the other side of the equation, we might ask why males would have ever become *providers* and *social fathers* when their best strategy for inclusive fitness appears to be promiscuity. Van den Berghe's analysis tends to represent marriage as a female institution in which males have little investment.

Although sociobiologists may have difficulty providing explanations of some areas of family behavior, they provide very clear explanations of areas that have proven difficult for other theorists. One of these is the basic question "Why do people have children?" From an exchange perspective, children are costly and provide few rewards. Sociobiology provides the unequivocal argument that having children maximizes inclusive fitness. Yet lurking around the corner are problems for this explanation because social change brings about the introduction of new and effective reproductive technologies not directly tied to the biological individual.

Also, keep in mind that many sociobiologists do not assume a deliberate and conscious attempt by members of any species to reproduce their genes per se. The only assumption they require, other than an assumption that humans desire to copulate and raise children, is that existing behaviors in a population are the result of differential reproduction. The principles of evolution work regardless of attitudes about our own or anybody else's genes. Social patterns that don't reproduce themselves disappear. What is most difficult is predicting which social patterns will be maladaptive before they disappear.

One of the most ambitious and systematic statements comes from Stephen T. Emlen, Jacob Gould Schurman Professor of Biology at Cornell University (the same professorship awarded Bronfenbrenner while at Cornell). Emlen (1995) argues that animal families share common properties that can be identified and developed as a set of theoretical propositions covering all animal families. He offers 15 propositions that allow us to predict such group phenomena as the stability of families. As Emlen states,

> I argue that knowledge of four basic parameters, (i) genetic
> relatedness, (ii) social dominance, (iii) the benefits of
> group living, and (iv) the probable success of independent
> reproduction, can explain many aspects of family life in birds
> and mammals. I suggest that this evolutionary perspective will
> provide insights into understanding human family systems as
> well. (p. 8092)

For example, Emlen argues that family stability is related to the opportunities for independent reproduction. So if an organism has very long periods of dependency on the parents, then family stability is enhanced. Likewise, once the young are capable of independence, the lack of opportunities to mate might also enhance family stability. Although Emlen does use the idea of inclusive fitness, it is not as central as in van den Berghe's early work on the family. Furthermore, Emlen's work has been seriously received by the social sciences (e.g., see Biblarz & Gottainer, 2000; Davis & Daly, 1997). Davis and Daly (1997) integrate nonreproductive caregivers into the theory proposed by Emlen, thus demonstrating the type of refinements that might be added by social scientists. In addition, Emlen and his evolutionary perspective are central to the perspective on single-parent families and marriage evolution being formulated by research projects such as "The Evolving Family: Family Processes, Contexts, and the Life Course of Children 2004–2007." Despite these advances, it remains to be seen whether a generation of family scholars that has lost contact with kinship studies and knows only assortative mating can see common cause with the more abstract evolutionary theory of the family. Not only is this theory broader than the immediate concern with American families, but it is even broader than our species as well.

Troost and Filsinger (1993) aptly characterize this biosocial area of theory as an emerging perspective. A recent review by Booth, Carver, and Granger (2000) supports this contention. Although Emlen's theory might prove very useful for family research, much of the recent biosocial family research has tended to move toward examination of hormonal differences and the inheritability of divorce. To date, however, much of this research has been based on correlational-type research and does not seem well integrated into the work of contemporary endocrinologists. In addition, this newer research effort does not seem to identify with explanations regarding inclusive fitness and evolutionary theory but clearly puts more emphasis on specific hormones as mediating between the individual's genetic endowment and the individual's behavior. The direction of this emerging area places greater emphasis on the biological underpinnings of humans and human society and on the fact that this biological substrate must be part of any complete ecological theory (see Belsky, 2001a, 2001b).

Human Ecology, Family, and Consumer Sciences

From its inception, home economics has been a form of human ecology. Richards's vision was that only through intelligent consumption and management of household resources could our society combat the waste and pollution of unbridled capitalism. She envisioned an application of scientific knowledge and principles to home management. These sentiments were given a more concrete framework by Paolucci, Hall, and Axinn (1977), who fostered the idea that families could affect significant outcomes at the macroscopic level by the management and control of their decisions.

Deacon and Firebaugh (1988) developed an ecological framework for family decision making. They view the family as a system interacting with its environment. Resources and some demands for family resources originate outside of the family. The family system is composed of individual personal subsystems and the family managerial subsystem. The family managerial subsystem contains both planning and implementing functions and results in demand responses and changes in resources as system output. Deacon and Firebaugh emphasize the embeddedness of the family system in the larger ecosystem and the interchanges that take place between these various levels. They stress resources, values, and information in family resource management and decision making that remain true to Richards's original vision.

Bubolz and Sontag (1993) argue that Richards's vision of a scientifically based family consumption unit missed the fact that family decisions ultimately reflect values. A proactive home economics profession, they argue, must likewise reflect a set of values. In this sense, because home economics is a practitioner field and not simply a field of studies, it cannot follow the value neutrality that Bubolz and Sontag identify with positivistic science. Thus, Bubolz and Sontag, as well as others such as Brown (1984), have rejected science as the appropriate model for knowledge and practice and favor a hermeneutic approach that includes the subjectivity of experience and valuing. Among the issues Bubolz and Sontag see as central to human ecology theory are a number of value-laden questions such as "What changes are necessary to bring about human betterment?" and "What should be done to realize such universal values for the common good as economic adequacy, equity in access to resources and opportunities, increased freedom and justice, and development of peace?" (1993, p. 429). It is interesting to contrast this approach with that of traditional scientists, who would first question if a universal set of values does indeed exist and would want to see evidence that these values are universal.

In some senses, Bubolz and Sontag's (1993) version of home economics is caught in a dilemma common to the "helping" professions. Home economics is dedicated to both the study of the ecosystem and to helping people. On one hand, home economists would like to build a theory of human ecology. On the other hand, they require that such a theory contain a statement of values, such as "equity in access to resources," so that practitioners have a clear notion of what the *common good* and *human betterment* represent. Scientists have in part attempted to remain value neutral because the juxtaposition between an accurate description and prediction of the way things are has largely been thought to be independent of our thinking about the way things should be. The name change of the American Home Economics Association to the American Association of Family and Consumer Sciences might signal the beginning of a resolution to the science versus service dilemma.

The practical implications for Home Economics research is demonstrated by research carried out by Perkins, Ferrari, Covey, and Keith (2005). They used the ecological approach to foster community collaborative efforts on behalf of children and families. The Community Coalitions in Action (e.g., Perkins et al., 2005) used both qualitative and quantitative approaches to investigate the patterns of collaborative community efforts in Michigan. They conclude that "an understanding of ecological theory can lead home economists/human ecologists to form collaborative relationships in the community to prevent problems and to create solutions for the situations facing children, youth and families" (p. 355).

Empirical Applications

Effect of Day Care on Young Children

The research on day care and its effects on young children has proven to be one of the most effective applications of ecological theory of the family. The ecological formulations of Bronfenbrenner (1979) have guided most of this research. Major studies include Belsky, Gillstrap, and Rovine (1984) in the United States and Goelman and Pence (1987) in Canada. Researchers in the Pennsylvania Infant and Family Development Project (Belsky et al., 1984) examined infant-mother attachment by using variables drawn from the micro-, meso-, and exosystems developed by Bronfenbrenner (1979; see Bretherton, 1993, p. 287). Findings from the work by Belsky and colleagues (1984) and the myriad other studies examining the ecological factors of child care appear to contradict previous research in the area of child care.

Belsky (1990) characterizes the newer research findings, first noting that the macrosystem environment in which these studies were conducted has changed over time: "Less than one-third of all mothers with an infant under one year of age were employed in 1976" but "by 1985 virtually one out of every two such women were working" (pp. 894–895). Belsky summarizes the current state of the literature:

> Children in any variety of child care arrangements, including center care, family day care, and nanny care, for the first year of life, are at elevated risk of being classified as insecure in their attachments to their mothers at 12 or 18 months of age and of being more disobedient and aggressive when they are from 3 to 8 years old. (p. 895)

Belsky and Eggebeen (1991) analyzed the National Longitudinal Survey of Youth and found greater noncompliance among children whose mothers were extensively involved in work early in the child's life. Although Belsky's (1990) claim has been replicated (Belsky, 2001a, 2001b) and is accepted by some academics, a significant number of critics offer empirical support for the position either that other factors might account for the differences in attachment or that no significant differences exist (see Demo & Cox, 2000; Greenstein, 1993). This debate has become more detailed and is summarized in the work of the National Institute of Child Health and Human Development (NICHD) Early Child Care Research Network (2005) and

Vandell et al. (2010). The 2010 report (Vandell et al., 2010) finds that the effects for child care found earlier in younger children continue into high school. The authors state that "more hours of nonrelative care predicted greater risk taking and impulsivity at age 15" (p. 737). There is little doubt that this debate about the long-term effects of day care will continue.

Child Maltreatment

Garbarino and Sherman (1980) argue that when the parent-child relationship is embedded in a community in which other adults with greater resources interact with the parent-child dyad, there is less child maltreatment than in socially isolated parent-child dyads. In *High-Risk Neighborhoods and High-Risk Families: The Human Ecology of Child Maltreatment,* Garbarino and Sherman (1980) cite ethological studies with isolated gorilla mothers and their infants and cross-cultural studies that suggest parental rejection of the child is inversely associated with social embeddedness. Garbarino and Sherman matched two neighborhoods, one high and one low in child risk, by racial composition and socioeconomic status. They state that about 40% of child maltreatment is associated with socioeconomic status, but there remain additional differences in child maltreatment. The hypothesis these researchers examined is that when socioeconomic status is controlled, child risk is associated with neighborhood characteristics.

The results support their contention that neighborhood characteristics are associated with levels of child maltreatment risk. Garbarino and Sherman (1980) describe the high-risk neighborhoods as being different from the low-risk neighborhoods on several dimensions. In low-risk neighborhoods, the children played with other children, and parents lent a helping hand with "coverage" of children so that stressed parents could recover. In high-risk neighborhoods, the children did not play with other children, and the parents expressed doubts that the neighborhood was a good place to raise children: "Family life is threatened from within and without. . . . A family's own problems seem to be compounded rather than ameliorated by the neighborhood context, dominated as it is by other needy families" (p. 194). Garbarino and Kostelny (1992) likewise view child maltreatment as a community problem. The presence of informal support networks in the community militates against child maltreatment. But as ecologists such as Burgess (1925) have pointed out, there is a tendency for neighborhoods to homogenize. This process leads Garbarino and Sherman (1980) to conclude that "we have repeated findings that ecological niches can 'make or break' risky families. The challenge to researchers and policymakers is to make the best of it" (p. 196). Their work continues to inform research on the role of community and neighborhood in the incidence of child maltreatment (e.g., Cicchetti & Valentino, 2006; Zielinsky & Bradshaw, 2006).

Critiques and Discussion

Regardless of the appealing logic of ecological theory and its seeming breadth and inclusiveness, there are some rather severe criticisms of both the logic and substance of this approach. The criticisms we broach here are not ones that can be dismissed by claims that the theory is too new or that these are simply areas that have not been adequately filled in as yet. Rather, many of the criticisms are directed at the logic of the explanation in general.

One of the basic notions in Hawley (1986) and Bronfenbrenner (1979, 1989) is that growth comes about by interchanges with the environment. Equally important is the question "How do decline and decay come about?" Hawley's (1986) *Human Ecology* contains chapters on growth, evolution, and expansion in time and space; chapters on decay, disintegration, and death are notably absent. Bronfenbrenner (1979) focuses so exclusively on child development that statements about environmental interaction and growth appear natural. Even with his later admission that the life course as well as child development need to be included in the model, there is no discussion of degeneration (Bronfenbrenner, 1989). Some ecological scholars address these issues and indeed go some distance in resolving the oversight. Most notable is the work by Hannan and Freeman (1984), who use the idea of structural size and attendant inertia to predict the ability of organizations to adapt to changing environments and the natural selection that results from their adaptive failure. These authors link the properties of the organization with adaptation and selection. The need remains to incorporate concepts such as aging and continuous decay into the ecological model.

Another major problem for ecological theory is the need to specify when ontogenetic causation changes to sociogenic causation. For example, a child may not learn toilet training at 2 months of age for reasons of ontogenetic maturation, but at some point in the life course of the organism, the same outcome (toilet training) switches from being ontogenetic to sociogenic. Another way of thinking about this is that there comes a time when the organism's responses are no longer determined by the organism's internal development but largely by social processes exogenous to the organism. The process of this changeover and its stages has not yet been identified by ecological theorists. Hawley (1986) provides a partial solution in his notion that an organization (such as a family) can switch from commensalistic to corporate functions. Bronfenbrenner (1979) incorporates this notion in relating the child to successively broader ecosystems. Yet the exact process and identity of this switch from genetic to social causality eludes us.

Somewhat similar to the above criticism is the question of levels of analysis. The problem is that there are few rules to guide the scholar as to when one level of analysis is appropriate rather than another. For example, if behavior is explained by gene pool variance, then when behavior changes rapidly, we would expect rapid changes in the gene pool. Now, imagine that violent crimes increase in a city in a short period of time, such as 3 years. We would be tempted to explain those changes in crime by changes in the gene pool or population, yet it is doubtful that gene pools change so rapidly with normal levels of migration. What, then, is the appropriate level of analysis; the individual, the group, the organization, or some other level?

A problem with the sociobiological variation of ecological theories is its limited predictive value. For example, we usually have to wait many generations before seeing whether a behavioral pattern is fit or adaptive. For this reason, empirical evidence is usually applied to outcomes that have already occurred rather than to outcomes that take place and are observed in the near-term future. This means that much of the explanatory power such theories have is ex post facto or post hoc rather than predictive.

Many critics claim that ecology is a sensitizing metaphor. For example, in home economics, some proponents show embedded circles as diagrams of ecological levels and interfaces, but critics claim these represent pretty circles but no theory. A theory must identify the process by which change occurs. Even Bronfenbrenner (1989) concedes that this is a rather large flaw in the theory. In his original contribution, Bronfenbrenner (1989) identified behavior as a function of the person interacting with his or her environment $(B = f \{PE\})$. He says, "The all-essential key to scientific discovery is missing. In all the preceding pages, what is there to substitute for the fateful 'f' in the formula? What is the process that the person and the context are to generate?" (p. 241). Bronfenbrenner also states that he is working on this problem, but as yet it remains a major question for ecological theorists.

Bronfenbrenner's (1989) task is complicated by the criticism that the logic underlying ecological theory is basically tautological or circular (Turner, 1991). For example, evolution is a form change brought on by adaptation and selection to change that in turn was brought on by evolution. One needs to ask if this is not defining change by change. It may not be a problem if there are sufficient precision and detail in the theory so that generalities such as *change* become more precisely specified as *evolution*, *adaptation*, and *development*. It also remains a problem that adaptation may be in terms of social organization or genetic selection. Among ecologists, only Emlen (1995) seems prepared to take on this challenge.

The notion of biological or ontogenetic development of the organism represents a richness that many sociological theories neglect. This allows for the inclusion of both internal and external dynamics of change. But the biological arguments from sociobiology and some ontogenetic arguments share a common flaw. Critics argue that because many of these claims and explanations are ex post facto in nature, any number of other plausible theories might also be true (including sociogenic theories). The way out of this criticism is to abandon claims that may appear reasonable on the surface but fail to lead to empirically testable predictions. For example, the claim that the male strategy for inclusive fitness is to maximize sexual partners might lead to cross-culturally testable hypotheses. But if this strategy is nothing other than a preference that is extremely malleable by the environment, then it would undoubtedly lead nowhere. This is what has happened to those ridiculous claims in the 1800s about the true *nature of man* and *natural law* theories. At the present time, the inclusion of biological factors holds great promise but also represents the threat of dragging ecological theory into the quagmire of ad hoc and ex post facto explanations that has been the bane of sociobiology.

Finally, there is criticism of building a value-laden human ecology theory (Bubolz & Sontag, 1993). It seems there is a choice to be made between producing a social science theory or a general value orientation. On one hand, it can be argued that all scientific theories entail some value orientation, and this may be the case. The problem we see is different. First, by definition, social science theories describe and predict. A value orientation may simply not meet the meaning or function of a scientific theory. There are philosophical theories, religious theories, theories of literature, and ideologies, none of which are scientific theories. Also, a value orientation may simply not be a social science theory. Second, value-oriented theories may be able to produce predictions, but we wonder whether predictions would be judged by their accuracy or by their desirability or value correctness. For example, Galileo's ideas were suppressed because they were politically incorrect, not because of the inaccuracy of his predictions.

Conclusion

In the final analysis, the ecological approach is at a youthful stage of its development. It has the necessary breadth and depth to offer a perspective on humans that is both biological and social. The possible unification of work from sociobiology (Emlen, 1995) with the ecology of human development (Bronfenbrenner, 2005) and Hawley's (1986) more organizational ecology offers some intriguing prospects for studying individual family members, the family as a group, and the general ecological context in which those groups function. It might well be that ecological theory will provide not only family scholars but also social scientists in general with the most powerful theoretical propositions possible. At present, however, we can only say that this promise remains a potentiality.

STUDY QUESTIONS

1. With climate change and global warming, we have seen increases in ecological disasters, such as storms, flooding, and drought. How is family ecological theory responding to these challenges? How should it respond?

2. One of the large problems for governments worldwide is to respond to migration. Which of the variations in ecological theory would best deal with this?

3. If you were a "new demographer" looking at changes in housing, how do you think carbon dioxide and nitrous oxide pollution relate to the demise of the single-family house and shopping centers?

4. Ecological theorists have not been at the forefront of our explanations of social and economic inequality. Can you think of reasons for this? (Hint: Carefully examine the intellectual traditions and the assumptions.)

5. If corporations start human economic settlements on Mars, does this theoretical approach help us understand the complex adjustments and interactions that would result?

Theory Construction and Emerging Theories

T he social sciences routinely deal with research methods in great detail. So, for example, students learn various ways of collecting and analyzing empirical data about families, and they learn the issues involved in making wise decisions during the research process. Much less attention is given to methods of theory construction and theorizing, the ways of reasoning and organizing ideas that help us understand and explain family life and other social phenomena. Professional journals with articles reporting research findings require authors to cover research methods in enough detail so that empirical studies can be replicated as well as being improved in the future. Although we would argue that there should be, there is neither a strict requirement nor a conventional way of reporting details about how data and methods connect with theory, other than the notion that research hypotheses should have some kind of link to broader explanations or a theoretical frame of reference.

In this chapter, we will explore ways of theorizing, general steps that can be taken in many fields, including the study of families, and explore some newly emerging theories in the field of family science. We will assume that there is a range of ways to theorize, and that they can be learned, evaluated, and practiced in a disciplined way.

Stages of Theory Construction

The process of theory building is often called *theory construction*. Theory construction is a process that cannot be easily communicated as a set of rules or an architectural blueprint. Theories develop deductively, inductively, and by a combination of these two processes (what C. S. Peirce termed *abduction*; see Buchler, 1955).

Roughly speaking, all theories go through two stages: a formative stage and a refinement stage. During the formative stage, the basic metaphor of the theory comes into sharper focus. This metaphor may eventually be so precise as to be expressed as propositions or even as mathematical models. During the refinement stage, the theory is increasingly subjected to testing, criticism, and application. As a result of these different activities, the theory will either become more refined, divide into variants, or fall into disuse along with the other theories on the trash heap of scientific history (e.g., early heliocentric theories of the universe).

All the theories in this book are beyond the formative stage. You can readily identify the metaphor of these theories, such as *clash* and *opposition* in conflict theory and *time-dependent change* in family developmental life course theory. Furthermore, these theories are sufficiently precise to offer us propositions and models. As we suggested in Chapter 2, however, theories may emerge from sources that are, at this time, not clearly identifiable. The theories in this book are clearly recognizable as theories in the second phase of theory construction.

The refinement stage is a difficult period in the life of a theory. Imagine that scientific theories, like people, have a birth, a life course, and an eventual death. The history of science clearly attests to the fact that there are no "true" scientific theories, at least not everywhere and forever. Even the theories currently occupying hallowed ground in physics, such as relativity theory, will eventually fall or be modified to achieve greater explanatory power and greater capacity to deal with the anomalies that plagued preceding versions and alternative theories. There is no one critical scientific test that leads to a theory falling into disuse; rather, it is typically an accumulation of contrary evidence or the gradual evolution or division into other theories that marks the demise of a theory.

Sometimes during the refinement stage there will be attempts to conduct crucial experiments using *strong inference*. This happens when there are two or more incompatible theories, or at least two incompatible hypotheses from different theories. By setting up an impartial study that allows each rival to be either true or false, but with only one winner and the rest losers, we ought to be able to reduce the number of inadequate theories in a field of study by confidently rejecting them. As glorious as this prospect might seem, we are not aware of any such crucial family experiments having been designed yet, let alone conducted. More attention in the future to this kind of research may be beneficial for theoretical hygiene.

Even if we consider theories with little, if any, empirical support, such as Freudian psychological theory, we sometimes find that the powerful metaphor in these theories continues to serve certain functions, such as therapeutic application. But when a theory cannot meet the standards of empirical plausibility demanded by science, it can no longer be regarded as a scientific theory but only as a general orientation. Thus, the theory that the Earth is flat was at one time widely accepted by the best minds of their time, but the theory has fallen into disuse and no longer can be regarded as an acceptable scientific theory (although groups such as the Flat Earth Society demonstrate that even theories that have been widely discredited can still have adherents).

We have said that all the theories in this book are in the refinement stage of development. Now we may ask if there is any way of comparing the adequacy and utility of one theory over another. The answer to this question is complex. If two theories are equally logical and have the same scope and breadth of explanation, then we could say that the theory that explains the most variance in a set of dependent variables is more adequate. But none of these *ifs* is ever exactly true. For example, is dialectical logic more "logical" than symbolic logic or Boolean algebra? There is really no answer here.

As we have seen, family theorists tend to attempt explanations of different levels of analysis and different dependent variables depending on the basic assumptions they make. And although scientists properly make demands about empirical testability and internal logical coherence, they do not and cannot justifiably claim that one set of assumptions is correct and all the other sets are wrong.

What we do know from Klein's (1994) study is that scholars who prefer certain family theories sometimes also prefer certain standards for judging them. At the most abstract and philosophical level, this would be equivalent to what Kuhn (1962/1998) has labeled incommensurability, meaning that theories speak very different languages, which makes any definitive test between two theories impossible. Though we disagree with Kuhn's analysis, there are nonetheless a few examples that might support his perspective. The clearest example of this is that family systems theorists favored practical utility more than other theorists. They also were more likely to favor standards that are more clearly associated with a critical philosophy of science than the other philosophies. This is rather interesting, for we mentioned earlier that Burr (1995) labeled family systems theory as being most consistent with an interpretive philosophy. Apparently, many family systems theorists would themselves place their theory more comfortably within the critical-emancipatory philosophy.

We encourage you to nurture your own opinions about which family theories are better and in what specific ways. Because we have argued that the result is most likely to be that all the theories in this book come out fairly strong and nearly equal overall, you may have to try a different way to find theories you would consider extremely adequate and extremely inadequate. Instead of starting with the more general theoretical frameworks, begin with a few specific books or articles by researchers who create or use a theory for a particular topic. By seeing how theories are applied at this very specific level, it should be easier for you to form opinions. Remember, however, that a few successes or a few failures are usually not enough to make sweeping judgments about an entire theoretical tradition or framework; theoretical refinement and evaluation, like all stages of science, is incremental.

Methods of Theory Construction

It should be useful to study how theories have been constructed in the past within formation and refinement stages. In addition, there may be methods available that seldom have been tried. We know much about how the higher level conceptual frameworks have evolved, but without a requirement that each theorist articulate how the theory was developed, it is mostly guesswork figuring out what actually happened to "birth" a theory.

In Chapter 2, we noted that there was a period of a dozen or more years (roughly 1967–1979) when formalization of theory took hold in the family field. This movement derived from efforts in the social sciences generally. In sociology alone, 10 theory construction textbooks were published in this period. Chronologically, they included Zetterberg (1965), Glaser and Strauss (1967), Stinchcombe (1968/1987), Blalock (1969), Dubin (1969), Mullins (1971), Reynolds (1971), Gibbs (1972), Hage (1972), and Chafetz (1997). These texts remain interesting today, for both their similarities and their differences.

The differences tend to be modest. Some were fairly basic in their coverage (e.g., Mullins, 1971; Reynolds, 1971), while others were more advanced and comprehensive (e.g., Hage, 1972; Stinchcombe, 1968/1987). They all used different topical examples, reflecting the authors' different areas of expertise. Most included causal explanations, with Blalock (1969) being adamant about them, while one argued against causal reasoning (Gibbs, 1972). One relied more than the others on induction from qualitative data (Glaser & Strauss, 1967).

Together, these texts were sufficient to constitute an intellectual movement. This collective effort seems to have been based on the shared observation that sociology had developed little theory to date. We needed to start from scratch, or else be much more formal about ideas that previously were informal, vague, imprecise, and subject to endlessly diverse interpretations. Formalists all argued that theories needed to be more self-consciously developed if the social sciences were to advance.

Were these suggestions heeded? Reviews are mixed. Years later, one of the earlier movement's participants, Hage (1994), lamented that formalization had faded away too quickly and that its virtues did not pass down to the next generation of scholars. This opinion may have been premature, however. Two of the texts were popular enough to be reissued (chronologically, Stinchcombe, 1968/1987; Reynolds, 2006), and one was dramatically revised (Corbin & Strauss, 1998). Perhaps more telling, three new theory construction texts with a multidisciplinary perspective have appeared in the last few years (chronologically, Shoemaker, Tankard, & Lasorsa, 2004; Bell, 2009; Jaccard & Jacoby, 2010). Hage was so enthusiastic about the efforts of Shoemaker and her colleagues that he wrote a laudatory foreword for their book.

In comparison with the earlier texts, the newer ones devote more attention to theorizing methods based on principles of creativity. Shoemaker et al. (2004) discuss 12 ways to be creative, while Jaccard and Jacoby (2010) discuss 26 ways. We offer just a few adapted examples here.

- *Imagine that something implausible is real.* For example, what if every child had three parents? What if every child had no parents? What if all marriages were required to be terminated after 5 years? Imagining things known to be untrue (counterfactuals) can sometimes improve our understanding of why true things that we take for granted are true and also whether or not they necessarily must be true.

- *Make extreme contrasts.* For example, consider this sentence: "All women are different, but all wives are the same." What does this potentially illuminate about the constraints of marriage? Might it apply as well to men and husbands?

- *Attribute a characteristic to an entity that probably cannot have it.* For example, what if every family had a personality? What might the elements of a group's personality be? Perhaps we can translate ideas across units of analysis, but trying to do it forces us to make sense of the meaning of ideas and who the appropriate actors are. Another common application concerns the difference between rates of events in a population and the likelihood that a particular individual will experience the same event. For example, can both of the following statements be true? (1) The higher the socioeconomic status of a couple, the less likely they are to divorce. (2) The higher the socioeconomic status of a population, the higher the divorce rate in that population is likely to be. Are these statements incongruent? How might they be reconciled?

The general rule about using techniques for stimulating creativity is that we cannot predict in advance which ones will yield useful theoretical ideas. So the more varied our techniques are, or perhaps the more often we use them, the more likely we are to generate an otherwise invisible theoretical insight.

Aside from the more provocative principles of creativity, virtually all the older and newer theory construction textbooks have relied heavily on the parts of a theory that we introduced in Chapter 1. At a minimum, all theories have concepts, statements that connect concepts, and relations among those statements. Notice that there is a difference between saying that theories have certain components and saying that they are built in a certain way. Simply having a hammer, some nails, and some wood doesn't tell you how to use these items together to create a piece of furniture.

The theory construction texts were written primarily to address situations where the goal was to create middle-range and lower level theories in substantive areas where little if any previous explicit theorizing had occurred. They emphasized the importance of clearly specifying all the essential elements, and they devoted some attention to ways of finding or creating, and organizing, the potentially useful components. This approach also was proposed when some theory existed in the area of study but was fuzzy or inconsistent. Box 10.1 contains a representative list of the kinds of questions addressed in these texts.

Box 10.1 Questions to Consider During Theory Construction

Concepts and Variables

1. What concepts are needed? Can they be found in existing literatures?
2. What does each concept mean? Are alternative meanings worth considering?
3. Which concepts vary, and what is their range of variation?
4. Which concepts capture structures and which capture processes?
5. What is the appropriate unit of analysis? Who are the relevant social actors?

Assumptions

1. What assumptions need to be made about the ideas in this theory?
2. Are different assumptions possible, and if not, why not?
3. Are any of the assumptions capable of being empirically disproven?

Propositions

1. What are the relationships within each pair of concepts and each pair of variables?
2. Is one relationship a subset of another relationship, or do they partially overlap?
3. Does one variable totally determine another variable, or is the strength of causal influence moderate?
4. Do any variables reciprocally influence each other? How does this work over time?
5. Are all effects linear, or are some nonlinear?
6. What are the boundaries of relevance, the scope conditions, for each proposition?

Strategies of Theory Construction

If an ample amount of source materials already exists at a particular level in the hierarchy of theoretical scope, we may want to start a new theorizing project there instead of going back to the basic building blocks of a theory. Hill (1971) outlined five principal theory construction strategies for the family field early in the theory construction era. Each has been fairly popular (e.g., Burr, Hill, Nye, & Reiss, 1979, Vols. 1 & 2), and each is still used today.

1. *Deducing Family Theories From More General Theories.* We have mentioned several times that most of our current family theories have been derived from more general theories in the social sciences. As new general theories are developed in the future, we would expect some to be eventually applied to families. It is also worth noting, however, that deriving inspiration from a general theory is possible without using formal deductive logic. Indeed, if you return to the lists of propositions in Chapters 3 through 9, you will see little evidence of formal deductive logic. This suggests that more work lies ahead for those who are deductively inclined, even if they start with current general theories. For example, it is not easy to start with propositions about individuals making rational choices and formally deduce other propositions about how small groups of interacting individuals, such as families, make rational choices.

So long as we are moving down by deduction from a broader to a narrower level, this strategy is applicable regardless of where we start or end in the hierarchy of theoretical scope. So, for example, we might start with a framework for family theory and end with a theory about family rituals. We have illustrated this movement with our empirical applications in previous chapters. Starting with theories that apply to all groups, organizations, or institutions, including families, is just one of several possibilities.

One issue that may arise when seeking source theories is the way they are grouped by scholars who assemble them. There are two common kinds of groupings. One is by general framework, including this book and others (e.g., Boss, Doherty, LaRossa, Schumm, & Steinmetz, 1993; Burr, Hill et al., 1979; Winton, 1995). The other common scheme is to arrange theories by substantive topic (e.g., Bengtson, Acock, Allen, Dilworth-Anderson, & Klein, 2005; Burr, 1973; Burr, Leigh, et al., 1979; Fine & Fincham, 2013). A strength of the frameworks approach is that it encourages rigorous applications of theory consistent with explicit assumptions. One limitation of the frameworks approach is that it may not reveal instances when lower level theories have drawn from multiple frameworks. One strength of the topics approach is that researchers tend to concentrate their expertise in one or two topical areas, so it is useful to know which middle-range and lower level theories already have been applied to a topic. One limitation of the topics approach is that it may discourage the integration of knowledge and encourage a fragmented view of the field.

2. *Codifying Partial Theories.* Many current theories about families are "partial" or incomplete in one of two ways. One is that they may address only part of a phenomenon. For example, a theory about dating among adolescents may tell us little about whether they get married, and it may not apply to divorced older adults who also are dating. Hill (1971) suggested that we could take several theories that are incomplete in this sense and combine them into, for example, a more comprehensive theory of mate selection or something even more general such as relationship formation. The other way in which theories are partial is that their explanations apply to a limited number of instances. We are especially likely to notice this when researchers test a theory and discover that they can explain only some of the differences that they observe. Again, the strategy needed to improve the situation is to combine the partial theories. If there are, for example, two or more theories of helping behavior among middle-aged siblings but each omits explanatory variables found in one of the others, the theories might well be eligible for combination. Although combining theories that are partial in either respect may be done intuitively, a more rigorous way is to first *codify* them; that is, clearly identify all the assumptions, concepts, and propositions and then try to link them in various ways that are logical and plausible. Hill (1971) also argued that merely formalizing partial

theories would represent progress. Clarity is thereby gained, and users of these theories benefit.

The more previous research and theorizing there has been in an area, the more complex is the task of identifying, codifying, and integrating partial theories. Fortunately, there are ways of comparing, simplifying, and elaborating ideas from multiple sources (e.g., Klein, 1973; Klein, 1976). In one such project, more than 400 propositions were located that involve the explanation of effective problem solving in families. It was possible to condense them down to a causal model with a small set of core propositions, stating, for example, that the type of family interaction influencing solution effectiveness depends on the nature of the problem (Klein & Hill, 1979).

3. *Borrowing From Other Fields of Study.* Because it is relatively difficult to invent any truly new idea that has never before been imagined, borrowing ideas is a fairly common practice. For example, systems theorists borrowed the idea of entropy from physics. Family development theorists borrowed the career concept from theories about labor force participation. Given that there are many specialized areas of study in the sciences, there is practically no limit to sources of ideas that might be transferred to the domain of the human family and molded into an existing or new theory.

It is also the case that family theorists often borrow from each other. Indeed, it has become such a common practice in the past few decades for theorists and researchers to blend elements of different family theories that it is becoming increasingly difficult to appreciate the origins and general themes in the newer theories. We return to this "food blender" phenomenon when we discuss the future in the next chapter. For now, it is enough to say that borrowing from each other's theories about the family is one good way for researchers to build a more comprehensive picture of families.

When borrowing ideas, it often helps to rely on metaphors and analogies. Because translating an idea from one area to another may be stretching the truth, it helps to consider both the merits and the limitations of any borrowed idea. For example, if we think about families responding to changes as if they were on a roller coaster, in what ways is that a helpful idea, and how might it be modified to be closer to the literal truth?

4. *Inducing From Empirical Research Generalizations.* Some empirical research is guided by preexisting theory; other research is not. In either case, particular studies tend to yield not only specific results but also more general statements that summarize the findings. Hill (1971) suggested that we could identify a somewhat topically bounded field, collect several reports of studies in that field, and, by inspecting them for similarities and differences, build a theory. Because research is an ongoing process and some topics may be more popular than others during a given period, it is likely that this strategy would result in only partial theories. Assuming that

these partial theories eventually became sufficiently adequate, however, we could shift to the second strategy above and continue the theory construction process.

Just as deduction can begin at any higher level in the hierarchy of theoretical scope and end at any lower level, induction can be applied going in the opposite direction, moving up instead of moving down. So empirical generalizations are just one starting point for inducing higher order theories. One popular induction strategy starts from raw observations—namely, the grounded theory approach first popularized by Glaser and Strauss (1967).

A much more quantitative approach to induction has emerged in recent years—namely, meta-analysis (e.g., Cooper, 2017). The theorist collects all the available quantitative research reports that try to explain variance in a common dependent variable. In a popular area, there might be dozens of studies with differing samples of participants, somewhat different sets of predictor variables, and other methodological similarities and differences. By systematically combining all the separate studies and treating them in unison, it is possible to come up with robust estimates of the effects of the most important casual factors. The technical side of meta-analysis can be difficult, so a concentrated study of this approach to synthesizing empirical data at a higher theoretical level is necessary.

Two precautions about induction are helpful to keep in mind, one concerning proving things and one about reasons things happen. Deduction is a method of proof. If the premises are true, the deduced conclusion must be true. Many philosophers have criticized the belief that induction also is a method of proof. Just because the first three swans you encounter are white doesn't prove that all swans are white. So, while we may reach a tentative conclusion based on induction, it must be taken as provisional. The more swans we see, the more likely our estimate of their color distribution will be accurate, but the future is not totally preordained by the past. Popper (1959) helped resolve the problem of induction by referring to it as a method of conjecture or discovery, not a method of proof, verification, or justification.

The other precaution involves the difference between reasons and causes. Whether or not they are scientists beholden to methods of seeking truth, everybody theorizes in a loose way about the world and their place in it. Using grounded theory with qualitative interviews, we are likely to encounter from interviewees their reasons for why things under study happen. It may be very valuable to induce and codify the reasons they give. We certainly can develop or apply a theory that is based on the notion that a family member's beliefs about causes influence that person's actions. It may even be that each family develops a set of shared beliefs about how some or all of the world works (e.g., Reiss, 1987). The precaution here is not to confuse reasons with causes. Believing that something is a cause does not make it a cause. Still, beliefs can be causes under the right circumstances, and as we saw in Chapter 4, this is a fundamental tenet in the symbolic interaction tradition.

5. *Integrating Concepts and Building Taxonomies.* The vocabulary of scientific concepts is always large and always growing. Some concepts get discarded or replaced along the way, of course, but certainly in an area of study with a growing population of theorists, researchers, and practitioners, the pool of potentially valuable concepts tends to grow as well.

The ongoing scrutiny of ideas and their meanings may not always result in new or improved explanations, or even better descriptions. But because concepts are at the core of every theory, and because language is dynamic rather than static, periodic attention to basic concepts that deal with actors, relations between actors, and actions themselves will inevitably influence the nature of scientific theories in any field, including family science.

Taxonomies are matrices of cross-classified concepts, allowing us to use two ideas in order to find a third idea at their intersection. Typologies are another useful conceptual tool because they reveal the hierarchy of inclusiveness that relates a broader concept with a narrower version of the same idea. Taxonomies and typologies are tools of clarification. It also sometimes helps to remember the difference between a word and its meaning. Different words can have the same or similar meanings, and a particular word can have several meanings. Because words and their meanings tend to emerge together from the endless necessity of human communication—because language is a human construction—there always is room to conceptualize ideas about families in both familiar and unfamiliar ways.

Today, as in earlier decades, it is an enormous task just to learn the meanings of all the technical terms that can be used in theories. Unlike the English language generally, there is no Webster's dictionary for concepts about the family, and different theories often use the same term to mean different things. There are many glossaries in many books, but there is no single common glossary that everyone is trained to understand. The fact that family theorizing is also undertaken by scholars who speak languages other than English obviously adds to the complexity of the nomenclature. In our judgment, we have reached the point, or perhaps merely remained at the point, at which words themselves are unreliable indicators of meaning or theoretical posture. For example, many family scholars use the word *system* without having any allegiance whatsoever to family systems theory. The same could be said about many other key concepts found in our theories. Hill's (1971) advice remains relevant today. By carefully studying our terminology and the various meanings of our concepts, we might be able to unveil and express the crucial ideas or invent new ones.

We have focused on various methods and five of the main strategies that are used to construct family theories, although it is likely that the inventory of useful tools will itself continue to grow as family scholars search for ways to improve the stock of knowledge. One helpful way to learn more about these strategies is to locate one or a few theoretical works in the literature, and then, instead of the usual practice of trying to figure out the content or product, study the work as a process; that is, see if you can identify the strategies and steps that the theorist used to craft the argument.

Emerging Theories

Although it might seem as though all of the good ideas have already been thought and nothing new could possibly remain for you to discover or create, new theoretical perspectives and models regularly emerge, both in family science and in related areas that can be applied to the study of families. Here, we will take a closer look at one such theory that has emerged relatively recently and increasingly is being used to understand families: queer theory.

Queer Theory

Queer theory began to see common usage as a theoretical and political framework in the 1990s, arising as an outgrowth of (and at times contested by; Lovaas, Elia, & Yep, 2006) lesbian, gay, bisexual, and transgender (LGBT) and feminist studies. Queer theory takes a postmodern and poststructuralist view of gender and sexuality, emphasizing self-reflexivity and that "subjectivities are multiple, fluid, and include agency, the ability to act, as opposed to a static, unified, view of the self, an object controlled by the dominant society" (Lovaas et al., 2006, p. 5). Queer theory was formally elaborated as a family theory by Oswald, Blume, and Marks (2005), and central to their argument was the concept of heteronormativity. Oswald et al. noted that the United States (and numerous other countries) espouses an "ideological composite" of gender, sexuality, and family binaries (cisgender/transgender, heterosexual/non-heterosexual, nuclear/non-nuclear), privileging cisgender and heterosexual individuals in nuclear families above other "deviant" individuals and families. Oswald et al. proposed that individuals and families that do not meet the cultural norm of heteronormativity engage in "queering" these statuses, "by challenging the gender, sexuality, and/or family binaries" (Oswald et al., 2005, p. 146). For example, gay marriage queers the sexuality binary by challenging the idea that marriage should be between a man and a woman; divorce, single parenthood, and polyamorous parenting queer the family binary by challenging the norm of nuclear biological families. By focusing on the privilege afforded to those whose acts and ideas fall under the umbrella of heteronormativity (and conversely, the disadvantage and oppression experienced by those outside of that domain), queer theory provides a lens for examining the power of social norms and expectations around gender and sexuality, and the ways in which individuals and families might challenge or uphold these norms through their identities and behaviors.

Recent calls have been made to expand queer theory beyond the original three binaries to include additional "contextual spheres" that individuals and families occupy, such as race, ethnicity, nationality, class, and disability, as well as the ways in which these spheres and the original binaries might evolve and shift over time, for both individuals and for societies (Allen & Mendez, 2018). Allen and Mendez noted that a shift in cultural views of gender and sexuality already had occurred in the decade since Oswald et al. (2005) first defined their construct of heteronormativity in families, and pushed for queer theory to expand to accommodate new definitions. For example, with the legalization of gay marriage, they argue that the United States has now shifted to "mononormativity" rather than strict "heteronormativity" in marriage, privileging monogamous relationships (including gay and lesbian ones) but leaving polyamorous relationships to remain as a "deviant" status. Too, with the increasing visibility of transgender individuals, they note that cultural "cisnormativity" has become more inclusive of transgender individuals if they "present" and are socially recognized as male or female, whereas genderqueer or nonbinary individuals remain on the "deviant" and unprivileged side of the binary. Finally, Allen and Mendez (2018) note that queering of families has resulted in "homonormativity," as shown by "gay and lesbian individuals seeking inclusion in, and the privileges granted by, traditionally heterosexual institutions such as marriage and parenting" (p. 76). By gaining access to and operating within the heteronormative system, some lesbian and gay individuals and families have gained access to greater privilege, but at the cost of leaving other individuals and families in the queer community outside the system and viewed as deviant. Whether such a shift is an advancement or a setback for the queer community is an ongoing debate in the field.

With its recent rise in popularity, queer theory has not been without its critics in family science (e.g., Doherty, Carroll, & Waite, 2006; Williams, 2006). Even in his discussion of the original Oswald et al. (2005) piece, Kurdek (2005) commented that "queer theory is not a theory with a well-articulated set of premises that enables one to make testable predictions that compete with those of other theories" (p. 162) but that, instead, it was better viewed as a "perspective." In this way, queer theory has faced some of the same criticisms as feminist theories, which is perhaps not surprising given its origins. Kurdek recommended that queer theorists go a step further and elucidate "queer methodology" (asking, for example, "whether quantitative methods are necessarily unqueer" [p. 162]), so that queer theory could make the aforementioned testable predictions that he viewed as crucial to both differentiating it from other family theories and advancing family science. Others (Few-Demo, Humble, Curran, & Lloyd, 2016) see queer theory as a natural and desirable progression of the ways that LGBT individuals and families have been conceptualized and queried over time in family science, moving from a place of exclusion and invisibility in research, to acknowledgement that LGBT individuals and families exist, to a focus on the disadvantage experienced by LGBT families, to full incorporation of queer and intersectional theories (and ultimately, they argue, to the use of queer theory to study all families, not just those who deviate from the norm).

Overall, queer theory appears to have passed through the formative stage and to be in the process of refinement. Time will tell whether it continues along this path to become a more *complete* theory in its own right, distinct from others, whether its component parts will be combined with or absorbed into other compatible perspectives, or whether it will eventually fall into disuse in favor of other perspectives.

Conclusion

There are other theories that may be emerging in the study of the family, yet these are undeveloped and may simply end up as extensions of existing theory. For example, gender theory (see Chapter 8) and emotion theory (see Chapter 4) both have potential to break from the frameworks within which they have developed and to emerge as distinct theories. At the current time, however, queer theory is the only nascent theory that can be seen as independent from current frameworks.

It is important that ideas and frameworks at all levels of theorizing continue to expand and change with our changing social world. Families might change in structure and purpose as a result of shifts in political and economic forces. Too, families might drive economic and political changes such as universal day care, which could change family functional emphases from early nurturance to companionship and support. Social theory must be dynamic, adaptive, and evolutionary, rather than static and stable, so that theory continues to be relevant.

STUDY QUESTIONS

1. What indicates that a theory has moved from a *formative* stage to a *conceptual* stage?

2. Explain why theories should change over time or be testable.

3. Queer theory has assailed *heteronormativity* as oppressive. Can you explain this?

4. Imagining theory is an important step in early theory construction. For example, if you are working from an assumption that everyone is guided only by her self-interest, the counterfactual opposite might be that everyone is guided by the welfare of others. Think about how that might change rational choice theory.

5. Scientists want our theories to be empirically testable. Recall from Chapter 1 why they want our theories to be testable. Now develop a theory about why students are concerned about grades. Let's say that students see grades as important to getting a good job. We could test this by seeing if employers examine grades of job applicants. Would this test yield useful information if it were true? And what if it were false?

CHAPTER 11

11

Epilogue

We have now traversed a considerable amount of theoretical territory. You have been introduced to the basic elements of theory in Chapters 1 and 2 as well as several family theories in Chapters 3 through 9. Chapter 10 has provided insights about theory construction and inductive approaches to theory. Now it is time for a comprehensive overview of family theory. A comprehensive overview, however, is not only a daunting task but also may well be impossible. The reason such a task might prove impossible is simply that a theory is never finished!

In the preceding chapters, we have presented theories as products of human thought. Although this is certainly one useful way to learn about theories, an overemphasis on the product may lead you away from the power of theories as tools to assist us in understanding our world. A tool analogy may help you appreciate our point here. Imagine you have a screwdriver. You can hold it up and examine it from different angles, note the color, the type of point, and so on. In this sense, you are examining the screwdriver as a product and a human construction. But your image of the screwdriver changes when you use it to screw in a screw, pry open a paint can, weed the garden, and so on. You might even find other new and helpful ways to use the screwdriver. Your appreciation changes when you use this tool to do things. The same is true of theories.

Any of the family theories you find in this book can be used for myriad tasks. These theories can be used to predict, interpret, explain, formulate questions, integrate research, make deductions, and lead us into novel areas of research. When we use them, we gain an understanding of theories that is unlike the rarefied experience of holding them up in isolation as objects for academic scrutiny.

Like the tools developed for carpentry or gardening, theories are often modified as they are used and as a result of their use. A researcher who tests a series of theoretically derived hypotheses may find some disconfirmed and others not disconfirmed, and these continue to be plausible. The researcher may then suggest modifications in the theory to make the theory more consistent with the findings. Although researchers often focus on a theory's ability to predict, theories are also used to interpret events that have already occurred. This after-the-fact (ex post facto) interpretation is what many of us consider to be the central component of explanation. We would like a good story about why or how something happened or usually happens. These interpretations of past events may also lead to modifications in theories. As we attempt to explain why Rod and Michelle are getting divorced or why our grandparents are extraordinarily frugal, we may find other dimensions and variables that are needed to make our story a plausible one.

Yet another way theories are modified is when practitioners use a theory to guide an educational, political, or therapeutic intervention. Often, practitioners discover inadequacies in theories that researchers might miss. All these tool users of theory may assist in modifying and improving family theory. This is the process of theory construction and reconstruction.

In presenting you with various family theories as *products,* we do not want to mislead you into thinking that these theories are finished artifacts of human thought. Nothing could be further from the truth. Because they are useful tools, theories are constantly being modified and refined. We are not saying that the core concepts and relations change constantly, but even those core concepts are not exempt from the process of theory building. In this last chapter, we discuss the current state of theory, the nature of theory construction, and how metatheory might assist us in moving the process of theory building and development forward in our field.

Metatheory and Theory Development

One major way to assist the refinement of theory is by using meta-analysis to assist in identifying the strengths and weaknesses of existing formulations. Meta-analysis proceeds by identifying specific dimensions on which a theory or theories are to be measured or evaluated. For example, we might ask if a theory has causal propositions or specifies core measures. We might also ask if a theory covers different levels of analysis or if the theory provides "dynamic" models. Although many of these dimensions might be foreign to you, the meta-analysis in our 1996 formulation (Klein & White, 1996) can provide a useful example of how such a method might work to identify strengths and weaknesses.

Klein and White (1996) and White (2004) provide an example of how metatheory assists in analyzing and improving theories. These authors identify three dimensions that they regard as critical for understanding how theories of the family function. The first dimension is the *level of analysis* (discussed in Chapter 9) on which the theory focuses. Although some theories discuss several different levels of analysis (e.g., individual, dyad, family group, social organization, and society), Klein and White initially just distinguished two levels: individual and greater-than-individual groups. These two levels of analysis are referred to as individualism and holism, respectively. Some theories focus almost exclusively on the individual; for example, exchange and choice theories focus on individual rational choices. On the other hand, other theories such as ecological and developmental theories focus on several levels, often assuming that the larger levels of population (ecological) or social institutional timing norms (developmental) are the major focus. The level of analysis constitutes an important element for the scope of explanation that a theory provides.

A second dimension used in this metatheoretical approach is the *source of causation*. The source of causation in family theory may be seen as originating from within the family group. For example, most family process theories and systems theories see the internal dynamics of the system as determining output or influences into the environment of the system. Theories that see the family group as having causal efficacy can be said to favor an *endogenous* view of causation. On the other hand, some family theories view the family as the recipient of influences from larger social forces. For instance, conflict theory and feminist theory tend to view the family as being moved by social forces, such as class conflict (Marx) or by institutional patriarchy (feminism). Such theories see cause as largely outside of or *exogenous* to the family group.

The final dimension is how the theory treats the concept of *time*. Although there are many ways of treating time in theoretical formulations, the two basic approaches are static and dynamic. A static approach to time basically assumes that social processes and causation happen more or less independently of time. For example, social exchange and choice models assume that all individuals across time and place weight rewards relative to costs for any given action. Certainly, long-term versus short-term rewards might be taken into account, but this is a static accounting. A dynamic theory, on the other hand, treats time as an essential causal agent. For example, developmental and life course theories assume that duration of time spent in a specific state affects outcomes. For example, the duration of time spent in a first marriage affects the probability of a first birth, and this relationship is not linear. Another example would be from systems theory, where the number of cycles of a positive feedback loop amplifies the system's error.

Reading Table 11.1, we caution readers that any such metatheoretical classification depends on the arguments that are launched to justify the classification. For example, we could argue that feminist theories are not dynamic but are more static and should appear in the same category with the functionalism and conflict frameworks. On the other hand, we have argued that feminism is more dynamic because we can view the terrain of feminism as constantly changing with time. Therefore, readers might make different arguments and even better arguments for alternative classifications in this table.

Table 11.1 Three-Dimensional Metatheory of Family Theories

Level of Analysis	Causation			
	Endogenous *Time*		Exogenous *Time*	
	Static	Dynamic	Static	Dynamic
Individualism	Exchange and Rational Choice	Symbolic Interaction	Role Theory	Feminism
Holism		Systems Theory	Conflict Functionalism	Ecological and Developmental Life Course Theories

Source: Adapted from Klein and White (1996) and White (2004).

What the table does assist us with is finding the weaknesses of theories. For example, we might ask exchange and social choice theorists whether there are any phenomena that cannot be explained by individual choices. If they insist on reducing all phenomena to the individual, then that provides a potential weakness for the theory. Another weakness appears to be the many social science theories about families that are not particularly dynamic. Such theoretical formulations might prosper from this recognition (for example, role theory) and suggest that future theoretical work be focused on a dynamic perspective of roles (see White, 2004).

As we stated at the outset of this section, there is no necessity to this particular metatheoretical view of family frameworks, and many others are possible. Furthermore, within any particular formulation, classifications are subject to argument and justification. The point of this section is that scholars can learn a great deal by comparing theories in a metatheoretical framework and identifying how one theory's strength might suggest avenues for addressing the weakness in other theories. This systematic approach has much to recommend it because it makes our thinking more formal and more easily scrutinized by the scholarly community.

The Future of Family Theory

It would be presumptuous of us to forecast what family theories and theorizing will be like as the 21st century unfolds. Perhaps if we had a good theory about how the social sciences develop over time, we would be willing to make predictions. Many such theories have been formulated by historians (e.g., Kuhn, 1962/1998), sociologists (e.g., Crane, 1972; Mullins, 1973), and psychologists (e.g., Maslow, 1966; Toulmin, 1972). No such theory has yet been used to explain why family science has developed as it has, although there are some suggestive hints in the works we cited toward the end of Chapter 2.

We already have discussed some strategies of theory construction that have been commonly used, and it is reasonable to expect that they will continue to be used. We do see particular developments and issues that we think will influence social science theory in this century.

Increasing Importance of Levels of Analysis

If there is one major change in social science theory and research, it is the area of levels of analysis. Certainly, theorists have bantered about such issues as community effects on child development and family effects on individuals; however, these were difficult to test because of multicollinearity and overlapping conceptions. The emergence of maximum likelihood estimation procedures and multilevel mixed models (http://www.spss .ch/upload/1126184451_Linear%20Mixed%20Effects%20Modeling%20 in%20SPSS.pdf) have provided tools that offer the researcher new ways to investigate effects on different levels of analysis and between levels. Previously, theorists had advanced multilevel ideas and were stalled by researchers' inability to measure these. Now, it is the theorists that are challenged to identify processes across levels of analysis and between levels.

Not only is theory challenged but it is also quickly becoming apparent that much of the progress that we make in philosophy, theology, biology, and many other areas of thought will be about emergent phenomenon. For example, the notion of *trust* is important at an individual level and dyadic level but also at a broader social level of *trust in our institutions*. Thus, understanding trust means defining and investigating it at these multiple connected levels.

Another dimension of multilevel analysis that will become more important is the study of emergent phenomena. There are many examples in science of emergence of higher order phenomena (think of the big bang and the emergence of gravity, suns, etc.), but the social sciences have been slower at investigating emergence because of an individualistic bias. As our thinking becomes more profoundly multilevel and nuanced we will find discussion of emergence involving connections between human feelings and emotions, robotics and intelligence, truthfulness and democracy.

Getting "Family" Into Social Theory

Family theorists sometimes face questions regarding the viability of family theory. One of the most interesting of these is the question "Is family theory necessary, or can we use any social science theory about groups to explain behavior in the family group?" This question suggests that theories designed expressly for the family may not be necessary or even desirable. Do we need family theory? Or can general social and behavioral science theories be applied to the family?

Given the previous discussion of emergence couples with the great diversity of family forms, we might approach family theory as a different kind of question. If general social theory can deal with an emergent social structure where there are individuals linked intergenerationally (e.g., older-younger generations) and with affinal contemporaries (cohabitants, marrieds), then we might not need family theory. However, the history of social theory is that it has either ignored the family (Weber, Durkheim) or not been able to account for the phenomena (e.g., Coleman, 1990). How can rational choice account for why people have children? How can conflict theory a la Marx account for why people have children or family?

Family theory does need to integrate more with larger social theories. At this point in history, it does not seem that existing social theories will be able to provide the same insights into family afforded by family theories. The basic assumption behind the argument that general theories about social groups can be applied to the family is that the family group does not differ from other social groups in any but trivial ways. It seems to us, however, that the family simply is not like any other social group, such as a work group or a friendship network. The family differs from other social groups in several important ways. We pointed out these unique properties in Chapter 1, and we encourage you to inspect them again. Clearly, the behaviors of family members have the potential for longer lasting effects in both the longevity of the family group and the historical and intergenerational nature of kinship. We argue that the family group is so different from other social groups that theories explicitly formulated about the family are likely to be necessary. We also expect that sociological and psychological theories will continue to be useful for family research and theory building.

Some existing theories have been useful to explain individual behavior in families, not because of family variables but because of individual variables. Other theories have been useful to explain how families are swept along on the powerful social tides of the larger society. These theories rely on the family being a group within the larger society but not a uniquely familial group. Psychological theories gain their usefulness by shedding light on how individual and relationship-level variables are related to the family group. Macro-level social theories provide insights about how institutional and social structural pressures may affect the family group.

What appears to be missing, however, is a theory focused on the family group as a group rather than a collection of individuals (micro) or one of many social organizations buffeted and determined by social processes (macro). Both micro- and macro-orientations fail to acknowledge and deal with the meso-level phenomena of the family group. We believe that such meso-level family theories are necessary to explain the unique and important properties of the family group. Genuine meso-level theory aimed at the family as a unique form of social group seems elusive, but we anticipate greater attention to this problem in the future.

Integrating

There always seems to be a tension, in family science as well as other sciences, between keeping things separate and pulling them together. The case for separation is straightforward. If phenomena really are different, it is important to know this. We illustrated this argument above by reemphasizing that because families are unique, we need special theories that fit family realities. The risk of ignoring differences is confusion, although some would argue that it is confrontation between incompatibilities that ignites creativity and change (e.g., dialecticians). In any case, one challenge in the future will be to create these family-focused theories. The *Journal of Family Theory and Review* has certainly provided an outlet for scholarly work on family theory.

An emphasis on pulling things together has been much more pronounced during the history of family theorizing. When we discussed strategies for theory construction, our emphasis was on organizing the theories and fragments of theories that exist and creating new theories out of them. There also is a much more profound kind of theoretical unification, which has periodically been the topic of great debates. The question is, "Should we attempt to take many or perhaps even all our existing theories about families and create a 'grand synthesis'?"

If such an effort were possible and successful, it would be a remarkable feat, not unlike the unified theory of matter in physics. But this idea of one encompassing theory of family life repeatedly meets with resounding resistance. Only occasionally is the resistance voiced by theorists with a fanatical devotion to their "favorite" family theory. Most family theorists, however, avoid the yes-or-no debate over integration. They steer a more moderate course, which is eclecticism. To be theoretically eclectic is to take pieces selectively, as the situation seems to warrant, from different perspectives, and blend them into something a little different.

During the nearly two decades of the conceptual frameworks era described in Chapter 1, a major lesson was learned by most family scholars. The big advantage of trying to array perspectives according to their similarities and differences is the discovery that novel combinations are sometimes possible. This spirit has continued with full force as we have moved into the refinement period of family theorizing. Eclectic theorizing is likely to continue as a principal activity in the future as well. In fact, if it continues much longer, the landscape of family theory may be nothing but milk shakes. Theories like those in this book will be ingredients, not the end products.

Even among those who are seeking meso-level family theory, a more selective kind of integration may bear fruit. Within some of the variants of the existing theories, we find some possible ways we might develop such a theory. For example, the structural conflict approach of Caplow's (1968) "coalition theory" allows the theorist to analyze group properties, such as cohesion, by means of variables such as the impermanence of coalition partners. If your opponent of today might be your ally of tomorrow, then we would assume greater cohesion than where allies and opponents are relatively permanent. Although coalition theory may assist in developing the structural aspects of the family group, it still neglects the time dimension and historicity of the family. Thus, although existing theoretical variants are not devoid of approaches to the meso level of the family, they need further development and integration by family scholars.

Clarification of Explanation and Understanding

A critical area of needless friction among researchers and theorists is about the goal of our endeavor as either explanation or understanding. This is a longstanding debate about the goal and the methods used in family research. Those in the interpretive approaches have emphasized that the goal of family scholarship is to understand people. The exact meaning of this usually ranges from offering the stories and perspective of actors to actually trying to create an empathic understanding of feelings, beliefs, and motives. On the other hand, positivistic sciences often focus the goal on measuring behaviors and prediction from theory. Most reasonable people will grasp that these are complimentary viewpoints. While it is important to record and predict actual behavior, that goal may be assisted by understanding the actors' perceptions and motives. Likewise, attaining an understanding of the actors perspectives might include what others in the larger community and nation are doing.

The friction results, however, when these two approaches clash over *facts*. As you may recall from the introduction to Chapter 1, a "fact" is, in most developed societies, a methodological finding. That is to say, we agree on a methodology to resolve competing claims. When those claims are about physical realities, we can rely on science. When those claims are about metaphysical reality, such as gods, demons, values, and so on, we rely on logic and argument to resolve disputes. However, a dispute is not resolvable by assuming that there are multiple realities or that there are alternative facts. This only prolongs dispute. For example, O'Connor and O'Neill (2000) state,

> Qualitative methodologies tend to move beyond a positivistic frame of reference which advocates that there is only one, "true" reality. Instead the notion of multiple realities is introduced. This concept opens the space for hearing the voices of others because it recognizes that in order to fully understand a particular phenomenon or process, ascertaining the perspectives of those who have experienced it is essential. (2000, p. 1)

While O'Connor and O'Neill (2000) are certainly correct about a full accounting of perspectives being essential for our understanding, the notion of multiple realities serves little use in resolving disputes. For example, even though there may be different perspectives within a lynch mob it is nonetheless one overall shared perspective that creates mob behavior and outcomes. Furthermore, individuals have motive and feelings, but we are less clear about moving this form of analysis to other levels of analysis, such as corporations and communities and even families.

It is important not to dismiss qualitative analysis as only important for understanding individuals in that institutional ethnography is an established methodology. What is important is that when it comes to resolving competing claims, there must be agreement on the method that would resolve those claims. Once the methodology for resolution is decided, science, scholarship, and argument can pursue a resolution. The alternative is chaos and loud voices because without agreement on methods of resolution, the resolution is either force or chaos, not reason.

Other voices are equally adamant about methods of resolving competing claims about facts. The feminist epistemologist Duran (1998) argues that if feminism rejects science, they better be in control of political power because that would be the only road to "truth." She points out that credible evidence presented in courts has led to a host of changes including cases of spousal abuse and child abuse (White 2005, p. 173). Even more strongly, Gross and Levitt (1994) argued that accepting multiple voices means that once again saying "the gods are angry" is as legitimate as scientific explanations. Indeed, they fear a new intellectual "dark ages." It is up to researchers, theorists, and politicians to supply a rational discourse to avoid these mistakes.

Conclusion

As we look back on the eight theoretical frameworks in this book and their many variants, we are struck by the amazing richness of the ideas. Not only do these theories deal with different levels of analysis but within any level of analysis, they often also deal with different dependent variables. Although we have said that we perceive a relatively underdeveloped area in meso-level theories about the family group, we are nonetheless impressed by the power and breadth that these seven theories provide researchers and practitioners.

At the conclusion of a work such as this, it is only natural that we should ask, "What has this book achieved?" Of course, it is gratuitous for the authors to answer this question. Time, colleagues, and successive generations of students will supply the answer in due course. But we hope that if this book achieves nothing else, it will serve to give you a glimpse of the "life of ideas" in which scholars participate. In this book, we believe we have introduced you to the world in which academics interested in understanding families dwell—that is, the life of ideas about families.

If we look at the history of science, it is not a particular research finding or a project that survives the test of time, nor even the reputations of people who produce them. Only basic ideas and theories survive over time. For most scholars, these ideas are what initially compelled them to join the academic enterprise and, indeed, it is this *life of ideas* that still furnishes the most significant but intangible rewards for many of us. We hope the theories and ideas you have encountered here will become integrated with the knowledge you have from other sources. As these ideas come together for you, forming a more complete picture of your world, your family, and especially other families, you should experience the same intrinsic rewards that we believe reside in the life of ideas.

References

Abbott, A. (1995). Sequence analysis: New methods for old ideas. *Annual Review of Sociology*, 93–113.

Acock, A. C., & Demo, D. H. (1994). *Family diversity and well being*. Thousand Oaks, CA: Sage.

Adams, B., & Steinmetz, S. (1993). Family theory and methods in the classics. In P. Boss, W. Doherty, R. LaRossa, W. Schumm, & S. Steinmetz (Eds.), *Sourcebook of family theories and methods: A contextual approach* (pp. 71–94). New York: Plenum.

Adamsons, K., O'Brien, M., & Pasley, K. (2007). An ecological approach to father involvement in biological and stepfather families. *Fathering: A Journal of Theory, Research, and Practice about Men as Fathers*, 5, 129–147.

Adamsons, K., & Pasley, K. (2006). Coparenting following divorce and relationship dissolution. In M. A. Fine & J. H. Harvey (Eds.), *Handbook of divorce and relationship dissolution* (pp. 241–261). Mahwah, NJ: Erlbaum.

Adorno, T. W. (1973). *Negative dialectics*. New York: Continuum.

Ainsworth, M. (1967). *Infancy in Uganda*. Baltimore, MD: Johns Hopkins Press.

Ainsworth, M., Blehar, M., Waters, E., & Wall, S. (1978). *Patterns of attachment*. Hillsdale, NJ: Erlbaum.

Aisenbrey, S., & Fasang, A. E. (2010). New life for old ideas: The "second wave" of sequence analysis bringing the "course" back into the life course. *Sociological Methods & Research*, 38, 420–462.

Albert, A., & Bulcroft, K. (1988). Pets, families, and the life course. *Journal of Marriage and the Family*, 50(2), 543–552. doi:10.2307/352019

Alcoff, L. (1995). Cultural feminism versus post-structuralism: The identity crisis in feminist theory. In N. Tuana & R. Tong (Eds.), *Feminism and philosophy: Essential readings in theory, reinterpretation, and application* (pp. 434–456). Boulder, CO: Westview.

Aldous, J. (1978). *Family careers*. New York: Wiley.

Aldous, J. (1990). Family development and the life course: Two perspectives on family change. *Journal of Marriage and the Family*, 52, 571–583.

Aldous, J. (1994). Someone to watch over me: Family responsibilities and their realization across the family lives. In E. Kahana, D. Beigel, & M. Wykle (Eds.), *Family caregiving across the life span* (pp. 42–68). Thousand Oaks, CA: Sage.

Aldous, J. (1996). *Family careers: Rethinking the developmental perspective*. Thousand Oaks, CA: Sage.

Aldous, J., & Hill, R. (1967). *International bibliography of research in marriage and the family, 1900–1964*. Minneapolis: University of Minnesota Press.

Alexander, J. C. (1985). Introduction. In J. C. Alexander (Ed.), *Neofunctionalism* (pp. 3–24). Beverly Hills, CA: Sage.

Allchin, D. (1998). Values in science and in science education. In B. Fraser & K. Tobin (Eds.), *International handbook of science education* (pp. 1083–1092). Dordrecht, The Netherlands: Kluwer Academic.

Allen, K. (2000). A conscious and inclusive family studies. *Journal of Marriage and the Family*, 62, 4–17.

Allen, K., Walker, A., & McCann, B. (2013). Feminism and families. In G. Peterson & K. Bush (Eds.), *Handbook of marriage and the family* (pp. 139–158). New York: Springer.

Allen, S. H., & Mendez, S. N. (2018). Hegemonic heteronormativity: Towards a new era of queer family theory. *Journal of Family Theory and Review, 10*, 70–86.

Allison, P. (1984). *Event history analysis: Regression for longitudinal event data.* Beverly Hills, CA: Sage.

Alwin, D. F., & McCammon, R. J. (2007). Rethinking generations. *Research in Human Development, 4*, 219–237.

Amato, P. R., Landale, N. S., Havasevich-Brooks, T. C., Booth, A., Eggebeen, D. J., Schoen, R., & McHale, S. M. (2008). Precursors of young women's family formation pathways. *Journal of Marriage and Family, 70*(5), 1271–1286.

American Psychiatric Association (APA). (1994). *Diagnostic and statistical manual of mental disorders* (4th ed., text rev.). Washington, DC: Author.

Andersen, M. (1991). Feminism and the American family ideal. *Journal of Comparative Family Studies, 22*, 235–246.

Anderson, S. A. (1988). Parental stress and coping during the leaving home transition. *Family Relations, 37*(2), 160–165. doi:10.2307/584314

Andreas, C. (1971). *Sex and caste in America.* Englewood Cliffs, NJ: Prentice Hall.

Arditti, J. A. (2012). Child trauma within the context of parental incarceration: A family process perspective. *Journal of Family Theory & Review, 4*(3), 181–219.

Arditti, J. A. (2015). Family process perspective on the heterogeneous effects of maternal incarceration on child wellbeing. *Criminology & Public Policy, 14*(1), 169–182.

Asai, S. G., & Olson, D. H. (2003). *Spouse abuse and marital system based on ENRICH.* Unpublished manuscript. Life Innovations, Minneapolis, MN. Retrieved from www.prepare-enrich.com/research

Asai, S. G., & Olson, D. H. (2004). Culturally sensitive adaptation of PREPARE with Japanese premarital couples. *Journal of Marital Family Therapy, 30*, 411–426.

Atwood, M. (2018, January 13). Am I a bad feminist? *The Toronto Globe and Mail.* Retrieved February 8, 2018, from https://www.theglobeandmail.com/opinion/am-i-a-bad-feminist/article37591823/

Baltes, P. (1987). Theoretical propositions of life-span developmental psychology: On the dynamics between growth and decline. *Developmental Psychology, 23*, 611–626.

Baltes, P., & Nesselroade, J. (1984). Paradigm lost and paradigm regained: Critique of Dannefer's portrayal of life-span developmental psychology. *American Sociological Review, 49*, 841–846.

Bartz, K., & Nye, F. I. (1970). Early marriage: A propositional formulation. *Journal of Marriage and the Family, 32*, 258–268.

Bateson, G., Jackson, D., Haley, J., & Weakland, J. (1956). Toward a theory of schizophrenia. *Behavioral Science, 1*, 251–264.

Becker, G. (1964). *Human capital.* Chicago, IL: University of Chicago Press.

Becker, G. (1981). *A treatise on the family.* Cambridge, MA: Belknap.

Bejenaru, A., & Roth, M. (2012). Romanian adoptive families: Stressors, coping strategies and resources. *Children and Youth Services Review, 34*(7), 1317–1324. doi:10.1016/j.childyouth.2012.03.011

Bell, D. C. (2009). *Constructing social theory.* Lanham, MD: Rowman & Littlefield.

Belsky, J. (1990). Parental and nonparental child care and children's socioemotional development: A decade review. *Journal of Marriage and the Family, 52*, 885–903.

Belsky, J. (2001a). Developmental risks (still) associated with early child care. *Journal of Child Psychology and Psychiatry, 42*, 845–859.

Belsky, J. (2001b). Marital violence in evolutionary perspective. In A. Booth & A. Crouter (Eds.), *Couples in conflict* (pp. 27–36). Mahwah, NJ: Erlbaum.

Belsky, J., & Eggebeen, D. (1991). Early and extensive maternal employment and young children's socioemotional development: Children of the National Longitudinal Survey of Youth. *Journal of Marriage and the Family, 53,* 1083–1110.

Belsky, J., Gillstrap, B., & Rovine, M. (1984). The Pennsylvania Infant and Family Project: I. Stability and change in mother-infant and father-infant interaction in a family setting at one, three, and nine months. *Child Development, 55,* 692–705.

Belsky, J., & Rovine, M. (1990). Patterns of marital change across the transition to parenthood. *Journal of Marriage and the Family, 52,* 5–20.

Bengston, V. L. (1977). *Reconstruction of family development theory: An exercise in the study of micro-social organizations through time.* Prepared discussion of the paper by R. Hill & P. Mattessich, Reconstruction of family development theories. Paper presented at the Theory Development and Methods Workshop, National Council on Family Relations, San Diego, CA.

Bengtson, V. L., Acock, A. C., Allen, K. R., Dilworth-Anderson, P., & Klein, D. M. (Eds.). (2005). *Sourcebook of family theory and research.* Thousand Oaks, CA: Sage.

Bengtson, V. L., & Allen, K. R. (1993). The life course perspective applied to families over time. In P. Boss, W. Doherty, R. LaRossa, W. Schumm, & S. Steinmetz (Eds.), *Sourcebook of family theories and methods: A contextual approach* (pp. 469–499). New York: Plenum.

Bergner, D. (2013). *What do women want? Adventures in the science of female desire.* New York: Harper Collins.

Berk, S. (1985). *The gender factory: The apportionment of work in American households.* New York: Plenum.

Beutler, I., Burr, W., Bahr, K., & Herrin, D. (1989). The family realm: Understanding its uniqueness. *Journal of Marriage and the Family, 51,* 805–816.

Bianchi, S., & Milkie, M. (2010). Work and family research in the first decade of the 21st century. *Journal of Marriage and Family, 72,* 705–725.

Bianchi, S. M., Robinson, J. P., & Milkie, M. A. (2007). *Changing rhythms of American family life.* New York: Russell Sage Foundation.

Biblarz, T. J., & Gottainer, G. (2000). Family structure and children's success: A comparison of widowed and divorced single-mother families. *Journal of Marriage and the Family, 62,* 533–548.

Blair, S., & Johnson, M. (1992). Wives' perception of the fairness of the division of household labor: The intersection of housework and ideology. *Journal of Marriage and the Family, 54,* 570–581.

Blair-Loy, M. (1999). Career patterns of executive women in finance: An optimal matching analysis. *American Journal of Sociology, 104,* 1346–1397.

Blalock, H. M., Jr. (1969). *Theory construction: From verbal to mathematical formulations.* Englewood Cliffs, NJ: Prentice-Hall.

Blau, P. M. (1964). *Exchange and power in social life.* New York: Wiley.

Blumer, H. (1962). Society as symbolic interaction. In A. M. Rose (Ed.), *Human behavior and social processes* (pp. 179–192). Boston, MA: Houghton Mifflin.

Blumer, H. (1969). *Symbolic interactionism.* Englewood Cliffs, NJ: Prentice Hall.

Blumstein, P., & Schwartz, P. (1983). *American couples.* New York: William Morrow.

Bohannan, P. (Ed.). (1970). *Divorce and after: An analysis of the emotional and social problems of divorce.* Garden City, NY: Doubleday.

Booth, A., Carver, K., & Granger, D. A. (2000). Biosocial perspectives on the family. *Journal of Marriage and the Family, 62,* 1018–1034.

Boss, P. (1988). *Family stress management.* Newbury Park, CA: Sage.

Boss, P. (1999). *Ambiguous loss: Learning to live with unresolved grief.* Cambridge, MA: Harvard University Press.

Boss, P. (2002). *Family stress management.* Thousand Oaks, CA: Sage.

Boss, P., Doherty, W., LaRossa, R., Schumm, W., & Steinmetz, S. (Eds.). (1993). *Sourcebook of family theories and methods: A contextual approach.* New York: Plenum.

Bott, E. (1957). *Family and social network: Roles, norms, and external relationships in ordinary urban families.* London, UK: Tavistock.

Bourdieu, P. (1980). Le capital social: Notes provisaires. *Actes de la Recherche en Science Sociales, 3,* 2–3.

Bourdieu, P. (1984). *Distinction: A social critique of the judgement of taste* (R. Nice, Trans.). Cambridge, MA: Harvard University Press.

Bourdieu, P. (1986). Forms of capital. In J. Richardson (Ed.), *Handbook of theory and research for the sociology of education* (pp. 241–260). Westport, CT: Greenwood.

Bowlby, J. (1953). *Child care and the growth of love.* London, UK: Penguin Books.

Bowles, S., & Gintis, H. (2002). The inheritance of inequality. *Journal of Economic Perspectives, 16,* 3–30.

Brannigan, A., Wanner, R., & White, J. (1981). The phenomenon of multiple discoveries and the re-publication of Mendel's work in 1900. *Philosophy of the Social Sciences, 11,* 263–276.

Bretherton, I. (1993). Theoretical contributions from developmental psychology. In P. Boss, W. Doherty, R. LaRossa, W. Schumm, & S. Steinmetz (Eds.), *Sourcebook of family theories and methods: A contextual approach* (pp. 275–297). New York: Plenum.

Breunlin, D. C. (1988). Oscillation theory and family development. In C. Falicov (Ed.), *Family transitions* (pp. 133–155). New York: Guilford.

Brinkerhoff, M., & Lupri, E. (1989). Power and authority in the family. In K. Ishwaran (Ed.), *Family and marriage: Cross-cultural perspectives* (pp. 213–238). Toronto, CAN: Wall & Thompson.

Broderick, C. (1971). Beyond the five conceptual frameworks: A decade of development in family theory. *Journal of Marriage and The Family, 33,* 139–160.

Broderick, C. (1993). *Understanding family process.* Newbury Park, CA: Sage.

Broderick, C., & Smith, J. (1979). The general systems approach to the family. In W. Burr, R. Hill, F. I. Nye, & I. Reiss (Eds.), *Contemporary theories about the family* (Vol. 2, pp. 112–129). New York: Free Press.

Bronfenbrenner, U. (1979). *The ecology of human development.* Cambridge, MA: Harvard University Press.

Bronfenbrenner, U. (1989). Ecological systems theory. In R. Vasta (Ed.), *Annals of child development* (Vol. 6, pp. 187–249). Greenwich, CT: JAI.

Bronfenbrenner, U. (Ed.). (2005). *Making human beings human: Bioecological perspectives on human development.* Thousand Oaks, CA: Sage.

Brooks, D., & Wiley, E. (1986). *Evolution as entropy: Toward a unified theory of biology.* Chicago, IL: University of Chicago Press.

Brotherson, S. E. (2007). From partners to parents: Couples and the transition to parenthood. *International Journal of childbirth education, 22*(2), 7.

Brown, M. (1984). Home economics: Proud past-promising future. *Journal of Home Economics, 76*, 48–54.

Brückner, H., & Mayer, K. U. (2005). De-standardization of the life course: What it might mean? And if it means anything, whether it actually took place. *Advances in Life Course Research, 9*, 27–53.

Bubolz, M., & Sontag, S. (1993). Human ecology theory. In P. Boss, W. Doherty, R. LaRossa, W. Schumm, & S. Steinmetz (Eds.), *Sourcebook of family theories and methods: A contextual approach* (pp. 419–448). New York: Plenum.

Buchler, J. (Ed.). (1955). *Philosophical writings of Peirce*. New York: Dover.

Buckley, W. (1967). *Sociology and modern systems theory*. Englewood Cliffs, NJ: Prentice Hall.

Bulcroft, R., Forste, R., & White, J. (1993, November). *An integrated model for studying the decision to breast-feed, duration of breastfeeding, and consequences for child health and development*. Paper presented at the National Council on Family Relations, Theory Construction, and Methodology Workshop, Baltimore, MD.

Bulcroft, R., & White, J. M. (1997). Family research methods and levels of analysis. *Family Science Review, 10*, 2–19.

Burgess, E. W. (1925). The growth of the city: An introduction to a research project. In R. Park, E. Burgess, & R. McKenzie (Eds.), *The city* (pp. 47–62). Chicago, IL: University of Chicago Press.

Burgess, E. W. (1926). The family as a unity of interacting personalities. *The Family, 7*, 3–9.

Burke, P. J. (Ed.). (2006). *Contemporary social psychological theories*. Palo Alto, CA: Stanford University Press.

Burr, W. R. (1973). *Theory construction and the sociology of the family*. New York: Wiley.

Burr, W. R. (1995). Using theories in family science. In R. Day, K. Gilbert, B. Settles, & W. R. Burr (Eds.), *Research and theory in family science* (pp. 73–90). Pacific Grove, CA: Brooks/Cole.

Burr, W. R., Day, R., & Bahr, K. (1993). *Family science*. Pacific Grove, CA: Brooks/Cole.

Burr, W. R., Hill, R., Nye, F. I., & Reiss, I. (Eds.). (1979). *Contemporary theories about the family* (Vols. 1 & 2). New York: Free Press.

Burr, W. R., Leigh, G., Day, R., & Constantine, J. (1979). Symbolic interaction and the family. In W. R. Burr, R. Hill, F. I. Nye, & I. Reiss (Eds.), *Contemporary theories about the family* (Vol. 2, pp. 42–111). New York: Free Press.

Caplow, T. (1968). *Two against one: Coalition in triads*. Englewood Cliffs, NJ: Prentice Hall.

Caplow, T., Bahr, H., Chadwick, B., Hill, R., & Williamson, M. (1983). *Middletown families: Fifty years of change and continuity*. Minneapolis: University of Minnesota Press.

Carlson, D. S., Kacmar, K. M., Wayne, J. H., & Grzywacz, J. G. (2006). Measuring the positive side of the work-family interface: Development and validation of a work-family enrichment scale. *Journal of Vocational Behavior, 68*, 131–164.

Carter, E., & McGoldrick, M. (Eds.). (1988). *The changing family cycle: A framework for family therapy* (2nd ed.). New York: Gardner.

Cavanagh, L., Compton, C. J., Tluczek, A., Brown, R. L., & Farrell, P. M. (2010). Long-term evaluation of genetic counseling following false-positive newborn screen for cystic fibrosis. *Journal of genetic counseling, 19*(2), 199–210. doi:10.1007/s10897-009-9274-4

Chafetz, J. (1997). Feminist theory and sociology: Underutilized contributions for mainstream theory. *Annual Review of Sociology, 23*, 97–120.

Chaulk, B., Johnson, P. J., & Bulcroft, R. (2003). Effects of marriage and children on financial risk tolerance: A synthesis of family development and prospect theory. *Journal of Family and Economic Issues, 24*(3), 257–279. doi:10.1023/A:1025495221519

Cheal, D. (1991). *Family and the state of theory*. Toronto, CAN: University of Toronto Press.

Chibucos, T. R., Leite, R. W., & Weis, D. L. (2004). *Readings in family theory*. Thousand Oaks, CA: Sage.

Chodorow, N. (1978). *The reproduction of mothering*. Berkeley: University of California Press.

Chomsky, N. (1965). *Aspects of the theory of syntax*. Cambridge, MA: MIT Press.

Christensen, H. (1964). Development of the family field of study. In H. Christensen (Ed.), *Handbook of marriage and the family* (pp. 3–32). Chicago, IL: Rand McNally.

Cicchetti, D., & Valentino, K. (2006). An ecological-transactional perspective on child maltreatment: Failure of the average expectable environment and its influence on child development. In D. Cicchetti & D. J. Cohen (Eds.), *Developmental psychopathology: Risk, disorder, and adaptation* (pp. 129–201). Hoboken, NJ: Wiley & Sons.

Clarke, R. (1973). *Ellen Swallow*. Chicago, IL: Follett.

CNN (Andrews, F., Peigne, Y., & Vonberg, J.; 2018 update, January 11). Catherine Deneuve denounces #MeToo in open letter. Retrieved February 8, 2018, from CNN, https://www.cnn.com/2018/01/10/europe/catherine-deneuve-france-letter-metoo-intl/index.html

Cochran, M., & Niego, S. (2002). Parenting and social networks. In M. H. Bornstein (Ed.), *Handbook of parenting: Vol. 4. social conditions and applied parenting* (pp. 123–148). Mahwah, NJ: Erlbaum.

Coleman, J. (1988). Social capital in the creation of human capital. In P. Dasgupta & I. Serageldin (Eds.), *Social capital: A multifaceted perspective* (pp. 13–39). Washington, DC: World Bank.

Coleman, J. (1990). *The foundations of social theory*. Cambridge, MA: Harvard University Press.

Coley, R., & Morris, J. (2002). Comparing mothers and fathers reports of father involvement among low-income minority families. *Journal of Marriage and Family, 64*, 982–998.

Collins, R. (1975). *Conflict sociology: Toward an explanatory science*. New York: Academic Press.

Coltrane, S. (2000). Research on household labor: Modeling and measuring the social embeddedness of routine family work. *Journal of Marriage and the Family, 62*, 1208–1233.

Conger, R., Conger, K., & Martin, M. (2010). Socioeconomic status, family processes, and individual development. *Journal of Marriage and Family, 72*, 685–704.

Connolly, J., & Friedlander, L. (2009). Peer group influences on adolescent dating aggression. *The Prevention Researcher, 16*, 8–11.

Connolly, J., Friedlander, L., Pepler, D., Craig, W., & Laporte, L. (2010). The ecology of adolescent dating aggression: Attitudes, relationships, media use, and socio-demographic risk factors. *Journal of Aggression, Maltreatment and Trauma, 19*, 469–491.

Cook, J., Tyson, R., White, J., Rushe, R., Gottman, J., & Murray, J. (1995). Mathematics of marital conflict: Qualitative dynamic modeling of marital interaction. *Journal of Family Psychology, 9*, 110–130.

Cook, K. (1975). Expectations, evaluations and equity. *American Sociological Review, 40*, 372–388.

Cook, K., & Yamaguchi, T. (1990). Power relations in exchange networks. *American Sociological Review, 55*, 297–300.

Cooley, C. H. (1902). *Human nature and the social order*. New York: Scribner's.

Cooley, C. H. (1909). *Social organization*. New York: Scribner's.

Cooper, H. (2017). *Research synthesis and meta-analysis* (5th ed.). Thousand Oaks, CA: Sage.

Corbin, J. M., & Strauss, A. L. (1998). *Basics of qualitative research: Techniques and procedures for developing grounded theory*. Thousand Oaks, CA: Sage.

Coser, L. (1956). *The functions of social conflict*. Glencoe, IL: Free Press.

Coser, L. A. (1974). *Greedy institutions: Patterns of undivided commitment.* New York: Free Press.

Cowan, P. A., & Cowan, C. P. (2000). *When partners become parents: The big life change for couples*. Mahwah, NJ: Erlbaum. (Original work published 1992)

Cox, M. J., Paley, B., Burchinal, M., & Payne, C. C. (1999). Marital perceptions and interactions across the transition to parenthood. *Journal of Marriage and the Family, 61*, 611–625.

Crane, D. (1972). *Invisible colleges: Diffusion of knowledge in scientific communities*. Chicago, IL: University of Chicago Press.

Crawford, D. W., & Fischer, J. L. (1993). Family developmental trajectories: Family timing and parent-child relations in young adulthood. *Home Economics Research Journal, 21*(4), 339–357. doi:10.1177/0046777493214001

Cristina d'Addio, A. Intergenerational transmission of disadvantage: Mobility or immobility across generations? A review of the evidence for OECD countries. *OECD Social, Employment, and Migration Working Papers No. 52*. Retrieved from http://www.oecd.org/els

Cromwell, R., & Olson, D. (Eds.). (1975). *Power in families*. New York: Halstead.

Crosnoe, R., & Elder, G., Jr. (2002). Life course transitions, the generational stake, and grandparent-grandchild relationships. *Journal of Marriage and Family, 64*, 1089–1096.

Crouter, A. C., Bumpus, M. F., Maguire, M. C., & McHale, S. M. (1999). Linking parents' work pressure and adolescents' well-being: Insights into dynamics in dual-earner families. *Developmental Psychology, 35*, 1453–1461.

Daly, K. (1996). *Families and time: Keeping pace in a hurried culture*. Thousand Oaks, CA: Sage.

Dannefer, D. (1984). Adult development and social theory: A paradigmatic reappraisal. *American Sociological Review, 49*, 100–116.

Dannefer, D., & Perlmutter, M. (1991). The life course perspective in current socio-behavioral research on development. *Research on Aging, 16*, 112–139.

Darwin, C. (1880). *The descent of man*. New York: D. Appleton.

Darwin, C. (1901). *On the origin of the species by means of natural selection*. London, UK: J. Murray. (Original work published 1859)

Davies, J. J., & Gentile, D. A. (2012). Responses to children's media use in families with and without siblings: A family development perspective. *Family Relations, 61*(3), 410–425. doi:0.1111/j.1741-3729.2012.00703.x

Davis, J., & Daly, M. (1997). Evolutionary theory and the human family. *Quarterly Review of Biology, 72*, 407–435.

Davis, K. (1947). Final note on a case of extreme isolation. *American Journal of Sociology, 52*, 432–437.

Davis, S., & Greenstein, T. (2013). Why study housework? Cleaning as a window into power couples. *Journal of Family Theory and Review, 5*, 63–71.

Day, R. D. (2005). Relationship stress in couples. In P. C. Mckenry & S. J. Price (Eds.), *Families and change*. Thousand Oaks, CA: Sage.

Day, R. D., Gavazzi, S. M., & Acock, A. C. (2001). Compelling family processes. In A. Thorton (Ed.), *The well-being of children and families: Research and data needs* (pp. 103–126). Ann Arbor: University of Michigan Press.

Deacon, R., & Firebaugh, F. (1988). *Family resource management: Principles and applications*. Needham Heights, MA: Allyn & Bacon.

de Beauvoir, S. (1953). *The second sex*. New York: Knopf. (Original work published 1949)

Demo, D. H., & Allen, K. R. (1996). Diversity within lesbian and gay families: Challenges and implications for family theory and research. *Journal of Social and Personal Relationships*, 13(3), 415–434. doi:10.1177/0265407596133007

Demo, D. H., & Cox, M. J. (2000). Families with young children: A review of research in the 1990's. *Journal of Marriage and the Family*, 62, 876–895.

De Reus, L. A., Few, A., & Blume, L. (2005). Multicultural and critical race feminisms: Theorizing families in the third wave. In V. Bengtson, A. Acock, K. Allen, P. Dilworth-Anderson, & D. Klein (Eds.), *Sourcebook of family theory and research* (pp. 447–450). Thousand Oaks, CA: Sage.

Dew, J. (2009). The gendered meanings of assets for divorce. *Journal of Family and Economic Issues*, 30, 20–31.

Dewey, J. (1925). *Experience and nature*. LaSalle, IL: Open Court.

Dilworth-Anderson, P., Burton, L. M., & Johnson, L. B. (1993). Reframing theories for understanding race, ethnicity, and families. In P. Boss, W. Doherty, R. LaRossa, W. Schumm, & S. Steinmetz (Eds.), *Sourcebook of family theories and methods:*

A contextual approach (pp. 627–645). New York: Plenum.

Doherty, W., Boss, P., LaRossa, R., Schumm, W., & Steinmetz, S. (1993). Family theories and methods: A contextual approach. In P. Boss, W. Doherty, R. LaRossa, W. Schumm, & S. Steinmetz (Eds.), *Sourcebook of family theories and methods: A contextual approach* (pp. 3–30). New York: Plenum.

Doherty, W. J., Carroll, J. S., & Waite, L. J. (2006). Supporting the institution of marriage: Ideological, research, and ecological perspectives. In A. S. Loveless & T. B. Holman (Eds.), *The family in the new millennium: World voices supporting the natural clan* (2nd ed., pp. 21–51). Westport, CT: Praeger.

Donnelly, D., Burgess, E., Anderson, S., Davis, R., & Dillard, J. (2001). Involuntary celibacy: A life course analysis. *Journal of Sex Research*, 38, 159–169.

Donovan, J. (1985). *Feminist theory*. New York: Frederick Ungar.

Drobnic, S., & Blossfeld, H. (2004). Career patterns over the life course: Gender, class, and linked lives. *Research in Social Stratification and Mobility*, 21, 139–164.

Drobnic, S., Blossfeld, H., & Rohwer, G. (1999). Dynamics of women's employment patterns over the family life course: A comparison of the United States and Germany. *Journal of Marriage and Family*, 61, 133–146.

Dubin, R. (1969). *Theory building: A practical guide to the construction and testing of theoretical models*. New York: Free Press.

Duran, J. (1998). *Philosophies of science/feminist theories*. Boulder, CO: Westview.

Durkeim, E. (1893/1984). *The division of labor*. NY: The Free Press.

Duvall, E. (1957). *Family development*. Philadelphia, PA: J. B. Lippincott.

Edlund, L., & Korn, E. (2002). A theory of prostitution. *Journal of Political Economy*, 110, 181–214.

Ehrenreich, B. (2000, April). Maid to order: The politics of other women's work. *Harper's Magazine*, pp. 59–70.

Eichler, M. (1988). *Families in Canada today: Recent changes and their social policy consequences* (2nd ed.). Toronto, CAN: Gage.

Ekeh, P. (1974). *Social exchange theory.* Cambridge, MA: Harvard University Press.

Elder, G. H. (1975). Age differentiation and the life course. *Annual Review of Sociology*, *1*, 165–190.

Elder, G., Jr. (1974). *Children of the great depression: Social change in life experience.* Chicago, IL: University of Chicago Press.

Elder, G. H. (1999). *Children of the great depression: Social change in life experience.* Boulder, CO: Westview Press.

Ellard, C. (2015). *Places of the heart.* NY: Bellevue Literary Press.

Ellison, C. G., & Bradshaw, M. (2009). Religious beliefs, sociopolitical ideology, and attitudes toward corporal punishment. *Journal of Family Issues*, *30*(3), 320–340. doi:10.1177/0192513x08326331

Elman, C. (1998). Intergenerational household structure and economic change at the turn of the century. *Journal of Family History*, 23, 417–437.

Emerson, R. (1962). Power-dependence relations. *American Sociological Review*, 27, 31–41.

Emerson, R. (1976). Social exchange theory. In A. Inkles, J. Coleman, & N. Smelser (Eds.), *Annual review of sociology* (Vol. 2, pp. 335–362). Palo Alto, CA: Annual Reviews.

Emlen, S. T. (1995). An evolutionary theory of the family. *Proceedings of the National Academy of Science, 92*, 8092–8099.

Engels, F. (1946). *The origin of the family, private property, and the state.* New York: International. (Original work published 1884)

Erikson, E. H. (1950). *Childhood and society.* New York: Norton.

Ervin, L. H., & Stryker, S. (2001). Theorizing the relationship between self-esteem and identity. In T. J. Owens, S. Stryker, & N. Goodman (Eds.), *Extending self-esteem theory and research: Sociological and psychological currents* (pp. 29–55). New York: Cambridge University Press.

Falicov, C. (Ed.). (1988). *Family transitions.* New York: Guilford.

Falicov, C. J. (2012). Immigrant family process. In F. Walsh (Ed.), *Normal family processes: Growing diversity and complexity* (pp. 297–323). New York: Guilford Press.

Farrington, K., & Chertok, E. (1993). Social conflict theories of the family. In P. Boss, W. Doherty, R. LaRossa, W. Schumm, & S. Steinmetz (Eds.), *Sourcebook of family theories and methods: A contextual approach* (pp. 357–381). New York: Plenum.

Featherman, D. (1985). Individual development and aging as a population process. In J. Nesselroade & A. Von Eye (Eds.), *Individual development and social change: Exploratory analysis* (pp. 213–241). New York: Academic Press.

Featherman, D., & Lerner, R. (1985). Ontogenesis and sociogenesis: Problematics for theory and research about development and socialization across the lifespan. *American Sociological Review, 50*, 659–676.

Feeney, J., Hohaus, L., Noller, P., & Alexander, R. (2001). *Becoming parents: Exploring the bonds between mothers, fathers, and their infants.* New York: Cambridge University Press.

Ferree, M. (1990). Beyond separate spheres: Feminism and family research. *Journal of Marriage and the Family, 52*, 866–884.

Few-Demo, A. L., Humble, A. M., Curran, M. A., & Lloyd, S. A. (2016). Queer theory, intersectionality, and LGBT-parent families: Transformative critical pedagogy in family theory. *Journal of Family Theory and Review*, 8, 74–94.

Fine, M., & Fincham, F. (Eds.). (2013). *Handbook of family theories: A content-based approach*. New York: Routledge.

Firestone, S. (1970). *The dialectic of sex*. New York: William Morrow.

Fischer, J., Zvonkovic, A., Juergens, C., Engler, R., & Frederick, H. (2013). Work, family, and well-being at midlife: A person-centered approach. *Journal of Family Issues*, 34, 305–311.

Fisher, R. (1958). *The genetic theory of natural selection*. New York: Dover.

Fitzpatrick, J., & Kostina-Ritchey, E. (2013). US families' adoption of Chinese daughters: A narrative analysis of family themes in children's books. *Family Relations*, 62(1), 58–71. doi:10.1111/j.1741-3729.2012.00745.x

Fitzpatrick, M. A. (1988). *Between husbands and wives*. Newbury Park, CA: Sage.

Flanagan, J., Holmes, S., & MacInnes, D. (2002). Advancing practice in family nursing across the cancer continuum. In D. Clarke, J. Flanagan, and K. Kendrick, (Eds.), *Advancing Nursing Practice in Cancer and Palliative Care* (pp. 117–139). Basingstoke, UK: Palgrave Macmillan. doi:10.1007/978-1-349-88882-5

Foa, U., & Foa, E. (1980). Resource theory: Interpersonal behavior as exchange. In K. Gergen, M. Greenberg, & R. Willis (Eds.), *Social exchange: Advances in research* (pp. 77–94). New York: Plenum.

Foschi, M. (1996). Double standards in the evaluation of men and women. *Social Psychological Quarterly*, 59, 237–254.

Foschi, M. (2000). Double standards for competence: Theory and research. *Annual Review of Sociology*, 26, 21–42.

Foschi, M., Lai, L., & Sigerson, K. (1994). Gender and double standards in the assessment of job applicants. *Social Psychological Quarterly*, 57, 326–339.

Fox, G. L., & Murry, V. M. (2000). Gender and families: Feminist perspectives and family research. *Journal of Marriage and the Family*, 62, 1160–1172.

Friedan, B. (1963). *The feminine mystique*. New York: Norton.

Friedan, B. (1981). *The second stage*. New York: Summit.

Fuller, S. (2008). Job mobility and wage trajectories for men and women in the United States. *American Sociological Review*, 53, 158–182.

Furstenburg, F. (2005). Banking on families: How families generate and distribute social capital. *Journal of Marriage and Family*, 67, 809–821.

Gaard, G. (Ed.). (1993). *Ecofeminism: Women, animals, nature*. Philadelphia, PA: Temple University Press.

Galton, F. (1952). *Hereditary genius*. New York: Horizon. (Original work published 1869)

Garbarino, J. (1992). *Children and families in the social environment* (2nd ed.). New York: Aldine de Gruyter.

Garbarino, J., & Kostelny, K. (1992). Child maltreatment as a community problem. *Child Abuse and Neglect*, 16, 455–464.

Garbarino, J., & Sherman, D. (1980). High-risk neighborhoods and high-risk families: The human ecology of child maltreatment. *Child Development*, 51, 188–198.

Gelles, R. (1994). Introduction to special issue on family violence. *Journal of Comparative Family Studies*, 25, 1–6.

Gerth, H., & Mills, C. W. (Eds. & Trans.). (1946). *From Max Weber*. New York: Oxford University Press.

Gibbs, J. (1972). *Sociological theory construction*. Hinsdale, IL: Dryden Press.

Gillath, O., & Karantzas, G. (2015). Insights into the formation of attachment bonds from a social network perspective. In V. Zayas & C. Hazan (Eds.), *Bases of adult attachment: Linking brain, mind and behavior* (pp. 131–156). New York: Springer New York. doi:10.1007/978-1-4614-9622-9_7

Gillath, O., Karantzas, G. C., & Selcuk, E. (2017). A net of friends: Investigating friendship by integrating attachment theory and social network analysis. *Personality and Social Psychology Bulletin*, 43(11), 1546–1565. doi:10.1177/0146167217719731

Gilligan, C. (1982). *In a different voice: Psychological theory and women's development.* Cambridge, MA: Harvard University Press.

Gilman, C. (1898). *Women and economics.* Boston, MA: Small, Maynard.

Gilman, C. (1910). *The home: Its work and influence.* New York: Charlton.

Glaser, B. G., & Strauss, A. L. (1967). *The discovery of grounded theory: Strategies for qualitative research.* Chicago, IL: Aldine de Gryter.

Glick, P. C. (1947). The family cycle. *American Sociological Review*, 12, 164–174.

Goelman, H., & Pence, A. (1987). Effects of child care, family, and individual characteristics on children's language development. In D. Phillips (Ed.), *Quality child care* (pp. 89–104). Washington, DC: National Association for the Education of Young Children.

Goffman, E. (1959). *Presentation of self in everyday life.* New York: Doubleday.

Goffman, E. (1974). *Frame analysis: An essay on the organization of experience.* New York: Harper & Row.

Goldberg, A. E. (2010). *Lesbian and gay parents and their children: Research on the family life cycle.* Washington, DC: APA Books.

Goldscheider, F., & Goldscheider, C. (1999). *Changing transition to adulthood: Leaving and returning home.* Thousand Oaks, CA: Sage.

Goode, W. (1959). Sociology of the family: Horizons in family theory. In R. Merton, L. Broom, & L. Cottrell (Eds.), *Sociology today* (Vol. 1, pp. 178–197). New York: Basic Books.

Goode, W., Hopkins, E., & McClure, H. (1971). *Social systems and family patterns: A propositional inventory.* Indianapolis, IN: Bobbs-Merrill.

Gordon, L. (1979). The struggle for reproductive freedom: Three stages of feminism. In Z. Eisenstein (Ed.), *Capitalist patriarchy and the case for socialist feminism* (pp. 107–136). New York: Monthly Review Press.

Gottman, J. M. (1979). *Marital interaction: Experimental investigations.* New York: Academic Press.

Gottman, J. M. (1993). A theory of marital dissolution and stability. *Journal of Family Psychology*, 7, 57–75.

Gottman, J. M. (1994). *What predicts divorce: The relationship between marital processes and marital outcomes.* Hillsdale, NJ: Lawrence Erlbaum.

Gottman, J. M., Coan, J., Carrere, S., & Sawnason, C. (1998). Predicting marital happiness and stability from newlywed interactions. *Journal of Marriage and the Family*, 60, 5–22.

Gottman, J. M., & Krokoff, L. (1989). Marital interaction and marital satisfaction: A longitudinal view. *Journal of Consulting and Clinical Psychology*, 57, 47–52.

Gottman, J. M., & Levenson, R. (1992). Marital processes predictive of later dissolution: Behavior, physiology and health. *Journal of Personality and Social Psychology*, 5, 295–318.

Gottman, J. M., Markman, H., & Notarius, C. (1977). The topography of marital interaction: A sequential analysis of verbal and non-verbal behavior. *Journal of Marriage and the Family*, 39, 461–478.

Gottman, J. M., & Notarius, C. I. (2000). Decade review: Observing marital interaction. *Journal of Marriage and the Family, 62,* 927–947.

Gottman, J. M., & Porterfield, A. (1981). Communicative competence in the nonverbal behavior of married couples. *Journal of Marriage and the Family, 43,* 817–824.

Gravenhorst, L. (1988). *A feminist look at family development theory.* New York: Guilford Press.

Greenstein, T. N. (1993). Maternal employment and child behavioral outcomes. *Journal of Family Issues, 14,* 323–354.

Greenstein, T. N. (1996). Gender ideology and perceptions of the fairness of the division of household labor: Effects on marital quality. *Social Forces, 74,* 1029–1042.

Gregory, A., & Milner, S. (2011). What is 'new' about fatherhood?: The social construction of fatherhood in France and the UK. *Men and Masculinities, 14,* 588–606. doi:10.1177/1097184x11412940

Grey, J. S. (2018, January 4). Reign of terror in matters of sex tempt backlash. *The Vancouver Sun* newspaper, p. A11.

Gross, P., & Levitt, R. (1994). *Higher superstition: The academic left and its quarrel with science.* Baltimore, MD: Johns Hopkins University Press.

Grzywacz, J. G., Almeida, D. M., & McDonald, D. A. (2002). Work-family spillover and daily reports of work and family stress in the adult labor force. *Family Relations, 51,* 28–36.

Gurmu, E., & Dejene, T. (2012). Trends and differentials of adolescent motherhood in Ethiopia: Evidences from 2005 Demographic and Health Survey. *African Journal of Reproductive Health, 16,* 162–174.

Gwartney-Gibbs, P. (1986). The institutionalization of premarital cohabitation: Estimates from marriage license applications, 1970 and 1980. *Journal of Marriage and the Family, 48,* 423–434.

Ha, N. (2014). Family life course development framework applied: Understanding the experiences of Vietnamese immigrant families. *Journal of Education and Human Development, 3*(4), 305–312. doi:10.15640/jehd.v3n4a27

Haack, S. (1998). *Manifesto of a passionate moderate: Unfashionable essays.* Chicago, IL: University of Chicago Press.

Hage, J. (1972). *Techniques and problems of theory construction in sociology.* New York: Wiley & Sons.

Hage, J. (Ed.). (1994). *Formal theory in sociology: Opportunity or pitfall?* Albany: SUNY Press.

Hall, A., & Fagan, R. (1956). Definition of systems. *General Systems, 1,* 18–28.

Hall, S. S., & Adams, R. (2011). Newlyweds' unexpected adjustments to marriage. *Family and Consumer Sciences Research Journal, 39*(4), 375–387. doi:10.1111/j.1552-3934.2011.02076.x

Han, S.-K., & Moen, P. (1999, March). Work and family over time: A life course approach. *Annals of the American Academy of Political and Social Science, 562,* 98–110.

Hannan, M., & Freeman, J. (1984). Structural inertia and organizational change. *American Sociological Review, 49,* 149–164.

Harding, S. (1986). The instability of the analytic categories of feminist theory. *Signs: Journal of Women in Culture and Society. 4,* 645–664.

Hardy, G. (1908). Mendelian proportions in mixed populations. *Science, 28,* 49–50.

Harris, J. N., Hay, J., Kuniyuki, A., Asgari, M. M., Press, N., & Bowen, D. J. (2010). Using a family systems approach to investigate cancer risk communication within melanoma families. *Psycho-Oncology, 19,* 1102–1111.

Haveman, R., & Wolfe, B. (1994). *Succeeding generations*. New York: Russell Sage.

Havighurst, R. (1948). *Developmental tasks and education*. Chicago, IL: University of Chicago Press.

Hawkins, A., Marshall, C., & Allen, S. (1998). The orientation toward domestic labor questionnaire: Exploring dual-earner wives' sense of fairness about family work. *Journal of Family Psychology, 12,* 244–258.

Hawley, A. (1986). *Human ecology: A theoretical essay*. Chicago, IL: University of Chicago Press.

Hays, S. (1996). *The cultural contradictions of motherhood*. New Haven, CT: Yale University Press.

Hays, S. (1998). The fallacious assumptions and unrealistic prescriptions of attachment theory: A comment on "Parents" socioemotional investment in children. *Journal of Marriage and the Family, 60,* 782–790.

Hazan, C., & Shaver, P. (1987). Romantic love conceptualized as an attachment process. *Journal of Personality and Social Psychology, 52,* 511–524.

Hechter, M. (1987). *Principles of group solidarity*. Berkeley: University of California Press.

Hellemans, A., & Bunch, B. (1988). *The timetables of science*. New York: Simon & Schuster.

Hempel, C. G. (1952). *Fundamentals of concept formation in empirical science*. Chicago, IL: University of Chicago Press.

Hempel, G., & Oppenheim, P. (1948). Studies in the logic of explanation. *Philosophy of Science, 15,* 135–175.

Hewitt, B., & de Vaus, D. (2009). Change in the association between premarital cohabitation and separation, Australia 1945–2000. *Journal of Marriage and Family, 71*(2), 353–361.

Heywood, L., & Drake, J. (Eds.). (1997). *Third wave agenda: Being feminist, doing feminism*. Minneapolis: University of Minnesota Press.

Hill, E. J., Erickson, J. J., Fellows, K. J., Martinengo, G., & Allen, S. M. (2012). Work and family over the life course: Do older workers differ? *Journal of Family and Economic Issues,* 1–13.

Hill, R. (1949). *Families under stress*. New York: Harper & Brothers.

Hill, R. (1951). Review of current research on marriage and the family. *American Sociological Review, 16,* 694–701.

Hill, R. (1958). Generic features of families under stress. *Social casework, 39,* 139–150.

Hill, R. (1966). Contemporary developments in family theory. *Journal of Marriage and the Family, 28,* 15–27.

Hill, R. (1971, August). *Payoffs and limitations of contemporary strategies for family theory systematization*. Paper presented at the National Council on Family Relations, Estes Park, CO.

Hill, R., & Hansen, D. (1960). The identification of conceptual frameworks utilized in family study. *Marriage and Family Living, 22,* 299–311.

Hill, R., & Rodgers, R. H. (1964). The developmental approach. In H. Christensen (Ed.), *Handbook of marriage and the family* (pp. 171–211). Chicago, IL: Rand McNally.

Hinckley, A. (1976). *Applied ecology*. New York: Macmillan.

Hobbes, T. (1947). *Leviathan*. New York: Macmillan. (Original work published 1651)

Hochschild, A., & Machung, A. (1989). *The second shift: Working parents and the revolution at home*. New York: Viking.

Hogan, D. (1978). The variable order of events in the life course. *American Sociological Review, 43,* 573–586.

Holman, T & Burr, W. (1980). Beyond the beyond: The growth of the family theories in the 1970's. *Journal of Marriage and the Family,* 42, 729–742.

Homans, G. C. (1961). *Social behavior: Its elementary forms.* New York: Harcourt, Brace & World.

Homans, G. C. (1964). Bringing men back in. *American Sociological Review, 29,* 809–818.

Homans, G. C. (1967). *The nature of social science.* New York: Harcourt, Brace & World.

Horkheimer, M. (1947). *Eclipse of reason.* New York: Oxford University Press.

Horkheimer, M. (1982). *Critical theory.* New York: Seabury Press.

Horkheimer, M., & Adorno, T. W. (2002). *Dialectic of enlightenment* (E. Jephcott, Trans.). Palo Alto, CA: Stanford University Press. (Original work published 1947)

Hosegood, V. (2009). The demographic impact of HIV and AIDS across the family and household life-cycle: Implications for efforts to strengthen families in sub-Saharan Africa. *AIDS Care, 21*(S1), 13–21.

Hostetler, A. J., & Cohler, B. J. (1997). Partnership, singlehood, and the lesbian and gay life course: A research agenda. *International Journal of Sexuality and Gender Studies, 2*(3–4), 199–230. doi:10.1023/A:102638582

Hostetler, A. J., Desrochers, S., Kopko, K., & Moen, P. (2012). Marital and family satisfaction as a function of work-family demands and community resources: Individual and couple-level analyses. *Journal of Family Issues, 33,* 316–340.

Howard, R. L. (1981). *A social history of American family sociology, 1865–1940.* Westport, CT: Greenwood.

Huang, Q., El-Khouri, B. M., Johansson, G., Lindroth, S., & Sverke, M. (2007). Women's career patterns: A study of Swedish women born in the 1950s. *Journal of Occupational and Organizational Psychology, 80,* 387–412.

Hughes, P. (2016). Using symbolic interactionism insights as an approach to helping the individual with Asperger's syndrome overcome barriers to social inclusion. *British Journal of Special Education, 43,* 60–74.

Huinink, J., & Feldhaus, M. (2009). Family research from the life course perspective. *International Sociology, 24*(3), 299–324.

Humphreys, T., & Herold, E. (2003). Should universities and colleges mandate sexual behavior? *Journal of Psychology and Human Sexuality, 15,* 35–51.

Huntington, S. P. (2007). *Clash of civilizations and the remaking of world Order.* New York: Simon & Schuster. (Original work published 1996)

Jaccard, J., & Jacoby, J. (2010). *Theory construction and model-building skills: A practical guide for social scientists.* New York: Guilford Press.

Jackson, D. D. (Ed.). (1974). *Communication, family, and marriage.* Palo Alto, CA: Science and Behavior Books.

Jacobs, J. A., & Gerson, K. (2009). *The time divide: Work, family, and gender inequality.* Cambridge, MA: Harvard University Press.

James, W. (1975). *Pragmatism: A new name for some old ways of thinking.* London, UK: Longmans.

James, W. (1983/1890). *The principles of psychology.* Cambridge, MA: Harvard University Press.

Johnson, M. P., & Ferraro, K. J. (2000). Research on domestic violence in the 1990s: Making distinctions. *Journal of Marriage and the Family, 62,* 948–963.

Josephson, W., & Pepler, D. (2012). Bullying: A stepping stone to dating aggression? *International Journal of Adolescent Medical Health, 24,* 37–47.

Kahneman, D., & Tversky, A. (1979). Prospect theory: An analysis of decision under risk. *Econometrica, 47,* 263–289.

Kahneman, D., & Tversky, A. (1984). Choices, values, and frames. *American Psychologist, 39*, 341–350.

Kamp Dush, C. M. K., & Taylor, M. G. (2012). Trajectories of marital conflict across the life course: Predictors and interactions with marital happiness trajectories. *Journal of Family Issues, 33*, 341–368.

Kantor, D., & Lehr, W. (1975). *Inside the family: Toward a theory of family process.* San Francisco, CA: Jossey-Bass.

Kingsbury, N., & Scanzoni, J. (1993). Structural-functionalism. In P. Boss, W. Doherty, R. LaRossa, W. Schumm, & S. Steinmetz (Eds.), *Sourcebook of family theories and methods: A contextual approach* (pp. 195–217). New York: Plenum.

Kitzman-Ulrich, H., Wilson, D., George, S., Lawman, H., Segal, M., & Fairchild, A. (2010). The integration of a family systems approach for understanding youth obesity, physical activity, and dietary programs. *Clinical Child and Family Psychology Review, 13*, 231–253. doi: 10.1007/s10567-010-0073-0

Klein, D. M. (1973, October). *Strategies of theory integration: A neglected area of theory construction methodology.* NCFR annual meeting, Toronto, CAN.

Klein, D. M. (1976, August). *Themes and perspectives in four emerging strategies of theory construction.* ASA annual meeting, New York.

Klein, D. M. (1994, November). *Theory as data: An investigation of ourselves.* Paper presented at the National Council on Family Relations, Theory Construction and Research Methodology Workshop, Minneapolis, MN.

Klein, D. M., & Aldous, J. (Eds.). (1988). *Social stress and family development.* New York: Guilford.

Klein, D. M., Borne, H., Jache, A., & Sederberg, N. (1979, August). *Family chronogram analysis: Toward the development of new methodological tools for assessing the life cycles of families.* Paper presented at the National Council on Family Relations, Theory Construction, and Research Methodology Workshop, Boston, MA.

Klein, D. M., & Hill, R. (1979). Determinants of family problem-solving effectiveness. In W. R. Burr, R. Hill, F. I. Nye, & I. L. Reiss (Eds.), *Contemporary theories about the family: Research-based theories.* New York: Free Press.

Klein, D. M., & White, J. M. (1996). *Family theories: An introduction.* Thousand Oaks, CA: Sage.

Koerner, A., & Fitzpatrick, M. A. (2002). Toward a theory of family communication. *Communication Theory, 12*, 70–91.

Kourany, J., Sterba, J., & Tong, R. (Eds.). (1999). *Feminist philosophies: Problems, theories, and applications* (2nd ed.). Upper Saddle River, NJ: Prentice Hall.

Krause, N., Ingersoll-Dayton, B., Liang, J., & Sugisawa, H. (1999). Religion, social support, and health among the Japanese elderly. *Journal of health and social behavior, 40*(4), 405–421.

Kuhn, M. (1964). Major trends in symbolic interaction theory in the past twenty-five years. *Sociological Quarterly, 5*, 61–84.

Kuhn, T. (1998). *The structure of scientific revolutions* (3rd ed.). Chicago, IL: University of Chicago Press. (Original work published 1962)

Kumagai, F. (1984). The life cycle of the Japanese family. *Journal of Marriage and the Family, 46*, 191–204.

Kurdek, L. A. (2005). Reflections on queer theory and family science. In V. L. Bengtson, A. C. Acock, K. R. Allen, P. Dilworth-Anderson, & D. M. Klein (Eds.), *Sourcebook of Family Theory and Research* (pp. 160–162). Thousand Oaks, CA: Sage.

Laibson, D., & Zeckhauser, R. (1998). Amos Tversky and the ascent of behavioral economics. *Journal of Risk and Uncertainty, 16*, 7–47.

Lamanna, M. (2002). *Emile Durkheim on the family*. Thousand Oaks, CA: Sage.

Lane, C., Meszaros, P., & Savla, J. (2016). Measuring Walsh's family resilience framework: Reliability and validity of the Family Resilience Assessment among women with a history of breast cancer. *Marriage and Family Review, 53*, 667–682.

Lareau, A. (2000). *Home advantage: Social class and parental intervention in elementary education*. Lanham, MD: Rowman & Littlefield.

Lareau, A. (2003). *Unequal childhoods: Class, race, and family*. Berkeley: University of California Press.

Lareau, A., & Goyette, K. (Eds.). (2014). *Choosing homes\Choosing schools*. NY: Russell Sage Foundation.

LaRossa, R. (1997). *The modernization of fatherhood: A social and political history*. Chicago, IL: University of Chicago Press.

LaRossa, R., & LaRossa, M. (1981). *Transition to parenthood: How infants change families*. Beverly Hills, CA: Sage.

LaRossa, R., & Reitzes, D. C. (1993). Symbolic interactionism and family studies. In P. Boss, W. Doherty, R. LaRossa, W. Schumm, & S. Steinmetz (Eds.), *Sourcebook of family theories and methods: A contextual approach* (pp. 135–163). New York: Plenum.

Lauster, N. (2016). *The death and life of the single family house*. Philadelphia, PA: Temple University Press.

Lee, M., Vernon-Feagans, L., Vazquez, A., & Kolak, A. (2003). The influence of family environment and child temperament on work-family role strain for mothers and fathers. *Infant and Child Development, 12*, 421–439.

Leon, A. M., & Knapp, S. (2008). Involving family systems in critical care nursing: Challenges and opportunities. *Dimensions of Critical Care Nursing, 27*, 255–262.

Levenson, R., & Gottman, J. (1983). Marital interaction: Physiological linkage and affective exchange. *Journal of Personality and Social Psychology, 45*, 587–597.

Levine, Phillip B. (2000, March). *The sexual activity and birth control use of American teenagers* (NBER Working Paper 7601). Cambridge, MA: NBER.

Levinger, G. (1965). Marital cohesiveness and dissolution. *Journal of Marriage and the Family, 27*, 19–28.

Levinger, G. (1966). Sources of marital dissatisfaction among applicants for divorce. *American Journal of Orthopsychiatry, 32*, 803–807.

Levinger, G. (1982). A social exchange view on the dissolution of pair relationships. In F. Nye (Ed.), *Family relationships: Rewards and costs* (pp. 97–122). Beverly Hills, CA: Sage.

Levy-Shiff, R., & Israelashvili, R. (1988). Antecedents of fathering: Some further exploration. *Developmental Psychology, 24*(3), 434–440.

Lévi-Strauss, C. (1969). *The elementary structures of kinship*. Boston, MA: Beacon.

Lewin, K. (1935). *A dynamic theory of personality*. New York: McGraw-Hill.

Lewis, R., & Spanier, G. (1979). Theorizing about the quality and stability of marriage. In W. R. Burr, R. Hill, F. I. Nye, & I. Reiss (Eds.), *Contemporary theories about the family* (Vol. 2, pp. 1–41). New York: Free Press.

Lichter, D. T., & Qian, Z. (2008). Serial cohabitation and the marital life course. *Journal of Marriage and Family, 70*, 861–878.

Liefbroer, A. C., & Dourleijn, E. (2006). Unmarried cohabitation and union stability: Testing the role of diffusion using data from 16 European countries. *Demography*, 43(2), 203–221.

Lillegard, N. (2003). Philosophy of social science. In J. Fieser (Ed.), *Internet encyclopedia of philosophy*. Retrieved September 2003, from www.utm.edu/research/iep/

Littlejohn-Blake, S. M., & Darling, C. A. (1993). Understanding the strengths of African American families. *Journal of Black Studies*, 23(4), 460–471. doi: 10.1177/002193479302300402

Liu, M. (2011). *Migration, prostitution, and human trafficking: The voice of Chinese women*. Vancouver, CAN: University of British Columbia Press.

Lively, C. E. (1932). *The growth cycle of the farm family* (Bulletin No. 51). Wooster: Ohio Agricultural Experiment Station.

Loomis, C. P. (1936). The study of the life cycle of families. *Rural Sociology*, 1, 180–199.

Lorber, J. (1998). *Gender inequality: Feminist theories and politics*. Los Angeles, CA: Roxbury.

Lorenz, K. (1966). *On aggression*. New York: Harcourt, Brace & World.

Lovaas, K. E., Elia, J. P., & Yep, G. A. (2006). Shifting Ground(s). *Journal of Homosexuality*, 52, 1–18. doi: 10.1300/J082v52n01_01

Lüscher, K., & Pillemer, K. (1998). Intergenerational ambivalence: A new approach to the study of parent-child relations in later life. *Journal of Marriage and the Family*, 60, 413–425.

Maconachie, M. (1989). Exploring the marital histories of some white South Africans. *South African Journal of Sociology*, 20(1), 47–52. doi:10.1080/02580144.1989.10432901

Magrabi, F. M., & Marshall, W. H. (1965). Family developmental tasks: A research model. *Journal of Marriage and the Family*, 27, 454–461.

Main, M., & Solomon. J. (1986). Discovery of an insecure-disorganized/disoriented attachment pattern. In T. B. Brazelton & M. W. Yogman (Eds.), *Affective development in infancy*. Norwood, NJ: Ablex.

Malthus, T. (1872). *An essay on the principle of population* (7th ed.). London, UK: Reeves & Turner. (Original work published 1798)

Mannheim, K. (1956). *Towards the sociology of the mind: An introduction*. Abingdon, UK: Routledge.

Marcuse, H. (1964). *One dimensional man*. Boston, MA: Beacon Hill.

Marini, M. M. (1984). Age and sequencing norms in the transition to adulthood. *Social Forces*, 63, 229–244.

Marks, N. F., & Lambert, J. D. (1998). Marital status continuity and change among young and midlife adults. *Journal of Family Issues*, 19, 652–686.

Marks, S. (1977). Multiple roles and role strain: Some notes on human energy, time, and commitment. *American Sociological Review*, 42, 921–936.

Marks, S., & MacDermid, S. M. (1996). Multiple roles and the self: A theory of role balance. *Journal of Marriage and the Family*, 58, 417–432.

Martin, P., Schoon, I., & Ross, A. (2008). Beyond transitions: Applying optimal matching analysis to life course research. *International Journal of Social Research Methodology*, 11(3), 179–199.

Martin, T. F. (2009, November). *A sequence analysis approach to family development theory*. Paper presented at the annual meetings of the Theory Construction and Research Methodology Workshop, National Council on Family Relations, San Francisco, CA.

Martin, T. F. (2014, November). *Advancing family theory through theoretical and methodological Advancement*. Paper presented at Theory Construction and Research Methodology

Workshop: Families at the Nexus of Global Change, NCFR, Baltimore, MD.

Martin, T. F. (2018). Family development theory 30 years later. *Journal of Family Theory & Review, 10*(1), 49–69.

Martindale, D. (1960). *The nature and types of sociological theory.* Boston, MA: Houghton Mifflin.

Marx, K. (1963/1852). *The Eighteenth Brumaire of Louis Bonaparte.* NY: International. (Original work published 1852)

Marx, K. (1992/1867). *Capital, Vol. 1: A critique of political economy* (B. Fowkes, trans.). NY: Penguin. (Original work published 1867)

Marx, K., & Engels, F. (1932/1845). *The German ideology.* London, UK: Lawrence & Wishart. (Original work published 1845–1846)

Marx, K., & Engels, F. (1971). *The communist manifesto.* New York: International (Original work published 1867)

Maslow, A. (1966). *The psychology of science: A reconnaissance.* Chicago, IL: Henry Regnery.

Mattessich, P., & Hill, R. (1987). Life cycle and family development. In M. B. Sussman & S. K. Steinmetz (Eds.), *Handbook of marriage and the family* (pp. 437–469). New York: Plenum.

Mauss, M. (1954). *The gift* (I. Cunnison, Trans.). New York: Free Press.

Maxymiv, S. D., & Blankemeyer, M. (2001). Bringing bereavement education into the family life education classroom. *Journal of Teaching in Marriage & Family, 1*(2), 18–33. doi:10.1300/J226v01n02_02

McAdoo, H. P., Martinez, E. A., & Hughes, H. (2005). Ecological changes in ethnic families of color. In V. Bengtson, A. Acock, K. Allen, P. Dilworth-Anderson, & D. Klein (Eds.), *Sourcebook of family theory and research* (pp. 191–202). Thousand Oaks, CA: Sage.

McCall, L., & Percheskie, C., (2010). Income inequality: New trends and research directions. *Annual Review of Sociology, 36,* 329–347.

McCubbin, H. I. (1979). Integrating coping behavior in family stress theory. *Journal of Marriage and the Family, 41*(2), 237–244. doi:10.2307/351693

McCubbin, H. I. (1980). Family stress and coping: A decade review. *Journal of Marriage and the Family, 42*(4), 855–871. doi:10.2307/351829

McCubbin, H. I., & McCubbin, M. A. (1988). Typologies of resilient families: Emerging roles of social class and ethnicity. *Family Relations, 2,* 247–254.

McCubbin, H. I., & Patterson, J. M. (1982). Family stress, coping, and social support. In H. I. McCubbin, A. E. Cauble, & J. M. Patterson (Eds.), *Family stress, coping, and social support* (pp. 26–47). Springfield, IL: Thomas.

McCubbin, H. I., & Patterson, J. M. (1983). The family stress process: The double ABC-X model of adjustment and adaptation. *Marriage & Family Review, 6,* 7–37.

McCubbin, H., Thompson, E., Thompson, A., & Futrell, J. (1999). *The dynamics of resilient families.* Thousand Oaks, CA: Sage.

McCubbin, M. (1999). Normative family transitions and health outcomes. In A. Hinshaw, S. Feetham, & J. Shaver (Eds.), *Handbook of clinical nursing research* (pp. 201–230). Thousand Oaks, CA: Sage.

McCubbin, M. A., & McCubbin, H. I. (1987). Family stress theory and assessment. In H. I. McCubbin & A. I. Thompson (Eds.), *Family assessment inventories for research and practice.* Madison: University of Wisconsin Press.

McCubbin, M. A., & McCubbin, H. I. (1989). Theoretical orientations to family stress and coping. In C. Figley (Ed.), *Treating families under stress.* New York: Brunner/Mazel.

McCubbin, M. A., & McCubbin, H. I. (1993). Families coping with illness: The resiliency model of family stress, adjustment, and adaptation. In C. Danielson, B. Hamel-Bissel, & P. Winstead-Fry (Eds.), *Families, health, and illness: Perspectives on coping and intervention.* New York: Mosby.

McGoldrick, M., Carter, B., & Garcia-Preto, N. (2011). *The expanded family life cycle: Individual, family, and social perspectives* (4th ed.). Boston, MA: Pearson.

McKenzie, R. (1924). The ecological approach to the study of human community. *American Journal of Sociology, 30,* 287–301.

Mead, G. H. (1934). *Mind, self, and society* (C. Morris, Introduction and Ed.). Chicago, IL: University of Chicago Press.

Mead, M. (1928). *Coming of age in Samoa.* New York: Morrow.

Mead, M. (1930). *Growing up in New Guinea.* New York: Blue Ribbon Books.

Mead, M. (1935). *Sex and temperament in three primitive societies.* New York: Mentor.

Mead, M. (1955). *Male and female.* New York: Mentor.

Mehrabian, A. (1972). *Nonverbal communication.* Chicago, IL: Aldine-Atherton.

Mehrabian, A., & Wiener, M. (1968). *Language within language: Immediacy, a channel in verbal communication.* New York: Appleton-Century-Crofts.

Menaghan, E. (1983). Marital stress and family transitions: A panel analysis. *Journal of Marriage and the Family, 45,* 371–386.

Menaghan, E. (1989). Role changes and psychological well-being: Variations in effects by gender and role repertoire. *Social Forces, 67,* 693–714.

Menaghan, E., & Parcel, T. (1990). Parental employment and family life: Research in the 1980's. *Journal of Marriage and the Family, 52,* 1079–1098.

Mendel, G. (1965). *Experiments in plant hybridisation.* London, UK: Oliver & Boyd. (Original work published 1865)

Merton, R. K. (1968). *On theoretical sociology: Five essays, old and new.* New York: Free Press.

Merton, R. K. (1973). *Sociology of science: Theoretical and empirical investigations.* Chicago, IL: University of Chicago Press.

Mesarovic, M. (1970). *Theory of hierarchical multi-level systems.* New York: Academic Press.

Milardo, R. M. (1982). Friendship networks in developing relationships: Converging and diverging social environments. *Social Psychology Quarterly, 3,* 162–172.

Milardo, R. M. (1987). Changes in social networks of women and men following divorce: A review. *Journal of Family Issues, 8,* 78–96.

Milardo, R. M. (1988). *New perspectives on family. Families and social networks.* Thousand Oaks, CA: Sage.

Milardo, R. M. (2005). Generative uncle and nephew relationships. *Journal of Marriage and Family, 67,* 1226–1236.

Milardo, R. M. (2010). *The forgotten kin: Aunts and uncles.* New York: Cambridge University Press.

Miller, J. G. (1978). *Living systems.* New York: McGraw-Hill.

Millet, K. (1970). *Sexual politics.* New York: Doubleday.

Minola, T., Brumana, M., Campopiano, G., Garrett, R. P., & Cassia, L. (2016). Corporate venturing in family business: A developmental approach of the enterprising family. *Strategic Entrepreneurship Journal, 10*(4), 395–412. doi:10.1002/sej.1236

Minuchin, S. (1974). *Families and family therapy.* Cambridge, MA: Harvard University Press.

Mishler, E. G., & Waxler, N. E. (1968). *Interaction in families: An experimental study of family processes and schizophrenia.* New York: Wiley.

Mitchell, J. (1972). *Woman's estate.* New York: Pantheon.

Modell, J. (1980). Normative aspects of marriage timing since World War II. *Journal of Family History, 5,* 210–234.

Moen, D., Bradford, K., Lee, T. R., Harris, V. W., & Stewart, J. W. (2015). After the honeymoon: The evolution of problem issues in Utah LDS marriages. *Marriage & Family Review, 51*(5), 396–417. doi:10.108 0/01494929.2015.1059787

Moen, P. (2003). *It's about time: Couples and careers.* New York: Cornell University Press.

Moen, P., Elder, G. H., Jr., & Lüscher, K. (Eds.). (1995). *Examining lives in context: Perspectives on the ecology of human development.* Washington, DC: American Psychological Association.

Moen, P., Kelly, E., & Huang, Q. (2008). Work, family and life-course fit: Does control over work time matter? *Journal of Vocational Behavior, 73,* 414–425.

Moore, M. (1989). Female lone parenting over the life course. *Canadian Journal of Sociology/Cahiers canadiens de sociologie, 14*(3), 335–352. doi:10.2307/3340608

Morris, C. (1934). Introduction. In G. H. Mead (Ed.), *Mind, self and society* (pp. ix–xxxv). Chicago, IL: University of Chicago Press.

Mullins, N. (1973). *Theories and theory groups in contemporary American sociology.* New York: Harper & Row.

Mullins, N. C. (1971). *The art of theory: Construction and use.* New York: Harper & Row.

National Institute of Child Health and Human Development (NICHD) Early Child Care Research Network. (2005). *Child care and child development.* New York: Guilford.

Neugarten, B., & Datan, N. (1973). Sociological perspectives on the life cycle. In P. Baltes & K. Warner Schaie (Eds.), *Lifespan developmental psychology: Personality and socialization* (pp. 53–69). New York: Academic Press.

Neugarten, B., Moore, J., & Lowe, J. (1965). Age norms, age constraints, and adult socialization. *American Journal of Sociology, 70,* 710–717.

Neuman, W. L. (1994). *Social research methods: Qualitative and quantitative approaches.* Needham Heights, MA: Allyn & Bacon.

Noller, P. (1984). *Nonverbal communication and marital interaction.* Elmsford, NY: Pergamon.

Noller, P., & Fitzpatrick, M. (1993). *Communication in family relationships.* Englewood Cliffs, NJ: Prentice Hall.

Nye, F. I. (Ed.). (1976). *Role structure and analysis of the family.* Beverly Hills, CA: Sage.

Nye, F. I. (1979). Choice, exchange, and the family. In W. R. Burr, R. Hill, F. I. Nye, & I. Reiss (Eds.), *Contemporary theories about the family* (Vol. 2, pp. 1–41). New York: Free Press.

Nye, F. I., & Berardo, F. (1981). *Emerging conceptual frameworks in family analysis.* New York: Praeger. (Original work published 1966)

Nye, F. I., White, L., & Frideres, J. (1969, October). *A partial theory of marital stability.* Paper presented to the National Council on Family Relations, Washington, DC.

O'Connor, D. L., & O'Neill, B. J. (2000). *Toward social justice: Teaching qualitative research.* Paper presented to the International Federation of Social Workers and the International Association of Schools of Social Work, Montreal, Quebec, CAN.

Ogburn, W. F., & Nimkoff, M. F. (1955). *Technology and the changing family*. New York: Houghton Mifflin.

Olson, D. (2011). Faces IV and the circumplex model: Validation study. *Journal of Marital and Family Therapy*, 37(1), 64–80.

Olson, D. H. (1972). Empirically unbinding the double-bind: Review of research and conceptual reformulations. *Family Process*, 11, 69–94.

Olson, D. H. (1995). Family systems: Understanding your roots. In R. Day, K. Gilbert, B. Settles, & W. Burr (Eds.), *Research and theory in family science* (pp. 131–153). Pacific Grove, CA: Brooks/Cole.

Olson, D. H., & McCubbin, H. I. (1982). Circumplex model of marital and family systems: V. Application to family stress and crisis intervention. In H. I. McCubbin, A. E. Cauble, & J. M. Patterson (Eds.), *Family stress, coping, and social support* (pp. 48–72). Springfield, IL: Charles C Thomas.

Olson, D. H., Russell, C. S., & Sprenkle, D. H. (1983). Circumplex model of marital and family systems: VI. Theoretical update. *Family Process*, 22, 69–83.

Olson, D. H., Sprenkle, D. H., & Russell, C. S. (1979). Circumplex model of marital and family systems: I. Cohesion and adaptability dimensions, family types, and clinical applications. *Family Process*, 18, 3–28.

O'Neill, J. (1995). *The poverty of postmodernism*. London, UK: Routledge.

Oppenheimer, V. (1988). A theory of marriage timing. *American Journal of Sociology*, 94, 563–591.

O'Rand, A. M., & Farkas, J. I. (2002). Couples' retirement timing in the United States in the 1990s: The impact of market and family role demands on joint work exits. *International Journal of Sociology*, 32(2), 11–29. doi:10.1080/15579336.2002.11770247

Ortega y Gasset, J. (1933). *Notas*. Madrid, SP: Espasa Calpe.

Osmond, M. (1987). Radical-critical theories. In M. Sussman & S. Steinmetz (Eds.), *Handbook of marriage and the family* (pp. 103–124). New York: Plenum.

Osmond, M., & Thorne, B. (1993). Feminist theories: The construction of gender in families and society. In P. Boss, W. Doherty, R. LaRossa, W. Schumm, & S. Steinmetz (Eds.), *Sourcebook of family theories and methods: A contextual approach* (pp. 591–622). New York: Plenum.

Oswald, R. F., Blume, L. B., & Marks, S. R. (2005). Decentering heteronormativity: A model for family studies. In V. L. Bengtson, A. C. Acock, K. R. Allen, P. Dilworth-Anderson, & D. M. Klein (Eds.), *Sourcebook of family theory and research* (pp. 143–155). Thousand Oaks, CA: Sage.

Paolucci, B., Hall, O., & Axinn, N. (1977). *Family decision making: An ecosystem approach*. New York: Wiley.

Park, R. (1925). The urban community as a spatial pattern and a moral order. *Publications of the American Sociological Society*, 20, 1–14.

Park, R., & Burgess, E. (1921). *Introduction to the science of sociology*. Chicago, IL: University of Chicago Press.

Parsons, T. (1937). *The structure of social action*. New York: Free Press.

Parsons, T. (1951). *The social system*. Glencoe, IL: Free Press.

Parsons, T. (1954). The kinship system in the contemporary United States. In T. Parsons (Ed.), *Essays in sociological theory*. Glencoe, IL: The Free Press.

Parsons, T. (1977). *Social systems and the evolution of action theory* (Vol. 62). New York: Free Press.

Parsons, T., & Bales, R. (1955). *Family, socialization and interaction process*. Glencoe, IL: Free Press.

Paton, D. (2002, March). The economics of abortion, family planning and underage conceptions. *Journal of Health Economics, 21*, 27–45.

Patterson, J. M. (1988). Families experiencing stress: I. The family adjustment and adaptation response model: II. Applying the FAAR model to health-related issues for intervention and research. *Family Systems Medicine, 6*, 202.

Patterson, J. M. (1989). A family stress model: The family adjustment and adaptation response. In C. N. Ramsey (Ed.), *Family systems in medicine* (pp. 95–118). New York: Guilford Press.

Patterson, J. M. (1993). The role of family meanings in adaptation to chronic illness and disability. In A. P. Turnbull (Ed.), *Cognitive coping, families, and disability* (pp. 221–238). Baltimore, MD: Brookes.

Patterson, J. M. (2002). Integrating family resilience and family stress theory. *Journal of Marriage and Family, 64*, 349–360. doi: 10.2307/3600109

Patterson, J. M., & Garwick, A. W. (1994). Levels of meaning in family stress theory. *Family Process, 33*, 287–304.

Pearson, K. (1909). *The scope and importance to the state of science of national eugenics*. London, UK: Dulau.

Peirce, C. S. (1905). What pragmatism is. *Monist, 5*, 411–436.

Perkins, D. F., Ferrari, T. M., Covey, M. A., & Keith, J. G. (2005). Getting dinosaurs to dance: Community collaborations as applications of ecological theory. In T. Chibucos & R. Leite (Eds.), *Readings in family theory* (pp. 345–357). Thousand Oaks, CA: Sage.

Pernice-Duca, F. (2010). Family network support and mental health recovery. *Journal of Marital and Family Therapy, 36*, 13–27.

Perry-Jenkins, M., Newkirk, K., & Ghunney, A. (2013). Family work through time and space: An ecological perspective. *Journal of Family Theory and Review, 5*, 105–123.

Perry-Jenkins, M., Repetti, R. L., & Crouter, A. C. (2000). Work and family in the 1900's. *Journal of Marriage and the Family, 62*, 981–998.

Peterson, G., & Bush, K. (Eds.). (2013). *Handbook of marriage and the family* (3rd ed.). New York: Springer.

Peterson, R. A., & Kern, R. M. (1996). Changing highbrow taste: From snob to omnivore. *American Sociological Review, 61*, 900–907.

Peterson, W. (1969). *Population* (2nd ed.). New York: Macmillan.

Piaget, J. (1952). *The origins of intelligence in children* (M. Cook, Trans.). New York: Norton.

Piketty, T. (2014). *Capital in the twenty-first century*. (A. Goldhammer, Trans). Cambridge, MA: Harvard University Press.

Pina, D., & Bengtson, V. (1993). The division of household labor and wives' happiness: Ideology, employment, and perceptions of support. *Journal of Marriage and the Family, 55*, 901–912.

Pirog-Good, M., & Stets, J. (Eds.). (1989). *Violence in dating relationships*. New York: Praeger.

Pollock, G. (2007). Holistic trajectories: A study of combined employment, housing and family careers by using multiple-sequence analysis. *Journal of the Royal Statistical Society: Series A (Statistics in Society), 170*, 167–183.

Popper, K. (1959). *The logic of scientific discovery*. New York: Basic Books.

Poster, M. (1978). *Critical theory of the family*. New York: Seabury.

Powers, W. (1974). *Behavior: The control of perception*. Chicago, IL: Aldine.

Price, S., McKenry, P., & Murphy, M. (2000). *Families across time: A life course perspective*. Los Angeles, CA: Roxbury.

Prigogine, I., & Stengers, I. (1984). *Order out of chaos*. New York: Bantam.

Pyke, K., & Coltrane, S. (1996). Entitlement, obligation, and gratitude in family work. *Journal of Family Issues, 17*, 60–82.

Rabuzzi, K. A. (1982). *The sacred and the feminine: Toward a theology of housework*. New York: Seabury.

Rada, C., & Olson, D. H. (2016). Circumplex model of marital and family systems (Faces III) in Romania. *Annuaire Roumain D'anthropologie, 53*, 11–29

Radcliffe, L. S., & Cassell, C. (2015). Flexible working, work-family conflict, and maternal gatekeeping: The daily experiences of dual-earner couples. *Journal of Occupational and Organizational Psychology, 88*, 835–855.

Rapp, R. (1982). Family and class in contemporary America: Notes toward an understanding of ideology. In B. Thorne (Ed.), *Rethinking the family* (pp. 168–187). New York: Longman.

Raush, H., Barry, W., Hertel, R., & Swain, N. (1974). *Communication, conflict, and marriage*. San Francisco, CA: Jossey-Bass.

Reiss, D. (1987). *The family's construction of reality*. Cambridge, MA: Harvard University Press.

Reynolds, P. D. (1971). *A primer in theory construction*. Indianapolis, IN: Bobbs-Merrill.

Reynolds, P. D. (2006). *A primer in theory construction*. Boston, MA: Allyn & Bacon.

Riley, M. W. (1998). *The hidden age revolution: Emergent integration of all ages*. Center for Policy Research (Paper 31). https://surface.syr.edu/cpr/31

Rindfuss, R. R., Swicegood, C. G., & Rosenfeld, R. A. (1987). Disorder in the life course: How common and does it matter? *American Sociological Review, 52*(6), 785–801.

Rodgers, R. H. (1964). Toward a theory of family development. *Journal of Marriage and the Family*, 262–270.

Rodgers, R. H. (1973). *Family interaction and transaction: The developmental approach*. Englewood Cliffs, NJ: Prentice Hall.

Rodgers, R. H., & White, J. M. (1993). Family development theory. In P. Boss, W. Doherty, R. LaRossa, W. Schumm, & S. Steinmetz (Eds.), *Sourcebook of family theories and methods: A contextual approach* (pp. 225–254). New York: Plenum.

Rodgers, R. H., & Witney, G. (1981). The family cycle in twentieth century Canada. *Journal of Marriage and the Family, 43*, 727–740.

Rodman, H. (1967). Marital power in France, Greece, Yugoslavia, and the United States. *Journal of Marriage and the Family, 29*, 320–324.

Rollins, B., & Feldman, H. (1970). Marital satisfaction over the family life cycle. *Journal of Marriage and the Family, 32*, 20–27.

Rosenblatt, P. C. (1994). *Metaphors of family systems theory: Toward new constructions*. New York: Guilford.

Rossi, P., & Berk, R. (1985). Varieties of normative consensus. *American Sociological Review, 50*, 333–347.

Rothbard, N. (2001). Enriching or depleting: The dynamics of engagement in work and family roles. *Administrative Science Quarterly, 46*, 655–684.

Rudner, R. S. (1966). *Philosophy of social science*. Englewood Cliffs, NJ: Prentice Hall.

Russo, N. F. (1998). Measuring feminist attitudes: Just what does it mean to be a feminist? [Editorial]. *Psychology of Women Quarterly, 22*, 313–316.

Sabatelli, R. M. (1988). Exploring relationship satisfaction: A social exchange perspective on the interdependence between theory, research, and practice. *Family Relations, 37*, 217–222.

Sabatelli, R., & Ripoll, K. (2004). An ecological exchange perspective on recent marital trends. In M. Coleman & L. Ganong (Eds.), *Handbook of contemporary families: Considering the past, contemplating the future.* Thousand Oaks, CA: Sage.

Sabatelli, R. M., & Shehan, C. L. (1993). Exchange and resource theories. In P. Boss, W. Doherty, R. LaRossa, W. Schumm, & S. Steinmetz (Eds.), *Sourcebook of family theories and methods: A contextual approach* (pp. 385–411). New York: Plenum.

Salmon, W. (1984). *Scientific explanation and the causal structure of the world.* Princeton, NJ: Princeton University Press.

Sassler, S. (2010). Partnering across the life course: Sex, relationships, and mate selection. *Journal of Marriage and Family, 72,* 557–575.

Saxeby, D., Rodriguez, A., & Margolin, G. (2013). Understanding conflict in families: Theoretical frameworks and future directions. In M. Fine & F. Fincham (Eds.), *Handbook of family theories: A content-based approach* (pp. 169–189). New York: Routledge.

Scanzoni, J. (1970). *Opportunity and the family.* New York: Free Press.

Scanzoni, J. (1972). *Sexual bargaining.* Chicago, IL: University of Chicago Press.

Scanzoni, J., & Szinovacz, M. (1980). *Family decision-making: A developmental sex role model.* Beverly Hills, CA: Sage.

Schoen, R. (1992). First unions and the stability of first marriages. *Journal of Marriage and Family, 54*(2), 281–284.

Schoon, I., Bynner, J., Joshi, H., Parsons, S., Wiggins, R. D., & Sacker, A. (2002). The influence of context, timing, and duration of risk experiences for the passage from childhood to midadulthood. *Child Development, 73*, 1486–1504.

Schoon, I., McCulloch, A., Joshi, H., Wiggins, R. D., & Bynner, J. (2001). Transitions from school to work in a changing social context. *Young, 9*, 4–22.

Schuham, A. (1967). The double-bind hypothesis a decade later. *Psychological Bulletin, 68*, 409–416.

Schuman, H., & Scott, J. (1989). Generations and collective memories. *American Sociological Review, 54*, 359–381.

Scott, J. (2013). *The Sage handbook of social network analysis.* Thousand Oaks, CA: Sage.

Scott, J. W. (1988). *Gender and the politics of history.* New York: Columbia University Press.

Scott, J., & Zac, L. (1993). Collective memories in Britain and the United States. *Public Opinion Quarterly, 57*, 315–331.

Seiffge-Krenke, I., & Pakalniskiene, V. (2011). Who shapes whom in the family: Reciprocal links between autonomy support in the family and parents' and adolescents' coping behaviors. *Journal of Youth and Adolescence, 40*(8), 983–995. doi:10.1007/s10964-010-9603-9

Serchuk, D. (2011, December 7). Happy country = Social mobility? *Forbes Magazine.* Retrieved from http://www.forbes.com/sites/daveserchuk/2011/12/07/happy-countrysocial-mobility/

Sexton, C., & Perlman, D. (1989). Couple's career orientation, gender role orientation, and perceived equity as determinants of marital power. *Journal of Marriage and the Family, 51*, 933–941.

Shams, M., & Björnberg, Å. (2006). Issues in family business: An international perspective. In P. Jackson & M. Shams (Eds.), *Developments in work and organizational psychology* (pp. 5–47). The Netherlands: Elsevier.

Shannon, C. E., & Weaver, W. (1949). *The mathematical theory of communication.* Urbana: University of Illinois Press.

Shelton, B. A., & John, D. (1996). The division of household labor. *Annual Review of Sociology, 22,* 299–322.

Shoemaker, P. J., Tankard, J. W., Jr., & Lasorsa, D. L. (2004). *How to build social science theories.* Thousand Oaks, CA: Sage.

Simmel, G. (1904). The sociology of conflict. *American Journal of Sociology, 9,* 490–525.

Simmel, G. (1950). *The sociology of Georg Simmel* (K. Wolff, Trans.). Glencoe, IL: Free Press.

Smith, D. E. (1992). Sociology from women's experiences: A reaffirmation. *Sociological Theory, 10,* 88–98.

South, S. (2001). Time-dependent effects of wives' employment on marital dissolution. *American Sociological Review, 66,* 226–245.

Spencer, H. (1880). *First principles.* New York: A. C. Burt.

Sprecher, S. (2001). Equity and social exchange in dating couples: Associations with satisfaction, commitment, and stability. *Journal of Marriage and Family, 63,* 599–613.

Sprey, J. (1979). Conflict theory and the study of marriage and the family. In W. R. Burr, R. Hill, F. I. Nye, & I. Reiss (Eds.), *Contemporary theories about the family* (Vol. 2, pp. 130–159). New York: Free Press.

SPSS. (2005). *Linear mixed-effects modeling in SPSS: An Introduction to the MIXED procedure.* Retrieved from http://www.spss.ch/upload/1126184451_Linear%20Mixed%20Effects%20Modeling%20in%20SPSS.pdf

Stets, J. (1992). Interactive processes in dating aggression: A national study. *Journal of Marriage and the Family, 54,* 165–177.

Stets, J. E. (2005). Emotions in identity theory. *Social Psychology Quarterly, 68,* 39–56.

Stets, J. E., & Turner, J. H. (Eds.). (2006). *Handbook of the sociology of emotions.* New York: Springer.

Stinchcombe, A. L. (1987). *Constructing social theories.* Chicago, IL: University of Chicago Press. (Original work published 1968).

Storaasli, R., & Markman, H. (1990). Relationship problems in the premarital and early stages of marriage: A test of family development theory. *Journal of Family Psychology, 4*(1), 80–98. doi:10.1037/0893-3200.4.1.80

Straus, M. (1994). State-to-state differences in social inequality and social bonds in relation to assaults on wives in the United States. *Journal of Comparative Family Studies, 25,* 7–24.

Stryker, S. (1964). The interactional and situational approaches. In H. Christensen (Ed.), *Handbook of marriage and the family* (pp. 125–170). Chicago, IL: Rand McNally.

Stryker, S. (1968a). Identity salience and role performance: The relevance of symbolic interaction theory for family research. *Journal of Marriage and the Family, 30,* 558–564.

Stryker, S. (1968b). Identity theory and role performance. *Journal of Marriage and the Family, 30,* 558–564.

Stryker, S. (1980). *Symbolic interactionism: A social structural version.* Menlo Park, CA: Benjamin/Cummings.

Stryker, S. (1987a). Identity theory: Developments and extensions. In K. Yardley & T. Honess (Eds.), *Self and identity: Psychological perspectives* (pp. 89–103). London, UK: Wiley.

Stryker, S. (1987b). The vitalization of symbolic interactionism. *Social Psychology Quarterly, 50,* 83–94.

Stryker, S. (1989). Further developments in identity theory: Singularity versus multiplicity of self. In J. Berger, M. Zelditch, & B. Anderson (Eds.), *Sociological theories in progress: New formulations* (pp. 35–57). Newbury Park, CA: Sage.

Stryker, S. (1991). Exploring the relevance of social cognition for the relationship of self and society: Linking the cognitive perspective and identity theory. In J. A. Howard & P. L. Callero (Eds.), *The self-society dynamic: Cognition, emotion, and action* (pp. 19–41). New York: Cambridge University Press.

Stryker, S. (1994). Identity theory: Its development, research base, and prospects. *Studies in Symbolic Interaction, 16,* 9–20.

Stryker, S., & Burke, P. (2000). The past, present and future of an identity theory. *Social Psychology Quarterly, 63,* 284–297.

Stryker, S., & Serpe, R. T. (1994). Identity salience and psychological centrality: Equivalent, overlapping, or complementary concepts. *Social Psychological Quarterly, 57,* 16–35.

Swann, W. B., Jr. (1987). Identity negotiation: Where two roads meet. *Journal of Personality and Social Psychology, 53,* 1038–1051.

Swann, W. B., Jr., De La Ronde, C., & Hixon, J. G. (1994). Authenticity and positivity strivings in marriage and courtship. *Journal of Personality and Social Psychology, 66,* 857–969.

Swann, W. B., Jr., & Read, S. J. (1981). Self-verification processes: How we sustain our self-conceptions. *Journal of Experimental Social Psychology, 17,* 351–372.

Sweet, L., Bumpass, L., & Call, V. (1988). *The design and content of the National Survey of Families and Households.* Madison: University of Wisconsin, Center for Demography and Ecology.

Swenson, D. (2004). *A neo-functionalist synthesis of theories in family sociology.* Lewiston, NY: Edwin Mellen Press.

Swenson, D. (2008). The personality system: Religion having an impact on the individual and the individual's influence on religion in familial settings. In *Religion and family links* (pp. 77–106). New York: Springer.

Szinovacz, M. (1987). Family power. In M. Sussman & S. Steinmetz (Eds.), *Handbook of marriage and the family* (pp. 651–694). New York: Plenum.

Taylor, D. (1997). The uneasy relationship between motherhood and feminism. In A. Jetter, A. Orleck, & D. Taylor (Eds.), *The politics of motherhood* (pp. 349–351). Hanover, MA: University Press of New England.

Teachman, J. D., & Crowder, K. (2002). Multilevel models in family research: Some conceptual and methodological issues. *Journal of Marriage and Family, 64,* 280–294.

Teachman, J. D., Paasch, K., & Carver, K. (1996). Social capital and dropping out of school early. *Journal of Marriage and the Family, 58,* 773–783.

Teachman, J. D., Paasch, K., & Carver, K. (1997). Social capital and the generation of human capital. *Social Forces, 75,* 1343–1359.

Teachman, J. D., & Polonko, K. (1990). Cohabitation and marital stability in the United States. *Social Forces, 69,* 207–220.

Teachman, J. D., Tedrow, L. M., & Crowder, K. D. (2000). The changing demography of America's families. *Journal of Marriage and the Family, 62,* 1234–1246.

Thibaut, J. W., & Kelley, H. H. (1959). *The social psychology of groups.* New York: Wiley.

Thomas, D. L., & Kleber, J. E. (1981). Comment on marital quality: A review of the seventies. *Journal of Marriage and the Family, 43,* 780–781.

Thomas, D. L., & Wilcox, J. E. (1987). The rise of family theory: A historical and critical analysis. In M. B. Sussman & S. K. Steinmetz (Eds.), *Handbook of marriage and the family* (pp. 81–102). New York: Plenum.

Thomas, W. I., & Thomas, D. S. (1928). *The child in America: Behavior problems and programs*. New York: Knopf.

Thompson, L. (1992). Feminist methodology for family studies. *Journal of Marriage and the Family, 54*, 3–18.

Thompson, L., & Walker, A. J. (1995). The place of feminism in family studies. *Journal of Marriage and the Family, 57*, 847–865.

Thomson, E., Winkler-Dworak, M., & Kennedy, S. (2013). The standard family life course: An assessment of variability in life course pathways. In A. Evans & J. Baxter (Eds.), *Negotiating the life course: Stability and change in life pathways* (pp. 35–52). London, UK: Springer.

Thornton, A., Axinn, W. G., & Xie, Y. (2007). *Marriage and cohabitation*. Chicago, IL: University of Chicago Press.

Tiedje, L., Wortman, C., Downey, G., Emmons, C., Biernat, M., & Lang, E. (1990). Women with multiple roles: Role-compatibility perceptions, satisfaction, and mental health. *Journal of Marriage and the Family, 52*, 63–72.

Touliatos, J. (Ed.). (1994). *Inventory of marriage and family literature* (Vol. 19). Minneapolis, MN: National Council on Family Relations.

Toulmin, S. (1972). *Human understanding: Vol. 1. General introduction and part 1*. Oxford, UK: Oxford University Press.

Troost, K., & Filsinger, E. (1993). Emerging biosocial perspectives on the family. In P. Boss, W. Doherty, R. LaRossa, W. Schumm, & S. Steinmetz (Eds.), *Sourcebook of family theories and methods: A contextual approach* (pp. 677–710). New York: Plenum.

Tuana, N., & Tong, R. (Eds.). (1995). *Feminism and philosophy*. Boulder, CO: Westview.

Tuma, N., & Hannan, M. (1984). *Social dynamics*. New York: Academic Press.

Turner, J. (1991). *The structure of sociological theory* (5th ed.), Belmont, CA: Wadsworth.

Turner, J. (1998). *The structure of sociological theory* (6th ed.). Belmont, CA: Wadsworth.

Turner, J. H., & Stets, J. E. (2005). *The sociology of emotion*. New York: Cambridge University Press.

Turner, R. H. (1970). *Family interaction*. New York: Wiley.

Turner, R. H. (1980). Strategy for developing an integrated role theory. *Humboldt Journal of Social Relations, 7*, 123–139.

Turner, R. H., & Colomy, P. (1987). Role differentiation: Orienting principles. *Advances in Group Processes, 5*, 1–47.

Valverde, M. (2012). *Everyday law on the street*. Chicago, IL: University of Chicago Press.

Vandell, D., Belsky, J., Burchinal, M., Steinberg, L., Vandergrift, N., & NICHD Early Child Care Research Network. (2010). Do effects of early child care extend to age 15 years? *Child Development, 81*, 737–756.

van den Berghe, P. (1979). *Human family systems*. New York: Elsevier North-Holland.

van Leeuwen, L. T. (1981). Early family sociology in Europe: Parallels to the United States. In R. L. Howard (Ed.), *A social history of American family sociology, 1865–1940* (pp. 95–139). Westport, CT: Greenwood.

Vannoy, D., & Phillber, W. (1992). Wife's employment and quality of marriage. *Journal of Marriage and the Family, 54*, 387–398.

von Bertalanffy, L. (1968). *General systems theory*. New York: George Braziller.

von Glasersfeld, E. (1987). *Constructivism: Wissen ohne erkenntnis and Declaration of the American Society for Cybernetics* (Working paper No. 87-1). Center for Systems Research, University of Alberta, Canada.

Voydanoff, P. (1987). *Work and family life*. Newbury Park, CA: Sage.

Voydanoff, P., & Donnelly, B. W. (1999). Multiple roles and psychological distress: The intersection of the paid worker, spouse, and parent role with the role of the adult child. *Journal of Marriage and the Family, 61,* 725–735.

Wadsworth, B. J. (1996). *Piaget's theory of cognitive and affective development* (5th ed.). New York: Longman.

Waldrop, D. P., Weber, J. A., Herald, S. L., Pruett, J., Cooper, K., & Juozapavicius, K. (1999). Wisdom and life experience: How grandfathers mentor their grandchildren. *Journal of Aging and Identity, 4*(1), 33–46. doi:10.1023/A:1022834825849

Walsh, F. (2015). *Strengthening family resilience.* New York: Guilford.

Walsh, F. (2016). *Strengthening family resilience* (3rd ed.). New York: Guilford.

Walster, E., & Walster, G. W. (1978). *Equity: Theory and research.* Boston, MA: Allyn & Bacon.

Warde, A., Wright, D., & Gayo-Cal, M. (2007). Cultural omnivourousness: Or, the myth of the cultural omnivore. *Cultural Sociology, 2,* 143–164.

Watt, D., & White, J. M. (1999). Computers and the family: A family development perspective. *Journal of Comparative Family Studies, 30,* 1–15.

Watzlawick, P., Beavin, J., & Jackson, D. (1967). *Pragmatics of human communication.* New York: Norton.

Weber, J. G. (2011). *Individual and family stress and crises.* Thousand Oaks, CA: Sage.

Weber, M. (1978). *Economy and society.* G. Roth & C. Wittich (Eds.). Berkeley, CA: University of California Press. (Original work published 1922)

Weinberg, W. (1908). Über den nachweis der Vererbung beim Menschen. *Jahreshefte des Vereins für vaterländische Naturkunde in Württemberg, 64,* 368–382.

Weininger, E., & Lareau, A. (2003). Translating Bourdieu into the American context: The question of social class and family-school relations. *Poetics, 31,* 375–402.

Westoff, C. (1978). Marriage and fertility in the developed countries. *Scientific American, 239,* 51–57.

White, H. (1963). *An anatomy of kinship.* Englewood Cliffs, NJ: Prentice Hall.

White, J. M. (1984). Not the sum of its parts. *Journal of Family Issues, 5,* 515–518.

White, J. M. (1987). Researching developmental careers: The career conformity scale. *Journal of Family Issues, 8,* 306–318.

White, J. M. (1991). *Dynamics of family development: A theoretical perspective.* New York: Guilford.

White, J. M. (1998). The normative interpretation of life course event histories. *Marriage and Family Review, 3/4,* 211–235.

White, J. M. (1999). Work-family stage and satisfaction with work-family balance. *Journal of Comparative Family Studies, 30,* 163–175.

White, J. M. (2004). *Advancing family theories.* Thousand Oaks, CA: Sage.

White, J. M. (2005). *Advancing family theories.* Thousand oaks, CA: Sage.

White, J. M. (2013). The current status of theorizing about families. In G. Peterson & K. Bush (Eds.), *Handbook of marriage and the family* (3rd ed., pp. 11–38). New York: Springer.

White, J. M., & Klein, D. M. (2002). *Family theories* (2nd ed.). Thousand Oaks, CA: Sage.

White, J. M., Martin, T. F., & Bartolic, S. (2013). *Families across the life course.* Scarborough, Ontario: Pearson Education Canada.

White, J. M., Martin, T. F., & Sayre, E. (2016). *Family structures and measurements for studying families: A project.* Paper presented at the Theory Construction and Research Methodology Workshop: Families and Human Rights: Promise and Vulnerability in the 21st Century, Minneapolis, MN.

White, J. M., & Teachman, J. D. (2005). Comment on "Multilevel methods in family research." In V. Bengtson, A. Acock, K. Allen, P. Dilworth-Anderson, & D. Klein (Eds.), *Sourcebook on family theories and methods* (pp. 307–313). Thousand Oaks, CA: Sage.

White, L. K., & Booth, A. (1991). Divorce over the life course: The role of marital happiness. *Journal of Family Issues*, 12, 5–21.

Whitehead, A. (1929). *Process and reality*. New York: Macmillan.

Wiener, N. (1948). *Cybernetics*. New York: Wiley.

Wilkinson, M. (1977, October). *Yes, Virginia, propositions can be derived from systems theory*. Paper presented to the National Council on Family Relations, Theory Construction, and Methodology Workshop, San Diego, CA.

Wills, J., & Risman, B. (2006). The visibility of feminist thought in family studies. *Journal of Marriage and Family*, 68, 690–700.

Williams, C. S. (2006). Theory, tradition, and contemporary marriage. In A. S. Loveless & T. B. Holman (Eds.), *The family in the new millennium: World voices supporting the natural clan* (2nd ed., pp. 21–51). Westport, CT: Praeger.

Willoughby, B. J., Hall, S. S., & Goff, S. (2015). Marriage matters but how much? Marital centrality among young adults. *The Journal of psychology*, 149(8), 796–817. doi: 10.1080/00223980.2014.979128

Wilson, E. O. (1975). *Sociobiology: The new synthesis*. Cambridge, MA: Harvard University Press.

Winton, C. A. (1995). *Frameworks for studying families*. Guilford, CT: Dushkin.

Wollstonecraft, M. (1975). *A vindication of the rights of woman*. Baltimore, MD: Penguin. (Original work published 1792)

Wood, J. (2013). Becoming gendered: Theories of gendering processes in early life. In M. Fine & F. Fincham (Eds.), *Handbook of family theories: A content-based approach* (pp. 301–315). New York: Routledge.

Wood, J. T. (1995). Feminist scholarship and the study of relationships. *Journal of Social and Personal Relationships*, 12, 103–120.

Xiao, J. (2013). Family economic well-being. In G. Peterson & K. Bush (Eds.), *Handbook of marriage and the family* (3rd ed., pp. 573–611). New York: Springer.

Yllö, K., & Straus, M. (1990). Patriarchy and violence against wives: The impact of structural and normative factors. In M. Straus & R. Gelles (Eds.), *Physical violence in American families: Risk factors and adaptations to violence in 8,145 families* (pp. 383–399). New Brunswick, NJ: Transaction Books.

Zaretsky, E. (1973). *Capitalism, the family, and personal life*. New York: Harper & Row.

Zetterberg, H. L. (1965). *On theory and verification in sociology*. Totowa, NY: Bedminster Press.

Zielinsky, D., & Bradshaw, C. (2006). Ecological influences on the sequelae of child maltreatment: A review of the literature. *Child Maltreatment 11*, 49–62.

Zimmerman, C. C. (1947). *Family and civilization*. New York: Harper.

Index

class conflict and, 176
coalition formation and, 180, 184, 187
competition/structural conflict
and, 179
concepts in, 179–183
conflict, as endemic, 178
conflict, as inevitable, 179
conflict, definition of, 179–180
conflict theory, development
of, 175–178
consensus and, 182–183
cooperation/competition,
social rules/norms and, 180
critical theory, development of,
193–195
critical theory of the family
and, 191–193
critiques/discussion of, 198–200
cultural omnivores and, 195
democratic groups, decision
process and, 185
dialectical historiography and,
31–32, 190–191
dialectical logic and, 175
dialectical materialism and,
32, 175, 176
division of labor, gender-based
nature of, 188–190, 225–227
domestic violence/wife assault
and, 195–197
emancipatory perspective and,
177, 199–200
empirical applications of, 195–198
family authority/power,
phases of, 187
feminism, development of, 200
focus/scope assumptions in, 178–179
gendered family roles and,
133, 189, 199, 208
habitus and, 194, 198
intellectual traditions and, 174–178
microresource conflict theory
and, 188–200
negotiation process and, 182, 183,
184–185, 188
norms of the situation and, 180
patriarchal social system and, 176,
184, 185, 196, 206, 218

power/authority and, 181–182
propositions in, 183–185
resources/capitals, power
and, 181–182
resource scarcity, distribution
inequities and, 183–184
self-interest motivations and,
174–175, 176, 178
single-cause theories and, 200
social contract, social order and, 70
social inequality and, 197–198
social structures, individual
oppression and, 181
structural conflict, associative/
dissociative forces and, 186–188
structure of the group,
dimensions in, 180–181
symbolic violence and, 181, 195
transmission of social class and, 178
variant theories and, 185–195
within-group conflict, resource
distribution inequities and
See also Family theories
Conflict-resource orientation, 49
Consensus, 182–183
Constantine, J., 146
Constructivist perspective,
155, 168, 170
Consumer sciences, 255–257
Contraception, 69, 253
Cook, K., 63
Cooley, C. H., 77, 82
Corporal punishment, 114
Coser, L. A., 135, 187, 188
Costs. See Rational choice/social
exchange framework
Couple dynamics
common goals and, 1, 2
first intercourse, probability of
marriage and, 5
See also Marriage
Covering law model, 14, 30
Covey, M. A., 256
Cowan, C. P., 108–109,
133, 134
Cowan, P. A., 108–109, 133, 134
Cox, M. J., 133
Creativity, 266–267

attachment theory, developmental
    ecological theory and, 251–252
bioecology of the family and,
    251, 252–255
biological/social variables, interaction
    of, 239–240
child care, effects of, 257–258
child maltreatment, neighborhood
    characteristics and, 258
chronosystem, development
    process and, 250
community collaborative
    efforts and, 256–257
concepts in, 241–244
consumer protection/education
    and, 255–257
critiques/discussion of, 259–261
dyads, developmental change/role
    specialization and, 245
ecological transition and, 250
ecosystems, definition of, 241
empirical applications of, 257–258
environmental resources, human
    dependency on, 240
eugenics and, 235–236, 238, 239
evolutionary perspective and,
    254–255
family demography, ecology
    and, 247–248
family processing system,
    transformed energy/information
    and, 245–246
focus/scope assumptions in, 239–241
hierarchical linear modeling,
    interaction effects analysis
    and, 250–251
human developmental ecology
    and, 238–239, 248–252
human development theories
    and, 106–107
human ecology framework
    and, 255–257
inclusive fitness principle
    and, 252–254
individual development and, 246
intellectual traditions and,
    235–239

levels of analysis in ecosystems
    and, 241–242, 259–260
metaphor and, 260
natural selection and, 236, 238,
    239, 243–244, 252, 259
nested ecosystems, levels
    of analysis of, 242
niches, ecosystem functions and, 242
ontogenetic/social development and,
    240, 243, 259
population analysis and, 247
population genetics and, 237–238
population growth, unconstrained
    situations and, 236
predictive value and, 260
propositions in, 244–247
settings/situations, distinctive
    behavior patterning and, 245
sociobiology of the family and,
    252–255, 260–261
spatial organization of human
    behavior and, 240–241
tautological logic and, 260
urban spatial arrangement and,
    235–236
value-laden theorizing and,
    256, 261
variant theories and, 247–257
See also Family theories
Ecological Society of America, 235
Economic capital, 62
Edlund, L., 68–69
Egalitarian authority, 184
Egalitarianism, 184, 226
Eggebeen, D., 257
Ego role enactment, 86
Ehrenreich, B., 226
Eichler, M., 217
Elder, G. H., Jr., 107, 120, 129, 250
Ellard, C., 248
Emancipatory perspective,
    177, 199–200, 205, 212–213
Emergence concept, 142
Emerson, R., 63
Emlen, S. T., 244, 252, 254–255, 260
Empirical research
    best practices and, 28

empirical research-based theorizing
and, 40, 130–131 (box)
evaluation criteria for, 19, 20 (table)
explanation/understanding,
clarification of, 286–287
family concept and, 18–19
family diversity/change and, 19
family group, characteristics of,
15–16, 70, 93
family group, focus on, 108–109,
111–112
folk wisdom, reliance on, 236
formal theory construction, models
of, 41–42
future of, 282–287
future of theory development,
282–287
history of, 39–45
ideology, intrusion of, 27–28
integrated concepts in, 285–286
intrafamily interactions/family life
focus of, 124
kinship structures and (box), 113
levels of analysis and, 280–281, 283
metatheory, theory development and,
280–282 (table)
modification of, 279–280
moral reform and, 39
multidisciplinary nature of, 266
parental socialization model and, 39
philosophies of science and,
23–26 (box)
pluralism, modern theory
development trends and, 42–44
post-postmodern theory development
and, 44–45
propositional format and, 40, 41–42
refinement/continued testing of, 264
social theory and, 283–285
systematic theory development
and, 40
time element in, 110–112
tool analogy for, 270
See also Conflict/critical theories
framework; Ecological
framework; Family; Family
theory construction; Feminist

framework; Life course
developmental framework;
Rational choice/social exchange
framework; Symbolic interaction
framework; Systems framework;
Theoretical frameworks
Family theory construction
borrowed ideas, food blender
phenomenon and, 271
emerging theories and, 274–276
empirical research generalizations,
induction from, 271–273
family system theory, interpretive
perspective and, 25, 26 (box)
formative stage of, 263–264
general theories, deduction of family
theories from, 269–270
incommensurability problem
and, 265
integrated concepts in, 273
levels of analysis/dependent
variables and, 247, 265
levels of theory, 280–281
meta-analytic approach and, 272, 280
metatheory, role of, 280–282 (table)
methods of, 265–268,
268 (box)–269 (box)
partial theories, codification
of, 270–271
queer theory and, 274–276
questions to consider during,
268 (box)–269 (box)
refinement stage of, 264
stages of, 263–265
strategies of, 269–274
taxonomies, construction
of, 273
See also Family theories;
Theoretical frameworks; Theory
Family therapy practice, 144, 161
Family values, 183–184
Family/work balance, 93–95
Farrington, K., 200–201
Fasang, A. E., 129
Featherman, D., 113
Feedback loops, 143, 146–147,
149, 152, 155

Fromm, E., 192
Functionalism, 33, 35–37, 38, 144, 156–157
Furstenburg, F., 57
Futrell, J., 133

Galton, F., 238
Game stage of socialization, 82
Garbarino, J., 250, 258
Gay marriage, 274–275
Gayo-Cal, M., 195
Gelles, R., 196
Gender
sex vs., 213
See also Feminist framework; Marriage; Roles; Symbolic interaction framework
Generalizable costs/rewards, 57–58, 71
Generalized exchanges, 64
Generalized other, 82, 84
General systems theory, 142, 144–145, 155–156
Gerson, K., 110
Gibbs, J., 266
Gillstrap, B., 257
Gilman, C., 206, 226–227
Glaser, B. G., 266, 272
Glick, P. C., 107, 128–129, 247
Goelman, H., 257
Goffman, E., 90, 91
Goode, W., 37, 41
Gordon, L., 210
Gottman, J. M., 101, 160, 164, 168, 169
Goyette, K., 193
Granger, D. A., 255
Great Depression, 107, 120, 205, 206
Great man theory, 62
Grey, J. H., 230
Gross, P., 287
Grounded theory, 31, 80, 272
Group solidarity. See Alliance formation; Coalition formation; Ecological framework
Groves, E., 40

Grzywacz, J. G., 135
Gurmu, E., 69
Gwartney-Gibbs, P., 122

Haack, S., 228
Habermas, J., 192
Habitus, 194, 198
Haeckel, E., 234
Hage, J., 266
Haley, J., 144
Hall, A., 147
Hall, O., 255
Hannan, M., 259
Harding, S., 211, 213
Hardy, G., 237–238
Haveman, R.
Hawkins, A., 225
Hawley, A., 236, 241, 242, 244, 245, 246, 249, 259
Hays, S., 252
Hechter, M., 62
Hedonistic calculus, 52
Hegel, F., 32, 175, 200
Hempel, C. G., 30, 43, 142
Hertel, R., 164
Heywood, L., 210
Hierarchical linear modeling (HLM), 250–251
Hill, R., 41, 42, 44, 107–108, 113, 128, 132, 133, 135–136, 199, 270–271, 273
Historiography, 31–32, 175, 190–191
Hobbes, T., 174, 176, 178
Hochschild, A., 225
Hogan, D., 108, 135, 248
Holman, T. B., 21
Homans, G. C., 13, 21, 57–58
Home economics, 256–257, 260
Homeostatic systems, 150
Horkheimer, M., 177, 192
Howard, R. L., 39–40
Hughes, H., 248
Human capital, 56, 57, 60
Human developmental ecology, 248–252
Human ecology framework, 255–257
Human trafficking, 69

comparator control system and, 150, 151, 154 (figure), 155

concepts in, 147–151

constructivist perspective, objective reality and, 147

critiques/discussion of, 168–170

deviation amplifying/dampening feedback and, 149

emergence concept and, 142

empirical applications of, 163–168

epistemological statement about, 146

equilibrium and, 36, 149–150

evolutionary perspective and, 142

fallacy of misplaced concreteness and, 147, 169

family adjustment and adaptation response model and, 166–168

family process theory and, 144, 160–162

family systems and, 143–145

feedback loops and, 146–147, 149

focus/scope assumptions in, 146–147

forecasting vs. prediction and, 168

general systems theory and, 142, 144–145, 155–156

global/general nature of, 168–169

goal hierarchies and, 152–154 (figure)

homeostatic systems and, 150

information science/technological developments and, 143

intellectual traditions and, 142–146

interconnectedness assumption and, 146

living/nonliving systems and, 145–146

marital/family communication systems and, 144, 160, 163–165

marital interaction system and, 164

modeling systems and, 168

neo-functional systems and, 156–158

permeability, degree of, 148

PREPARE/ENRICH tool and, 165–166

propositions in, 151–155

reality, systems as not, 147

reification error and, 147, 169–170

rules of transformation and, 148–149

social network analysis and, 162

subsystems and, 36, 150–151

system, definition of, 147–148

systems levels and, 150

universal principles, search for, 142

variant theories and, 155–162

variety, systems adaptability/viability and, 149, 152

wholesystem perspective, deep understanding and, 146

See also Family theories

Tankard, J. W., Jr., 266

Tautological reasoning, 72–73

Taxonomy construction, 273

Teachman, J. D., 193, 248

Tedrow, L. M., 248

Teleological values, 29

Theoretical frameworks

best practices and, 28

causal model of explanation and, 30, 271

conceptual frameworks, identification of, 40–41

covering law model of explanation and, 14, 30

critical perspective and, 26 (box)

explanation function of, 13–14

formal theory construction, models of, 41–42, 186

ideology and, 27–28, 227

interpretive perspective and, 25, 26 (box)

knowledge, characterization of, 5, 6, 12

overview of, 19–21

philosophers of science and, 24

philosophies of science and, 23–26 (box)

pluralism, modern theory development trends and, 42–44

positivist perspective and, 25, 26 (box)

post-postmodern theory construction and, 44–45

pragmatic positivism and, 25

pragmatism and, 25, 29, 30, 77

About the Authors

James M. White is professor emeritus of sociology at the University of British Columbia where he taught for 35 years. He is known internationally for his book, *Dynamics of Family Development*, which has been published in both the United States (1991) and Japan (1994). He is the author of five books, including *Advancing Family Theories* (2004), and numerous journal articles appearing in such journals as *Journal of Family Issues, Journal of Social and Personal Relationships,* and *Journal of Marriage and Family*. He is past editor of the *Journal of Comparative Family Studies* and is on numerous editorial boards. He is past president of the Northwest Council on Family Relations and past chair of the Theory Construction and Research Methodology Workshop (TCRM). He is an honorary fellow of the National Council on Family Relations.

Todd F. Martin is associate professor in the Department of Sociology and dean of the Faculty of Humanities and Social Sciences at Trinity Western University. He is coauthor of *Families Across the Life Course* (2012). He holds degrees in theology, family studies, and sociology. His work has been published in journals such as the *Journal of Adolescent Research, International Migration Review,* and *Journal of Family Theory and Review*. He has also contributed to edited volumes on the topic of fertility as well as work and family interaction. His current research is on cohabitation, adolescent religious socialization, and union dissolution. Currently, he is the managing editor of *The Journal of Comparative Family Studies*. He is a member of the National Council on Family Relations and active in the Theory Construction and Research Methodology Workshop.

Kari Adamsons is an associate professor of Human Development and Family Studies at the University of Connecticut. She holds a master's and PhD in human development and family studies, and a BA in psychology. Her work has been published in journals such as the *Journal of Family Psychology, Parenting: Science and Practice,* and the *Journal of Family Theory and Review*. Her research focuses on fathering, coparenting, and identity theory. She is an associate editor for the *Journal of Social and Personal Relationships* and a member of the editorial board for the *Journal of Family Theory and Review*. She is the current chair of the Research and Theory section of the National Council on Family Relations, and she is a past chair of the Theory Construction and Research Methodology Workshop.